THE ORIGINS OF PHILOSOPHY IN ANCIENT GREECE AND ANCIENT INDIA

Why did Greek philosophy begin in the sixth century BCE? Why did Indian philosophy begin at about the same time? Why did the earliest philosophy take the form that it did? Why was this form so similar in Greece and India? And how do we explain the differences between them? These questions can only be answered by locating the philosophical intellect within its entire societal context, ignoring neither ritual nor economy. The cities of Greece and northern India were in this period distinctive also by virtue of being pervasively monetised. The metaphysics of both cultures is marked by the projection (onto the cosmos) and the introjection (into the inner self) of the abstract, all-pervasive, quasi-omnipotent, impersonal substance embodied in money (especially coinage). And in both cultures this development accompanied the interiorisation of the cosmic rite of passage (in India sacrifice, in Greece mystic initiation).

RICHARD SEAFORD is Emeritus Professor of Ancient Greek at the University of Exeter. His books include commentaries on Euripides' *Cyclops* and on Euripides' *Bacchae*, as well as *Reciprocity and Ritual* (1994), *Dionysos* (2006), *Money and the Early Greek Mind* (Cambridge University Press, 2004), and *Cosmology and the Polis* (Cambridge University Press, 2012). A volume of his selected papers has recently been published entitled *Tragedy, Ritual, and Money in Ancient Greece* (Cambridge University Press, 2018).

THE ORIGINS OF PHILOSOPHY IN ANCIENT GREECE AND ANCIENT INDIA

A Historical Comparison

RICHARD SEAFORD
University of Exeter

CAMBRIDGE
UNIVERSITY PRESS

CAMBRIDGE
UNIVERSITY PRESS

Shaftesbury Road, Cambridge CB2 8EA, United Kingdom

One Liberty Plaza, 20th Floor, New York, NY 10006, USA

477 Williamstown Road, Port Melbourne, VIC 3207, Australia

314–321, 3rd Floor, Plot 3, Splendor Forum, Jasola District Centre, New Delhi – 110025, India

103 Penang Road, #05–06/07, Visioncrest Commercial, Singapore 238467

Cambridge University Press is part of Cambridge University Press & Assessment,
a department of the University of Cambridge.

We share the University's mission to contribute to society through the pursuit of
education, learning and research at the highest international levels of excellence.

www.cambridge.org
Information on this title: www.cambridge.org/9781108730815

DOI: 10.1017/9781108583701

First published 2020
First paperback edition 2024

A catalogue record for this publication is available from the British Library

ISBN 978-1-108-49955-2 Hardback
ISBN 978-1-108-73081-5 Paperback

Contents

Preface — *page* ix
The Ancient Texts — xi
Translations — xii
Anglicisation of Sanskrit — xiii
List of Abbreviations — xiv

PART A: INTRODUCTORY — 1

1. Summary — 3
2. Explanations — 7
   - 2§A Explananda — 7
   - 2§B A Shared Indo-European Origin? — 8
   - 2§C Influence? — 9
   - 2§D The Advance of Reason? — 14
   - 2§E Individual Property and Monetisation — 17

PART B: THE EARLIEST TEXTS — 39

3. Sacrifice and Reciprocity in the Earliest Texts — 41
   - 3§A The *Rigveda* — 41
   - 3§B Homer and Hesiod — 43
4. Self, Society and Universe in the Earliest Texts — 49
   - 4§A Constructing the Self — 49
   - 4§B Organs of Consciousness in Homer — 54
   - 4§C Organs of Consciousness in the *Rigveda* — 57
   - 4§D Society and the Self in the *Rigveda* and Homer — 60
   - 4§E Monism — 62
   - 4§F Projection and Introjection (Interiorisation) — 67

PART C: UNIFIED SELF, MONISM AND COSMIC CYCLE IN INDIA 71

5. The Economics of Sacrifice 73
5§A Sacrifice and Society 73
5§B The Cosmic Economy of Vedic Sacrifice 78
5§C The Individualisation of Vedic Sacrifice 82
5§D From Gift to Payment 90
5§E Individualisation in India and Greece 97

6. Inner Self and Universe 102
6§A From Diversity to Wholeness 102
6§B Loka and *Sarva* 110
6§C Inner Self in *Bṛhadāraṇyaka Upaniṣad* 1.1–4 114
6§D Prana, Atman and *Manas* 118

7. The Powerful Individual 125
7§A Kshatriyas and Individualism 125
7§B The Interiorisation of Autocracy 137

8. The Formation of Monism 143
8§A Monism between the *Rigveda* and the *Upanishads* 143
8§B From Correspondences to Monism 145
8§C Monism in the Five Earliest *Upanishads* 151
8§D Monism and Immortality 161
8§E Chapter 6 of the *Chāndogya Upaniṣad* 162

9. The Hereafter 167
9§A The Earliest Beliefs 167
9§B From Ritual Action to Metaphysical Merit 168
9§C Metaphysical Merit and Repeated Death 170
9§D Metaphysical Merit and Cyclical Hereafter 172
9§E Renunciation: Ajivikism, Jainism and Buddhism 180
9§F The Factor of Monetisation 190

10. Reincarnation and Karma 193
10§A Reincarnation: A Cross-Cultural Perspective 193
10§B Cyclicality 199
10§C Karma 202
10§D Lineage and Caste 213

PART D: UNIFIED SELF, MONISM AND COSMIC CYCLE IN GREECE 217

11. *Psuchē* and the Interiorisation of Mystery-Cult 219
11§A The Interiorisation of Ritual in India and Greece 219

11§B Mystery-Cult and the *Psuchē* Before 400 BCE 221
11§C The Interiorisation of Mystery-Cult in Herakleitos 223
11§D The Interiorisation of Mystery-Cult in Parmenides 225
11§E The Interiorisation of Mystery-Cult in Plato 230

12. Monism and Inner Self 235
12§A Greek Monisms 235
12§B From Reciprocity to Monism 240
12§C Monism and the Unitary Inner Self 242
12§D Fire: Herakleitean, Zoroastrian, Vedic and Buddhist 244

13. Money and Inner Self in Greece 253
13§A Money and Universe 253
13§B The *Psuchē* of Achilles 254
13§C Death as Economic Transaction 257
13§D Herakleitos 261
13§E Abstract Value and Inner Self 265

14. Community and Individual 271
14§A Circulation and Abstraction, Community and Individual 271
14§B Reason, Mystery and Money 280
14§C Ritual and Money 285
14§D Reincarnation 289

15. Plato 294
15§A The Platonic Inner Self 294
15§B Reflexivity and Subjectivity 304
15§C Chapter 7 of the *Chāndogya Upaniṣad* 311

PART E: CONCLUSION 315

16. The Complex Imagining of Universe and Inner Self 317
16§A Monetisation and Other Factors 317
16§B Differing Perspectives on Money 321
16§C Brahman and the Parmenidean One 329

17. Ritual, Money, Society and Metaphysics 332
17§A Universe and Inner Self 332
17§B Why Did the Greeks Not Have Karma? 342

Bibliography 347
Index of Principal Ancient Passages 362
Index 366

Preface

This book is for Indologists and Hellenists, but also for non-specialists, including those who appreciated my *Money and the Early Greek Mind* (Cambridge University Press, 2004), the argument of which I here recapitulate, develop and extend. I regard my socio-economic mode of explanation there of the Greek intellectual revolution as vindicated here by its power to explain the striking similarities (and differences) between the Greek and Indian intellectual revolutions. The conclusions of my 2004 book have received attention from anthropologists and historians of religion among others, but relatively little from classical scholars, who are generally uninterested in explaining the preconceptions behind ancient metaphysics. However, even those averse to my socio-economic perspective may, I hope, be stimulated by the numerous interconnections I make between early Indian and early Greek thought to view one or the other of them (or both) in a new light.

My five years of immersion in the rich and complex culture of ancient India, after four decades of writing about ancient Greece, have been an experience beyond compare. Such ambitious interdisciplinarity cannot represent the extent and profuse untidiness of the relevant material, and it risks various kinds of vulnerability. Because my knowledge of Sanskrit (and of the Pali of Buddhist texts) is no more than rudimentary, I devoured the relevant ancient texts in English translation, but subsequently examined the original language of the passages that I quote. For essential help in this often formidable undertaking I am in debt to the linguistic skills of Richard Fynes, and to the Arts and Humanities Research Council, which financed our collaboration. Simon Brodbeck and Christopher Gill have most helpfully read sections of the book. I am grateful also to the anonymous referees for their useful suggestions, and for answers to specific queries to Douglas Berger, Joel Brereton, Jonardon Ganeri, Richard Gombrich, Terry Hardaker, Stephanie Jamison, Joanna Jurewicz, Tim Lubin, Patrick Olivelle, Alexis Pinchard, Chiara Robbiano, Joseph Russo, Jens Schlieter, Shaul Tor, Herman Tull and Alex Wynne. Special thanks go to Phiroze Vasunia for organising in London a seminar on an early draft of some chapters, and to all those who participated in the discussion. I have also had the pleasure and benefit of numerous conversations on the subject of India and Greece with Richard Stoneman. By far my greatest debt, as she well knows, is to Laura Casimir.

The Ancient Texts

This book concerns a wide range of ancient texts from Greece and India. The chronology of the Greek texts is much better known than that of the Indian, where throughout the period with which we are mainly concerned (defined in 2§A) the texts were transmitted orally and we have no precise dates for anything whatsoever: for discussion of the approximate chronology of my Indian texts see 2§E and 4§E.

Many of my Indian texts belong to the vast body of religious Sanskrit texts known as the Vedas, which are considered *śruti* ('heard', i.e. divinely revealed). They are divided into four collections, the *Rigveda*, *Yajurveda*, *Samaveda* and *Atharvaveda*, each of which contains four major kinds of text: *Samhitas* (ritual utterances), *Aranyakas* and *Brahmanas* (prose commentaries on ritual, sometimes with quasi-philosophical content) and *Upanishads*, in which philosophical content has largely excluded commentary on ritual.

To some of these texts I give special attention. The earliest Vedic text is the collection of verse hymns contained in the *Rigveda.* There is rich quasi-philosophical content in the *Śatapatha Brāhmaṇa*, which is also one of the latest of the *Brahmanas* and so relatively close in time to the early *Upanishads*, of which the earliest and most substantial are the *Bṛhadāraṇyaka Upaniṣad* and the *Chāndogya Upaniṣad.* I will also use the (non-Vedic) texts of Buddhism and Jainism. In Greece my main focus will be on Homeric epic, presocratic philosophy (especially Herakleitos and Parmenides) and Plato.

Translations

Translations of Greek texts are generally my own. For Indian texts I use translations listed in the bibliography: for the *Rigveda* Jamison and Brereton, for the *Pañcaviṃśa Brāhmaṇa* Caland, for the *Śatapatha Brāhmaṇa* Eggeling, for the *Upanishads* Olivelle, for the *Majjhima Nikāya* Bhikkhu Ñaṇāmoli and Bhikkhu Bodhi, for the *Questions of Milinda* Rhys Davids.

Anglicisation of Sanskrit

Common personal and place names, and names of castes, sects and common texts are anglicised (without diacritics), as are the following concepts:

atman (self: meaning discussed at 4§C, 6§D)
brahman (universal principle or power: 5§C; to be distinguished from the priests called Brahmins or Brahmans)
karma (derived from Sanskrit *karman*: 7§A)
loka (world: 6§B)
prana (breath, inner faculty: 4§C, 6§D)

Abbreviations

A.	Aeschylus
AA	*Aitareya Āraṇyaka*
AB	*Aitareya Brāhmaṇa*
AN	*Aṅguttara Nikāya*
AU	*Aitareya Upaniṣad*
AV	*Atharvaveda Saṃhitā*
BG	*Bhagavad Gītā*
BU	*Bṛhadāraṇyaka Upaniṣad*
CU	*Chāndogya Upaniṣad*
DN	*Dīgha Nikāya*
DK	Diels, H. and Kranz, W. (eds.) *Die Fragmente der Vorsokratiker*, 6th edn, Berlin, 1951
D.L.	Diogenes Laetius, *Lives of the Philosophers*
E.	Euripides
EIR	ethicised indiscriminate reincarnation (see 2§A)
FGrH	F. Jacoby (ed.), *Die Fragmente der Griechischer Historiker*, Berlin and Leiden, 1923–58.
fr.	fragment
Hdt.	Herodotos
Hklt.	Herakleitos
JB	*Jāiminīya Brāhmaṇa*
JUB	*Jāiminīya Upaniṣad Brāhmaṇa*
KaU	*Kaṭha Upaniṣad*
KB	*Kauṣītaki Brāhmaṇa*
KRS	Kirk, G.S., Raven, D., and Schofield, M. (1983). *The Presocratic Philosophers*. 2nd ed. Cambridge U.P.
KU	*Kauṣītaki Upaniṣad*
MaiU	*Maitrāyaṇīya/Maitrī Upaniṣad*
MN	*Majjhima Nikāya*
MS	*Maitrāyaṇī Saṃhitā*

MU	*Muṇḍaka Upaniṣad*
PB	*Pañcaviṃśa Brāhmaṇa*
Pl.	Plato
Plut.	Plutarch
PrU	*Praśna Upaniṣad*
RV	*Rigveda* (*Ṛigveda Saṃhitā*)
SB	*Śatapatha Brāhmaṇa*
S.	Sophokles
SU	*Śvetāśvatara Upaniṣad*
TA	*Taittirīya Āraṇyaka*
TB	*Taittirīya Brāhmaṇa*
TS	*Taittirīya Saṃhitā*
TU	*Taittirīya Upaniṣad*

PART A

Introductory

CHAPTER 1

Summary

This book is devoted to a unitary argument, but over such a wide range of material that I offer the reader preliminary guidance in this chapter, beginning with an overview.

The next chapter (concluding Part A) presents explanations of the similarity between the earliest philosophy in India and Greece. Part B describes the polytheist reciprocity that, among an elite, was replaced in both cultures by monism. Part C centres on the main factors behind this replacement in India: the individual *interiorisation* of what I call the cosmic rite of passage, and *monetisation.* Part D describes the similar factors behind the similar development of ideas in Greece. The conclusion (Part E) summarises and explores the variety of factors behind the new imagining of universe and inner self.

Although Part C focuses mainly on India and Part D mainly on Greece, I have made frequent attempts throughout the book to explain the similarities and differences between the intellectual transformations in the two cultures. Some references to the Greek material in Part C will be fully appreciated only after the analogy between the Greek and the Indian intellectual transformations has become clear in Part D. Possible early misgivings about my position on monetisation as an important factor behind the intellectual transformations are addressed in Part E.

There follows a brief summary of each chapter.

Chapter 2 describes the set of metaphysical ideas that, roughly speaking, arose at about the same time in India and Greece and nowhere else (2§A). For the sake of clarity, right from the start I expose the weaknesses of several kinds of explanation, in particular the widely popular assumption of 'influence' (2§C), while also setting out the evidence for the *socio-economic* transformations that I regard as the most important but relatively neglected factor (2§E).

In Part B, Chapter 3 describes how there is in the earliest texts of both cultures (*Rigveda*, Homer, Hesiod) a variety of anthropomorphic deities whose goodwill is to be elicited by offerings and praise, against a background combination of pastoralism and agriculture, with no money and very little commerce.

Chapter 4 concerns the construction of the inner self in the *Rigveda* and in Homer. The comprehensive, bounded inner self with which we are familiar, but which is in fact given to us not by nature but as a construction in some societies but not in others (4§A), is found neither in Homer (4§B) nor in the *Rigveda* (4§C). Its absence can be correlated with polytheist reciprocity (4§D), whereas its subsequent development (i.e. of atman and *psuchē*) can be correlated with various kinds of *monism*, of which there are a very few slight occurrences in the latest section of the *Rigveda* (4§E). The explanation I will give of these developments requires a preliminary description here of the phenomena of cosmisation (cosmic projection) and interiorisation (introjection) (4§F).

In Part C, Chapter 5 begins with similarities and differences between Vedic and Greek sacrifice, notably the centrality to Greek sacrifice of the communal meal that was absent from Vedic sacrifice (5§A), in which the cycle of nature, the payment of metaphysical debt and the rite of passage to heaven and back each forms a cosmic cycle driven by necessity (5§B). The *individualisation* of the Vedic sacrifice, along with its *interiorisation* and *automatisation* (5§C), cannot be explained without taking into account the factor of monetisation (5§D). Individualisation in India and Greece has different cultural consequences (5§E).

Chapter 6 describes the construction of the unified inner self and its relation to the universe. A movement from diversity (inner, cosmic and political) to wholeness is found in the mythic-ritual complex of both cultures, notably in the strikingly similar myths of Prajapati and Dionysos (6§A). The wholeness of the inner self correlates with the wholeness of the world obtained by sacrifice (6§B). The formation of the unified inner self (atman) as cosmogony is described in the opening of the *Bṛhadāraṇyaka Upaniṣad* (6§C). The relation of atman to other candidates for the role of unified inner self, prana and *manas*, is described (6§D).

Chapter 7 describes a distinctively Indian phenomenon. The participation of individual autocrats (Kshatriyas) in the dialogues of the early *Upanishads* is associated with new metaphysical doctrines that will be shown to reflect monetisation (7§A). The social power that is interiorised in the construction of the unified inner self is in India (mainly) autocracy, whereas in Greece – where kingship is in decline – it is (mainly) monetary value (7§B).

The first three chapters of Part C have focused on the inner self. The remaining three focus on cosmology.

Chapter 8 describes the development of the various forms of *monism* (material, personal, mental, abstract) after the *Rigveda* (8§A). The traditional correspondences, between ritual and what ritual controls, tend to collapse into a single identification, of subject with object (8§B), making for the prominence and coalescence of mental monism and abstract monism in the early *Upanishads* – under the influence of universal abstract *value* (8§C). Awareness of the unity of all things (monism) is associated with immortality (8§D). The monistic tendency is illustrated by focus on a single passage (CU 6: 8§E).

Chapter 9 describes the earliest extant Indian beliefs about the afterlife (9§A), which were superseded by the idea of individually accumulated metaphysical merit accompanied by the danger of repeated death (9§C) and develops into the idea of subjection in the hereafter to a repeated cosmic cycle (9§D). All this prefigures the combination of individually accumulated karma with the universal cycle of reincarnation (*saṃsāra*), from which escape was sought by various forms of renunciation (9§E). An important factor in these developments was the individual accumulation and universal circulation of money (9§F).

Chapter 10 begins with a critique of the best existing attempt (by Obeyesekere) to explain the origins of what I call ethicised indiscriminate reincarnation (EIR) in India and in Greece. But in my view any successful explanation cannot exclude monetisation (10§A), which also contributes to the importance of cyclicality in reincarnation (10§B), and to the advent of the widespread and persistent idea of individually accumulated karma (10§C). This requires reflection on the different roles of kinship in Greece and India (10§D).

In Part D the main focus moves from India to Greece. Chapter 11 compares the interiorisation of the cosmic rite of passage in India (sacrifice) and Greece (mystic initiation) (11§A), identifies the importance of the soul (*psuchē*) in mystic initiation (11§B), which is interiorised in Herakleitos (12§B), in Parmenides (11§C) and in Plato (11§D). This Greek interiorisation promoted ideas akin to the coalescence of mental with abstract monism promoted by the interiorisation of the cosmic rite of passage in India.

Chapter 12 classifies Greek monism with the same four categories as used for India (12§A), and describes the transition – also found in India – from reciprocity to monism (12§B), which is closely associated with the new inner self (12§C). The element of fire in universe and inner self allows cross-cultural comparison that includes Zoroastrianism and Buddhism (12§D).

Chapter 13 describes the projection (13§A) and interiorisation (introjection) of abstract value. The idea of the comprehensive inner self as constituting a person's identity is first indicated in the Homeric Achilles' evaluation, in a crisis of reciprocity, of his *psuchē* (13§B), which is also the first of many passages in which death is envisaged as an economic transaction (13§C), for instance in Herakleitos, who is also the first to focus on the nature of the living *psuchē* (13§D) and who also exemplifies the Greek interiorisation of unifying abstract value (13§E).

Chapter 14 describes the opposition within early Greek metaphysics between the ontological privileging of (communal) circulation and of (individually owned) abstract value (14§A). Our three key processes of abstraction, monetisation and ritual are assessed as factors in the production of Parmenidean 'reason' (14§B), a combination facilitated by the similarities between money and ritual (14§C), both of which contribute to the Greek doctrine of reincarnation, which was taught in mystic initiation and involved a cosmic projection (cosmisation) of monetised circulation (14§D).

Chapter 15 discusses the various features of the Platonic inner self (soul, *psuchē*), in particular its interiorisation of controlling abstract value and of the master-slave relationship (15§A). We then take a detour through linguistics, the history of *reflexivity* in Greek and Sanskrit, to provide independent evidence for our view of monetisation as a factor in the emergence of the unitary inner self (15§B), which is then related to the influence of monetised self-sufficiency on a continuous passage of the *Chāndogya Upaniṣad* (15§C).

In the concluding section (Part E), Chapter 16 emphasises the complex diversity of factors that shaped the Greek and Indian intellectual revolutions (16§A), describes the metaphysical consequences of a variety of perspectives on money (16§B) and accounts for the differences between brahman and the Parmenidean One (16§C). Chapter 17 sets out the historical factors behind the differing conceptions in India and Greece of the interrelation of universe with inner self (17§A) and the absence from Greece of karma (17§B).

CHAPTER 2

Explanations

2§A Explananda

I define 'philosophy' as the attempt to explain systematically, and without relying on superhuman agency, the fundamental features of the universe and the place of human beings in it. This is not the only possible definition,[1] but is the most revealing one for our period, in which we find the advent of 'philosophy' (or something very like it) in Greece, India and China – and nowhere else.

I must also define (to the extent possible) 'our period'. For Greece it is from Homer to Plato, who died circa 348 BCE. For India it is from the *Rigveda* to 326 BCE, one of the very few dates in early Indian history and a convenient end point for us as it is when Alexander crossed the Indus, after which influence between the cultures became much more likely. Both end dates are inevitably somewhat arbitrary, not least because Indian texts are notoriously undateable. But the five earliest *Upanishads* (*Bṛhadāraṇyaka*, *Chāndogya*, *Taittirīya*, *Aitareya*, *Kauṣītaki*) were (along with the earlier Vedic texts) probably produced before 326 BCE. I will also use later texts when they shed light on our period.

We find in our period in both cultures as ingredients of 'philosophy' certain specific ideas, including (a) that beneath appearances all things are, in fact, a single entity (monism) that may be entirely *abstract*; (b) that knowledge of the unitary (not just imperceptible but) *incorporeal* inner self is central both to understanding the world and to achieving well-being; and (c) ethicised indiscriminate reincarnation (EIR), by which I mean the belief that after death we acquire a new bodily identity

[1] E.g. for Jurewicz (2016a: 14–15) philosophy is an overall explanation, with a coherent conceptual structure, of basic questions; this does not exclude superhuman agency, with the result that 'philosophy' occurs – she claims – in the *Rigveda*, but also – I suggest – in mythology in general.

(human or animal) whose desirability depends on the ethical quality of our previous existence.

I will attempt to explain why a similar complex of fundamental ideas occurs at about the same time in two cultures remote from each other (and nowhere else). Even the individual ideas that form the components of the complex are at this time barely found elsewhere. Moreover, we will find that in both India and Greece this new world-view developed out of an earlier, very different one that is also similar between the two cultures. Describing and explaining these and other similarities (and differences) will shed new light on both cultures, even though for both we depend at all times largely on texts written by a small male elite and have only very limited knowledge of the practices and beliefs of the vast majority of people.

In the next three sections of this chapter I discuss three kinds of explanation that have been offered for intellectual similarities between Greece and India in our period. They have, I argue, very little explanatory power. What has much more explanatory power is – I claim – the fact that both societies were, in the crucial period, undergoing significant socio-economic change, and in particular attaining a degree of *monetisation* that had at the time been attained by no other society (with the possible exception of China).[2] The rest of the book gradually accumulates the evidence for this claim, starting with a description of the monetisation itself, and of the concomitant developments of cities, of commerce and of individual property (2§E).

2§B A Shared Indo-European Origin?

There are numerous similarities between Greek and Indian culture that are best explained by their common Indo-European heritage. But our set of new metaphysical ideas cannot be attributed to a common Indo-European heritage, because of the *combination* of the following considerations. (1) Although prominent in both cultures within the period circa 600–326 BCE, the ideas are almost entirely absent from the earliest texts (the *Rigveda*, Homer and Hesiod), even though these texts are of great length and embody a wide range of concerns. (2) We will see that in both cultures certain new ideas *relate to each other* in a way that suggests that they

[2] The most recent conference publication on the Axial Age (Bellah and Joas 2012) largely ignores both economics and *detailed* intercultural comparison: an exception is the statement by Arnason (Bellah and Joas [2012] 347) that my approach in Seaford (2004) 'merits a discussion that has hardly begun'. The influences of monetisation on metaphysics have been better understood in the study of Christian thought: e.g. Kaye (1998) and Singh (2018).

belonged to a *single* intellectual *development* that began later than the earliest texts, which were in turn produced later than the separation of the European from the Indian branch of the Indo-Europeans. (3) Nothing remotely like this development occurred autonomously in any other of the many Indo-European societies. Why not? (4) The ideas are fundamental beliefs about the nature of the universe and of the self, quite different in kind from the *forms or structures* (linguistic, social, numerical, narrative) that may well embody a shared Indo-European heritage.

This last distinction is tested by the claim of Pinchard (2009) that it is possible to affiliate Platonic *ontology* to the *Rigveda*, more specifically the intelligible world of ideas in Plato to the speech (especially 'noms secrets') of the gods. True, the idea of a hidden reality that is somehow superior to the visible world, and can be revealed in speech, is shared by the *Rigveda* and Plato, as well as (in various forms) by many other cultures. But we do not find in the *Rigveda* anything like the systematic ontological distinction, in Plato, between on the one hand the changing material realm of the senses and on the other an unchanging, intelligible and more fully real realm in which abstract forms depend somehow – for their being, intelligibility and value – on a single supremely real abstract entity that is sometimes called the form of the good.

This is not to say that Pinchard's wide-ranging exploration of various questions and issues has no substance, or that the Indo-European inheritance is entirely irrelevant to my enquiry: indeed, I will not infrequently adduce it.[3] It is just that its explanatory power is limited.

2§C Influence?

As the shared metaphysics does not occur before our period, and then in our period only in India and Greece, it is most unlikely that it was diffused from any third culture, be it Indo-European or, say, Mesopotamian or Egyptian. There is another possibility, that the similarity of ideas was a result of direct or indirect contact between India and Greece. How likely was this?

It became a fanciful commonplace in antiquity to derive doctrines of Greek thinkers from contact with the Orient. Pythagoras, for instance, was said to have learnt from Egyptians, Persians, Chaldaeans, Phoenicians, Jews and Indians, as well as Celts and Iberians.[4] But we do not in fact have reliable reports of there being any Greeks beyond the Indus, or Indians in

[3] 3§B, 6§B, 9§D, 12§D, 16§A. [4] Riedweg (2005) 7–8.

Greece (except briefly in Xerxes' army), before Alexander crossed the Indus in 326 BCE.[5] And so those who believe that ideas were transmitted between India and Greece before 326 BCE tend to claim that Indians and Greeks might easily have met in the Achaemenid empire.

Precisely such a meeting is imagined by Herodotus in his colourful account of Darius I interviewing some Indians, in the presence of Greeks, about their treatment of the dead (3.38). It is from soon after 522 BCE, when Darius I became king, that we first hear of the presence of Greeks at the Persian court,[6] and Greeks are also mentioned in the Persepolis tablets of Darius' reign.[7] Herodotus records Darius settling groups of Greeks in his empire: the Barcaeans in Bactria, Milesians near the mouth of the Tigris (493 BCE) and Eretrians near Sousa (490 BCE).[8] There is further such evidence for the reign of his successor Xerxes.[9]

As for the Indian side, after the decline – early in the second millennium BCE – of the trade between Mesopotamia and the Indus valley,[10] the evidence for contact between the two regions is relatively sparse and never undisputed,[11] until the Achaemenid period. In about 518 BCE Darius extended[12] his empire to the Indus area, after an exploratory voyage down the Indus by Skylax of Caryanda.[13] From the time of Darius goods were brought to Persia from India,[14] and texts found at Persepolis mention the presence of Indians in Persepolis or Susa.[15] In the reign of Xerxes (from 486 BC) Indians bringing tribute were represented in the Persepolis reliefs, and there was an Indian contingent in the army that invaded Greece.[16]

In the Indian texts that certainly belong before 326 BCE there is not a single reference to anything Greek.[17] The earliest Greek

[5] The least obviously fantastical is the anecdote (of which there is no trace in Plato, Xenophon etc.) that in Athens an Indian laughed at Socrates for studying human life in ignorance of things divine (Aristoxenus F53 Wehrli = Eusebius *Preparation* 11.3.8).

[6] Syloson of Samos and Demokedes of Croton: Hdt. 3.125, 129–37, 139–41.

[7] Briant (2002) 506.

[8] Hdt. 4.204; 6.20; 6.120.

[9] This includes the much later story, disbelieved by some, that Xerxes settled the Milesian Branchidai in a small town in Sogdiana: Curtius Rufus 7.5.28–35; Plut. *Moralia* 557b; Strabo 517–18, 634.

[10] Wright (2010) 215–25, 314.

[11] Karttunen (1989) 15–31.

[12] As for Cyrus, Nearchus (F3a; Arrian *Anabasis* 6.24) states that he planned to invade India but did not get beyond the Gedrosian desert. Cf. Megasthenes FGrH 715 F11a, F14.

[13] Hdt. 4.44 (cf. 3.94). In inscriptions Darius includes in his possessions Gandhara and Sind. For a discussion of the unanswerable question of precisely what Darius controlled, see Karttunen (1989) 34–8.

[14] E.g. ivory: Briant (2002) 172.

[15] Koch (1993) 36–8; Giovinazzo (2000/1) 59–76. Cf. Hdt. 3.38.

[16] Hdt. 7.65, 86, 113; 9.31.

[17] The first mention is perhaps *yavana* ('Greek') in the *Aṣṭādhyāyī* of Panini, which may be borrowed from Old Persian *yauna* (Panini was from Gandhara in the north-west). But even this is not certainly dateable to our period: Bronkhorst (2007) 177 with bibliography. Greeks are mentioned also in the *Assalāyana Sutta* (MN 2.149), but again we cannot say that this predates Alexander: e.g. Bronkhorst

reference[18] to anything Indian is in the geography of Hekataios of Miletos (born around the middle of the sixth century BCE), who mentioned names of places and of peoples in the Indus area.[19] He had available to him writing by Skylax. Subsequently, in the period before 326 BCE, there are isolated references to India in various Greek authors, as well as the surviving treatment of India by Herodotus and substantial fragments of the lost treatment of India by Ctesias.[20]

Herodotus says that Asia is inhabited as far as India: east of India the country is uninhabited and nobody knows what it is like (4.40). Elsewhere he states that east of India there is an uninhabitable desert of sand (3.98): this is presumably the large Thar desert now shared by Pakistan and India. We may infer that for Herodotus and his Greek contemporaries, knowledge of (what we call) the Indian subcontinent does not extend much beyond the Indus valley. What Herodotus then does tell us about India (3.98–105) contains much fantasy (especially the giant gold-digging ants) and some information that may reflect reality. One tribe practises cannibalism, another vegetarianism. His source for the ants is 'the Persians'.

Ctesias was a Greek doctor at the Persian court in the last years of the fifth century BCE. He was said to have written in his *Indika* about the justice of the Indians, their customs, their high regard for their king and their disdain for death.[21] But what survives of the work consists almost entirely of marvels. His claim that the sun appears ten times larger in India than in any other land[22] would surely be denied by anyone who had been to India. Despite his time at the Persian court, and his claim to have 'seen' Indians,[23] Ctesias seems, so far as we know, to have had no closer acquaintance with India than did Herodotus. It is significant that even at the end of the fifth century India was largely unknown even by Greeks who published on the subject. Nor do any other mentions of India before 326 BCE indicate any closer acquaintance.

We can conclude that the possibility of *philosophical ideas* passing between Greeks and Indians before 326 BCE was very small. Nowhere in the pre-326 BCE reports on India or on writers on India is there any reference to an *idea*, or to *ideas in general* (though there are references to

(2011a) 35–6. And so the mention of Greeks in the inscriptions of Ashoka may be the earliest (mid-third century BCE). On the lack of interaction, see further Halbfass (1988) 18, 20.

18 Unless the reference to 'Indian stones' attributed to Epimenides (DK3 B25 = FGrH 457 F19.8) was earlier, which is most unlikely.

19 FGrH 1 F294-9.

20 English translations of all these texts (except Hdt. 3.97–106) are collected by Arora (1996) 111–54.

21 FGrH 688 F45 (16), (30). 22 FGrH 688 F45 (12). 23 FGrH 688 F45 (19); cf. F45bα.

customs), not even in the many references to India in Aristotle. Even after 326 BCE there is no – or hardly any – certain Greek knowledge of fundamental Indian beliefs or vice versa.[24]

Although travellers have always acquired the language needed for their purposes (e.g. trade),[25] there is no evidence of any Greek *author* of our period knowing any foreign language at all (let alone Sanskrit). The most likely form of influence between remote cultures was of narratives, artefacts or practical innovations. But even for these there is in our period no evidence connecting Greece and India (though practical skills may well have been indirectly transmitted, as I explain at the end of 2§E). Moreover, the early *Upanishads*, which are closest to early Greek thought, were produced not in the area least remote from the Greeks (around the Indus) but a long way eastwards, in the area of the Ganges. The claim that there was intellectual influence between Greece and India derives not from the historical probability of such influence but from the striking similarities between some Greek and some Indian ideas. But it is yet another obstacle to this hypothesis of influence that nothing like these ideas appears anywhere in the vast area between Ionia and the Ganges.[26] In general a factor promoting the possibility of influence is that the influential ideas are superior to those of the recipients, or at least seem to the recipients to be superior. It is hard to see how this would be true of the ideas listed in 2§A.

The assumption of influence is seductive, unexamined common sense: firstly because it seems to solve at one blow the conundrum of how strikingly similar ideas appear at about the same time in Greece and India; and secondly because it accords with assumptions derived from a later world in which communications are easy, influence is pervasive and for centuries there have existed contexts of interaction (or domination) in which fundamental ideas are transmitted. Scholars who have never asked themselves whether there might be a relation between the nature of a society and the metaphysics it produces (or adopts) are likely to project unconsciously onto the ancient world the conditions of their own world, in which intellectual influence – transmitted

[24] The (contemptuous) account by Megasthenes (FGrH 715 F33) is in this respect unimpressive, as are also Greek mentions of the Indian gymnosophists.

[25] Known examples of Persian acquired by Greeks in the classical period (for practical purposes) are Histiaios (Hdt. 6.29.2), Themistokles (Thucydides 1.138.1), perhaps Alkibiades (Athenaeus 535e) and Laomedon (Arrian *Anabasis* 3.6). There were, no doubt, may others. Translators working for the Persians may have been Greek.

[26] In particular, there is neither monism nor reincarnation. For further fundamental differences between Persian beliefs and those shared by Greece and India, see McEvilley (2002) 122–6.

internationally in publications and conferences – seems to occupy an autonomous sphere of its own.[27]

But the assumption of influence leaves basic problems unsolved. One is the difficulty of showing, or even plausibly imagining, how the necessary contact occurred between these remote areas, despite the complete lack of evidence. This problem would be less severe with visual images, narratives and descriptions of various kinds, which might indeed be easily transmitted between travellers from remote cultures. But we have already noted that before 326 BCE there is in fact no evidence of anything even of this kind reaching India from Greece, and most of what reached Greece from India were *incredibilia*. As for the adoption by one culture of the *fundamental metaphysical ideas or methods of enquiry* of another, more substantial contexts of interaction (or rather domination) are required.

But even if it could be shown that such substantial contexts existed, or that fundamental ideas migrated, a major problem would remain. If Parmenides or Parmenideans had arrived on the banks of the Ganges, they might have received an appreciative hearing. Do those who incline to explain all similarities by influence believe that they would have received an equally appreciative hearing on the banks of the Thames? And how do we explain that Greek metaphysical ideas had no effect on any of the societies in the vast area between India and Greece? At this point we are approaching the insight that a society will receive *fundamental* ideas from another society only if it *has a need and a place* for them, whether because it has become dominated by that other society or because in its basic form it sufficiently resembles the society in which the ideas were produced. Between Greece and India in our period there was no relation of domination (or even of contact), but there was a similarity in basic societal form at least as great as that between Greece and any other society. What this means is that, even if there was influence (in one direction or the other), which of course in principle cannot be completely disproved, it was made possible by the similarities between Greek and Gangetic society – an insight blocked by the widespread assumption of mere 'influence'.

The shared ideas arise too late to be attributed to a common Indo-European heritage, but earlier than any likelihood of influence between Greece and India. We are therefore forced to ask the questions not often asked. Why and how did these strikingly similar ideas arise independently

[27] From numerous examples I cite Beckwith (2015), who has the honesty to (a) *reject explicitly* the manifest truth that 'two figures saying similar, or even identical things, in different parts of the world, is never enough to establish direct influence' (xi), and (b) admit that such similarities are, unless we suppose influence, (for him) 'mysterious'.

in the two cultures? Can the same method account for the shared shape of the new ideas? And, as the new ideas are similar but not identical, can we use the same method to explain the differences? When we have answered these questions in the affirmative, we will see that answers involving common origin or influence are as unnecessary as they are mistaken. This will also have the further consequence that – because the Indian and Greek ideas are so similar – any historical explanation that applies to the one but is manifestly impossible for the other will be at a disadvantage even for the culture to which it is not manifestly inapplicable. For instance, for the genesis of Greek philosophy Eric Havelock (1963) argued for the importance of *literacy*, Robert Hahn (2001) for the importance of *monumental stone architecture.* But in India very similar ideas to those of early Greek philosophy clearly predate both these inventions.

Finally, I must note here the claim by McEvilley (in the only comprehensive account of the similarities between presocratic philosophy and the *Upanishads*) that there is one similarity that is so close that we are *forced* to suppose influence: this I deal with in 9§D(8).

2§D The Advance of Reason?

In a 1998 lecture entitled 'Why is There Philosophy in India?'[28] Johannes Bronkhorst began by establishing that there was a tradition of serious rational enquiry in Greece and in India but not in China. This leaves the Greek and Indian as the only independent traditions of rational debate. How did they originate? For Greece he follows the political explanation of Geoffrey Lloyd,[29] to which I will return below. But for India he admits that the political explanation cannot work: 'We are not at all sure that anything like the Greek city-state ever existed in ancient India.' He maintains instead that 'the original impulse for the development of Indian rational philosophy came from Buddhism', and that 'the Buddhists of North-West India adopted the method of rational debate and enquiry from the Greeks'.[30] With this claim, which may be justified, I will not be concerned because it is about what occurred well after our period.

But what about the early *Upanishads*? They do not – he maintains – contain rational argumentation, and so are not philosophy, and so do not impede his claim that the Indians acquired philosophy from the Greeks.

28 Bronkhorst (1999). In Bronkhorst (2016) he restates the argument in a broader context.
29 He cites in particular Lloyd (1979) Chapter 4.
30 For Schlumberger (1972) the earliest Buddhist thought was an 'offshoot' of Epicureanism (see Halbfass in Bechert [1995] 207–9).

This approach of Bronkhorst is perfectly legitimate. But it means that he omits from his explananda what are, on my definition of philosophy, striking similarities between early Greek and early Indian philosophy. And indeed, if rational argumentation arrived in India from the Greeks, then probably it did so only because there was already in India what I call philosophy: there was no comparable enrichment (as opposed to replacement) of numerous other cultures that the Greeks had contact with in the area. Moreover, in much of what survives of presocratic philosophy, as in the early *Upanishads*, there is no rational argumentation. The most substantial instance of it is in the fragments of Parmenides, to whom I will return after first examining Bronkhorst's description of an Indian instance.

He describes three stages in the development of the doctrine of karmic retribution. I do not need to reproduce the details. What matters is that each of these stages uses rationality to modify the doctrine so as to make it more intelligible. 'They did so because they saw no other way to account for a dogma which they accepted as certain: the dogma of karmic retribution.' Bronkhorst neither claims that rationality had any role in producing the dogma itself nor comments on this lack. However, it cannot be claimed that the three modifications that he selects to exemplify philosophy as rational enquiry have more impact on the final doctrine than does the initial irrational dogma. Bronkhorst identifies philosophy with rational argumentation, but philosophical conclusions never derive *merely* from rational argumentation.

This point can now be applied to Parmenides. He seems to deduce that all that exists is one, abstract and invariant in space and time (eternal, unchanging, unmoving, homogeneous). This bizarre conclusion is of course not a result of mere deduction (as *cogito ergo sum* etc. is sometimes imagined to be), but is rather implicit as a *preconception* from the beginning of (and during) the chain of deduction (14§A). The conclusion (abstract monism) is no more the result of mere reasoning than karmic retribution is the result of mere reasoning. None of the fundamental ideas discussed in this book as shared by Greeks and Indians can be said to be the product of reason. They are *preconceptions*, whose origins we will in due course investigate.

Lloyd's political explanation of the genesis of Greek philosophy implies that reasoning is a natural human activity, which had previously been *inhibited*: once political freedom arrived in Greece, the argument goes, rational enquiry was released from inhibition and allowed to flourish. Following Lloyd, Bronkhorst writes that:

> It is noteworthy to what extent the features most characteristic of what I have proposed to call a tradition of rational inquiry – primarily free and uninhibited discussion of all issues even in areas which might encroach upon other sources of authority – appear to be intimately linked to the political situation of Greece at the time. It is precisely inhibitions, the fear to encroach on other sources of authority, which would seem to prevent traditions of rational debate and inquiry from coming about in the majority of human societies.[31]

I have argued at length elsewhere for the inadequacy and inconsistency of Lloyd's explanation of the Greek development.[32] Here I add briefly the point that the implication of the argument – that reason-impeding inhibition was the universal fate of humankind until the sixth-century polis – is implausible.

Consider, for instance, a band of hunter-gatherers, who are subject to no political authority beyond the egalitarian band. On seeing certain marks on the ground, they infer that a certain animal is nearby. And noticing that the marks occur with a certain frequency, they infer that the animal is limping, and so will be easy prey. They also speculate on the origin of fire: it must have been brought to them from the fire in the sky, for which the divine thief and humankind must have had to pay a price, namely alienation from the gods and suffering in general. All this is reasoning, which occurs equally in repressive and non-repressive societies. It produces conclusions that others may use reason to dispute, producing other conclusions. And it cannot be said to be less *fundamental* than the reasoning of Parmenides. True, hunter-gatherers do not produce what we call *philosophical* reasoning. For instance, Parmenides argues that what exists cannot derive from what does not exist (DK28 B8.7–10), rather as a pre-Buddhist Indian text (CU 6.2.2) asks 'How can what is existent be born from what is non-existent?' We feel that with Parmenides reasoning has almost reached the degree of *abstraction* that will allow it – not long afterwards, with Plato and especially Aristotle – to reflect on itself. However, what is new – in both Parmenides and (independently) the early *Upanishads* – is not the use of reason but the *degree of generalising abstraction* with which it is employed.[33]

To conclude, Bronkhorst may be right to suppose Greek influence on early Buddhist reasoning (after 326CE), but this cannot explain any of our explananda (2§A); and the purely negative explanation of the advent of reason (absence of inhibition) does not work.

[31] Bronkhorst (1999) 13. [32] Seaford (2004) 176–87. [33] 8§E, 14§B.

2§E Individual Property and Monetisation

I must start by defining monetisation, as *development towards a single entity (money) whose only or main function is to be a general means of payment and exchange and a general measure and store of value*. It is important to bear this (relatively narrow) definition in mind, as the word is often used vaguely or with other legitimate meanings. It is also important to distinguish money and monetisation from coinage. Coinage is one form of money, but there have been others: in particular, it is likely in both Greece and India that before the introduction of coinage precious metal acquired, to some extent, at least some of the four functions of money in the definition of monetisation just given. Monetisation may be a gradual process, which is likely to be speeded up and completed by the introduction of coinage with its convenience of numerous standardised units that do not require testing and weighing at every transaction.

(1) India

The society of the *Rigveda* is semi-nomadic, without towns or money or writing, and with only a few slight indications of commerce.[34] Subsequent Vedic literature contains almost no mention of towns and cities but some mentions of commerce:[35] this is in sharp contrast to the urban, commercial and monetised environment manifest in some early Buddhist texts. The contrast arises in part perhaps from geographical and chronological differences, but also probably from the well-documented Brahminical rejection of urban life,[36] as one instance of what Uma Chakravarti calls the 'rigidity and utter distance from reality' of the 'Brahmanical model', which is 'weakest in explaining the political-economic domain'.[37] Such *ideological omission* is commonplace, for instance in Homer.[38] Olivelle notes that the *Upanishads* contain very few agricultural images, but many from crafts, suggesting a milieu of 'court and crafts, rather than village and agriculture'.[39]

In any event, archaeology tells us that there was rapid and considerable urbanisation in the sixth and fifth centuries BCE. Of the six cities selected

[34] This is of course not to say that no exchange occurred. In their translation Jamison and Brereton (2014) use the word 'merchant' twice (1.112.11 *vaṇije*, 5.45.6 *vaṇig*), but it is unclear what exactly the Sanskrit refers to. Bargaining is indicated at 4.24.9.

[35] Collected by Rau (1957) 28–9, to which add esp. AV 3.15.

[36] Bronkhorst (2007) 251–5; Thapar (1984) 93; Pande (1995) 315; Gombrich (2006) 56; Lubin (2005) 79–80. The rejection was explicit in the early *Dharmasūtras*.

[37] Chakravarti (1987) 119. [38] Seaford (2004) 53–4 [39] Olivelle (1996) xxix.

by Buddhist tradition as fit to receive the remains of the Buddha – Campa, Kasi, Kausambi, Rajagriha, Saketa and Sravasti – all except Saketa are also the earliest urban centres known from archaeology (along with Ujjain). The cities clearly stated by their excavators to have been fortified by 550 are Campa, Kasi, Rajagriha and Ujjain.[40] These early cities extend throughout a vast area, with Kasi and Campa on the river Ganges, Kausambi on the river Yamuna, Sravasti to the north in Kosala, Rajagriha to the south-east in Magadha and Ujjain to the south-west in Avanti.

As for the period 550–400 BCE, Erdosy describes an exceptionally large increase in the size of the sites in the Allahabad district, producing *inter alia* 'towns providing a full complement of manufacturing activities' but dwarfed by the capital city of Kausambi.[41] It is worth adding that Megasthenes, who visited the Mauryan king Chandragupta around 300 BCE, wrote that there were so many Indian cities (*poleis*) that he could not give the exact number. The Mauryan capital Palibothra (Pataliputra) was – he writes – eighty stades long and fifteen stades wide, and its wall had five hundred and seventy towers and sixty-four gates (FGrH 715 F18a).

The layout of towns and cities is not well known before the third century BCE. Large urban settlements are not necessarily pervaded by commerce, because they may be the sites of centralised redistribution, as were the prehistoric riverine cities of ancient Egypt, Mesopotamia and (almost certainly) the Indus valley.[42] But in those areas the economic centralisation is reflected in the archaeological record, whereas by contrast in the towns and cities of the Ganges area – where there seems to have been continuity of layout from the beginning[43] – there are market places,[44] 'a striking absence of monumental public buildings'[45] and 'little evidence for a citadel or acropolis distinct from the residential area . . . the absence of large-scale warehouses or granaries in these towns again suggests that political authority was still relatively decentralised'.[46] This is precisely the kind of context – decentralised exchange in growing towns and cities (i.e. between strangers) – in which we would expect monetisation. The clearance of jungle

[40] Erdosy (1995) 109–10, 115. [41] Erdosy (1995) 107.

[42] The absence of decipherable texts from the Indus valley civilisation makes certainty impossible, but archaeology reveals river-dependent agriculture (as in Mesopotamia and Egypt), evidence for centralised (as well as for independent) production, no evidence for anything indicating money (but numerous seals, as in Mesopotamia and Egypt) and cities with large non-residential buildings (often taken to be granaries) and public works requiring centralised planning: e.g. Wright (2010) 33, 117–27, 183–5, 236–7, 240–2, 271. Where we have archaeobotanical evidence, it suggests the central role of the city (Harappa) in 'storage, trade, and the centralisation and control of the food supply': Weber (2003) 194. In 2014 a large building claimed to be a granary was discovered at Rakhigarhi.

[43] Erdosy (1995) 111. [44] Thapar (1984) 99. [45] Thapar (1984) 91. [46] Thapar (1984) 99.

opened up fertile areas far from rivers, some cities were located for their proximity to raw materials absent from the alluvial plains (especially iron ore)[47] and massive quantities of iron slag in several sites suggest 'full-time craft specialisation and production for a wide market'.[48] The widespread accessibility of iron (unknown in the *Rigveda*) surely increased the efficiency of jungle-clearing and of the resulting agriculture. The economy of the northern Indian cities in our period was – somewhat like the Greek polis but unlike e.g. Egypt and Mesopotamia – commercial (as well as basically agricultural) rather than redistributive.

A fourth-century origin is possible, some would say likely, for the earliest Buddhist texts,[49] which refer to manufacture, specialised skills, inter-city trade, individual property, rich merchants, market towns, shops and the use of money, including coinage and money-lending at interest[50] – true though it is that this picture may have been enhanced during the oral transmission of these texts through the Mauryan and post-Mauryan periods. Urbanisation continued in the third century BCE,[51] but by the fourth century BCE had already – archaeology suggests – advanced to the point at which social relations had been transformed by commerce, at least in the towns and cities.

Part of this historical development is the development of *individual property*. In his detailed study of the society implied by Vedic prose texts, Rau detects 'a tendency for family property to be dissolved into private shares'.[52] Uma Chakravarti argues that in the *gaṇa-saṅghas*[53] land was held collectively, and that their collapse belonged to the 'same phenomenon' as the emergence of 'an economy based on the individual holding of land and organised around the *gahapati*'.[54] Romila Thapar writes of the *gahapati* (a householder) as 'deriving his land through the breaking up of the lineage-held lands into family ownership', and of 'erosion of the lineage system with the eventual arrival of the notion of private ownership of land and of the development of commerce as more than just exchange'.[55] In the earliest law codes the rules of inheritance combine the principle of individual property with elements of clan solidarity: the son of a legitimate

47 Kosambi (1951) 195; Erdosy (1995) 82, 113. 48 Erdosy (1995) 112.
49 Much of the *Vinaya* and of the four *Nikāyas*: Gombrich (2006) 20–21; (2013) 95–110; Pande (1995); Chakravarti (1987) 2–4.
50 E.g. Thapar (1984) 90–104; Chakravarti (1987) 20–22; Bailey and Mabbett (2003) 15–18, 24, 56–76.
51 Emphasised by Bailey and Mabbett (2003) 83–4.
52 Rau (1957) 50; also Kosambi (1951) 186; (1965) 100–101.
53 Non-monarchical societies, generally on the periphery of the Ganges plain.
54 Chakravarti (1987) 91–2, 177; similarly Thapar (1984) 76, 78; Kosambi (1965) 100–1.
55 Thapar (1984) 88–9, 36; Kosambi (1965) 101.

marriage must inherit, and belongs to his father, and in the absence of sons other relatives must inherit.[56]

A central feature of decline in an early Buddhist account of the past is the dividing up of the rice fields into individual property.[57] According to Erdosy private ownership of land, which was recognised for the first time in a passage of the *Taittirīya Saṃhitā* (2.2.1), probably originated in the granting of lands (or their revenues) by powerful individuals to Brahmins (e.g. CU 4.2.4–5),[58] which combined with other processes to 'hasten the emergence of private property out of communal (lineage) ownership'.[59] The *Brahmanas* tell of a priest officiating in a sacrifice that bestows power on an individual who conquers the whole earth, which he promises to the priest; but the earth herself objects that no mortal can give her away:[60] This story expresses on the one hand the politico-economic potential of the extreme individualism inherent in the sacrificial interaction of Brahmin and Kshatriya (a phenomenon to which I will return below), and on the other hand resistance to the (resulting) individualisation of the land.

The *Śatapatha Brāhmaṇa*[61] mentions a sacrifice in which the entire property of an individual is given away for 'all one's property is (a manifestation of) totality'.[62] At BU 1.5.15 a man is said to consist, in being identified with Prajapati, of sixteen parts: 'his fifteen parts consist merely of his wealth, while his sixteenth part is his atman. He is like a wheel, with his atman as hub and his wealth as rim (or plate) .' A little later the atman is compared to the hub and rim, and the spokes compared to all the gods, all the worlds, etc.:[63] i.e. the unity of self with wealth is expressed with the same image as the unity of self with universe. Later still the atman, as the controller, lord and ruler of all, is also called 'the dike separating these worlds so that they would not mingle with one another' (4.4.22). Dike (*setu*), explains Olivelle, 'probably refers to the raised earthen boundaries across paddy-fields that both allow one to walk across wet land and mark the boundaries between properties'. The power of the self and the order of the universe are characterised by individual property.

How do we date this textual evidence? The chronology of middle and late Vedic texts is notoriously obscure. For the *Brahmanas* 'the 10th-7th century may for the main texts be a reasonable conjecture',[64] with the

[56] *Dharmasūtras*: *Apastamba* 2.13–14; *Gautama* 28; *Baudhayana* 1.11.11–14; *Vasistha* 17.81–3. For the chronology of these texts, see this section below. See also the later *Laws Of Manu* 9.104–220.
[57] *Aggañña Sutta* (DN 27.18–20, pp. 412–13 Walshe). [58] Erdosy (1988) 93–4.
[59] Erdosy (1995) 114. [60] AB 8.21; SB 13.7.1.15. [61] 4.6.1.15; 13.6.2.9.
[62] Gonda's (1982–3: 6) translation of *sarvaṃ vai sarvavedasaṃ*.
[63] BU 2.5.15; similar are CU 7.15.1 and KU 3.8. [64] Gonda (1975) 360.

Śatapatha Brāhmaṇa (generally regarded as one of the latest of the *Brahmanas*) often assigned to 800–600 BCE. For the earliest *Upanishads* (*Bṛhadāraṇyaka* and *Chāndogya*), 'the seventh to sixth century BCE may be reasonable, give or take a century or so' (Olivelle).[65] The absence in them of Buddhist influence has been thought to provide a *terminus ante quem*. And so because Olivelle favours the downdating of the death of the Buddha to 375–55 BCE,[66] 'then the dates of the early *Upanishads* should be pushed forward a century or so', i.e. perhaps to as late as the fourth century BCE. It is not impossible that even this is too early, for we do not have to suppose that the Vedic and Buddhist milieux were interconnected so early that the *Upanishads* would have to be influenced by Buddhism in the lifetime of the Buddha. After all, Buddhism seems to have been the product of an urban milieu, which Brahmins were hostile enough to ignore. This hostility also means that the absence of towns from the early *Upanishads* cannot be used to date the *Upanishads* earlier than the archaeological record for towns. And instances of Upanishadic influence on Buddhist texts cannot be dated as early as the lifetime of the Buddha. Moreover, there is no evidence for writing in India before the Ashoka inscriptions of the mid-third century BCE,[67] and the writing down of the early *Upanishads* may have first occurred centuries later.[68]

The movement of population into towns and cities was in all likelihood accompanied by a tendency towards the dissolution of kinship groups and of traditional culture, and by an increase in impersonal institutions, commerce, specialisation and individual property.[69] One would also expect these developments to favour the convenience of using certain items – eventually a single item – as means of exchange and as measure and store of value, and this incipient monetisation to spread to some extent into the countryside. Money is made possible by,

65 Olivelle (1996) xxxvi. Both these *Upanishads* are compilations of originally independent texts and have certain passages in common.

66 For the consensus on downdating the death of the Buddha, see esp. the numerous works edited or written by Bechert (e.g. 1995, 2001), for whom (2001) the Buddha must have died between 420 BCE and 350 BCE; for Gombrich (2006: 32) the date is between 422 BCE and 399 BCE. For subsequent disagreement (with a survey of some recent scholarship), see e.g. Loeschner (2012) 138–9.

67 Except perhaps in the north-western area, under Achaemenid influence: script (probably Aramaic) is mentioned in the *Aṣṭādhyāyī* of Panini, which is dated anywhere from the mid-fifth century BCE to after our period (2§C n.14). For detailed treatment, see Falk (1993); the date of the graffiti in *brahmi* subsequently discovered in Anuradhapura in Sri Lanka (early fourth century BCE?) remains controversial (Thapar 2002a: 163); see also Gombrich (2006) 54.

68 This allows Bronkhorst (2007) to argue that their final form was much later than is generally supposed.

69 E.g. Ghosh (1973) 37.

and promotes, the development of individual property. Especially conducive to *individual* possession is the ease with which precious metal money can be transferred, transported, stored and concealed. Whether incipient monetisation in northern India used gold or silver (or both), or even some other item, is impossible to say. Gold and silver were – unless buried and never recovered – always too valuable to be left for archaeology to discover. Is there any evidence for money in the middle and late Vedic texts?

Payments (or gifts?) are either for sacrifice (in the *Brahmanas*) or for wisdom (in the early *Upanishads*). The *dakṣiṇā* (the fee given to the sacrificial priest) took the form of cows, gold, clothes or horses;[70] and in the *Bṛhadāraṇyaka Upaniṣad* and *Chāndogya Upaniṣad* specified numbers of cows (generally a thousand) are given for wisdom.[71] Such variety counts against the existence of a general means of payment. Wealth is not specified in terms of money: for instance, a man with a certain kind of knowledge 'becomes a big man on account of offspring and livestock' (CU II.2). There are in these texts few indications[72] of anything with the *functions* of money as *general* means of payment and exchange, measure of value or store of value. And there is no mention of coinage.

Cows are often given together with gold. Gold and silver are frequently mentioned in early Indian texts, silver first in the middle Vedic period.[73] Gold was used in various ways in ritual, where it had various associations, especially – given its incorruptibility – with immortality[74] (as in Greece). Gold and silver are more lasting than all commodities, but silver less so than gold. And the comparative newcomer silver had negative associations,[75] which for Falk 'explains why the Brahmins did not usually accept silver as gift at sacrifices'.[76] Gold (or occasionally silver) given to the priests might be specified as of quantified weight,[77]

70 Biardeau and Malamoud (1976) 174–5; SB 4.3.4.24–7. At e.g. SB 2.2.3.28 (= 4.5.1.15) the fee is specified as gold, for 'this is a sacrifice to Agni, and gold is Agni's seed . . . Or an ox, for such a one is of Agni's nature as regards its shoulder . . .'

71 BU 2.1.1; 4.1.2–7; 4.3.14–16, 33; 4.4.7; CU 4.2.1–4; also AB 7.3.15–16. The cow might be a unit of value already in the RV (Thapar [1984] 25), as in Homer. Cf. RV 4.24.10 'Who for ten cows acquires from me this Indra who is mine?'

72 I discuss some below. Also, the mention of a buried treasure of gold at CU 8.3.2 may suggest that gold was used, at least sometimes, as a store of value. At RV 9.112.2 a smith seeks a man who has gold, but from the context (different people seeking different things) it appears that he seeks it as *material*.

73 Ctesias, writing at around the end of the fifth century BCE, says that India contains gold, much silver and silver-mines (FGrH 688 F45 (26)).

74 Gonda (1991). 75 E.g. AV 8.13.7; TS 1.5.1.1. 76 Falk (1991) 111.

77 E.g. SB 12.7.2.13; 13.2.3.2; 13.4.1.6–7; 13.4.2.10 (silver); 13.4.2.13; TB 1.8.9.1; 1.7.8.2; TS 2.3.11.6; MS 1.6.4; 2.2.2; etc.: Prasad (1966) 165.

and it might be given in pieces,[78] or even pieces of uniform quantified weight.[79] The *Pañcaviṃśa Brāhmaṇa* (18.3.2) specifies what should be given on various ritual occasions:

> (a piece of) gold weighing 12 *manas* [measures]; ... (a piece of) gold of 24 *manas*; ... 2 (pieces) of 24 *manas* ... 4 pieces of 24 *manas* (with the 4 increasing at subsequent performances to 8, then 16, then 32, then 64, then 128) ... 2 pieces of 128 *manas* ... 4 pieces of 128 *manas* ... 8 pieces of 128 *manas* ... 16 pieces of 128 *manas* ... 100 oxen ... a golden plate (as ornament to be worn round the neck) ... a (golden) wreath ... 32 pieces of 128 *manas* ... 64 pieces of 128 *manas* ... 128 pieces of 128 *manas*.

Janaka, king of Videha, plans a sacrifice, at which he intends to give lavish gifts to the priests, and to the assembled Brahmins he declares that the most learned man of them should drive away a thousand cows, to the horns of each of which are attached ten pieces[80] of gold.[81] Even in its association in ritual with immortality gold might take the form of a thousand pieces.[82] Pieces of precious metal (especially if of uniform quantified weight) look like proto-money. The new kind of exchange – of wealth for wisdom rather than *dakṣiṇās* for sacrifice – allows the question that Janaka then asks one of the Brahmins (Yājñavalkya), 'Do you want cows or subtle disputations?', to which Yājñavalkya replies 'Both, your majesty'. Yājñavalkya amasses much wealth. Another Brahmin, Usasti, when hired to perform a sacrifice as a result of his superior knowledge, insists on being paid the same amount as the priests who had been performing it (CU 1.10–11). To these slight indications of monetisation we will return in 7§A.

We cannot expect in the early history of money a specific word for it. Long after the Greek polis was pervaded by coinage there was no such word:[83] it was 'gold' to which Herakleitos attributed the function of money as a general means of exchange (B90). In middle and late Vedic texts we may also have to reckon with a factor of archaising conservatism. The exchange of wisdom for 'a thousand cows' in the *Upanishads* has an

78 Cf. 'ten golden balls have I gained already from Divodāsa' as early as RV 6.47.23.

79 SB 5.4.3.26; 5.5.5.15.

80 Sanskrit *pāda* (meaning foot, both a part of the body and a measurement, as in English; also means a quarter). 'Gold' is understood. This may be influenced by, but is significantly different from, RV 8.65.10: 'The king is giver to me – of dappled cows (with horns) wrapped in gold.'

81 BU 3.1.1. The synthesis of pastoral with metallic wealth occurs in Greek mythology, for instance in the famous golden fleece.

82 SB 8.7.4.7–11: having constructed the fire-altar (i.e. Agni), the sacrificer bestrews him with a thousand pieces of gold (*hiraṇyaśakalaiḥ*), thereby making him immortal ('a thousand means everything: with everything he thus confers upon him immortality, that highest form').

83 Seaford (2004) 16, 88–95.

archaising (even pre-agricultural) feel about it,[84] rather like the evaluation of prestige objects in terms of a hundred cows (along with the absence of money) in Homer.[85] Our long list of golden pieces of quantified standard weights in the *Pañcaviṃśa Brāhmaṇa* is varied by a single specification of a hundred cows (along with a gold ornament). As we have seen, the Brahmins of this era suspected silver, rejected urban life and omitted to mention the towns and cities that were being created around them.[86] And so they may also have omitted to mention explicitly the monetisation that was centered in those cities, just as they subsequently did in *Upanishads* that were certainly produced centuries after monetisation. Moreover, money tends to dissolve distinctions between groups separated by status (as indicated in an early Buddhist text: 10§C), and so was likely to be ignored or rejected by Brahmins. Another fundamental innovation that they ignored (somewhat later) was writing.

But it is possible to reject money and yet be profoundly (if only unconsciously) influenced by it, rather as Plato separates the guardians of his ideal polis from the polluting circulation of money but requires them to be told that they have divine gold and silver coinage (χρυσίον . . καὶ ἀργυρίον) in their souls (*Republic* 416e). In the *Upanishads* there is barely any awareness of what lies outside their tradition, be it urbanisation, monetisation or other religious movements. But it would be difficult for the Brahmins to lead lives entirely isolated from the rapidly self-replicating convenience of money. They received wealth from non-Brahmins, and sacrifice itself required provisions. And in fact we will see in certain middle Vedic passages indirect evidence for money. For instance,[87] the necessity for the Brahmins to engage in (undesirable) monetised commerce is, I suggest, beautifully expressed in the following ritual enactment described at SB 3.3.3.1–7.

A priest (Brahmin) purchases a vital ingredient of the sacrifice, soma.[88] He bargains with the soma-seller, 'therefore any and everything is vendible

[84] Cf. RV 10.98.4: 'O Indra, give a thousand (cows) . . .'; Heesterman (1993) 79: 'The horizon of the Veda remained that of a cattle-keeping warrior world', and sacrifice, having acquired transcendence, seems 'strangely impervious to the world around it'.

[85] A difference is that the world in which Homeric epic originated was certainly premonetary, although it may have had the chance to ignore money during the long period of transmission before it reached its final form.

[86] On the non-recognition or exclusion of commerce as part of the Indo-European inheritance, see Hénaff (2010) 66–72.

[87] See also the narratives of Prajapati (5§D) and Raikva (7§A).

[88] The buying of soma is an episode in the surviving *agnicayana* ritual filmed by Fritz Staal in 1975: www.youtube.com/watch?v=RYvkYk7GvJo.

here'. That is to say, the bargaining is imagined to be the origin of universal commerce. The priest's first offer is of one sixteenth of a cow, which however he agrees is insufficient: 'Yes, King Soma is worth more than that; but great, surely, is the greatness of the cow'; he then lists the various good things that come from the cow. That is to say, after first accepting the principle of commercial *quantification*, he then implictly rejects it by irrelevantly praising the quality and variety of the cow.

He then offers instead a hoof, and finally the whole cow. This the soma-seller accepts, saying 'name the kinds!', to which the priest responds by offering a *variety* of goods: gold, a cloth, a goat and various cows. This is explained as the origin of *bargaining*:

> And because they first bargain and afterwards come to terms, therefore about any and everything that is for sale here, people first bargain and afterwards come to terms.

Moreover:

> the reason why only the priest enumerates the virtues of the cow, and not the soma-seller those of the soma, is that soma is already glorified, since soma is a god.

The soma transcends – and is exempted from – the new, unprecedented *explicitly self-interested* process of bargaining that is universal in commerce:

> The priest then makes (the sacrificer) say on the gold 'You, the pure, I buy with the pure', for he indeed buys the pure with the pure, when (he buys) soma with gold,

and similarly (in place of 'pure') 'brilliant' and 'immortal'. This reflects the importance of gold as means of exchange. But here the gold is personalised, and praised not for its monetary value but as itself having the purity, brilliance and immortality of the soma for which it is exchanged. The equivalence of gold and soma is here not *quantitative* (exchange-value) but endowed with the *qualities* (use-value) with which gold is used in Brahminical *ritual*. Niketas in the *Kaṭha Upaniṣad* (2.3) is commended for accepting a gold disc for ritual use rather than 'as a thing of wealth'.[89] All this is – in this context – a reaction against the vulgar (mere) quantification that defines monetised commerce. The inevitability of the commercial act is acknowledged, but assimilated to ritual.[90] The metal offered is accordingly gold, which had long been valued in ritual, rather than silver,

[89] Bodewitz (1985) 20–1.

[90] Such assimilation is facilitated by the fact that Vedic sacrifice itself involved exchange.

which besides being inauspicious was (or subsequently became) the main metal of the earliest Indian coins.

The priest then transfers the cow from soma-seller to sacrificer, by offering gold as compensation, but then:

> draws (the gold) back to the sacrificer, and throws it down, with, 'Ours be thy gold!', whereby he (the sacrificer) takes unto himself the vital energy, and the soma-seller gets only the body.

The priest here reasserts his control of the transaction, on behalf of the sacrificer, who receives not only the cow but also the (abstract) vital energy of the gold, the invisible power that it bestows on ritual, whereas the soma-seller is left with nothing but its (merely corporeal) body.[91] This ritualised absorption by the sacrificer of the incorporeal power (vital energy) separated from the body of the gold illustrates a phenomenon that will be important for our overall argument: the convergence of the incorporeal (abstract, invisible) power of money with the invisible power of ritual.

To summarise: the enactment (a) expresses the tension between quantification and pre-monetary value (quality); (b) identifies Vedic ritual as the authoritative origin of (self-interested) commercial practice; (c) nevertheless expresses the Brahmins' sense of superiority to monetised commerce – despite their need to engage in it – by absorbing it (including the abstract value of money) into their ritual.[92] Another ritual that presents itself as the origin of monetary practice (the monetary power of gold), which it absorbs into itself, will be described in 5§D (TB 3.11.8).

Later in the *Śatapatha Brāhmaṇa* (5.5.5.16) a *dakṣiṇā* of three gold *śatamānāni* – pieces of a hundred (*śata*) measures (*mānāni*) each – is presented to the Brahmin,

> for the Brahmin neither performs nor chants nor recites (like the other priests), and yet he is an object of respect. And with gold they do nothing, and yet it is an object of respect: therefore he presents to the Brahmin three *śatamānāni*.

'Do nothing' with the gold may seem to mean that it was not used in ritual. But why not? In fact in the *Śatapatha Brāhmaṇa* gold objects are frequently

91 A later text adds that the gold is again taken away forcibly from the Soma-seller by the priest, and the seller is driven away: *Kātyāyana Śrautasūtra* 7.8.27.

92 From Greece I know of nothing of precisely this kind. Instead, Greek texts may express the collision and synthesis of ritual and money (e.g. Seaford [2012a] 125–36), and Aristophanes' *Wealth* dramatises the abject dependence of ritual on money.

prescribed for ritual use, especially as symbolising immortality. As we saw, Niketas is commended for accepting a gold disc for ritual use rather than as a thing of wealth. At 5.4.3.24–6 two round gold *śatamānāni* are put to ritual use *as well as* given to the Brahmin as *dakṣiṇā*. 'Do nothing' may imply rather the Brahminical hostility to having to use gold in *exchange*, especially as the uniform quantification of the gold pieces implies their suitability for exchange. The *inherent* symbolic value of gold is (in contrast to its exchange value) *respected*, just as a Brahmin is respected when doing nothing. Another aspect of this comparison occurs at 14.3.1.32:

> as to the *dakṣiṇā*, the gold plate he gives to the Brahmin; for the Brahmin is seated, and gold is *settled*[93] *glory* (my emphasis).

There is a resemblance here with the (ideological) self-sufficiency of the wealthy Greek individual expressed in the imagined self-sufficiency of monetary value.[94]

The gold of the *dakṣiṇā* ideally was used in ritual or perhaps just hoarded, but sometimes would have to be given in exchange, as with the soma-seller, in which case there would be tension between inherent and exchange value, resulting – we have seen – in the preliminary extraction and retention of the true value of the gold then given in exchange. This solution was not confined to gold: at SB 14.1.1.32 we learn that

> if they bring up to him a *dakṣiṇā* he must not, at least on the same day, make over these (objects) to any one else lest he should make over to some one else that glory which has come to him; but rather on the morrow, or the day after: he thus gives it away after having made that glory his own, whatever it be – gold, a cow, a garment, or a horse.

We may conclude that the Indian texts we have discussed generally ignore money while showing signs of its encroachment (as we shall show also for presocratic philosophy). The production of these texts may have extended into, or even largely occurred in, the fifth century BCE (or even later). The urban environment (at least) may well have been already monetised from the beginning of the fifth century, and in the second half of the century may have known coinage. But a full picture of pervasive monetisation is provided by texts that are probably somewhat later:[95] (a) some early

[93] *śayānaṃ*, literally 'lying', i.e. (like the seated Brahmin) not moving. [94] 11§D, 14§A.

[95] The Hathigumpha inscription from Orissa, which records building works paid for by hundreds of thousands (of coins?), is of uncertain date (probably the second or first century BCE).

Buddhist texts, (b) the *Dharmasūtras* and (c) the *Arthaśāstra* attributed to Kautilya, each of which I will now discuss.

(a) There is evidence that Buddhists associated with merchants early on. The financier Anāthapiṇḍika, said to be a companion of the Buddha, in buying land for the Buddhist *saṅgha* covered it with gold (pieces).[96] The episode is from a text. Its representation in sculpture of the second century BCE from Bharhut shows a cartload of coins. The earliness of the narrative (from the *Vinaya*, which may date back to the fourth century BCE)[97] is supported by its expression in *concrete* terms of money's *initially* mysterious power of equivalence (compare the ransom of Hektor's body with an equivalent weight of gold, dramatised in Aeschylus' *Phrygians*). In another passage of the *Vinaya* the ban on Buddhist monks travelling in the rainy season is relaxed for a monk in a caravan or on a ship, presumably accompanying Buddhist merchants.[98]

(b) A survey of the evidence published in 1999 puts the upper limit of the *Āpastamba Dharmasūtra* at the beginning of the third century BCE, the composition of *Gautama* and the *Baudhāyana* between the beginning of the third to the middle of the second, and the *Vasistha* 'somewhat later';[99] though others have dated them all much earlier. The *Āpastamba* mentions the lending of money at interest.[100] The *Gautama* also mentions the lending of money at interest,[101] and specifies units of value (*māsas* and *krsnalas*, probably coins) as interest[102] and as fines.[103] The *Baudhāyana* (1.10.21) and the *Vasistha* (92.50) specify interest in *māsas*. And the *Vasistha* mentions tolls (for crossing a river) in *māsas* and in *kārsapanas*, and tax in *kārsapanas*.[104]

(c) The *Arthaśāstra* presents a more detailed picture of monetised society. However, though it knows gold, it never mentions gold coins. Gold coins were first produced in India by the Kushan Vima Kadphises, who ruled from the end of the first century CE to the beginning of the second. And so we can date the information on coinage in the *Arthaśāstra* to no later (and perhaps much earlier) than this period.[105] It refers to the minting of coins with 25 percent copper (2.12.24), which, Falk notes, 'applies to punchmarked coins of the Mauryan period, not to earlier and not to later coins'.[106]

96 *Vinaya* 2.158–9; Gombrich (2006) 54; Fynes (2015).
97 Gombrich (2006) 92–6; (2013) 95–102.
98 So Gombrich (2013) 27; *Vinaya* 1.152.
99 Olivelle (1999) xxv-xxxiv.
100 1.18.22; 1.19.1; 1.27.10.
101 10.6; 11.31; 12.36; 15.18.
102 12.29.
103 12.8; 12.18; 22.23.
104 19.21–2; 19.36.
105 Olivelle (2013) 27–9; cf. Bronkhorst (2011a) 67–70.
106 Falk (1991) 112–13, 115.

In the *Arthaśāstra* the *pana*, a silver coin, was worth 16 copper *māsakas* and 128 of the smallest copper coins (each worth half a *kakani*). The payment for washing garments of the highest value was one *pana*, for coarse garments one or two *māsakas* (4.1.22). Clearly coins were used for everyday transactions. They were minted and controlled by the state,[107] and were widely used for the purposes of government. For instance, the size (in *panas*) of a fine for theft is determined in part by the value (in *panas*) of the property stolen (4.9.9–11). Taxes were sometimes paid in cash and sometimes in kind.[108]

The *Arthaśāstra* contains a fascinating passage of dialogue[109] in which it is first claimed that what is fundamental is an army: with an army one may (besides military success) amass a treasury, whereas without a treasury one may still raise an army (with forest produce, land or individual plunder). Kautilya (to whom the whole treatise is ascribed) then disagrees:

> For the treasury serves as the foundation for the army. When there is no treasury, the army goes over to the enemy or kills the lord. The treasury facilitates offensive operations; it sustains religious activities and sensual pleasures. According to the requirements of place, time and task, however, either the treasury or the army is of greater moment; for the army is instrumental in acquiring and protecting the treasury, whereas the treasury is instrumental in acquiring and protecting both the treasury and the army. A calamity affecting the treasure is more serious, because all material objects originate from the treasury.

The qualified primacy here of money (rather than the army) as source of all else reflects the process of thoroughgoing monetisation. The *Arthaśāstra* illustrates the interpenetration of the universal power of money with the universal power of the state. It has been plausibly argued that a key factor in the origin and spread of coinage, in India and in Greece, was its use for the payment of soldiers, who at some stage might be best rewarded with numerous equal portions of durable value.[110] In the *Arthaśāstra* (5.3.14) the professional soldier is well paid, with a salary of 500 *panas* (the commanders earn much more). The standing army may have been made possible (and then necessary) by the increasing size of states in northern India from the sixth century BCE, and by monarchical centralisation.[111] Indeed this development, culminating in the establishment of the Mauryan empire over most of the subcontinent from the late fourth

[107] E.g. 2.12.24–6; 4.1.44–8. [108] E.g. 2.12.25; 2.35.1; 2.15.8 [109] 8.1.42–52; cf. 2.12.37.
[110] For Greece references are in Graeber (2011) 426 n.11, for India 428 n.35.
[111] Thapar (2002b) 27 associates standing armies with the monarchies (rather than the *gaṇa-saṅghas*).

century BCE, seems to be reflected in the transition from the regionally circulating silver punchmarked coins (mainly with from one to four marks), to the universal circulation of those with five marks (found across the entire subcontinent).[112]

The references to coins in early Indian texts are undateable.[113] The earliest date we have is from a Roman text: circa 325 BCE, when according to Curtius Rufus[114] tribute of marked silver (*argentum signatum*) was paid by the king of Taxila to Alexander, but even this may be stamped bullion rather than coinage.

What about the survival of the coins themselves? Our concern is with the silver punchmarked coins that appeared, along with urbanisation, at first mainly in the central Gangetic basin.[115] But some have argued that Indian coinage began in the north-west. A hoard found at Chaman Hazouri in Kabul contains Gandharan silver punchmarked coins, Greek coins, so-called 'bent bar' coins and imitations of Greek coins (including an imitation of an issue of Athenian coins that began in the 390s). Cribb (2005) argues that (a) the Gangetic silver punchmarked coins were derived from the Ghandaran (rather than vice versa), (b) the Ghandaran were in turn modelled on Graeco-Persian coins, (c) the attempts to push the dating of the earliest Gangetic coins much further back than the mid-fourth century (archaeological context, varieties and phases of the coins, weight loss through use, correlation of historical events) are all fatally flawed, (d) an introduction of silver coinage from outside the subcontinent would explain the fact that there is hitherto no evidence for the monetary use of silver: gold and pieces of gold are far more at home in Vedic India than is silver, and yet the indigenous production of gold coins began only towards the end of the first century CE.

It is indeed not unlikely that the *idea* of coinage spread from Greece to India. But Gangetic coinage was not accompanied by any other known Greek influence, and there was a substantial difference between the Greek and the Gangetic techniques of producing coins.[116] It is likely that – as in Greece[117] – Gangetic coinage was preceded by monetisation using precious

[112] See e.g. the good recent account by Bhandare (2012).

[113] The earliest mention seems to be (unsurprisingly) in the northwest, by Panini (*rūpya*: Falk [1991] 115), but may be later than our period (2§C n.13). Words in (possibly) earlier texts that have been claimed to mean coins may in fact refer to ornaments (e.g. *niṣka*) or weights (*śatamāna*): Prasad (1966); Sirkar (1968) 48–61. And they may have been for *thesaurisation*, storage for prestige not exchange.

[114] *Life of Alexander* 8.12.42. [115] Hardaker (2019).

[116] Greek coins are stamped, whereas Indian are punched (often several times).

[117] Seaford (2004) 93.

metal: this is what is suggested by the indications of money (but not coins) that we have seen in the *Brahmanas* and early *Upanishads*, and pre-existing monetisation would facilitate the adoption of coinage. Such early monetisation was – remote from existing areas of monetisation – likely to have been largely *endogenous*.

Two further points require emphasis. Firstly, a date earlier than the mid-fourth century for the earliest Gangetic coins cannot, *pace* Cribb, be excluded. According to Erdosy, the radiocarbon dating of Northern Black Polished Ware suggests that 'the introduction of coinage into the subcontinent could be dated to 400 BCE at the earliest'.[118] More recently, and more importantly, Hardaker (2019) has provided a detailed book-length study of the coins themselves, of their method of manufacture, symbology and weight systems. This leads him to date the earliest coins of Magadha (Magadha Series 0) at circa 430 BCE or a little earlier, with the very earliest of all the Gangetic coins a little earlier than that.[119] The story of Anāthapiṇḍika (above) implies the existence of numerous coins in the lifetime of the Buddha (late fifth century BCE).[120]

Secondly, in the Gangetic region the relatively low value of small silver coins (in contrast to Achaemenid gold coins) made possible from the beginning their use in everyday transactions, as is suggested also by the large numbers of surviving silver coins.[121] The rapid advent of large numbers would result from their adoption by states, perhaps – we have seen – to pay soldiers.

Monetisation represents the gradual transfer of power from interpersonal relations to objective embodiment of a universal. Growing stability and volume of exchanges will gradually make it convenient for there to be recognition of a particular substance as generally exchangeable and as providing a measure of value. This may also tend to produce the idea of *abstract value* (embodied in the substance). This process is monetisation, which does not require there to be coinage, true though it is that monetisation may be facilitated and promoted by coinage, and that coinage is – especially as its conventional value is generally greater than its metallic value – likely to advance further the idea of abstract value (or abstract Being). The kind of urbanisation and commercialisation manifest in the archaeological record in the sixth and fifth centuries BCE was – we noted – very likely to have been

[118] Erdosy (1995) 105; cf. 113. [119] See also Gupta and Hardaker (2014) 44–9. [120] Fynes (2015).

[121] They were according to Hardaker 'in their time perhaps even more plentiful than the Roman denarius, judging from the numbers that survive today': Gupta and Hardaker (2014: 19; Gupta 1966: 7; Hardaker 2019) claim to have identified more than 600 varieties of silver punchmarked coins, which suggests millions of coins.

accompanied by monetisation, which would have made possible the emergence, or introduction – perhaps from as early as the mid-fifth century BCE – of large numbers of coins, many of them of a value low enough to be for everyday commercial use.[122] It was also the sixth and fifth centuries BCE that may have produced our versions of the texts in which we have detected the earliest signs of monetisation.

The uncertainties of chronology should not obscure the certainty of the radical transformation of the Gangetic area, manifest from both archaeology and texts, around the middle of the first millennium BCE. In the semi-nomadic, basically pastoral and relatively egalitarian society of the *Rigveda* there is no indication of any of the components of this radical transformation: widespread sedentary agriculture, states based on territory, (individual) property in land, widespread commerce, cities, money and coercive interpersonal relations (debt, dependence, enslavement) based on vast inequality of individual property.

Such radical transformation could not be unaccompanied by radical metaphysical and spiritual change. But even those who allow that the new world-view was likely to have been generated by historical change describe the connection in general terms, such as nostalgia for a simpler past, an escapist response to disruption or the new individualism of the merchant. I do not claim that these and other claims lack all truth, but that they are inadequate. The connection between the new socio-economic form and the *content* of the new metaphysics is much more detailed than has been has realised. And much the same is true of Greece. For Greece our relatively good knowledge of the chronology of the earliest monetisation and of the genesis of 'philosophy' allows us to observe the simultaneity of the two, whereas for India our relative ignorance of chronology prevents us from doing so. However, what we can state for India is that there is *nothing that excludes* the hypothesis that the period of monetisation coincided with the period of metaphysical transformation that we have independent reasons to regard as influenced by monetisation. Moreover, there is, roughly speaking, a *spatial* correlation between the metaphysical transformation and the earliest coinage: they both occurred in the Gangetic area, not least in 'Greater Magadha' (7§A).

A broader context for this development is provided by a review of modern sociological data by Greenfield (2009), in which she uses the opposition between *Gemeinschaft* and *Gesellschaft*. What for her

[122] Low value: e.g. Hardaker (2011) 211–12. This is despite the fact that in the early period fractions are quite small in number in relation to the full denominations.

distinguishes the *Gemeinschaft* model from the *Gesellschaft* model is that the former is rural, small scale, homogeneous and self-contained, with low division of labour, low technology, a subsistence economy (as opposed to a money-based economy), illiteracy and lifelong interdependence of kin. On the often-observed historical movement from *Gemeinschaft* to *Gesellschaft* she concludes (401) that

> a review of empirical research demonstrates that, through adaptive processes, movement of any ecological variable in a *Gesellschaft* direction shifts cultural values in an individualistic direction and developmental pathways toward more independent social behavior and more abstract cognition—to give a few examples of the myriad behaviors that respond to these sociodemographic changes.

Against this widespread pattern observable in the twentieth century we should set the distinctiveness of Gangetic society in the sixth and fifth centuries BCE, and in particular the *aversion* of the (in some ways dominant) Brahminical culture to the newly swollen cities. Nevertheless, the daily encounters with strangers characteristic of the relatively commercialised space of the city are inherently likely to produce the *individualisation* and *more abstract cognition* that Greenfield selects as examples of the effect of the movement of any ecological variable in a *Gesellschaft* direction.

(2) Greece

The chronology of the earliest coinage in Greece is not undisputed, but is much more straightforward than in India, and I have set out the evidence for it elsewhere.[123] There is no trace of coinage in Homer. It became widespread from the early sixth century BCE in the city-states of Ionia, from where it spread across the Greek world. This produced, already in the sixth century BCE, the Greek polis as the earliest society known to be pervasively monetised (through coinage).[124]

One effect of monetisation is to facilitate the development of individual property, a development for which – again – we have more Greek evidence than Indian in this period. In Athens of the classical period, from which we derive most of our Greek evidence, the property of a household is generally inherited by the legitimate sons. The very few apparent exceptions to this

[123] Seaford (2004) chapters 6 and 7.

[124] See Seaford (2004) 318–37. It is not impossible that China was pervasively monetised earlier (16§A n.4).

practice are exceptional also in other respects.[125] There is therefore a sense in which the property belongs to the household rather than to its individual owner, in practice and sentiment if not in the letter of the law. And although land at Athens could be sold, nevertheless – as Todd observes – 'to sell off ancestral estates is in the orators the characteristic behaviour of a man who is wasting rather than investing the proceeds'.[126]

There are indications that individual ownership had in the past been weaker. According to Aristotle 'there used to be laws in many city-states forbidding the sale of the first allotments' (i.e. the land originally allotted to households).[127] The implication is that these laws were no longer current in the time of Aristotle. Plato refers to 'lawgivers of old' who passed a law giving a man freedom to bequeath his property as he liked (*Laws* 922e). At Athens individual ownership was advanced by a law attributed to Solon, which allows a man to bequeath his property as he wishes unless he has legitimate sons.[128] Plutarch (*Solon* 21.2) describes Solon's law thus.

> He (Solon) was esteemed also for his law concerning wills. Previously no will could be made, but the *chrēmata* (property) and *oikos* (household) had to remain in the *genos* (extended family, clan). But he allowed a man, if he had no children, to give his property to whom he wished, ranking *philia* (friendship) above *suggeneia* (kinship) and *charis* (favour) above necessity, and made the *chrēmata* into the *ktemata* (possessions) of the *echontes* (those who have it).

The property of the childless man would, before Solon, revert to the *genos*, i.e. perhaps something like the *ankhisteia* as known from classical Athens, the legally defined group of kin who had, in default of direct heirs, not only rights of inheritance[129] but also obligations in case of homicide.[130] The kinship group was, to a considerable extent, envisaged as a unit in relation not only to property but also to self-defence.

It has been shown in detail by Glotz[131] that in archaic Greece individual ownership emerged from clan ownership along with the emergence of individual responsibility from clan responsibility. Clan responsibility can be 'passive' (for transgression) or 'active' (to take action against the

[125] Lacey (1968) 131–2; Todd (1993) 225–6; Harrison (1968) 151–2. On 'the sort of prejudice against dividing property by will which still existed in the early fourth century' see the passages cited by Harrison (1968) 149 n.3.
[126] Todd (1993) 246, giving as examples Isaios 5.41–7 and Aeschines 1.95–105. Note also Pl. *Laws* 923a.
[127] Aristotle *Politics* 1319a9.
[128] Demosthenes 46.14; Plut. *Solon* 21.2; Isaios 3.68; 6.9, 28; 10.9; *Constitution of the Athenians* 35.2 (attributed to Aristotle).
[129] E.g. Aristophanes *Birds* 1660–6. [130] Todd (1993) 217–18.
[131] Glotz (1904); see also the comparative study by Fauconnet (1928).

transgressor). Although revenge may be taken on the kinship group of the killer,[132] and the idea of inherited guilt persisted throughout antiquity,[133] the responsibility of the clan tended to be of the active kind.[134] In circa 621 BCE Drakon passed a law that included a definition of the group of the victim's relatives that should share the prosecution (for unintentional homicide), and specified as follows the conditions for their pardon of the transgressor:

> If there is a father or brother or sons, pardon is to be agreed by all, or the one who opposes it is to prevail; but if none of these survives, by those up to the degree of first cousin, if all are willing to agree to a pardon; the one who opposes is to prevail.[135]

The polis defines and ultimately controls the process of dealing with homicide. The group of kin are divided into two groups, and power of veto is bestowed on the *individual* kinsman. It has been suggested that this indicates disintegration of the kinship group.[136] The dual meaning of the word αὐθέντης ('murderer' and 'master') restricts both violence and mastery (both once belonging to the clan) to an individual (αὐτός, component of αὐθέντης). The dispute about compensation for a killing described on the Homeric shield of Achilles has been interpreted as being between relatives of the victim.[137]

Of the laws of Drakon Solon retained only the law on homicide. Solon did, however, give to any citizen the right to initiate legal proceedings on behalf of an injured party.[138] What category of cases this involved is uncertain. But it is significant that the author of the *Constitution of the Athenians* (9.2) attributed to Aristotle regards the measure as one of the three most democratic features of the Solonian constitution. Plutarch (*Solon* 18.5) says that it accustomed the citizens to feel each others' suffering as if parts of one body. In so far as injured parties might hitherto have relied on help from kin, then here again Solonian legislation tends to shift power from kin to individual citizen. Similarly, in the religious sphere,[139] it has been argued that Solon transformed the *Genesia* from a private ritual celebrated on days specific to each *genos* into a public festival celebrated

132 E.g. *Iliad* 24.734–8.
133 E.g. Solon 13.25–32; Thucydides 1.126; Pl. *Republic* 364c1, 366a7; Parker (1983) 198–206; Glotz (1904) 560–83.
134 Glotz (1904) 47–59.
135 *Inscriptiones Graecae* 1 (3rd edn., Berlin) 104; I reproduce the translation of Gagarin (1981).
136 Glotz (1904) 324; Gagarin (1981) 164.
137 *Iliad* 18.498–500; Gagarin (1981) 13–16.
138 This is very likely to be indeed one of Solon's laws: Rhodes (2006).
139 Note also Solon's funerary legislation: Seaford (1994) 101.

on a single day.[140] If so, then here again the extended kinship group (*genos*), whether real or fictive, loses function to the individual participating in the polis.

Solon's laws included specifications of sums of money (in uncoined silver), as rewards, penalties and prices to be paid for victims in public sacrifices. I suggest that the various shifts (visible in Solonian legislation) from kinship group to individual are related to the fact that this society has – in sharp contrast to Homer and Hesiod – begun to use money. Precious metal money – being easily obtained, accumulated, stored, transported and concealed – lends itself to *individual* ownership. In particular, the tendency of money to be individually owned contrasts with the tendency of immoveable wealth to belong to the household. This can be illustrated from the Attic orators.

For instance, in a speech of Lysias (32) the brothers Diodotos and Diogeiton treat their inheritance in two ways: it is significant that they divide up the 'invisible wealth' and hold the 'visible wealth' in common. (The former includes money and the latter includes land.) Diodotos then makes a large amount of money through commerce, presumably by using his share of the invisible wealth (4), marries Diogeiton's daughter and has children by her. When Diodotos is subsequently killed in action (in 409 BCE), Diogeiton becomes guardian of Diodotos' children, and (claims Lysias) fraudulently appropriates much of their estate for himself. 'He seems at no time to have thought to establish the wealth as visible (φανερὰν καταστήσων τὴν οὐσίαν), but rather to keep their property for himself' (23). Indeed, making the wealth visible, in particular by buying land, would have impeded his individual appropriation of it. As it is, the appropriation is facilitated by the fact that the wealth consists entirely of money (6, 14–15, 21–22). He is accused of putting money above his daughter, his (deceased) brother and their children (17).

Why did the developments described in this section occur at about the same time in Greece and India? I confine myself to noting that practical innovations are more likely to travel between remote cultures in our period than are metaphysical ideas. For instance, the new widespread availability of iron has been claimed as a precondition for the efficient ground-clearing and ploughing that permitted the growth of rain-fed agriculture in Greece and (alongside irrigation) on the north Indian plains, which in turn – along with other factors – permitted in the middle of the first millenium BCE a new kind of urbanisation in which relatively autonomous cities could

140 Jacoby (1944); Davies (1988) 379; Seaford (1994) 108.

interact with each other not only by land but by sea (Greece) and river (India). Iron (unlike the components of bronze) is found almost everywhere, and knowledge of how to produce it would eventually be transmitted across cultures. It is the gradual diffusion of such practical skills, rather than any diffusion of metaphysics, that may help to explain *indirectly* the simultaneity of similar metaphysical developments in Greece and India (and China). The indirectly transmitted practical skills may even have included the use of a general means of exchange along trade routes, or even the idea of producing coins.

PART B

The Earliest Texts

CHAPTER 3

Sacrifice and Reciprocity in the Earliest Texts

3§A The *Rigveda*

Sacrifice, which occurs in many cultures, I define broadly as the ceremonial offering of sustenance to deity (often by killing an animal) in a carefully articulated process that may contain other features such as sustenance for the human participants. We need to make sense of the similarities and differences in the performance and functions of sacrifice in ancient Greece and ancient India in the context of these two societies taken (so far as possible) as a whole. In this chapter we focus on the earliest evidence for sacrifice, on the one hand in the *Rigveda*, produced for the most part before 1000 BCE in the north-western region of the Indian subcontinent, and on the other hand in Homer and Hesiod, produced in Greece from the eighth to the sixth century BCE but containing some earlier material.

In both societies sacrificial offerings are of central importance and give access to the gods. The cult activity with which most of the *Rigveda* is concerned is the giving of food, drink and praise to gods in the hope of eliciting benefits in return.[1] Because the gods are powerful and on the whole benign, it is pointless to try to *force* them to bestow the benefits, which are therefore merely requested.[2] 'As the gods desire, just so will it be' (RV 8.28.4). The relationship between men and gods can be described therefore as *reciprocity*, by which I will mean voluntary requital.

[1] Detail in Oberlies (2012) 232–40; Keith (1925) 259.

[2] Keith (1925) 260–1, who draws a distinction in this respect between the RV and the *Brahmanas*; Krishan (1997) 8. Oberlies (2012) 232 notes (434 n.1) that the idea of such force does occur in some passages of the RV, but attributed to a rival, and that the 'tenor' is that such a thing cannot happen: see 3.45.1 and 8.2.6. Some hymns, mainly in the late tenth book, rely on the inherent power of words and ritual actions: Oberlies (2012) 311–14.

The god most frequently invoked in the *Rigveda* is the god of warfare, Indra, to whom about a quarter of the 1,028 hymns are dedicated. This frequency of Indra, and his cosmic power, reflects a society in which warfare is closely allied with the fundamental economic activity. Where, as in the *Rigveda*,[3] the main form of wealth is cattle, prosperity may depend not only on tending the cattle (a relatively undemanding task) but also on four other much more demanding activities: raiding others for cattle; defending cattle against raids; winning pasture; and defending pasture.[4] The *Rigveda* contains numerous prayers to Indra for the possession of cattle and numerous allusions to cattle raids.[5]

Success in warfare often depends on a single unquestioned source of command.[6] The power of the war-leader over the community, and over the enemy, may be imagined as unlimited and therefore *universal*, and accordingly the necessity of imagining the power as cosmic shapes the god Indra:

> Who made firm the wavering earth, who settled the quaking mountains, who gave the midspace wider measure, who propped up the heaven – he, O peoples, is Indra (2.12.2).

In the same hymn we hear – along with his cosmic power – of his social and military power:

> under whose direction are the horses, under whose the cows, under whose the nomadic bands, and under whose all the chariots, who has given birth to the sun and who to the dawn, who is the guide of the waters – he, O peoples, is Indra (7) . . . Without whom peoples do not win, whom they call upon for help as they fight (9).

In warfare, declares another hymn, 'whoever has Indra – they win'.[7] On his own he mobilises the people (7.19.1). The narrative of his release of the waters by overcoming the dragon Vrtra in one hymn (1.32) ends with the statement that Indra is king of all, and in another (4.19) starts with his elevation to the kingship by the other gods (4.19). He is in the *Rigveda* constantly invited by means of praise, prayer and offerings (especially of *soma*). Because he unites the community and leads them against external enemies, it is from afar that he is summoned.[8] He is asked to support the

[3] E.g. Oberlies (2012) 14.

[4] The cultural and religious similarities with semi-nomadic cattle economies in twentieth-century east Africa are discussed by Lincoln (1981).

[5] Oberlies (2012) 16.

[6] *Iliad* 2.204 'Having many kings is not good: let there be one commander.'

[7] 8.16.5: cf. 2.12.8: 'whom the two war-cries, clashing together, call upon in rivalry – the enemies on both sides, here and over there'; 6.47.17; 8.37.6.

[8] Oberlies (2012) 102.

king (e.g. 10.173; cf. 174), who should be, like Indra, also poet and seer.[9] Man fuses with god,[10] social and military power with cosmic power. In a society of semi-nomadic herding, beset by violent conflict between groups, the well-being of each individual may seem to depend primarily on the universal power of a leader who is a god.

3§B Homer and Hesiod

Most of the hymns of the *Rigveda* were produced centuries before the earliest extant Greek literary texts (Homer and Hesiod). But there are – despite the differences of genre, period and cosmology – some striking similarities. An example, which has been related to the shared Indo-European origin of the two cultures, is that Indra in the *Rigveda* and Zeus in Hesiod's *Theogony* each uses a thunderbolt to defeat a serpentine monster in a cosmic battle,[11] and in each case the victory is associated with the god becoming king of the gods.[12]

Another important but less observed example is provided by the reciprocal relationship of men to gods, what I call polytheist reciprocity. In Homer, as in the *Rigveda*, sacrifices are regularly accompanied by requests to the gods,[13] and there are even similarities in the form of what is said: the appeal to the god to listen, the inclusion of their epithets and of their whereabouts.[14] In both Homeric epic and the *Rigveda* (and the Vedas generally) places of sacrifice are only temporary. Although the offerings are for the gods, the human participants consume much or most what is offered.[15] In the *Rigveda* nourishment for the gods may be provided by sending it to the sky, ascending with the smoke – rather as in Homeric sacrifice (*Iliad* 1.317). Alternatively, the gods may be invited to the place of offering. Or both methods may occur together, as at RV 7.11.5:

> Agni, convey the gods hither to consume the oblations. Let those whose chief is Indra find elation here. Place this sacrifice here in heaven among the gods.

[9] Oberlies (2012) 24–5.

[10] Oberlies (2012) 22–7; Whitaker (2011) 9; Kuiper (1960) argues that rich patrons may have personified Indra as distributor of wealth.

[11] This is very often alluded to or described in RV: see e.g. 1.32; 1.80; 3.30; 4.17; 8.82; Hesiod *Theogony* 820–68.

[12] For this last detail, see RV 1.32.15; 8.12.22; 8.86.10; 10.147.2; Hesiod *Theogony* 881–5.

[13] E.g. *Iliad* 1.451–6; 2.412–8; 3.276–91; 3.298–301; 16.233–48; 19.258–65; *Odyssey* 3.55–61; 3.445–6; 14.423–4; 15.258.

[14] Oberlies (2012) 234–7. [15] Oberlies (2012) 279.

The Greek gods do in Homer sometimes descend to earth, albeit not for a meal (they do descend for a meal in the subsequently attested *theoxenia*[16]). These similarities between the *Rigveda* and Homer should be seen in the context not only of a common Indo-European heritage but also of broadly similar economies. Both texts imply a pre-monetary society in which cattle are important and there is some agriculture.[17]

However, the societies implied by the texts are also different. Whereas in the *Rigveda* there is a complete absence of towns and temples, and almost no indication of commerce, in Homer these are largely but not entirely absent. Similarly, there is some state organisation in Homer[18] but none in the *Rigveda*,[19] although even in the *Rigveda* we can see tendencies *towards* state formation.[20] Whereas the people of the *Rigveda*, in their need for pastures,[21] are subject to an 'alternation of peaceful settlement, struggle, and further migration',[22] Homeric society is more settled, with incipient urbanisation. This may help to explain why, whereas the warrior Indra is the king of the gods, the Greek god of war, Ares, is – in Homer and subsequently – a relatively minor figure in the Olympian pantheon. The Greek king of the gods, Zeus, is in Homer not a warrior but a patriarch who rules both a relatively ordered and static world and the Olympian gods, who form – in contrast to the collection of gods in the *Rigveda* – a single family.[23]

In what follows I select three issues in which the Indian and Greek texts are similar while also being interestingly different: (1) the imagining of universe and society in terms of each other, (2) the relationship of the personal power of Indra and Zeus to the universal order and (3) the *failure* of reciprocity.

[16] Burkert (1985) 107; Parker (2011) 102–4.

[17] E.g. Jamison and Brereton (2014) 6. The RV lacks a deity of agriculture (4.57 is exceptional); in Homer Demeter and Dionysos are mentioned but unimportant. The agriculture evidenced in the RV contains no mention of rice, and does not imply permanent settlement: Rau (1997); Whitaker (2011) 4: 'The text does not indicate that the tribes were concerned with the permanent control of territory or state formation, though these become post-*Rigvedic* concerns. Conflict appears to have occurred because of the pressures of seasonal migrations. The need for food and water led to cattle raiding and competition for natural resources (such as access to grazing grounds and waterways), which escalated into open warfare and claims to chieftainship and sovereignty.'

[18] Seaford (1994).

[19] For the RV Whitaker denies that there was any concern with state-formation (see n. 17 above); also Proferes (2007): 'in the absence of both permanent territorial identity and institutional state administration, segmentary kinship structures must have served as the fundamental organisational principle . . .' (23, also 15 and 19).

[20] Proferes (2007) 10–13. [21] 6.19.12 calls on the god in battle for offspring, cattle and water.

[22] Oberlies (2012) 17. [23] Deussen (1915) 104.

(1) The transcendence of social power in premodern societies is often extended over the whole universe. In the *Rigveda* the king has cosmic power[24] and we have seen both that he may be identified with a god and that a god may be imagined as a king. In Homer and Hesiod Zeus is a patriarchal monarch, but kings are not imagined as cosmic autocrats or identified with gods, and even their association with gods is relatively weak.[25] In Homer the Olympian gods, rather than embodying the power of the cosmos, seem merely to occupy a privileged sphere within it.

This difference between the *Rigveda* and the Greek texts is attributable in part perhaps to their difference in genre: the *Rigveda* consists of hymns, which may express the emotion of a group or political community, and may invite the presence of gods, whereas from Greece we have panhellenic *narratives*. But it is also attributable to the relative weakness of the monarchy in Greece, a weakness that is indeed a theme of both the Homeric epics. The difference is significant. In India the universal power of the ruling individual became a model for the inner unity of the individual generally (7§B), whereas in Greece the political community emerging from the decline and disappearance of monarchy was embodied in rituals (sacrifice and mystery-cult) that indirectly promoted a conception of the individual as a *participant* in the universe (rather than, as in India, obtaining it or being equivalent to it).

(2) A hymn to Indra and Varuna describes the functions of the two gods:

> The one [Indra] smashes obstacles in the battles; the other [Varuna] ever guards his commandments (RV 7.83.9).

On the basis of this and other passages[26] of the *Rigveda* Oberlies describes a *complementarity* of the two gods: Indra is devoted to *battle* and to the creation of the world in its *natural* state, whereas Varuna creates and preserves the world *order* (sometimes called *ṛta*).[27] Varuna presides over oaths, vows and obligations, and punishes wrongdoing.[28] In his task of enforcing social ethics he is joined especially by the god Mitra,[29] and they both belong to a group of gods known as the Adityas.[30] Because the natural

[24] Proferes (2007) 20, 39, 48, 73, 76, 96, 105, 142.

[25] Exceptional is *Iliad* 2.101–8 (Agamemnon's sceptre derives from Zeus). Note also *Odyssey* 19.109–14 (abundance on land and in the sea results from a just king, cf. Hesiod *Works and Days* 225–47).

[26] Esp. 7.82.4–6; 7.85.3; 4.33.10.

[27] Oberlies (2012) 101–3; similarly e.g. Whitaker (2011) 10.

[28] Oberlies (2012) 103, 136–9.

[29] Oberlies (2012) 104–5, 132–4.

[30] RV 6.51.4: 'givers of good dwelling'.

and social orders are imagined in terms of each other, upholding the one is inseparable from upholding the other.[31] There is a hymn in which a king identifies himself simultaneously with both Varuna and Indra, after which Varuna claims to have upheld heaven on the seat of *ṛta* and is said – as possessor of *ṛta* – to have spread wide the threefold earth, and Indra claims that men call on him in battle (4.42.3–5). What is claimed here by the king is kingship in both peace and war.

Oberlies uses numerous passages of the *Rigveda* to align Varuna and the Adityas with the relative peace of the *kṣema* (settlement),[32] and to align Indra with the warfare inherent in the *yoga* (harnessing, i.e. onward movement).[33] If this is right, then with the subsequent transition in the Ganges area from semi-nomadism to permanent settlement,[34] and eventually urbanisation, we would expect the role and status of Indra to decline, and that is indeed what we find. It is also worth noting that in the Iranian west, in early Zoroastrianism, the *daevas* (in India the Devas, led by Indra) had sunk to the status of demons: they are described as 'all spawned from evil thought' (*Yasna* 32.3), and in the later Avesta Indra turns up as a demon.[35] The moral dualism of early Zoroastrianism has been described as 'a universalization of a concrete political and social situation in which a peaceful pastoral and cattle-breeding population was constantly threatened by the inroads of fierce nomadic tribes'.[36]

In Homer we do not find the complementarity – exemplified by Indra and Varuna – between physical power and socio-cosmic order. True, Zeus – as monarch of a relatively stable world – does have a role as guardian of behavioural norms, but it is a very limited one (mainly as protector of suppliants and of guests and as guarantor of oaths), and on the whole the Olympians neither act morally themselves nor enforce morality among mortals. On the other hand, there are occasional mentions of female deities whose role is to enforce behavioural norms and who can constrain the Olympians. The anger of the Erinues (Furies) causes defeat for Ares (*Iliad* 21.412–3). Poseidon, in dispute with his elder brother Zeus, is told that 'the Erinues always follow the elder' (*Iliad* 15.204). Poseidon responds (209) by claiming to have an equal share (*isomoron*) with Zeus, namely an equal

31 Oberlies (2012) 133–4.

32 Another god aligned with the settlement is Agni, in his role as master of the house: Oberlies (2012) 113, 118–20.

33 Oberlies (2012) 17–21, 101–5, 137.

34 This transition may be embodied in the horse sacrifice (*aśvamedha*), before which the horse has for a year to be guarded wherever it roams (SB 13.1.1ff.; 5§A n.15). In Greek myth Kadmos was told to found Thebes where a wandering cow first lay down.

35 Zaehner (1961) 37, 39, 65–6, 88.

36 Zaehner (1961) 34.

inheritance (187–9), and to be provided with the same *aisē*. Both Aisē (or Aisa) and Moira are female deities whose names originally meant *share* (in distribution)[37] but came to mean *destiny*. Zeus' desire to save from death men whose *aisē* it is to die is disapproved of by the other gods.[38] In the *Rigveda* Bhaga, whose name means share, has a special responsibility for the distribution of goods, as well as a more general responsibility for the order of the world.[39] Here, too, as in Greece, there is an element of *female* cosmic ordering: Bhaga belongs – along with Varuna, Mitra and other deities that order human society – to the Adityas, a group named after their mother the goddess Aditi. Further, the Adityas, the Erinues and Moira belonged to the primeval order imagined as preceding the coming to power of Zeus and Indra.[40]

Where in the *Rigveda* there tends to be *complementarity* between sovereignty and moral order, in Homer the relation is, rather, of *opposition*. True, the female limits on the power of the Olympians are marginal, but they were probably once more prominent,[41] as they are the fifth-century BCE tragedy *Prometheus Bound*,[42] in which the recently acquired power of the tyrannical Zeus is limited by destiny as decided by Moira and the Erinues (511–18), to the benefit of Prometheus. Prometheus belongs (like Varuna) to the older generation of gods, the Titans, and is the son of the goddess Themis (*themis* means right established by custom).

And so the moral order is in our period associated with the female and with the primeval in Greece and (to a lesser extent) in India; but in India there is nothing like the Greek *opposition* between the deities of moral order (and Prometheus, saviour of mankind) and the cosmic autocrat.

This fundamental difference leads to another. The opposition probably yielded, at the end of the (lost) Prometheus trilogy, to *reconciliation*, which may well have involved the acquisition by humankind of the virtue of justice. Similarly, Aeschylus' *Oresteia* dramatises the conflict and eventual reconciliation between Zeus and Apollo on the one hand and the older[43] female deities Moira and the Erinues on the other (and between the norms

[37] Seaford (2004) 51. [38] *Iliad* 16.441; 22.179. [39] Oberlies (2012) 131–2.

[40] The Adityas were a subgroup of the Asuras, who were older than the gods (Devas): e.g. BU 1.3.1; 5§A; Oberlies (2012) 94–6, 101, 138; Kuiper (1975). In the AV and *Brahmanas* the Asuras are almost always a group hostile to the gods, but earlier, in the RV, the word sometimes occurs in the singular and can mean something like 'ruler': Hale (1986). It seems that with their victory over the Asuras the Devas are joined by Varuna: see esp. RV 10.124.5 (Hale [1986: 88] notes linguistic evidence 'that this hymn is as late as any in the RV'). Cf. RV 1.151.4; 5.63.3; 7.21.7; 7.36.2; 7.65.2; 8.25.3–4; 8.96.9; 10.53.4; 10.82.5; 10.157.4.

[41] Seaford (2012) 51; Thomson (1961) 345–6. [42] Wrongly attributed to Aeschylus.

[43] *Eumenides* 173, 335, 778, 808, 838, 872; also 961, 1046.

each side represents). The opposition is thus absorbed into the Greek *systematisation* of gods, which we earlier correlated with *state organisation* – a correlation now confirmed by the fact that in the *Oresteia* the reconciliation of the Olympians with the Erinues is inseparable from the founding of a basic element of state organisation, the law court. Such cosmic projection of the polis is inconceivable in India.

One of the warriors whom Zeus is prevented by female destiny from saving is Hektor, which brings us to our third point of comparison between the *Rigveda* and Homer, the failure of reciprocity.

(3) Zeus considered rescuing Hektor from being slain because Hektor had burnt for him many thigh-pieces of oxen (*Iliad* 22.169–72). But the sacrifices were in the end ineffective. And indeed the ineffectiveness of a particular offering to the gods, or at least of the prayer that accompanies it, is more than once made explicit by the Homeric poet.[44] Such ineffectiveness was surely also familiar to the poets of the *Rigveda*, who comment on the fickleness of Indra, his helping some but not others, and even on doubt as to his existence.[45] However, and in contrast to Homer, none of this is necessarily inconsistent with the belief that Indra always helps those who offer him enough.

In Homer, moreover, there is a failure of reciprocity (voluntary requital) not only in the divine sphere but also in the human sphere. The crisis of the *Iliad*, the withdrawal of Achilles from battle, results from a breakdown in the reciprocity that should govern the relationship between the leader of the Trojan expedition (Agamemnon) and a fighting participant (Achilles).[46] Similarly, in the *Odyssey*, the crisis of reciprocity consists in the suitors' abuse – in abnormal circumstances – of a system of feasting that should be governed by reciprocity.[47] And in both cases the offer of gifts to resolve the crisis is ineffective. The centrality to Homeric epic of the failure of interhuman reciprocity expresses, in my view, a *historical* decline of reciprocity as a governing social principle. I will argue that in India, too, reciprocity lost its centrality, and that in both societies the decline of interhuman reciprocity was a factor in metaphysical transformation: in the transformation of the reciprocity imagined as existing between men and gods, and in the advent of the unitary inner self and of monism. But for this purpose we must first, in the next chapter, examine conceptions of the individual and indications of monism in the earliest texts.

[44] See also *Iliad* 2.419–20; 6.311; 16.249–52; *Odyssey* 9.551–5. [45] RV 6.47.17; 8.37.6; 8.100.3.
[46] Seaford (1994) 65–72. [47] Seaford (1994) 57–9.

CHAPTER 4

Self, Society and Universe in the Earliest Texts

4§A Constructing the Self

What is a person or self? We start with a debate, in modern analytical philosophy, between Sorabji and Parfit.

Sorabji maintains that 'a person is something that has psychological states and does things; for short that *owns* psychological states and actions' (emphasis in the original).[1] Parfit, on the other hand, asks us to imagine the idea of thoughts, experiences and acts occurring in a body: to operate with this idea alone is to lack the concept of a person, but is none the worse for that. Although thinkers exist, 'we cannot deduce, from the content of our experiences, that a thinker is a separately existing entity . . . we could fully describe our thoughts without claiming that they have thinkers'.[2]

In opposing Parfit, Sorabji relies heavily and frequently on the concept of 'ownership' of psychological states and actions. Ownership is socially sanctioned possession. Sorabji, in order to separate out the person from her thoughts, uses 'ownership' as a metaphor – but for what? Ownership is an exclusive *invisible* (abstract, socially imagined) relationship of a person to a separate entity (in contrast to possession, which implies physical control).

Is it clear from introspection or observation that a person is an entity separate from (and so 'owns') her thoughts etc.? No, for if it were clear, it could not be the point of disagreement that it is between Parfit and Sorabji. Parfit regards 'ownership' as a way of speaking that adds nothing important. Indeed, he imagines beings who believe that 'there are persisting bodies and related sequences of thoughts, experiences, and acts', but who do not have the concept of a person. Such beings could be taught the concept of a person, and would learn that they were persons, without having to give up any of their previous beliefs.[3]

[1] Sorabji (2006) 265. [2] Parfit (1984) 225. [3] Parfit (1999) 260–1.

It is generally true that we bring to observation preconceptions that influence the observation, and this is especially so in introspection. Because my thought of 'ownership' may be used to organise my thoughts, and because moreover it is indeed easy to *imagine* my thoughts as invisibly somehow mine and yet in a sense separate from me, my thoughts seem to have an 'owner', i.e. an entity separate from thoughts, even though the precise nature of this entity is unclear and even its existence is disputed. In this way the question of whether I am the owner of my thoughts may seem to answer itself.

Similarly, the question of whether consciousness is *unitary* may seem to answer itself: the introspection that tries to answer this question is itself unitary.[4] Bayne concludes a recent book on the unity of consciousness as follows[5]:

> The only thing that plays the self role – indeed perhaps the only thing that *could* play the role of self – is a merely intentional entity . . . the owner of an experience is nothing 'over and above' a virtual object – indeed the same virtual object around which that experience is structured . . . In generating a virtual self the cognitive architecture underlying the stream of consciousness also ensures that the self is represented as the owner or bearer of those experiences that are responsible for its very existence . . . like the creatures of the writer's imagination, there is nothing more to the nature of the self than what we take there to be.

This approach transcends the difference between Parfit and Sorabji. But it leaves undiscussed the question of whether this 'cognitive architecture' is universal or culture-specific.

This distinction is ignored in the debate between Parfit and Sorabji on the nature of the person (by implication the person always and everywhere). True, Parfit imagines beings who do not have the concept of a person but who do believe in persisting bodies, etc. But these are purely imaginary beings. Nor does Sorabji consider the possibility that there are or have been actual people who would find it difficult or impossible to envisage the individual as the 'owner' of his experiences – because of beliefs such as that I contain more than one inner self, or that I embody the 'soul' of my grandfather or because of social realities such as the absence of (a developed concept of) individual ownership. Some socio-economic formations do not have our concept of a person (as Sorabji defines it), not

[4] Although a substantial minority of people believe that they possess more than one inner self: e.g. Braude (1995).

[5] Bayne (2010) 290–4.

because they fail to *notice* it but because they do not *need* it. He correctly claims that our ethics require us to think of there being a *person* who deserves credit or blame.[6] But there have also been societies in which credit and blame, as well as property, belongs primarily to the kinship group. Later in this chapter we will see that in the *Rigveda* and in Homer (as in numerous other cultures) different kinds of inner self or entity of consciousness may coexist in (what we call) the same person. Different cultures (and phases of cultures) construct persons differently, depending on what they are constructed *from* and *for*. And they use various subjective experiences (dreaming, imagining oneself elsewhere, etc.), or objective observations (of the reflection or shadow of a body,[7] of others losing consciousness, etc.) to arrive at the idea of a personal entity that is physically distinct from the body and that we call a *soul*, but which may be imagined as a physical object such as a bird.

In a word, the ontological debate between Parfit and Sorabji ignores the *anthropology* of the self,[8] for instance the role of ritual in the forming of the idea of a person,[9] the duality of biological and social inner selves[10] or the work of Arbman and his followers on the remarkably widespread distinction between (in the same person) on the one hand the 'free soul', which wanders freely from the unconscious body, and on the other hand one or more 'body souls', which endow the body with life and/or consciousness.[11] Then there is the conceptual polarity – applied in particular to Melanesia – between individual and 'dividual':

> In the simplest terms, the individual is considered to be an indivisible self or person. That is, it refers to something like the essential core, or spirit of a singular human being, which, as a whole, defines that self in its particularity. To change, remove or otherwise alter any part of that whole would fundamentally alter the 'self'; she/he would then be, effectively, a different person. By contrast, the dividual is considered to be divisible, comprising a complex of separable—interrelated but essentially independent—dimensions or aspects. The individual is thus monadic, while the dividual is fractal; the individual is atomistic, while the dividual is always socially embedded; the individual is an autonomous social actor, the author of his or her own actions, while the dividual is a heteronomous actor performing

[6] Sorabji (2006) 275. [7] For this in the Vedas, see Keith (1925) 404; Oldenberg (1894) 527.

[8] They both discuss Buddhism, but only so as either to refute it (Sorabji 2006: 278–97) or to find in it supportive arguments (Parfit 1984: 273, 280, 502–3).

[9] Pioneered by Mauss (1938). [10] E.g. Berger (1967) 83–4.

[11] Arbman (1926) and (1927). Ethnographic accounts of the self (and of cosmology) would be germane to my investigation but expand unacceptably this monograph. I return briefly to Arbman in 4§C, 6§D and 13§B.

> a culturally written script; the individual is a free-agent, while the dividual is determined by cultural structures; the individual is egocentric, and the dividual is sociocentric.[12]

It has in fact become an anthropological norm to see the person generally as both individual and dividual, with the Melanesian person closer than the Western person to the dividual end of the spectrum. From the rich anthropological literature I have space for a single example. LiPuma describes the arrival of Westerners among the Maring of New Guinea as creating contexts for the expression, legitimation and empowerment of the individual aspect of personhood. For instance:

> an implicational logic runs from the appearance of the tradestore to the emergence of the individual aspect of personhood. The tradestore implies the right of private property, exemplified by a decline in the obligation to share, and private ownership is in turn a metaphor for privacy, or the self-containment of the person that is an index of individuality.[13]

'Ownership', which we saw used by Sorabji as an implicit metaphor, is by LiPuma here explicitly called a 'metaphor', for the person. But metaphors comparing two knowns should be distinguished from 'metaphors' using the image to construct the unknown.[14] It is not that the pre-existing individual person is compared to individual property, but that individual ownership of property is interiorised so as to imagine or construct the (otherwise unimaginable) individual person.

We are not transposing a Melanesian development to ancient India or ancient Greece. When in the twentieth century (Western) money and pervasive individual ownership were introduced or promoted by a colonial power, its recipients sometimes modified (without eliminating) its individualising effect by channelling money into traditional exchange relations or using their traditions as barriers against the all-pervasiveness of money.[15] But ancient societies that were *endogenously* monetised (India, Greece, China) – without alien (and alienating) cultural influence from elsewhere – did not of course have *this* kind of defence against the new developments, and so may even have been *more* radically transformed by them. In any event, the ethnographic data does at least establish the

[12] Smith (2012). [13] LiPuma (1998) 74. Cf. 13§C.

[14] See 10§C, also 8§B, 8§C, 9§F, 10§B, 10§C, 11§A n.5, 14§B n.9.

[15] This has become an anthropological commonplace since Parry and Bloch (1989) called into question the assumption that the introduction of (Western) money corrodes social relations by promoting possessive individualism. The more complex reality is revealed by more detailed studies: e.g. Hutchinson (1996) and the essays in Akin and Robbins (1999).

possibility that the advance of the individual aspect of personhood may be promoted by the development of individual property and money. After all, Melanesia is not exceptional:

> The western conception of the person as a bounded, unique, more or less integrated motivational and cognitive universe; a dynamic centre of awareness, emotion, judgement and action organised into a distinctive whole and set contrastively against other such wholes and against a social and natural background is, however incorrigible it may seem to us, a rather peculiar idea within the context of the world's cultures.[16]

On the other hand, what nature does provide all cultures with is the individual human body, which is the easily identifiable basis of numerous 'personal entities' in all the languages of the world. I will be referring to the *self* (as opposed to *others*), the *individual* (as opposed to *society*), the *subject* (as opposed to *object*) and the *soul* (as opposed to *body*). *Person* is close to self and to individual, and *mind* is close to soul. Whereas the soul is *physically* distinct from the body, the subject and self are *conceptually* distinct from the body. In the construction of the distinction between *subject* and object introspection is likely to be a factor. And the construction of the distinction between *self* and others may be promoted by certain kinds of social organisation and practice, which may also provide *models* for imagining the self.

An example of such a model is provided by what has been argued is an important stage in the development of modern Western individualism, namely the 'possessive quality' of seventeenth-century individualism:

> its conception of the individual as essentially the proprietor of his own person or capacities, owing nothing to society for them. The individual was seen neither as a moral whole, nor as part of a larger social whole, but as an owner of himself. The relationship of ownership, having become for more and more men the critically important relation determining their actual freedom and actual prospect of realizing their full potentialities, was read back into the nature of the individual.[17]

This historical process – the spread of individual property along with the interiorisation of ownership – resembles what we will argue is crucial for the development of the Greek inner self. A significant difference is that the seventeenth-century context for the emerging idea of the individual was the reaction of political debate to possibilities of ownership based on economic advances that went beyond anything in the ancient world. The

[16] Geertz (1984) 59. [17] Macpherson (1962) 3.

Greek individual, by contrast, shaped in part by the communal ritual and coined money of the polis, was indeed generally 'part of a larger whole'. In the modern absence of this larger whole it is eventually – in modern individualism – by virtue of a merely abstract humanity that each human is irreplaceable, equal and free.

4§B Organs of Consciousness in Homer

It was long since demonstrated by Bruno Snell that in Homer there is no word for an organ of comprehensive consciousness or inner self (including thought, emotion and sensation) corresponding roughly to our 'mind' or 'soul'.[18] *Noos* refers (mainly) to intellectual capacity,[19] and there are various words for organs of thought or emotion (notably *thumos*, *kēr*, *ētor*, *prapides*, *phrēn*, *kradiē*), some of which are associated with parts of the body. Sullivan concludes her study of all seven of them in early Greek literature thus: 'in their entirety these entities do not simply compose what we would call somebody's "personality" or "self". It is true that individuals may find in each a seat of many of their deepest qualities but none adequately expresses the full person.'[20] In Homer the semantic convergence and metrical interchangeability of some of these terms[21] do not suffice to show that they have become semantically identical.[22]

There has been repeated criticism of Snell for his *teleological* conception of the development of the idea of the mind and for his discussion of Homeric *agency*. I have no concern with these aspects, and on the whole agree with the criticisms. But another common criticism[23] of Snell fails. This is the criticism that – because in Homer individuals obviously take decisions, have thoughts, do things and are distinguished from each other – there is therefore in Homer a *concept* of inner self without there being a *word* for it.

[18] Snell (1960) 1–22. [19] Jahn (1987) 117–22. [20] Sullivan (1995) 76. [21] Jahn (1987).

[22] Note e.g. the criticisms of Jahn by van der Mije (1991); Jeremiah (2012) 15 n.11: 'metrical felicity does not determine semantic/idiomatic felicity, meaning that listeners will not accept a strange psychological expression simply because it satisfied metre. Though in time metre may well have facilitated the production of synonymy between the terms, their provenance must ultimately have been outside the epic language'. Clarke (1999) 64 rightly notes that the metrical evidence 'does not mean that they [the metrically interchangeable terms] are semantically identical'. However, he then adds that Homer has a notion of a 'single apparatus' for which he uses them as 'interchangeable labels'; but the semi-corporeality of the Homeric organs of thought/sensation (shown by Clarke) favours neither internal conflict nor a comprehensive inner self, which may require abstraction.

[23] E.g. Sharples (1983); Sullivan (1988) 6; Williams (1993) 21–6; Gaskin (1990) 4. An excellent recent defence of Snell on this point is by Jeremiah (2012) 11–15. Note also the indirect support for Snell in 15§B below. For more on the soul or mind in Homer, see e.g. Claus (1981) 11–47.

Where there is no word for a concept, this is either because there is no concept, or because the concept is merely incipient, not yet sufficiently formed to generate a corresponding word. We cannot say which of these applies to the absence from Homer of a word for the inner self. But whichever it is, what we can be sure of is that the acquisition of a word not only (by marking *need* for the word) indicates the *importance* of the concept, it also *familiarises* the concept and facilitates *thinking about* the concept, which in turn facilitates the *development* of the concept. True, people in Homer take decisions and do things; but there is no interest in (no mention of, no periphrasis for, no description of, no focus on, no construction or reification of) a unitary entity of comprehensive consciousness, and no distinction between it and the body, whereas in later Greek texts we frequently find all these things. Critics of Snell do not attempt to explain this absence because – generally lacking anthropological as well as historical perspective – they tend to assume that our unitary entity of consciousness is universal, and so regard its absence from Homeric (and Hesiodic) *language* as relatively insignificant and undeserving of explanation.

Moreover, even the mere concept of a comprehensive inner self (if there was one) is likely to be marginalised, if not entirely excluded, by the existence of various differently named organs or entities of thought or emotion. Some of these entities in Homer are sometimes represented as physical organs with specific locations in the body. It has been argued, on the one hand, that in Homer 'the stuff of thought and emotion is one with the stuff of the physical body',[24] and on the other hand that 'certain of the psychic terms (in particular *noos*, *thumos* and *phrēn*)[25] seem to have lost their predominantly physical connotation, and to have become more what we would call faculties', with the result that 'the person in Homer still seems to view these psychic terms as having some physical nature, but one that is indeterminate'.[26]

Certainly in the Homeric individual there are several entities of consciousness. Moreover, it is *implied* that the individual is himself a conscious entity separate from each of them, an entity denoted occasionally by the pronoun *autos*.[27] For instance, a man may converse with something within

[24] Clarke (1999) 126.

[25] These three terms have no precise equivalents in English. *Noos* and *phrēn* (plural *phrenes*) are often translated 'mind', whereas *thumos* is often an organ of emotions such as courage.

[26] Sullivan (1988) 8–9.

[27] αὐτός seems to mean different things depending on context. Russo (1992), writing on *Odyssey* 20.24, claims that it denotes 'the "whole" psychological entity in opposition to its constituent impulses',

him called *kradiē* ('heart') or *thumos*.[28] And a detailed study of *phrenes* in Homer concludes that 'the relationship that a person has to *phrenes* is one in which *phrenes* are subordinate to him or co-operate with him'.[29] Conscious entities may, like parts of the body, be called *philos*, which refers much more commonly to other (closely related) individuals. An instance is the line that occurs several times in the *Iliad*: 'But why did *philos thumos* converse with me thus?'[30]

Another way in which the inner space is modelled on interpersonal relations is that the conscious entities are themselves often open to influence or compulsion effected by other (divine) persons,[31] who sometimes put something into them as if it were an object or even a gift: for instance, Athena 'put' into the *phrenes* of Penelope to appear to the suitors, and 'gave' strength and courage to Diomedes.[32] It has accordingly been claimed that:

> even what seems to us a highly personal achievement, a thought say or an impulse, is imagined in the *Iliad* as a gift received . . . man does not confront an outside world with a different inner selfhood, but is interpenetrated by the whole, just as he on his part by his action and indeed by his suffering penetrates the total event.[33]

To the extent that there is in Homer any conception of inner space,[34] it is often permeable by personal (divine) intervention.

The Homeric *psuchē* plays no part in living consciousness, but acquires consciousness on the death of the body.[35] As a result, it may *contrast* with the person (imagined as his body). In the opening lines of the *Iliad* the

contrasting its reference to mere corpses at *Iliad* 1.4. But at *Odyssey* 20.24 αὐτὸς ἑλίσσετο refers to Odysseus' *bodily* movement, true though it is that – because it comes after a description of his emotions – it implies a broader sense of self than at *Iliad* 1.4.

[28] E.g. *kradiē* at *Odyssey* 20.23; for *thumos* see below. An organ like *thumos* may embody manifestations both of the *biological* self (e.g. energy) and of the interiorised *social* self (e.g. conversation).

[29] Sullivan (1988) 195.

[30] *Iliad* 11.407, 17.97, 21.562, 22.122, 385. The *thumos* is *philos* also at *Iliad* 5.155, 7.31, 11.342, 20.412; *Odyssey* 13.40, 14.405. *Philos* is also applied frequently to the *ētor* and the *kēr*. Modern translations inevitably use or add 'my'. Agamemnon 'trusted' (his) *phrenes* (*Iliad* 9.119).

[31] Russo (2012) corrects earlier attempts to downplay this phenomenon in Homer.

[32] *Odyssey* 18.158; *Iliad* 5.2.

[33] Fränkel (1975) 80.

[34] Cf. Holmes (2010) 59 on 'boundaries of the self'.

[35] I suspect that the immortality of *psuchē* long predates Homeric epic. But the way in which it is presented in Homeric epic seems to be influenced specifically by two practices: (a) the recitation of epic itself, in which it is the glorious deeds of heroes in this life that are perpetuated: accordingly, Achilles both prefers this life to the underworld and yet chooses early death with its consolation of glory; (b) the pouring of blood into the earth for the dead: accordingly, the dead in the Homeric underworld are insubstantial, and acquire some capacities by drinking blood (see esp. *Odyssey* 11.36, 50, 96–8, 153, 232, 390).

wrath of Achilles sent many *psuchai* of heroes to Hades, but gave 'them (*autous*)' to (be eaten by) the dogs and birds.[36] A person is distinct from his *psuchē*.

It may nevertheless also come close to being identified with the person. The *psuchē* of the slain Patroklos, appearing to Achilles, resembles Patroklos in appearance and voice, and has memory, emotion, thought and will (*Il.* 23.65–92). It seems to be Patroklos minus his actual body. In being separable from the body, and yet somehow almost identifiable with the person, *psuchē* can develop into something like a second self within the body, and then develop further into what it is in Plato: the subject, the comprehensive centre of the person, the invisible entity of unitary consciousness that originates decision and action (15§A). This Platonic subject is also *immortal*. From being in Homer conscious only in the next world, the *psuchē* was extended to *living* consciousness, but without thereby losing the capacity to refer to the dead or to the force that keeps the living alive. It has this wide range of meanings in – for instance – Athenian tragedy.[37] A special effect is created by their combination, as when Antigone says that her *psuchē* 'died long ago'.[38]

To conclude, Homeric inner space has no unity. It is modelled not on a single relationship such as ownership of property,[39] but rather on the relationships of the individual to his body parts and to other individuals.

The Platonic *psuchē*, by contrast, is constituted by self-collected awareness, of the unity with oneself that requires the inner self to be a comprehensive (even if partitioned) entity. Why and how did this transition occur? The answer can only be historical, not merely lexical.

4§C Organs of Consciousness in the *Rigveda*

The main words in the *Rigveda* that have been claimed to mean 'soul' or 'mind' or 'self' are *prāṇa* (prana), *asu*, *jīva*, *manas* and *ātman* (atman).[40]

[36] *Iliad* 1.3–4.

[37] Sullivan (1997) 145–51; (1999) 181–4; (2000) 111–12. *Psuchē* identified with living person: S. *Philoktetes* 712; E. *Medea* 247, *Hippolytus* 259, *Iphigeneia in Tauris* 882; cf. e.g. Hdt. 7.153.4; Pindar *Pythian* 3.61; 4.122.

[38] S. *Antigone* 559–60. This evokes the (usually temporary) participation of the mourner in the state of the dead, as does A. *Septem* 1033–4.

[39] 'Homeric man does not *have* a mind, rather his thought and consciousness are as inseparable a part of his bodily life as are movement and metabolism': Clarke (1999) 115. The main exception will prove to be illuminating: 13§B.

[40] *Puruṣa*, which will later mean self or consciousness, in RV occurs only in the late tenth book: 10.90 (as cosmic man) and 10.51.8.

The difficulty of determining the meaning or meanings of each of these words is sometimes considerable, and has produced much difference of scholarly opinion. *Prāṇa* occurs ten times in the *Rigveda* (as noun or in verbal form), in each case referring to breath, which leaves the body at death (3.53.21). *Asu* occurs ten times, mostly translatable as 'life', but is 'more than just life. It is the soul which leaves the body and produces death in the case of lasting absence.'[41] *Jīva*, with twenty-three occurrences, also generally means 'life'.[42] *Prāṇa*, *asu* and *jīva* refer to what gives the body life, and may leave the body, but do not function in the body as organs of consciousness:[43] in these respects they are like the Homeric *psuchē*. All are – in the terminology of Arbman (4§A) – 'free souls'.

By far the most commonly mentioned organ of consciousness in the *Rigveda* is *manas*, which occurs more than two hundred times, and is translated by such words as 'mind', 'spirit', 'Geist' and 'Sinn' (in Arbman's terminology a 'body soul'). It may be described as concentrated, eager, inclined to give, god-devoted, gratified,[44] and so on. It often embodies the required mental attitude of god or worshipper.[45] In the late tenth book it acquires a new variety of roles.[46] But no question is ever asked about its nature[47] and almost nothing is ever predicated of it ('*manas* is x').[48] It is far from being an organ of comprehensive consciousness that unites thought, perception and emotion.[49] It leaves the body only in a cluster of three late passages[50] (thereby – in Arbman's

41 Bodewitz (1991) 43–5. Grassmann (1873: 155a) gives the meanings 'leben, lebensfrische, lebenskraft, geisterleben'.

42 Exceptional is 1.164.30 (from the unique riddle hymn in the relatively late first book): 'the living one (*jīva*) keeps moving by the will of the dead one; the immortal one shares the same womb with the mortal one'.

43 The dead are addressed not as *asu* or prana or *jīva* or *manas*, but as 'forefathers' etc.: Oldenberg (1894) 529.

44 1.33.11; 1.54.5; 1.55.7; 1.93.8; 1.134.1.

45 Similarly in the earliest Iranian literature, the Gathas, the first person is used (with a strong ethical interest), but there is no interest in the nature of the self.

46 Esp. 57.3–6 and 58 the *manas* summoned; 60.10 the *manas* brought back from the realm of the dead; 81.4 'in your *manas* ask about . . . (creation)'; 90.13 the moon is born from the *manas* of *Puruṣa*; 129.4 'from *manas* there evolved desire, which existed as the primal semen'; 130.6 'seeing with my *manas* as my eye, I think of the ancient ones who offered this sacrifice'; 10.191.3 'Common to them all is the solemn utterance, common the assembly, common their *manas* along with their perception.'

47 The closest is from the unique riddling hymn in the relatively late first book (1.164.18): 'Showing himself to be a poet, who will proclaim this here: from whence has divine thought (*manas*) been born?'

48 Rather than just attributed to it. Possible exceptions are 10.164.1 'of many kinds is the *manas* of the living', and 6.9.5 'the *manas* (of Agni) swiftest among (all) those that fly'.

49 Oberlies concludes that in the RV the concept of a single soul is unknown, rather man has a plurality of 'souls': (2012) 335.

50 10.57.3–6 (it is summoned); 10.58; 10.60.10 (a claim to have brought someone's *manas* from Yama, i.e. from death).

terminology – becoming also a 'free soul'). What does leave the body at death is not said to be conscious or immortal. The afterlife is corporeal, and a new body may be required.[51] In 10.16 it is the body of the dead man that Agni is to lead to heaven, whereas his atman ('breath') merely goes to the wind just as his eye goes to the sun and his limbs to the plants.

Of special interest, given its subsequent history, is atman. A recent study of its twenty-two occurrences in the *Rigveda* and forty-eight in the *Atharvaveda* claims to detect a development in which the meaning of *ātman* develops – roughly speaking – from 'vital breath' to 'self'.[52] This represents a consensus, from which there has been dissent.[53] At any rate the variety of things that are identified with – or have – atman in the *Rigveda*[54] implies a broader, perhaps more abstract sense than 'breath',[55] and a greater range of meanings than *prāṇa*, *asu*, *jīva* and *manas*: the words used to translate it include not only 'breath', 'wind', 'soul' and 'spirit', but also 'self'[56] and 'body',[57] which already (as in later texts) suggest a sense of the individual, of the *self* as opposed to others.[58]

In the *Upanishads* there is a central focus on the nature of the atman, an organ of comprehensive consciousness that is in various passages described as unitary, comprehensive, incorporeal, fundamental, the real person, immortal, all-controlling, unknowable and identical with the universe. In the *Rigveda* neither *jīva* nor prana nor *asu* nor *manas* nor *ātman* has any of these characteristics. Mental phenomena are generally mentioned as *instruments* in a limited range of achievements (notably travelling towards – or in some way associating with – the gods),[59] and may be regarded in

51 Oberlies (2012) 333–4. 52 Orqueda (2015), who gives earlier bibliography.

53 Deussen (1915) 285 disputed the usual derivation of atman from the Sanskrit root *an-*, 'to breathe', deriving it instead from the roots *a* (as in *aham*, 'I') and *ta*, 'this', meaning 'this I', the self. Such a derivation, he contends, accounts – better than the derivation from 'breath' – for the meaning 'body' as well as 'soul'. Moreover, the closely related form *tman* is in its seventy-eight occurrences in the RV always a pronoun or adverb (except perhaps at 1.63.8, where it seems that Indra is asked to bestow it on his worshippers). Against Deussen see Keith (1925) 450–1.

54 Of the sun (1.115.1), earth (1.164.4), sacrifice (9.2.10; 9.6.8), clouds (9.74.4), plants (10.97.4), disease (10.97.11), food (10.107.7).

55 Although 'essence', favoured for some passages by Jurewicz (2007) 127–30, goes too far if it implies a systematic distinction between essence and appearance.

56 Although Orqueda (2015) maintains that 'it is difficult to support that the reflexive meaning is already present in the RV given that there is only one passage that exhibits the properties of a reflexive (RV 9.113.1c), attributed to the most recent period.'

57 NB 'from your hair, and from your nails, / from your whole atman I drive your illness away' (10.63.5).

58 On atman in SB meaning the totality of a person's existence (both mental and physical) see Tull (1989) 150 n.32.

59 E.g. 1.77.2; 1.168.1; 1.184.2; 2.21.6; 2.23.6; 2.26.3; 3.19.3; 3.39.1; 3.62.12; 4.3.15; 4.20.4; 4.21.11; 4.32.15; 4.41.8; 6.49.5; 6.51.6; 7.10.2; 7.23.4; 7.57.2; 7.88.1; 8.45.26; 8.61.1; 8.102.2; 9.75.4; 9.95.3.

material terms: for instance, gods 'send our ghee-covered insight to its goal'.[60]

4§D Society and the Self in the *Rigveda* and Homer

The *Rigveda* and Homeric epic are different kinds of text. The former consists of hymns – mainly accompanying offerings – to deities, whereas the latter is narrative that describes offerings and prayers among much else. The former generally shows us mortals in a specific relationship with deity, whereas the latter describes a great variety of events that involve various relationships of mortals with each other and with deity. But in both texts the relationship of mortals with deity is one of reciprocity, and neither of them has a place for a unitary organ of consciousness by which the individual self is defined. In the *Rigveda* there is no suggestion of interior space. In Homer there is a limited sense of interior space, which is permeable by personal (divine) intervention. In neither the *Rigveda* nor Homer is there anything like the later Upanishadic, Herakleitean and Platonic descriptions, involving spatial terms, of atman and *psuchē* as entities of comprehensive consciousness.[61]

In the kind of society described in the *Rigveda* the well-being of each individual depends primarily on the power of the group to obtain and defend cattle and land. This power itself depends on the coherence and the confidence of the group in warfare. The coherence may require loyalty to a single human leader, and the confidence may require belief that it is also being led by an all-powerful god (Indra). Other contexts require other gods as focuses of unity. Varuna presides over certain kinds of agreement, Agni over the household. Bhaga has a role to play in the distribution of goods. And so on. The actions and beliefs that contribute exclusively to the well-being of a single individual are less important and less visible than the collective actions and collective beliefs on which each individual depends. Such collective beliefs include the importance of maintaining the goodwill and presence of certain powerful individuals. The powerful individuals are in the *Rigveda* for the most part gods, but in the society that produced the *Rigveda* the code of reciprocity between the weak and the strong obtained also within the human sphere.[62]

60 1.2.7 *dhiyaṃ ghṛtācīṃ sādhantā*; cf. e.g. 2.3.2; 8.63.1; 10.39.4. The inadequacy of the material conception of mind and thought is strikingly expressed at 1.164.37: 'I do not understand what sort of thing I am here: though bound, I roam about in secret by my thinking'.

61 E.g. BU 2.1.20; CU 3.14.2–4; Hklt. B36, 45, 77, 118. The soul is compared to a spider in both BU 2.1.20 and Hklt. B67a.

62 E.g. RV 10.33; 10. 117; 10.173; Thapar (1984) 26; Whitaker (2011) 8; 'in the human realm, poets [of the RV] repeatedly praise wealthy patrons, lords, and chieftains for their financial support and

In such a society what matters is not individual interiority but *power* and *relationship with power,* expressed in requests and hymns in order to obtain wealth, victory, health, long life and progeny. Even the requests and hymns derive, like poetic inspiration in Homer, from the gods themselves.[63] It is significant that by far the most common word for an organ of consciousness, *manas*, frequently occurs to express the required attitude of god or worshipper. True, this is hardly surprising given that the *Rigveda* consists of hymns, but the hymns contain much narrative as well as descriptions of very various kinds, and their performance seems to have had a significant *social* function.[64]

This contrasts with a society in which the well-being of the individual depends considerably on commerce, and especially with a *monetised* society, in which the possession of money frees the individual *in principle* (albeit not necessarily in practice) from the need for all socially defined relationships (reciprocity, kinship, ritual, etc.), and in which therefore the individual may seem to depend entirely on his own actions and beliefs, to be an entirely self-sufficient *self* (as opposed to others) and *subject* (as opposed to objects). As we will see most clearly in Greece, it is such conditions that promote the emergence of the idea of a unitary organ of consciousness by which the individual self is defined. For an organ of consciousness can only be imagined as unitary if it is imagined as bounded, and (though open to external influences) as the motivator of its own thoughts and actions. Such boundedness, imagined self-sufficiency, is conducive to the development of *introspection.* Further, inasmuch as money may seem able to acquire all goods, its impersonal power seems to be *universal.* The people of the *Rigveda* needed Indra in one context, Varuna in another, Agni in another, and so on. But where a single thing, the power of money, is effective in all contexts, the corresponding cosmic belief tends towards monotheism or monism (the belief that all things are a single entity).

The idea of the unitary inner self (atman, *psuchē*) as central to understanding the world was one of the four fundamental ideas listed in 1§A, all four of which are almost entirely absent from the *Rigveda*, Homer and Hesiod. Moreover, these are not the only striking differences between the

protection and, in turn, command the gods to give these men prosperity, victory, sons, and a long life'; Whitaker (2011) 45: 'The notion that men should seek protection and generosity from Agni and Indra also parallels the ideal relationship shared among men as ritual patrons (*sūrí-*) are frequently defined in terms of their largesse, while also being called protectors of men (*nṛpātṛ-*)'; Whitaker (2011) 87–96. RV 8.22.17–18 asks whether the source of a great bounty is a god or a king.

63 RV 1.37.4; 1.105.15; 1.164.37–9; 2.9.4; 3.34.5; 4.11.3; 5.42.4; 6.1.1; 7.97.3; 8.42.3; 9.95.2; 10.98.7.

64 Whitaker (2011) 165 concludes that the ideology of RV 'demands that all men within the tribe participate in *sóma* rituals—whether they did is another matter—and expects that they will accept Ṛgvedic social, economic, and political ideals, relationships, and practices as normative'.

earliest texts and subsequent developments in both cultures. For instance, the remark that in the *Rigveda* 'nowhere can we find the tiniest suspicion of a wish to renounce the material world in favour of some spiritual quest'[65] applies no less to Homer and Hesiod. All these fundamental ideas are interrelated, and form a complex whose emergence is sufficiently similar in the two cultures to make the differences also significant.

4§E Monism

The idea of the comprehensive inner self is almost entirely absent from the *Rigveda* and Homer, and so is monism. The two ideas (two of our four explananda: 2§A) will then in both cultures develop together, and may even be described as complementary aspects of the same development.

By 'monism', which can be used with various meanings, I mean the belief that all things are a single entity (so that diversity is mere appearance, or no more than diversity of aspect or of mode). The single entity may be personal or impersonal, and imperceptible or perceptible: their combination gives rise to the four (potentially overlapping) subdivisions of monism proposed below. It is neither the only possible such classification nor an end in itself, but merely a tool for understanding the similarities and differences between Indian and Greek thought, which is not to claim that it was in the mind of the thinkers:

(1) (impersonal, generally perceptible). *Material monism:* all that exists is a single material entity.
(2) (personal, perceptible). *Personal (including anthropomorphic) monism*: all that exists is a single person, who may be stated or assumed (unless there are indications to the contrary) to be anthropomorphic.
(3) (personal, imperceptible). *Mental monism* I use to refer to *one or both* of its two distinct aspects: all that exists is an organ of consciousness (mind), or all that exists is the content of consciousness (subjectivity), neither of which are perceptible objects. In the ancient texts it is usually but not always clear which aspect (or both?) is meant.
(4) (impersonal, imperceptible). *Abstract monism*: all that exists is a single abstract entity that – being abstract – can be apprehended only by the mind.

Mental monism (3) may seem to be a kind of personal monism (2) inasmuch as the mind belongs to a person: the difference is that in

[65] Doniger (1981) 229.

personal monism the whole person is imagined from the outside, whereas mental monism reifies the *inner* self or its content. It is nevertheless sometimes difficult to distinguish them: for instance, atman is variously translated 'body', 'self' or 'soul'.

Finally, the schema requires two further qualifications. Firstly, what I have so far called monism (the belief that all things *are* a single entity) would be described more precisely as *present monism*, to distinguish it from *primordial monism* (the belief that all things *were in the beginning* a single entity). Secondly, there are beliefs that resemble monism while falling short of it, for instance that several (not all) entities have a special relationship (identity, emergence, transformation, dependence) with a single entity; or that everything belongs to (or depends on) a single system united by a single entity. For such beliefs I use the umbrella term *reductionist*, in that they tend to reduce a series of entities to a close relationship with a single entity. Reductionism can be divided into the same categories into which we divide monism.

In Homer and Hesiod there is no trace of *present* monism. Mortals and immortals inhabit a world completely differentiated into land, sea, underworld, sky and everything else. Two passages might be thought to embody *primordial* monism. The god Sleep says that he would easily lull to sleep the streams of river Okeanos, 'who is the begetter (γένεσις) for all (πάντεσσι)' (*Iliad* 14.244–6). Inasmuch as this suggests procreation, πάντεσσι seems to refer merely to all that *lives*,[66] and so the passage may not in fact embody (personal) primordial *monism*. The other passage is Hesiod *Theogony* 116: 'first of all there came into being Χάος (chasm or gap), and then broad-breasted Earth ...' This, too, should probably not be called primordial monism. Χάος is not described, and it is unclear what is meant by it: it may well be an *event* (the separation of earth from sky) rather than an entity.[67]

As for the *Rigveda*, on our broad definition of reductionism there is much reductionism in *Rigveda*,[68] but the instances of the reductionist tendency producing *monism* (by reducing *all* things to one thing) are very few. There are, it is true, several passages of the *Rigveda* that have been claimed to state or imply the unity of all things.[69] But many of them

66 Similar is *Iliad* 14.200: 'Okeanos begetter of gods and mother Tethys'. 67 KRS 34–46.

68 On this tendency see Deussen (1915) 103–27. The relative universality of Agni in the RV I associate – following Proferes (2007) – with a historical development, the ritual fire expressing the universality of sovereignty. A later more embodied instance of the tendency of sovereignty to be imagined as universal is Rock Edict 13 of Ashoka (third century BCE), which claims that the king has achieved conquest by *dharma* even in the Hellenistic monarchies.

69 Comparably, Jurewicz (2010) proposes for the RV an abstract 'general model of reality transformation', but the model 'operates only conceptually and is never expressed in words explicitly but is implied ...' (39). On the problematic idea of a merely implicit concept (in Homer), see 4§B.

turn out, on examination, not to do so. Three hymns do state or imply a single *origin* – or something close to it – for all things (*primordial* monism).[70] And there is a single instance of (personal) *present* monism at 10.90.2: 'The Man (*Puruṣa*) alone is this whole (world): what has come into being and what is to be.' This hymn then narrates that the gods created the world by sacrificing *Puruṣa*, and that the parts of his dismembered body became the *varṇas* ('colours', sometimes translated as 'castes'), parts of the cosmos and gods. This looks more like primordial personal monism, and creates a plurality that seems inconsistent with the present monism stated earlier in the hymn.

Such seeming inconsistency is to be expected where what may appear to be monism – or rather monotheism – is not a considered doctrine but an expression of praise, of the importance of the praised. Most hymns of the *Rigveda* are designed to praise a single god, which can result in what has been called 'monotheism of the moment'.[71] Praise may take the form of identifying a deity with other deities,[72] and with other things, as at 1.89.10:

> Aditi is heaven. Aditi is the midspace. Aditi is the Mother; she is the father, she the son. Aditi is the All Gods, the five people. Aditi is what has been born, Aditi what is to be born.[73]

This is neither monism nor even monotheism, but personal reductionism.

Our four instances of monism in the *Rigveda* (one present, three primordial) all come from book 10,[74] which is the latest book of the *Rigveda*.[75] And so the *Rigveda* indicates *a historical transition from polytheism to monism*. Especially telling is 10.90, which contains not only the only instance of present monism but also three other fundamental ideas of which there is no clear mention elsewhere in the *Rigveda*, but which will subsequently acquire great importance:

[70] 10.72.2 (abstract?: on *sat* see 8§C); 10.121.1, 9 (the golden embryo), 7 (material: waters); 10.129.2 (personal), 3 (material: waters), 4 (subjective): see 8§E n.16; 10.129.6 states, significantly, that the gods are latecomers.

[71] Oberlies (2012) 88–9; Deussen (1915) 104 notes that the gods of the RV do not have a community as on Olympos, but that each of them stands on its own height, and when he is approached the other gods recede into the background.

[72] E.g. 1.164.46; 2.1.3–7. Other passages in which monism or something like it has been erroneously identified are 1.164.4 (Sharma [1972] 32), 4.40.5 (Sharma [1972] 39–40), 10.81 and 82 (Keith [1925] 437–8).

[73] Although elsewhere in the RV Aditi is a mother (of cosmic significance esp. at 10.72), anthropomorphic or bovine.

[74] See note 5 above. [75] Witzel (1997a) 264–5; Oberlies (2012) 37, 39, 347 n.6.

(a) the system of three Vedas (9).

(b) the system of four *varṇas* (11–12).[76] Its absence from the main body of the *Rigveda* suggests that 10.90 is the product of a comparatively late historical situation, in which the societal importance of the *varṇa* system – with the semi-nomadism of lineages now replaced by sedentary and centralised differentiation of roles – has developed to the point at which it requires cosmogonic legitimation.[77] A *Rigveda* lacking legitimation of the Vedas and *varṇas* would in a certain historical phase be unacceptable. This makes it likely that the interval between the main body and 10.90 (at least) was considerable: why otherwise would the *varṇa* system be so important in the cosmogony of 10.90 and yet completely absent from the rest of the *Rigveda*? Not only was the tenth book 'the latest part of the *Rigveda* and apparently its most fluid', but also – although the *Rigveda* seems to have been put together in its current form (though containing earlier material) at the beginning of the first millennium BCE – verses could be added to it no less than some five hundred years later, after the creation of the *Sākala Padapātha*.[78] Moreover it was first written down many centuries (probably) after that. A substantial downdating of the final form of the *Rigveda* (and of Vedic literature in general), based in part on the recognition of its use of archaic language,[79] is argued for by Bronkhorst (2007). Even if Bronkhorst is mistaken in this, there is nothing to preclude the final form of 10.90 postdating the *Brahmanas* or even the early *Upanishads*. And the same is true of verses elsewhere in book 10 that are at odds with the rest of the *Rigveda*.

The fundamental importance of the Vedas and of the *varṇas* is in 10.90 legitimated by their emergence from the cosmogonic sacrifice. And the systematicity of the *varṇas* is expressed by the identification of each of the four *varṇas* with a bodily part of *Puruṣa* (Man), who is identified with the whole world. The plurality of the *varṇas* has developed from present monism. This seems – I have noted – inconsistent. But such inconsistency may have (as inconsistency often does) an unspoken rationale. Perhaps this – the only instance in the *Rigveda* of present monism – was introduced (or adapted) to

[76] There are slight prefigurations of the *varna* system in 8.35–7: Jamison and Brereton (2014) 1.58.

[77] As at SB 2.1.4.12.

[78] Jamison and Brereton (2014) 1.17; Gonda (1975) 15. RV 10.95 was known at the time of SB to have had fewer verses than at present: Bronkhorst (2007) 340.

[79] Bronkhorst (2007) 176–80.

legitimate the system of *varṇas* by lending it comprehensive unity. This in turn depends on the third fundamental but unique feature of 10.90:

(c) The *transformation* of the sacrificed *Puruṣa* into the universe. The parts of the universe, and even the leading gods Indra and Agni, are born from parts of his body.

The late tenth book also provides the only other occurrence of the word *puruṣa* in the *Rigveda* (51.8), as well as the closest conception to (c) – in a funerary hymn (16) in which the dead man is addressed thus (verse 3):

> Let your eye go to the sun, your life-breath (atman) to the wind. Go to heaven and to earth as is fitting. Or go to the waters, if it has been fixed for you there. Take your stand in the plants with your limbs.

This conception of the afterlife is unique in the *Rigveda*. Unique also, from the same hymn, is that the dead man is conveyed 'to the place of those whose (ritual) actions are well-done' (verse 4)[80]; and the next verse seems to prefigure the universal doctrine of reincarnation, of which the only other possible indication (9§A) is also provided by the tenth book; 14.8 exhorts the dead man to:

> unite with forefathers, unite with Yama (Death), with what has been sacrificed and bestowed in the highest distant heaven. Having left behind the imperfection, come home again. Unite with your body in your full lustre.

'What has been sacrificed and bestowed' is *iṣṭāpūrta*, the result or merit of sacrifices and gifts,[81] a word that occurs only here in the *Rigveda* but prefigures an idea that we will see later to be fundamental.[82]

To conclude, it is, in the *Rigveda*, only in a handful of hymns in the late tenth book that we find ideas that will later be fundamental: present monism, the Vedas, the *varṇas*, personal monism, the sacrificial victim as the universe, reincarnation and afterlife merit. The idea of the dead individual joining other *persons* in the afterlife (gods, forefathers) occurs throughout the *Rigveda*.[83] What the tenth book then adds is the idea of the dead individual united with something *impersonal*, be it elements of the universe (10.16.3) or merit obtained by sacrifice (10.14.8). This is relatively *individualist*, inasmuch as in joining the

[80] *Sukṛtām ulokam*, which occurs nowhere else in RV; ritual actions: Gonda (1966) 132.
[81] Keith (1925) 409. [82] 5§D, 9§B, 9§D. [83] 6§B, 9§A.

*im*personal the individual is ultimately isolated from other individuals. More obviously individualist is the first of many identifications – in later texts – of man with the universe in 10.90.[84] Even in the cycle of reincarnation, also fleetingly prefigured in the tenth book, the individual is isolated (10§A).

4§F Projection and Introjection (Interiorisation)

I have called Indra the cosmic projection of the war-leader. As the concept of cosmic projection or cosmisation (I will use the terms synonymously) will be important to my overall argument, I should make clear here what I mean by it.

A lucid account is given by the sociologist Peter Berger (1967): 'there is an inherent logic that impels every nomos [meaningful human order] to expand into wider areas of meaning. If the ordering activity of society never attains to totality, it may yet be described as totalising' (20). 'Cosmisation' is the process through which 'nomos and cosmos appear to be co-extensive' (25). In Indra war-leadership is cosmised, in Zeus patriarchal monarchy, in sacrifice gift-exchange.

Berger notes that the continuing reality of the socially constructed world:

> depends on specific social processes, namely those processes that ongoingly reconstruct and maintain the particular worlds in question. Conversely, the interruption of these social processes threatens the (objective and subjective) reality of the worlds in question (45).

And so each socially constructed world requires a social base, or 'plausibility structure', for its continuing existence. I maintain that the radical metaphysical transformations that are the theme of this book arose largely from the interruption, for elites in India and Greece, of the existing plausibility structure. In particular the tendency for personal power to be replaced – as social power – by the universal, invisible and impersonal power of *money* was in both societies a factor in the creation of a new plausibility structure and accordingly a new metaphysics.

The cosmisation of money as totalising power-entity is unusual. Zeus is a monarch, and may directly legitimate human monarchy, whereas e.g. Herakeitean fire, which I argue involves the cosmisation of money, is *not* money, and cannot directly legitimate money. This distinction reflects the

[84] With even a suggestion of *mental monism* (verse 13): Tull (1989) 53.

unprecedented nature of the new power being cosmised. A king embodies and exercises his own personal power (legitimating or coercive) at the summit of a structure, and it is accordingly in this form that monarchy is cosmised. But the power of money consists in its abstract value, which depends – for its prime purpose of transferability in *exchange* – on its absolute abstraction from all particular persons, things, places and structures. Indeed, it is imagined as unchanging only by virtue of being abstracted from circulation, from human acts of exchange (14§A). And so whereas this socially transcendent, unchanging abstractness of monetary power may be cosmised (12§B), as may its individual ownership (10§C) and legitimating function (10§C, 14§A), what cannot be cosmised is the multifarious human process of exchange, the devolution of power to all individual owners of money. Or rather, the only way in which exchange may be cosmised is by shedding its human agency so as to become the impersonal power of universal self-*transformation* exemplified by Herakleitean fire, combining immanence with transcendence. Even the cosmisation of monarchy is subjected to some abstraction: it is unlikely to include the king's mortality, the specificities of his family life, etc.

Berger describes only the *legitimating* function of cosmisation, and mainly *religious* cosmisation, which is for the most part personal, although he does allow the possibility of abstract (impersonal) cosmisation, giving as an example the legitimising power of the Chinese *dao* (34–5), to which I will return briefly in 16§A. But cosmisation may also aim to achieve the *intelligibility* of the cosmos (unknown universal power imagined in terms of universal power that is known) and *control* of the cosmos (e.g. in Vedic sacrifice[85]).

Cosmisation for Berger belongs to the very general process of 'objectivation', the attainment by products of human (physical and mental) activity of 'a reality that confronts its original producers as a facticity external to and other than themselves' (4). This is accompanied by the equally general process of 'internalisation', which is 'the reappropriation of this same reality, transforming it once again from the structures of the objective world into structures of subjective consciousness'. Here, too, I add, a special case is money. The exclusion of human agency from the abstractness of money permits and promotes not only its totalising *projection* but also its totalising internalisation (I will use the synonyms 'interiorisation' and 'introjection'): the power of money, a unifying abstraction activated by

[85] 5§C, 8§B.

and empowering the unitary subject, becomes a model for imagining the unitary subject as a whole. Why and how this happens will emerge as we proceed.

Finally, the importance I assign to the cosmisation of money must be qualified by the considerations set out in 16§A.

PART C

Unified Self, Monism and Cosmic Cycle in India

CHAPTER 5

The Economics of Sacrifice

We now turn to the Vedic sacrifice, and to its concomitant metaphysics, as represented in texts subsequent to the *Rigveda*. This will involve noting some similarities with the Greek material, but also considerable differences.

5§A Sacrifice and Society

In both cultures there is a belief that men and gods once feasted together, and that this was ended by a transgression, resulting in the current relative remoteness of access to the gods in sacrifice.

Hesiod (*Theogony* 535–60) narrates that when men and gods feasted together, Prometheus divided the meat into two portions, the best meat wrapped in skin and paunch, and the bones covered with fat. Zeus chose the latter, which became forever after the portion given to the gods in the sacrifice, while mortals eat the best meat. But Zeus was angered by Prometheus' trick, and the institution of the practice of sacrifice put an end to the practice of men and gods feasting together.

In India:

> Once the gods and men lived together in the world. Everything that men did not have, they demanded from the gods: 'We do not have this! Give it to us!'. The gods disliked all these demands, and disappeared (SB 2.3.4.4).

Their disappearance affected the sacrificial feast, which attempts to re-establish contact:

> And indeed both the gods and men, and the fathers drink together and this (i.e. the sacrifice) is their symposium; of old they drank together visibly, but now they do so unseen (SB 3.6.2.26).

The narrative of Prometheus' sacrificial trick in Hesiod is followed immediately by his bringing fire to men, with the result that Zeus punishes

Prometheus and gives to mortals the beautiful evil of woman. The next episode is the conflict of the Olympian gods with the older deities, the Titans. This resembles in certain respects the Indian conflict between one group of gods (Devas) and another (Asuras). In both myths a newer group that represents order unites[1] to defeat an older group[2] that represents disorder. The victory is won not so much by physical force as by knowledge or mental ability,[3] as well as by the help of a significant individual: the gods are joined by Prometheus and by Prajapati, each of whom is associated with the sacrifice as well as standing for humankind.[4] The myth is aetiological of the current state of the world, in which disorder is held in check by order[5] but there is also badness.[6]

In the context of this striking set of similarities, two differences between the myths are instructive.

Firstly, in India the mortals make unsuccessful demands on the gods, but in Greece Prometheus succeeds in acquiring the best sacrificial meat for mortals. Accordingly, central to the Greek sacrifice – but not the Vedic – was the communal meal, a distinction that we will see to be significant.

Secondly, the conflict between Devas and Asuras occurs *by means of – and for control of – the sacrifice.*[7] The Asuras were defeated because of their inferiority in the sacrifice.[8] The relationship of military power to Brahminical power is expressed in the Brahminical texts as the containment of the former by the latter. In Hesiod's *Theogony*, by contrast, the establishment of sacrifice as a result of the trickery of the Titan Prometheus is – though immediately followed by the conflict of gods with Titans – nevertheless separate from that conflict. Moreover, the Greek agent of the sacrificial transgression, Prometheus, brings to mortals not only fire from heaven but 'all their techniques',[9] whereas the closest Indian equivalent – the bringing of fire from heaven by Mātāriśvan[10] – has no such significance.

1 Proferes (2007) 51–2; Hesiod *Theogony* 617–63.

2 Asuras older than Devas: BU 1.3.1; Oberlies (2012) 95–7; 2§B.

3 TS 5.3.11.1 (spells or commands); AB 4.6.1 (spells); SB 1.5.4.6–11 (speech); PB 18.1.1; Lévi (1898) 36, 58; A. *Prometheus Bound* 211–15. Prajapati's knowledge is of *numerical equivalences*: 5§C.

4 Prometheus: [A.] *Prometheus Bound* 216–18; Prajapati: Lévi (1898) 53–5.

5 Lévi (1898) 55–6; Biardeau and Malamoud (1976) 25; Hesiod *Theogony* 729–33.

6 In Greece the badness is the Titanic nature of humankind, in India the evil with which the Asuras riddled the faculties, namely the disagreeable things a person says, smells, sees, hears and thinks (BU 1.3.1–7; CU 1.2.1–7).

7 Lévi (1898) 36–61; BU 1.3.1–7; CU 1.2.1–7; Proferes (2007) 107–10 on RV 10.124. Whereas the Greek giants try to ascend to heaven by piling one mountain on another (Pelion on Ossa), the Asuras try to do so by building an altar (SB 2.1.2.13–17).

8 Lévi (1898) 54–6.

9 [A.] *Prometheus Bound* 506.

10 RV 1.93.6; 1.128.2; 3.5.10; 3.9.5; 6.8.4. Against this parallel, and for a different translation of 3.9.5, see Kuiper (1971).

Mortals are established by Prometheus in a distinct sphere in which their control of nature through technology on the one hand distinguishes them from animals and on the other compensates for their separation from the gods.[11] True, with sacrifice the Greeks could open a line of communication with deity, but this is generally from the separate human sphere, whereas the Vedic sacrifice was more inclusive of the universe. Accordingly, another distinctively Greek idea was the reconciliation of the champion of humankind (Prometheus) with the cosmic autocrat (Zeus), with its broadly *political* dimension (3§B).

This marks, already, a general distinction between Greece and India – in the words of Halbfass:

> there is no tradition of explicit and thematic thought about man as man in India, no tradition of trying to define his essence and to distinguish it from other forms of life ... There is, in general, nothing comparable to that tradition in the West which has its roots in ancient Greek as well as biblical sources and leads through the Renaissance and Enlightenment periods to the growing anthropocentrism of modern western thought.[12]

The *differences* between the new (and remarkably similar) metaphysical thought in India and in Greece will be related on the whole to its greater closeness in India to the priestly performance of ritual (16§C, 17§A).

Further, in the Vedic sacrifice there is nothing comparable to the Greek idea of sacrifice that, performed though it may be by an individual, is performed nevertheless on behalf of the group or community – for instance 'on behalf of the Athenians'.[13] Moreover, the Indian sources do not mention any communal *organisation* of the sacrifice.[14] True, the royal horse-sacrifice (*aśvamedha*) is said to ensure security of possession (*yogakṣema*) for the people (*prajānām*).[15] But even in the royal consecration (the *rajasūya*), on the one hand the king is 'for the Vedic ritualist nothing more than a common sacrificer, *yajāmana*', and on the other hand he is 'the universe itself ... he

[11] At SB 2.1.2.13 the sacrificer dons a linen garment 'to be complete'. For in doing this 'it is verily his own skin that he puts on. For this same skin that is presently on the body of the cow was once on man.' For the gods, noting the fundamental importance of the cow, gave it man's skin to enable it to bear the rain, the cold and the heat. Here, man uniquely acquires culture as compensation for deficiency in his nature, as in Plato's Protagoras. But in India, in contrast to Greece, the transition to culture forms part of the *sacrifice*.

[12] Halbfass (1991) 266. [13] Parker (2005) 95–7.

[14] Apart from some temporary groups that disband after the sacrifice: Heesterman (1993) 35. Keith (1925) 258: 'there is no public cult, merely the carrying out of offerings for princes and other men wealthy enough to employ professional priests, and the performance of a much simpler cult by the householder himself'.

[15] SB 13.1.4.3; 13.1.9.10; cf. 13.5.4.24; 3§B n. 34.

impersonates the cosmic tide of regeneration and decay'.[16] There is in Heesterman's book-length study of the *rajasūya* no mention of the state.[17] The long *rajasūya* 'is not concerned with society or polity but exclusively with the metaphysical fate of the single sacrificer as a private individual'.[18]

In the *Rigveda* the gods distribute portions,[19] and there is mention of sacrificial shares[20] and of something like 'ritual community',[21] but hardly any explicit mentions of a communal meal.[22] In subsequent texts, after the offerings are burnt for the gods the human participants do eat what is left, but the function of this eating is not so much a communal meal as the destruction of the offerings by the fire of digestion: it is as representing the gods that the priests and sacrificer eat the offerings, thereby ensuring the total destruction of the victim, from which are expected greater goods such as heaven after death.[23] Malamoud notes that:

> the *Brahmanas* say nothing about the communal character that sharing the same dish among several eaters ought in principle to have. There are no teachings telling us that the circle of table-companions forms a society; nor anything to suggest that the status and social function of the eater are sufficiently altered by the quality or quantity of the share he is allocated.[24]

This is crucially different from the Greek sacrifice.

This lack of communal function and communal enactment does not mean that the Vedic sacrifices never produced general benefit

16 Heesterman (1957) 3, 224.

17 The closest to an exception is the TB (1.7.3.1) stating that the ratnins (the king's subordinates) 'extend to him the realm' (Heesterman [1957] 50): but even here, as in mentions of the people at large (*vis-*, Heesterman 52–3), the focus is on the king (e.g. 76: 'the ratnins, as "the limbs of kingship" are united by the human king'; similarly 55–6, 102, 155). On the *triṣaṃyukta* ('triply connected') sacrifice performed by the king (SB 5.2.5) 'it seems as though the sacrificer concentrates in himself the three forces, emblematic of the three varnas and constituting the social universe of Vedic India: dominion, cattle and priesthood.' (Heesterman 46). He also suggests that 'the people had been gradually excluded from the ritual, in which it could no longer participate' (226).

18 Heesterman (1993) 69. Some scattered texts conferring benefits on the king are collected at Gonda (1975) 286.

19 E.g. 1.22.7; 1.24.5; 1.92.15 1.103.6; 1.109.5; 1.123.3; 1.130.1; 2.1.4; 2.27.12; etc.

20 E.g. 1.20.8; 1.156.5 (of truth); 1.162.12; 2.26.1; 3.60.1; etc.

21 E.g. 1.60.3; 9.82.4 (*vṛjane*: enclosure, settlement, people in the settlement).

22 I have found only 2.1.4; cf. 8.1.23. Of cult in the RV Oberlies (2012) 249–53 does write of a comprehensive commensality of all the participants ('eine umfassende Kommensalität aller beteiligten'), but in fact all the passages of RV he cites are concerned with who is to drink first; none of them bring out commensality.

23 Biardeau and Malamoud (1976) 22.

24 Malamoud (1996) 171, 317 n.7; Keith (1925) 273–4. But sometimes parts are allocated to particular officiants, which might affirm the status of the eater. Malamoud (170) describes the preoccupation 'how best to proceed so that the parts resulting from the division of the [sacrificed] body might reconstitute themselves to form a living whole'.

(e.g. indirectly, as fertility imagined as from the gods) or large-scale collaboration or social and political significance. But such collaboration and such significance were produced by the complex and substantial *exchanges* that occurred – again in contrast to Greek practice – *within* the Vedic ritual of sacrifice.

In the pre-monetary society described by Homer we find goods allocated to mortals in four ways: (a) the sacrificial distribution of meat, (b) interhuman reciprocity (exchange of gifts and benefits), (c) redistributive (centralised) reciprocity (notably of booty by the leader) and (d) sale/purchase. Of these, (d) is marginal and rare, but will in later texts increase, while (a) and (b) are represented as unproblematic, contrasting with the crises created by (c).[25]

In Indian texts later than the *Rigveda*, (a) the sacrificial distribution of meat is without social significance,[26] whereas in Homer it is marked by the ordered egalitarianism of the communal meal,[27] a practice that will be crucial for the development of the state (polis).[28] Indeed the presence of an incipient polis distinguishes Homeric epic not only from the *Rigveda* (3§B) but also from the Vedic texts in general. Moreover, (b) interhuman reciprocity, (c) the distribution of booty and elements of (d) sale/purchase, all of which in Homer occur outside – or even contrast with – the sacrifice, are all found *within* the Vedic sacrifice.

As for the use of booty in sacrificial distribution (c), Heesterman[29] maintains that:

> conquest of wealth and *dakṣiṇā* distribution are two poles of the same process, and that the conquest of wealth and the *dīkṣā*[30] are closely connected.

The sacrificial distribution of booty would lend considerable economic significance to sacrifice,[31] and indeed the sacrificial gifts (or payment) called *dakṣiṇās* were often of considerable economic value. Some of the evidence for Heesterman's claim is early, from the *Rigveda*, for instance

[25] Seaford (2004) Chapter 2.

[26] AB 7.1 does detail distribution of the parts of the sacrificed animal (as a way of reaching heaven), but only among the priests.

[27] The indications in Homer of the combination of (a) and (c) – i.e. centralised redistribution with a ruler providing victims – are rare and slight: Seaford (2004) 76.

[28] Seaford (2004) 39–47, 81–7.

[29] Heesterman (1959) 249; see also Heesterman (1957) 162–6; Whitaker (2011) 87–90.

[30] The rite of passage preliminary to the sacrifice: Heesterman (1993) 160–1; Lévi (1898) 102–8. For chariot-driving in the *dīkṣā*, and the *dīkṣita* as 'bent on booty', see Heesterman (1993) 163.

[31] E.g. SB 13.5.4.24 (the *aśvamedha*).

in the conception of the *dakṣiṇā* as a booty-winning (*vājayantī*) chariot.[32] But we also hear in later texts of looted goods serving as *dakṣiṇās.*[33]

The giving of *dakṣiṇās* by a sacrificer to officiants is a central event of the sacrifice. *Dakṣiṇās* are (5§D) ambivalent between (b) gifts and (d) commercial payment, and this ambivalence has caused debate as to whether the *dakṣiṇā* is part of the sacrifice or payment for it.[34] The two main socially integrative practices of Homeric society – interhuman reciprocity and sacrifice – occur in different contexts: the former creates or sustains a bond between two individuals, the latter unites a group. The contrasting practice of gift-exchange *within* the Vedic sacrifice goes with the control of certain sacrifices by a priestly caste, or rather with the all-powerful complementarity (or synarchy) of Brahmins and Kshatriyas, by which in return for providing sacrificial access to deity the Brahmins receive from the Kshatriyas wealth and protection.[35] To this difference in their socio-political locations most of the major differences between Greek and Vedic sacrifice can be related.

5§B The Cosmic Economy of Vedic Sacrifice

Vedic sacrifice is not performed by a community but is the achievement of an individual (the *yajāmana*) for himself,[36] with the help of priestly officiants. Why does he sacrifice? Here is one motive:[37]

> Indeed, whoever exists, he, in being born, is born as a debt (*ṛṇa*) to the gods, to the sages (*rishis*), to the fathers, and to men. For, inasmuch as he is bound to sacrifice, for that reason he is born as a debt to the gods: hence when he sacrifices to them, when he makes offerings to them, he does this (in discharge of his debt) to them (SB 1.7.2.1–2).[38]

32 RV 5.1.3; 1.123.5; see also 1.80.6; 3.53.6; 5.65.3, 6.4.8, 6.5.3, 6.55.2; etc.: Heesterman (1959) 249.

33 Heesterman (1957) 162–6; (1959) 248–9, 255; *Apastamba Śrauta Sūtra* 10.18.4ff.; *Kāṭhaka Saṃhitā* 28.6, 81.7; *Lātyāyana Śrauta Sūtra* 9.1.14–18.

34 Biardeau and Malamoud (1976) 166–97; Malamoud (1998) 45. Historical transition from the former to the latter: Heesterman (1959) 258.

35 See e.g. BU 1.4.11; Biardeau and Malamoud (1976) 29; Dumont (1980) 66–7; Smith (1990).

36 Biardeau and Malamoud (1976) 157–8.

37 In RV the gods collect debts (e.g. 2.23.17; 2.27.4) or may send them away (2.28.9; 4.23.7). Cf. 10.135 (the need for debts to be forgiven at death?).

38 The passage then explains that being bound to study (the Veda), he is born as a debt to the *rishis*; being bound to wish for offspring, he is born as a debt to the forefathers; and being bound to practise hospitality, he is born as a debt to men. Cf. TS 6.3.10.5; TB 6.3.10.5; AV 6.117.3 (TB 3.7.9.8); AB 7.3.13 (23.1).

> Indeed, even in being born, man, by his own self (atman), is born as a debt (*ṛṇa*) to death. And in that he sacrifices, he thereby redeems (*niṣkrīṇīte*[39]) his atman from death (SB 3.6.2.16).

The real offering is the sacrificer himself, for whom the animal or vegetal offerings are substitutes:[40]

> Now, when he performs the animal offering, he thereby redeems (*niṣkrīṇīte*) his atman – male by male, for the victim is a male, and the sacrificer is a male.[41]

In the sacrifice the sacrificer pays his debt to the gods,[42] not least by substituting an animal for himself. And besides being thereby freed from his metaphysical debt, the sacrificer is transformed. This is another major motive for sacrifice. The sacrificer is reborn, divinised,[43] and taken up to the sky. He must then return to earth, in what is a victory over death, but not before entering and obtaining a loka to which he will go when he dies.[44] (For the meaning of loka, see 6§B.)

The sacrifice is envisaged as an *economic transaction*: the sacrificer gives offerings or gifts that absolve him from debt. There are two kinds of offering or gift. According to SB 2.2.2.6:

> there are two kinds of gods; for, indeed, the gods are the gods; and the Brahmins who have studied and teach sacred lore are the human gods. The sacrifice of these is divided into two kinds: oblations constitute the sacrifice to the gods; and *dakṣiṇā* that to the human gods.[45]

The *dakṣiṇā* 'establishes, or is expressive of, a generative alliance between the giving and receiving parties':[46]

39 Middle voice (krī- means to buy).

40 Biardeau and Malamoud (1976) 19, 161, 193; Hubert and Mauss (1898) 32; Lévi (1898) 132–3; Tull (1989) 1.

41 SB 11.7.1.3. So, too, Prajapati, the projection of the individual sacrificer, 'having given himself up to the gods, created that counterpart of himself, to wit, the sacrifice . . . By this . . . sacrifice he redeemed his atman from the gods' (SB 11.1.8.2–4).

42 Biardeau and Malamoud (1976) 194; Lévi (1898) 131. For an account of the logic of debt to the gods that emphasises the need to reciprocate for goods already received (notably human power over the natural world), see Hénaff (2010) 155, 183–7.

43 Lévi (1898) 103–6; Biardeau and Malamoud (1976) 193; Tull (1989) 106.

44 Lévi (1898) 87–90, 130–1; Biardeau and Malamoud (1976), 190–5; Tull (1989) 113–15; Collins (1982) 47–8; Gonda (1966).

45 See also SB 4.3.4.4; TS 1.7.3.1; Gonda (1965) 215; Biardeau and Malamoud (1976) 166, 190; Lévi (1898) 82.

46 Heesterman (1959) 245.

> According to Brahmanic ritual theory, the sacrificer ransoms the merit of the sacrifice through the giving of sacrificial gifts (*dakṣiṇās*) to the priests who perform the ritual.[47]

'No offering should be without a *dakṣiṇā*' (SB 4.5.1.16), the sacrifice is not a sacrifice without it[48] and rejection of a *dakṣiṇā* creates serious disorder.[49] At BU 3.9.21 sacrifice is founded on the *dakṣiṇā* – because, according to Malamoud:[50]

> the *dakṣiṇā* is the act by which the sacrificer makes – of the voyage that takes him beyond his mortal condition – a going followed by a return. It is the assurance of this return that the sacrificer pays for when he pays, with the *dakṣiṇā*, for the services that he demands from the officiants.

Accordingly, *dakṣiṇās* have a special relationship to (a) the self, and (b) the universe.

(a) In general gifts in premonetary societies are often imagined as somehow embodying their donor to a greater extent than in monetised societies, thereby creating a personal bond between donor and recipient that is not created by money (13§C). 'The sacrificer when distributing the *dakṣiṇās* is considered to give himself', with the *dakṣiṇās* substituting for various parts of himself for the various priests.[51] Further:

> becoming himself, the sacrificer frees himself from death; . . . what he offers becomes his self in the hereafter; when he goes away from this world it calls after him, saying: Come, here I am, your atman (SB 11.2.2.5–6).[52]

(b) Already in RV 10.107 we find, along with *Dakṣiṇā* personified, cosmic as well as earthly returns for giving *dakṣiṇās.* Sacrifice creates and maintains the universe. It recreates cosmogony, the gods and ancestors are present and the *Brahmanas* constantly proclaim the correspondence or identity of elements of the ritual with parts of the

[47] Tull (1989) 35, citing KB 15.1; SB 4.3.4.5–6, 5.1.11–12. See also SB 2.2.2.7 and KB 15. 1, both quoted by Biardeau and Malamoud (1976) 193–3.

[48] Biardeau and Malamoud (1976) 163–6, 190. [49] Heesterman (1959) 244–5.

[50] Malamoud (1998) 42 (my translation from the French).

[51] Heesterman (1959) 243, citing *Āpastamba Śrauta Sūtra* 13.6.4–6; *Hiraṅyakeśi Śrauta Sūtra* 10.15; cf. JB 2.54.; Tull (1989) 46; Biardeau and Malamoud (1976) 187.

[52] Cf. also e.g. PB 4.9.19 'At a *sattra* the *dakṣiṇā* is the (person) self'; SB 11.1.8.6; AB 5.5.28 (xxv 8); also, the sacrificer is, having distributed a thousand cows, 'emptied out' and in need of being 'filled up' again (like his prototype Prajapati): SB 4.5.8.6–9; Heesterman (1959) 246–7. Cf. also the *Brahmayajña* sacrifice, which has as *dakṣiṇā* the breath, which is the self: TA 2.16–17; Biardeau and Malamoud (1976) 187.

universe.[53] When the sacrifice was killed, the gods invigorated it with the *dakṣiṇā*.[54] The *dakṣiṇās* serve as a bridge to heaven.[55] The sacrifice is a boat or a chariot, and the *dakṣiṇā* is the driver of the chariot, or its internal links.[56]

The close connection of the *dakṣiṇā* to the cosmic journey on the one hand and the self on the other is manifest at SB 1.9.3.1:[57]

> That sacrifice goes to the world of the gods, after that goes the *dakṣiṇā* which he gives [to the officiants], and holding on to the *dakṣiṇā* is the sacrificer.

The sacrificer, according to Heesterman:

> like his prototype Prajapati, incorporates the universe and performs the cosmic drama of disintegration and reintegration [we will describe this in 6§A] . . . he ascends to heaven and returns to the earthly world again . . . the *dakṣiṇā* is closely bound up with this process in all its stages . . . the *dakṣiṇās* represent the sacrificer himself, who by distributing himself performs Prajapati's cosmogonic role . . . The picture that arises is that of a continuous stream of *dakṣiṇā* wealth which is dispersed by the sacrifice and then returns to the sacrifice to be renewed again. This cyclical process of the *dakṣiṇās* is closely woven into the ritual cycle.[58]

On the basis of passages indicating the cosmic circulation of the *dakṣiṇā* Heesterman concludes that:

> the *dakṣiṇā* is the material manifestation of the cyclical course of the universe as it is represented in the ritual.[59]

The idea of cosmic cyclicality – be it of souls, cosmological processes, time or history – is frequent in India and Greece but almost entirely absent from the earliest texts (*Rigveda*, Homer, Hesiod), and so the existence of natural cycles is not a sufficient condition for it. Malamoud sees the sacrificial cosmic process as an *economic* process, driven by the need for *payment*:

> The *dakṣiṇā* is the price to pay so that the profane body of the sacrificer returns to its possessor. Having to return to his being, to ensure the certainty

53 Lévi (1898) 10, 77, 81–2; Biardeau and Malamoud (1976) 19, 158, 168–9; Tull (1989) 1, 69.

54 SB 2.2.2.1–2; 4.3.4.1–2. 55 MS 4.8.3; *Kāṭhaka Saṃhitā* 28.4; Heesterman (1959) 252.

56 SB 2.3.3.15; MU 1.2.5–6; PB 16.1.3; AB 6.35; Biardeau and Malamoud (1976) 190–2.

57 As an example of a continuous text illustrating some of these themes see TS 1.4.43 (followed by its prose *Brāhmaṇa*, TS 6.6.1).

58 Heesterman (1959) 246–8; PB 20.15.6–8; 20.15.9–11; 20.16.1; 20.16.9; 21.1.1–8; 21.1.9 (cf. 16.8.6); 21.1.10; JB 2.242–3; 2.246; 2.248–9; 2.252; TS 7.1.5; 7.1.6.1–4; AB 6.15.11; SB 4.5.8.6–9.

59 Heesterman (1959) 257. Sacrifices as endless circle: Lévi (1898) 81; sacrifices as embodying cosmic circulation: Biardeau and Malamoud (1976) 23–4.

> of refinding it; these procedures are inscribed in the general economy of debt and ransom which, in Brahmanism, govern not only the individual life of men but also the whole organisation of the world, and notably the sacrifice.[60]

In the 'whole organisation of the world' another necessary cosmic cycle, in which the sacrifice participates, is the cycle of fertility. Sacrifice nourishes the gods, who send the rain that nourishes plants and – thereby – animals, humans and (through sacrifice again) the gods.[61] The notion is sometimes expressed in the *Brahmanas* that:

> the smoke of the oblational fire goes up to heaven and returns again as rain from the clouds so as to make the earth bear fruit. This represents a perfect, automatically effective circulation between the human and the heavenly worlds, set in motion by man through his sacrificial fire. But this applies to smoke in general, not exclusively to the smoke of the burnt offering. Moreover, the gods are not necessarily involved in the automatism of the circulatory chain.[62]

Debt, the sacrificial rite of passage, and nature – each forming a cycle driven by necessity – influence and inform each other, are imagined in terms of each other. Whereas the cosmic economy of Greek sacrifice consists of offerings to elicit divine requital, the cosmic economy of Vedic sacrifice is more complex. In India there is exchange (or a cycle of exchanges) between the human participants as well as between this world and the world of the gods, but these two kinds of exchange do not form separate spheres: to the officiants the sacrificer gives *dakṣiṇās*, which – some texts imply – embody (or even drive) the cosmic cycle. What is given, acquired, exchanged or circulated comprises three kinds of goods: *dakṣiṇās*, offerings to the gods and the fruits of the sacrifice, which include goods in the afterlife. The exchange and circulation of goods is projected onto the universe. Typical features of the cosmic rite of passage, such as rebirth (and dismemberment: 6§A), coalesce with the circulation of goods.

5§C The Individualisation of Vedic Sacrifice

The sacrifice as presented in the *Brahmanas* and *Śrauta Sūtras* centres on the single *yajamana*, who is the sole beneficiary. But 'underneath the

[60] Biardeau and Malamoud (1976) 194 (my translation from the French). For the importance of debt bondage in ancient India, see Chakravarti (1985).

[61] Biardeau and Malamoud (1976) 24.

[62] Heesterman (1993) 12, citing SB 5.3.5.17; 7.4.2.22.

classical system', according to Heesterman, 'a different, older pattern can be discerned'.[63]

The differences detected by Heesterman in the older pattern are threefold. It was characterised by *exchange*, by the participation of the *group* and by *conflict or competition*. I confine myself here to one or two of Heesterman's examples of each of these three elements.

Firstly, *exchange* is exemplified thus:

> At the acme of the ritual, the moment of birth, when the *dakṣiṇās* are distributed, a reversal takes place; the *dīkṣita* (one who has undergone the preliminary rite of passage known as *dīkṣā*) patron sheds his death impurity and is reborn a pure Brahmin. The Brahmin on the other hand takes over the burden of death. Whereas the pivot of the classical ritual is represented by the single *yajāmana*, the preclassical ritual is based on a complementary pair. This pair, through an exchange and the reversal of roles, maintains the continuity of the cosmos.[64]

Secondly, this *dīkṣita*-Brahmin pair stands for two opposed *groups*. In the Black Yajurveda we find – in the soma sacrifice known as *ahina* – a group of *dīkṣitas* faced in the ritual by a group of non-*dīkṣitas*. 'The cooperation of two opposed groups, which is not mentioned in the White Yajurveda any more, belongs to the pre-classical system.'[65]

Thirdly, Heesterman provides evidence that such cooperation might include *conflict or competition*.[66] For example, 'that ritual competition was a normal phenomenon is indicated by the fact that the full- and new-moon sacrifices are characterised in the older *Brahmanas* as *samṛtayajña*, "competing sacrifice"'.[67] Another example is the 'concord' sacrifice (*saṃjñāneṣṭi*), which was 'manifestly intended to be performed by rival groups in order to unite them under a common leader', and was transformed into a ritual performed by a single *yajāmana*, who wants non-participants in the ritual to agree to his leadership.[68] We noted in 5§A that the Indian mythical conflict between two groups (Devas and Asuras) differed from the similar Greek myth by being *within and for the sacrifice*. Another myth of

[63] Heesterman (1985) 26–44; (1993) *passim*. [64] Heesterman (1985) 28.

[65] Heesterman (1985) 28. [66] See esp. Heesterman (1993) 40–3, 49, 52, 137–40, 201–3.

[67] Heesterman (1993) 40–1.

[68] Heesterman (1985) 29, 34; (1993) 40: 'sacrifice is not just concerned with conflict. It *is* conflict writ large'; 42: 'sacrifice has to be agonistic: throughout the ancient Indian *śrauta* ritual the contest has left its mark. The disturbing and destabilising effect of sacrifice makes itself manifest in its fiercely agonistic character.'

conflict between groups within and for the sacrifice is between the Adityas and the Angirases.[69]

The marginalisation of exchange, conflict and the group within the sacrifice results in its *individualisation*, which – prefigured in the late tenth book of the *Rigveda* (4§E) – has its subsequent mythical expression in the figure of Prajapati:

> Prajapati, the cosmic man and incorporation of the classical ritual doctrine, is the prototype of the single *yajāmana*, who performs without the intervention of a rival party and for his sole benefit the ritual of cosmic renewal.[70]

The *Jāiminīya Brāhmaṇa* narrates the competition of Prajapati and Death through rival sacrifices. Prajapati wins by discovering the symbolical and numerical equivalences (*saṃpad*, *saṃkhyāna*):

> He managed in the end to win not because he was a stronger, better equipped contender and sacrifice – the two are explicitly said to be equally strong – but exclusively through his 'vision' of *saṃpad* or *saṃkhyāna* and the intricate arithmetic involved in establishing the symbolic equivalences.[71]

The result is that:

> now there is no ritual competition (*saṃsava*); what was the second sacrifice (of Death), that waned; the sacrifice is only one; Prajapati alone is the sacrifice (JB 2.69–70).

Heesterman describes the development thus:

> Everything now depends on the correct execution of the automatically working ritual. This has led to an excessive development of ritual 'science', but nevertheless it was a breakthrough in that it set the individual free from the oppressive bonds of reciprocity which tied him to the others, the rivals. This was achieved through the symbolic and numerical equivalences. Where there was opposition, now there is equivalence. Through his knowledge of the equivalences, the *yajāmana* not only becomes the cosmic man Prajapati but also, like Prajapati, he assimilates Death. 'Death becomes his self', and thus he conquers recurring death (*punarmṛtyu*).'[72]

Remarkable about this process of individualisation is that it might not – and sometimes did not – stop before everything was absorbed into the individual. What is required for an 'automatically working ritual'

[69] Heesterman (1993) 37–41. In Homer the order of sacrifice contrasts with battle, and sacrificial slaughter is never used as a metaphor for battle. In contrast, for the interpenetration of sacrifice and battle in the *Mahābhārata* see Heesterman (1993) 27–8, 43.

[70] Heesterman (1985) 33. [71] Heesterman (1993) 54.

[72] Heesterman (1985) 33–4; (1993) 3, 54–8.

performed by an individual is neither reciprocity with other participants nor the intervention of deity but rather knowledge of its correct performance and of the connections (*bandhus*) between elements of the ritual and elements external to the ritual.[73] For *bandhus* Cavallin uses the term 'ritual correspondence', which he defines as 'a relation between two or more entities, which connects them in a way that makes it possible to influence one of them through the ritual manipulation of the other (or to explain e.g. the use of one entity in terms of the other)'.[74] Knowledge of the correspondences is knowledge that *controls*,[75] knowledge not only of the sacrifice but of the correspondence of elements of the sacrifice with elements of the person and of the universe, extending to knowledge of the universe as a whole.

Individualisation advances to the point at which such knowledge amounts to absorption of the universe into the individual, identification of the universe with the individual self. The relations of complementarity and exchange between *yajāmana* (sacrificer) and officiant are transformed into relations that 'can only be realised in terms of fusion into a single unit'.[76] There is increased individual control of what was once uncontrollable circulation.[77] The prototype of the individual sacrificer, Prajapati, is also officiant, sacrifice, victim, universe, atman,[78] creator of everything and himself everything.[79] In performing the sacrifice the individual may be identified with Prajapati, and may become everything.[80] 'The classical doctrine implies', notes Heesterman, 'that the *yajāmana*, through knowledge of the equivalences, becomes the integral cosmos, realising in himself, and thereby mastering, the cosmic alternation of life and

73 For a discussion of this relation, and of the various ways in which it has been translated and interpreted (identification, correspondence, equivalence, resemblance), see Cavallin (2003a) 6–33; Smith (1989) 31–8, 46–9.

74 Cavallin (2003a) 7–8. He gives as an example AV 2.33.2: 'If he desire of a man, "Let me deprive him of the lordly power", he should recite the hymn in the middle of the Nivid [a text]; the Nivid is the lordly power, the hymn the people; verily thus he deprives him of the lordly power.'

75 BU 6.1.4 (similar CU 5.1.4): 'When a man knows the correspondence, whatever he desires is fulfilled for him.' CU 1.1.10: 'Only what is performed with knowledge, with faith, and with awareness of the *upaniṣad* (hidden connection) becomes truly potent.'

76 Heesterman (1985) 34.

77 E.g. on the fear that the offered sacrifice will not come back again see Heesterman (1985) 32; on the sacrifice staying with (or becoming the self of) the *yajāmana* see Heesterman (1985) 34 ('instead of the transversal axis of the reciprocal relations with the others, everything is now concentrated on the vertical axis of the individual life, or lives, of the single *yajāmana*); 'the *dakṣiṇās* no longer circulate but stay in the same place' (Heesterman [1985] 36); Cf. Heesterman (1993) 38–9.

78 E.g. SB 4.6.1.1.

79 6§A; see also the Brahmanic texts collected and discussed by Lévi (1898) 13–30.

80 E.g. SB 4.5.7.1; 3.3.4.5–11; 13.6.1.1; 13.7.1.1. At SB 6.1.1.5–6 Prajapati is created out of seven individuals.

death'.[81] The control of the cosmos by the individual, once achieved by ritual embodying reciprocity with divine powers, is now achieved by the mental absorption of the cosmos into himself.

Heesterman's argument for the individualisation of the sacrifice at the expense of exchange, conflict and the group is supported by considerable evidence.[82] One objection to it is that he does not use the *Rigveda*, in which – it has been maintained – there is very little evidence for his postulated early phase of sacrifice.[83] However, there is evidence for the ritual background of the *Rigveda* hymns as agonistic.[84] Certainly they contain numerous mentions of contests (in particular chariot races and verbal contests), for which the help of deity is invoked. And Proferes notes *competition* between *groups*:

> a number of common motifs in the *Rigvedic* liturgies that have in common the idea that multiple groups invoke the soma-drinking deities simultaneously. These include passages in which the liturgical songs are depicted as competing against each other ... for the gods' attention; other passages in which rival worshippers ... seek to win the exclusive presence of the gods at their own rite; and still others that explicitly refer to 'rival invocations' (*vihava, vívāc*) or that refer to rival groups simultaneously invoking ... the same deity.[85]

A more substantial criticism is surprise at 'how little interest Heesterman displays in situating the Vedic and pre-Vedic religious culture that he hypothesises in a socio-historical context'.[86] Let us take for instance the question of why the individualisation occurred. Heesterman speculates that the origin of 'ritual thought' is to be found in a 'problem before the ancient ritualists', which was 'to break through the vicious circle of mutual dependence':

> They had to find a way permanently to overcome death and secure the continuity of life. The solution that presented itself to them was to short-circuit the bilateral pattern of exchange and reversal by cutting out the

[81] Heesterman (1985) 39. We may add that in practice the *yajāmana* would depend on the knowledge of the ritual specialist.

[82] Jamison (1996) is critical of Heesterman's conclusions, but refers to his 'profound knowledge of Vedic ritual texts'. To her criticisms I would add that conflict associated with sacrifice may derive from the need to *imagine* the disorder excluded by the actual performance of the ritual – e.g. at KB 11.3 (cf. SB 11.6.1.1–13; 12.9.1.1; JB 1.26; 1.42), in which negative reciprocity has been replaced by individual control (Malamoud [1996] 165), but the replacement is *imaginative*, not historical. (For other instances of revenge averted in the sacrifice, see Malamoud [1996] 164–8).

[83] Jamison (1996) 104; Minkowski (1996) 343; Whitaker (2011) 163–5.

[84] The controversy on this point is well summarised, with bibliography, by Proferes (2007) 5–6.

[85] Proferes (2007) 5 (also 44–5, 67, 70). Examples I have found of sacrificial rivalry in RV are 1.162.1; 1.173.10; 3.31.15–18; 3.35.5; 4.25.2–6; 4.39.5; 4.58.10; 5.3.6; 6.52.1–2; 7.24.2; 7.32.11–14; 7.34.6; 7.93.3; 8.31.5–6; 10.71.7–8; 10.128.1–4. See further Kuiper (1960).

[86] Minkowski (1996) 343.

> other, the rival party. The elimination of the rival brought the cosmic cycle of life and death in one hand; thus the single *yajāmana* was enabled to deal ritually with death without incurring the risk involved in the ambivalent co-operation with others.[87]

But why did this problem, and the attempt to resolve it, occur when and where they did? The answers to these crucial questions cannot, *pace* Heesterman, be inferred merely from within the practice of sacrifice and its associated ideas. If we are to understand why a set of ideas becomes problematic enough to require transformation, we must look rather at changes in its environment.[88] In doing so I will be presenting a cumulative case for *monetisation* as an important factor in the new metaphysics.

Heesterman is not the only scholar to describe and emphasise the process of individualisation. In his study of the *Rigvedic Brahmanas* Cavallin[89] concludes that 'the tendency is that the sacrificer also becomes the goal of the ritual activity'. And there are, according to Tull, a number of passages in the *Brahmanas* that:

> indicate that the Brahmanic thinkers recognised two types of sacrifice: the traditional sacrificial format and a form of sacrifice that emphasises the individual to the point of excluding the priests and perhaps even the gods.[90]

At SB 10.5.4.16 the world attained by knowledge is the place where sacrificial gifts (*dakṣiṇās*) do not go. For Tull this constitutes an 'experience independent of the ritual specialist', which in the *Upanishads*:

> continues in the development of the interiorised sacrifice; its unfragmented nature, centering entirely on the individual, is thus mirrored in the conditions of the afterlife.[91]

SB 11.2.6.13–14 distinguishes between the one who sacrifices for the gods (*devayājin*, 'god-offerer') and the one who sacrifices for the self (*ātmayājin*, 'self-offerer').[92] Better is the *ātmayājin*:

> 'Who is the better one, the self-offerer, or the god-offerer?' Let him say, 'The self-offerer;' for a self-offerer, doubtless, is he who knows, 'This my (new) body is formed by that (body of *Yajña*, the sacrifice), this my (new) body is procured thereby.'[93]

[87] Heesterman (1985) 32; (1982) 260.

[88] Heesterman does raise the possibility, but only fleetingly, that the growth of agriculture may have been a factor: (1985) 106, 124–5.

[89] Cavallin (2003a) 230.

[90] Tull (1989) 39; Heesterman (1993) 82, 216.

[91] Tull (1989) 36.

[92] On this passage see Bodewitz (1973) 304.

[93] For the self-offerer as *created by the sacrifice as a composite* (of the Vedas and offerings), cf. KU 2.6; AB 2.40.1–7; cf. also TU 2.7.1; AU 2.3; Collins (1982) 53–4.

The *devayājin* on the other hand:

> is as the inferior who brings tribute to the superior, or like a man of the people who brings tribute to the king: indeed, he does not win such a place (in heaven) as the other.

Whereas the *devayājin* attains the benefit of the sacrifice through the intercession of the gods, the *ātmayājin* attains it directly.[94] This distinction is another symptom of individualisation, and introduces an economic dimension. If the *devayājin* is like the inferior who brings tribute to the superior, the implication is that the *ātmayājin* is like the economically autonomous individual. Among the ritual prescriptions that make up most of the *Śatapatha Brāhmaṇa* the gods are frequently mentioned; but in the *Bṛhadāraṇyaka Upaniṣad*, which forms the concluding section of the *Śatapatha Brāhmaṇa*, they appear far less. At BU 1.4.10 one man knows 'I am brahman', and becomes this whole world, and 'not even the gods are able to prevent it'. He is contrasted with one who worships another deity, thinking 'he is one and I am another'. The latter does not understand, and relates to the gods as livestock do to men, and so 'it is not pleasing to the gods when men know this'. Like those who pay tribute to their superiors, animals serve the economic interests of men, and some sacrificers benefit gods. On the other hand 'if someone venerates himself alone as his world, that rite of his will never fade away, because from his very self he will produce whatever he desires' (1.4.15). Metaphysical autonomy is economic autonomy, in the sense of fulfilling desire independently of others. The marginalisation of deity by the impersonal omnipotence of money was in both India and Greece more likely to occur among intellectuals whom money had made independent of others, namely an economic elite.

What is this 'brahman' with which the autonomous man identifies himself? Connected it seems with the verb *bṛh-*, 'to grow, swell, expand', in the *Rigveda* brahman refers to invisible power, generally created in ritual (especially by ritual utterance).[95] Subsequently it has various senses, as

[94] The *ātmayajña* sacrifice, performed for the self, has been described as playing an important role in the development of the sacrifice for the breaths, the *prāṇāgnihotra*, in which 'the pranas-fires became the object rather than the instrument of the rite, i.e. they became the deities or deity in and to which one sacrificed. This external manifestation of the divine object of the rite (which in fact was identical with the sacrificer's self) could easily be interiorised' (Bodewitz [1973] 304, 330). On the *prāṇāgnihotra*, see also Heesterman (1993) 214: 'turning the meal into a sacrifice, performed in and by himself alone, he sets himself free from the surrounding world and eats his meal in sovereign independence . . . It is a ritualistic act that points toward man's capacity to transcend the world and ultimately himself.' On atman and pranas, see 6§D.

[95] Gonda (1950) 13–14, 40–2, 58; Cohen (2008) 46–8.

personal[96] or impersonal, as the real (*satya*),[97] and even as material.[98] Overall its meaning, as of *sukṛta* and *karman* (7§A), tends to develop from action to entity, from ritual to what is controlled by ritual (i.e. most or all things).[99] Smith writes of a transition in its meaning 'from the *Rigveda* (where the meaning tends to centre on the transcendental potency of hymn or formula), through the ritual texts (where it describes the power of sacrificial activity), to the Upanishadic literature (where it is more generally conceived as the ultimate principle of all being)'.[100] Already in SB (11.4.4.1–7) one may achieve union with it and participation in its world (through offering sacrificial food). In the early *Upanishads* it becomes – like *karman* subsequently (7§A) – completely detached from ritual, coming to mean an entity that is universal, fundamental to all else, distinct and yet all-pervasive,[101] the source and destination of things,[102] eternal and invisible,[103] 'without a before and an after, without an inner and an outer'.[104] With the tendency for Prajapati to be progressively superseded by brahman as the highest principle,[105] the *invisibility* of brahman tends to become universal impersonal *abstraction*; and the questions arise of what exactly brahman is and how it is to be accessed.[106] It is like buried golden treasure that people frequently walk over without discovering,

96 E.g. SB 11.2.2.3 (quoted below, 16§B n.1); Cohen (2008) 46. In order to protect the gods against the Asuras, the mighty Indra requires as his ally Brahman, personalised as Brihaspati (SB 9.2.3.3).

97 True, real, actual, genuine, honest, good.

98 BU 5.4.1 Brahman is *satya*; TB 2.8.9.3–7: brahman is the wood, the tree, from which the earth and sky are carved (answer to question at RV 10.81.4); also AB 8.28 (wind).

99 TB 2.8.8.8–10; SB 7.3.1.42; cf. 10.4.1.9; 13.6.2.7; TB 3.12.9 the whole world created through brahman; Deussen (1915) 240–70. Brahman as the Veda: SB 6.1.1.8. A good account of brahman is in Smith (1989) 72.

100 Smith (1989) 71.

101 E.g. SB 11.2.3.3: 'Then the Brahman itself went up to the sphere beyond. Having gone up to the sphere beyond, it considered, "How can I descend again into these worlds?" It then descended again by means of these two – Form and Name . . . as far as there are Form and Name so far, indeed, extends this (universe).'

102 TU 3.1.1: 'That from which these things are born; on which, once born, they live; and into which they pass upon death – seek to perceive that! That is brahman!'

103 See e.g. Deussen (1915) 240–70; Smith (1989) 72; e.g. BU 1.4.10; 2.5.1–4; 4.1.7; 4.4.7, 17, 18.

104 CU 2.5.19.

105 Deussen (1915) 204, 257–65; Keith (1925) 443–4, 449–50. On the similarity between Prajapati and brahman, see Smith (1989) 70. Nothing is greater than *brahman*: SB 10.3.5.10 (a status it may already have in some passages of the AV: Edgerton (1965) 24.n.2). The unknowability and power of brahman is the theme of the later *Kena Upaniṣad* (= JUB 4.18–21). Note the primordial monism of brahman at SB 11.2.3.1.

106 Brereton (1990: 118) calls brahman in the *Upaniṣhads* 'an open concept', 'the designation given to whatever principle or power a sage believes to be behind the world and to make the world explicable'.

'for they are led astray by the unreal'.[107] As such, it is able to fuse with the (universal, impersonal, invisible) power of money, producing a concept distinct on the one hand from pure Being (the existent) and from a specific substance on the other – and hence without a Greek equivalent.

5§D From Gift to Payment

In 5§C we described Heesterman's account of the marginalisation of reciprocity by individualism, and extended it with the distinction between the traditional sacrificer (for the gods) and the sacrificer for the self. Sacrificing for the self is also recommended at SB 9.5.2.12–13:

> Now who performs these [rites] for another, he causes these oceans [the rites] to dry up [for himself]; those dried up, his metres are dried up; after the metres, the world (loka); after the world, the atman; after the atman, (his) children and cattle, Indeed he becomes poorer daily who performs these rites for another ... now who does not perform these [rites] for another becomes more prosperous daily. Indeed this [rite] is his divine, undying atman; who performs these rites for another gives his divine atman to another. Only a dried trunk remains.

To sacrifice for another rather than for yourself makes you poorer. This suggests a world in which reciprocity (voluntary requital) is in decline: giving does not necessarily elicit corresponding benefits in return, and so may impoverish the giver.[108] In such a world prosperity may be attained through the individual autonomy bestowed by the possession of money, an autonomy that marginalises even the gods. The advance of commercial exchange, and of the monetisation that facilitates commercial exchange, is likely to marginalise the traditional practice of reciprocity.

There are various respects in which positive reciprocity (gift-exchange) is distinct from commercial (including monetised) exchange:[109]

(1) In reciprocity requital is voluntary, or at least imagined as voluntary, whereas in a commercial exchange, once it is agreed, payment is obligatory.
(2) In reciprocity there is no requirement for equivalence between goods, but connections between donor and recipient are established or confirmed.

[107] CU 8.3.2; cf. AV 2.1.1: 'Vena beholds That Highest which lies hidden, wherein this All resumes one form and fashion'.
[108] Cf. Heesterman (1993) 210. [109] I discuss this opposition further in 13§C.

(3) In commerce the ownership and alienation of goods (or money) is absolute. By contrast, the embodiment of the donor in the gift is exemplified by the identification of sacrificer both with the victim offered to the gods and with the dakṣiṇās offered to the officiants.[110]

(4) Reciprocity generally[111] creates a *series of discrete relationships* between parties (individuals or communities), as for instance does Homeric gift-exchange, whereas commerce is facilitated by a single universal equivalent, which – especially if embodied in a circulating substance (e.g. precious metal) – may seem to be the (passive or active) vehicle of a *universal cycle*.

(5) From reciprocity the *quantification* of equivalence is on the whole absent, whereas commerce depends on quantified equivalence between the goods (or goods and money) exchanged. We are reminded that the new autonomous individual, Prajapati, prevails by his knowledge of the 'intricate arithmetic' of numerical equivalences, which are a frequent feature of the ritual prescriptions in the *Brāhmaṇas*.[112] An early reaction to the power of quantified individualism occurs in a late hymn of the *Rigveda* (10.117), which first praises reciprocity ('the wealth of one who gives does not become exhausted, and the non-giver finds no one to show mercy . . . he who eats alone has only evil'), and then suggests that power and autonomy do not correlate with *quantity*.[113]

These descriptions represent ideal types of reciprocity on the one hand and commerce on the other. In practice they merge along a spectrum, which is reflected in the metaphysical realm of sacrifice. On this spectrum, the gift may become *compulsory*, as *tribute*, which is used negatively to characterise gifts to the gods (5§C).

The 'two kinds of gods' – gods and Brahmins – when they are satisfied by oblations and *dakṣiṇās*, respectively (5§B), 'put the sacrificer in a state of

110 5§B: this dispersal of the sacrificial self was perhaps a factor in the *identification of the sacrificer with the sacrifice*. Prajapati is both sacrificer and sacrifice (6§A).

111 True, in some instances of reciprocity there is a single or dominant kind of object given (for instance shells in the Kula exchange), which accordingly seems to create a universal cycle and so to have *some* of the features of money. And reciprocity may be transformed not only into the universal cycle of money but also, in different conditions, into the top-down redistribution such as occurred in ancient Egypt and Mesopotamia.

112 Gonda (1975) 373–4.

113 Verse 8: 'The one-footed [=sun?] has stridden further than the two-footed [=man?]; the two footed overtakes the three-footed [=old man?] from behind. The four footed [=dog?] comes at the call of the two-footed ones as it watches over the fivefold ones [=herds?], staying by them.' Jamison and Brereton note that this 'suggests that sheer quantity isn't the measure of power and effectiveness: the more "feet" an entity has, the less its autonomy and power'.

bliss' (SB 2.2.2.6). Here the model is of reciprocity: the gods, satisfied by gifts, voluntarily requite the sacrificer, as in the *Rigveda*. But sacrifice may also seem to be, at the other end of the spectrum, an *automatic cycle*.

Some passages manifest a combination of (or ambivalence between) on the one hand gift-exchange and on the other hand the impersonal necessity and individual accumulation of absolute property characteristic of commerce. For instance, a mantra at a funeral by a relative of the dead proclaims:

> leave the clothing that you have worn down here, think of your *iṣṭāpūrta*, of the *dakṣiṇā*, how it was given by you often among your connections (TA 6.1.1).

Iṣṭāpūrta is etymologically connected with sacrifice, and could refer to the result of sacrifice, but came to refer not only to material wealth in this world[114] but also to the totality of merit accumulated (not only by sacrifice)[115] in the addressee's life (other than by asceticism) for advantage in the beyond.[116] It:

> appears to be a synonym for *nidhi* (treasure), deposit in heaven, consisting of religious merit, something on a man's credit side in the invisible world or in the life hereafter.[117]

It is at TA 6.1.1 cited along with the gift (*dakṣiṇā*) given among connections (including priests). Just as a man may either accumulate individual property for himself or use it as gift to create useful connections with others, so a donor in this life may thereby obtain in the next life either a store of accumulated merit (*iṣṭāpūrta*) or reciprocal benefit (notably bliss) from recipients of the gift (*dakṣiṇā*).

The transition from gift to individually earned merit/substance in the imagined beyond surely did not occur independently of the same transition (monetisation) in this world. I will pursue this theme further in Chapter 9. The association of religious merit with individualisation is much later made explicit, in the *Laws of Manu* (9.111): brothers may live together, 'or they may live separately if they wish for religious merit; for religious merit increases in separation, and so separate rituals are conducive to religious merit'.

The *dakṣiṇā* is in some respects a gift: it should be given freely without bargaining (SB 9.5.2.16) such as accompanied the purchase of soma (2§E),

114 Source references in Krishan (1997) 33. 115 Halbfass (2000) 59; Krishan (1997) 4–5.
116 Biardeau and Malamoud (1976) 165 (excluding asceticism); Keith (1925) 250, 409, 478.
117 Krishan (1997) 5.

and create interpersonal connection.[118] The essential act of the sacrificer is the abandoning (*tyāga*) of something belonging to him.[119] But on the other hand the requital was regarded as automatic rather than voluntary,[120] and in this respect it resembles a commercial transaction. It is as *payment* that the *dakṣiṇā* is widely understood as assuring the autonomy of the sacrificer in relation to the officiants;[121] and, indeed, it became a model for other kinds of payment.[122] Ambivalence between the voluntary requital of true gift-exchange and the impersonal necessity characteristic of commerce is manifest in passages in which the effectiveness of gifts is stated without any mention of requital from their recipients (although it is not explicitly excluded). For instance a line of a late hymn of the *Rigveda* (10.107.8) seems to mean that the *dakṣiṇās* put their donors in possession of this whole world and heaven.[123] In JB 2.278 the man who knows is able to reach heaven by gift-giving (*dānena*) and by religious exertions (*sramena*). And in BU (6.2.16) people are said to 'win heavenly worlds' in three ways, 'by offering sacrifice (*yajñena*), by giving gifts (*dānena*), and by performing austerities (*tapasā*)'.

It was once the exchange of *gifts* that maintained the order of the universe.[124] And whereas, according to Heesterman, the 'pre-classical system based the life- and prosperity-furthering function on periodically alternating exchanges and reversals', the classical ritual by contrast 'is supposed to produce its results (broadly speaking the furtherance of life and prosperity) automatically without an intervening agency'.[125] If so, then the ambivalence of the *dakṣiṇā* between gift and payment is to be understood historically, as – roughly speaking – a *transition* from gift to payment. Similarly, whereas in the *Rigveda* sacrifice generally *propitiated* the gods, subsequently divine agency was – we have seen – diminished by privileging the power of knowledge, and by preference for the *ātmayājin* over the *devayājin*. Sacrifice in the *Brahmanas* has been characterised as working –

118 Heesterman (1959) 242–5. 119 Biardeau and Malamoud (1976) 19, 72.

120 Heesterman (1959) 242–5. 121 Malamoud (1998) 43 (cf. 45).

122 Biardeau and Malamoud (1976) 193, 197 (at 169 they emphasise that the giving of *dakṣiṇās* is precisely a purchase of service); Malamoud (1998) 45–6.

123 The passage is admittedly obscure, meaning something like 'he grants this entire world and all heaven from *dakṣiṇās*'.

124 Gonda (1965) 214: 'Both god and worshipper give and receive, both participate in the powerfulness of what may be called a circular process on which the maintenance of the world-order as well as the continuance of life depends'; Biardeau and Malamoud (1976) 168–9. On the erstwhile exchange between sacrificer and Brahmin Heesterman (1985) 28 notes that 'the preclassical ritual is based on a complementary pair. This pair, through exchange and the reversal of roles, maintain the continuity of the cosmos'.

125 Heesterman (1985) 31.

as magic may do – through internal necessity, independently of the gods.[126] The metaphysical debt to the gods, incurred by birth and paid by sacrifices, seems more like an impersonal necessity than requiring a gift designed to create goodwill. As for the Greeks, the holiness of sacrifice and prayer was in the age of money characterised in Plato as 'a kind of commercial art between gods and men' (*Euthyphro* 14e).

The transformation of the sacrifice described in great detail by Heesterman is not just a matter of individualisation. Whereas the older kind of ritual 'derives directly from the transposition of worldly tension and strife to the sacrificial arena', and there is visible redistribution of the goods of life, the new kind of ritual:

> is not dependent on the participation of others ... It stands apart in sovereign independence ... it transcends the surrounding world[127] ... deals with the invisible (*adṛṣṭa*). The effect, the 'fruit' it promises to the faithful sacrificer, comes about in an invisible way[128] ... The expert officiants who receive the *dakṣiṇā* wealth are not held to any reciprocity ... When the service is rendered and the salary received there is no longer reciprocity or mutual obligation ... The ritual is supposed to produce its result automatically ... but the way in which the effect should come about is hidden from our view... It [*śraddhā*] has come to mean the unquestioning faith in the efficacy of the ritual. As such it has no social content. But the connection it still shows with the *dakṣiṇā* points in the direction of an original social context of gift-giving and alliance.[129]

This combination of sovereign independence, transcendence, fruitful but invisible power (*adṛṣṭa*), replacement of reciprocity by payment, automatism, the transition from the interpersonal confidence of gift-exchange to a general confidence in impersonal efficacy: it will emerge that all this is – along with individualisation, interiorisation, monism, and the individual autonomy bestowed by knowledge of *numerical equivalences* (5§C) – precisely what one would expect of the effect of monetisation. But this is unnoticed by Heesterman.[130]

126 Lévi (1898) 129.
127 Blezer (1992: 22) emphasises that this new transcendence is 'part and parcel of a more comprehensive and irrevocable development in Indian thought, rather than only the outcome of the deliberations of some firepriests', but does not attempt to explain the development.
128 Biardeau and Malamoud (1976) 150 distinguish between the explicit invisibility of the effect of the sacrifice and the explicit visibility of the *dakṣiṇā*.
129 Heesterman (1993) 77–8; cf. 186–7.
130 Heesterman elsewhere (1985: 35) notes that 'individualisation implies that the individual has to be all lest he be nothing'. Cf. the all-or-nothing logic of monetisation (Seaford [2004] 249 on Parmenides B8.33), and the 'practical solipsism' introduced by money (Sohn-Rethel [1978]).

'Sacrifice', he notes, 'and especially animal sacrifice, is very much a public, social affair, as one would expect it to be. Cattle keeping and cultivation, given their ultimate purpose of providing food and survival, cannot be solitary affairs.'[131] But with the advance of the invisibly automatic at the expense of voluntary requital (reciprocity), the individual sacrificer had less need for interpersonal confidence, for the goodwill of the officiants, even for the goodwill of the gods. What he required was confidence in impersonal efficacy, and *knowledge* (especially of the correspondences). His mental power becomes increasingly central to the sacrifice (and so to the universe), with the final result that he – either his body or his mental power – absorbs the sacrificial ritual itself.[132] Sacrifice is *interiorised.*[133]

The gift, whether to god or man, is given so as to elicit the goodwill of the recipient. But the payment of money is merely an agreement to exchange impersonal power (embodied in the money) for goods or services, and can successfully occur without any goodwill. And so money seems to embody universal power whose deployment depends entirely on the self-directed will of its owner. Moreover, whereas gifts preserve some relation (memory, gratitude, obligation) to their donor, money belongs absolutely to its owner. The invisible power of money is impersonal, but expresses the will of its individual owner. Indeed, it is through his money that its individual owner enacts his will. The result is that the invisible power of money, though universal, may seem nevertheless to belong to the inner self of its owner. In Greek texts the autonomous, unitary inner self is to some extent modelled on the abstract power-substance of money (Chapter 13). The power of money is interiorised.

This aspect of monetisation is also likely to influence ideas about sacrificial ritual. Firstly, wealth sent in sacrifice to heaven to elicit the goodwill of the gods may tend to become wealth accumulated in heaven by the individual sacrificer for his own use (Chapter 9). Secondly, monetisation helps to explain the interiorisation of sacrifice. The power of the individual sacrificer is expressed in the correspondences imagined between elements of the ritual and elements of the world outside it (including himself). But with the single thing, money, the individual may obtain all

131 Heesterman (1993) 43.

132 As preliminary to such interiorisation, note how several passages of SB 'suggest a subtle shift in the meaning of *bandha*, from the physical binding of the animal to that of a metaphysical binding of the animal to the sacrificer' (Tull [1989] 74).

133 A natural concomitant of this development is the detachment of some sacrifices from the season cycle: cf. Heesterman (1985) 41.

goods and services, and do so more successfully than with ritual. The power of money – individualising but universal, interiorised but direct – comes to influence the way in which the traditional power of the individual sacrificer is imagined.

This is reflected in a story in the *Taittirīya Brāhmaṇa* (3.11.8). Prajapati, desiring offspring, practised asceticism, and emitted gold. He threw the gold into the sacrificial fire three times, but each time it did not please the fire. So he threw the gold:

> into himself, into his heart, into the omnipresent fire. That pleased it. Therefore gold is the smallest of (all) valued objects; (and) being of service, it is the dearest (of all valued objects), for it is born of the heart.

This *identifies interiorisation of the sacrificial fire with the (interiorised) power of gold as money*. It is the monetary power of gold that both *interiorises* it and makes it the *dearest* and the *smallest* valued object ('smallest' because of the high value of a small amount). Moreover, this internal fire is (in contrast to the sacrificial fire), like money '*omnipresent*'. Prajapati then keeps the *dakṣiṇā*, consisting of gold, for himself, because he finds nobody to give it to, and thereby increases his own ability: this, too, embodies the self-directed power of money. I will return to this passage in 9§C.

Prajapati is sacrificer and sacrifice, as well as being himself everything (5§C, 6§A). The interiorisation of sacrifice is the interiorisation of the whole world. This is promoted by three factors: firstly, the traditional power of the sacrificer to obtain 'worlds' (lokas: 6§B); secondly the new, interiorised *universal* power of money; thirdly the identification of the sacrificer with his gifts and with the sacrifice.[134] The cosmic reach of the traditional sacrificer with his gifts is monetised and interiorised.

These developments in the Vedic sacrifice are not reproduced in Greek sacrifice, in which the only wealth involved, the sacrificed animals, were not sent to heaven but consumed in a communal meal that contrasts with the individualism of the Vedic sacrifice. Greek animal sacrifice, lacking the transference of individual wealth characteristic of the Vedic sacrifice, was not transformed by monetisation. Nevertheless, the Greek sacrifice could be economically significant, and its egalitarian distribution of spits meat to each individual contributed to the *genesis* of coined money (5§E).

[134] 5§D n.3; 8§A n. 12.

5§E Individualisation in India and Greece

The experience of the individual subjected to the cosmic rite of passage to the afterlife and back (Vedic sacrifice, Greek mystic initiation) was in some respects similar in the two cultures. In both he is imagined as sacrificial victim, but is replaced by an animal.[135] In India he might be subjected to the preliminary *dīkṣā*, in which he is transformed into an embryo;[136] and this passive isolation contrasts with the divine power with which he emerges from the *dīkṣā* as sacrificer.[137] As a preliminary to the most famous of mystic initiations, at Eleusis:

> every initiand was required to sacrifice a 'mystic piglet' 'on his own behalf'. Individual offerings were commonplace in Greek religion, but at collective rituals one animal or group of animals was commonly brought 'on behalf of' all; the individualism of the *Mysteries* stands out by contrast, and reflects their character as a preparation for another individual experience, death.[138]

But what happens next at Eleusis has no counterpart in (what we know of) India: in the mystic rehearsal of death the individual passes from anxious individual isolation to joyful incorporation into a group (14§A).

In India the individualism of the sacrificer is marked by economic transactions. The large number and high value of the oblations and *dakṣiṇās* gave the sacrifice considerable economic significance, both for the individual[139] and for society as a whole.[140] The most frequently mentioned *dakṣiṇās* are 'gold, the cow, clothing, the horse'.[141] The *dakṣiṇā* became the model for payment in general, rather as the word for sacrificer (*yajāmana*) gave rise to the general word for employer (*yajman*),[142] and sacrificial exchange might be envisaged as legitimating commercial exchange.[143]

The various interpretations of the *dakṣiṇā* all aim, according to Malamoud, to show that by paying the *dakṣiṇā* the sacrificer

> assures his autonomy in relation to the officiants; he marks the salutary distance without which he will lose himself, by a kind of absorption, in the being on whom he so closely depends.[144]

135 For Greece, see Seaford (1994) 282–4, for India 5§B.
136 AB 1.3; Lévi (1898) 103–5; Heesterman (1993) 160–1.
137 Lévi (1898) 106; Biardeau and Malamoud (1976) 194.
138 Parker (2005) 342–3.
139 Heesterman (1993) 39: 'On the pragmatic level sacrifice means the redistribution of the material goods that one needs to maintain life. Life, property, and honor imperceptibly shade off into each other so as to form the inextricable cluster that constitutes the person.'
140 Thapar (1984) 32, 63–7, 92–3.
141 Biardeau and Malamoud (1976) 175.
142 Biardeau and Malamoud (1976) 183, 197.
143 Malamoud (1998) 49–50.
144 Malamoud (1998) 43 (cf. 45).

Such individual autonomy is precisely what distinguishes commercial exchange from the personal relationship established by gift-exchange. It is taken by Anspach (1998) to derive from a dynamic internal to the sacrifice: by paying the *dakṣiṇā* to the officiant the sacrificer not only ensures that the benefit of the sacrifice comes to himself but also, by ending his relation with the officiant, that the pollution of the sacrificial killing does not pass from the officiant to himself. Similarly, Heesterman maintains that, in the pre-classical sacrifice, when the *dakṣiṇās* were distributed the officiant took over the burden of death pollution from the sacrificer (5§B).

Anspach sees in this internal dynamic of the sacrifice the origin of the individual autonomy of monetised exchange.[145] Any truth in this excessive claim would obtain only for India. Moreover, if Vedic sacrifice gave rise to monetised exchange, then we cannot explain what caused this to happen when it did, any more than we can explain the developments described by Heesterman by the internal dynamic of the sacrifice. Credit must go to Anspach for his (unusual) connection of sacrifice to monetised exchange. But he has it the wrong way around. Monetised exchange arises outside the Vedic sacrifice (2§E), and influences it in the way that I have begun to explain.

On the other hand the individualism of the Vedic sacrifice, which goes far beyond the moment of payment selected by Anspach, does not arise *merely* from the influence of commercial exchange. Rather, pre-existing sacrificial individualism made it receptive to (and was intensified by) the individualising influence of commercial exchange. To understand the roots of this sacrificial individualism, and its difference from Greek individualism, we need to step back for a moment to obtain a broad perspective on the basic differences between the two cultures.

Egyptian geography – a long fertile strip bounded by desert – enabled and required the theocratic political unity capable of organising the production and distribution of the vast wealth arising from the annual inundation of the Nile. In theocratic Mesopotamia a similar point applies to the Tigris and Euphrates, but the fertile area was larger and less desert-bound than in Egypt, and accordingly political unification of the whole area occurred much later. After the clearing of the forests of northern India the fertile area – within the confines of mountains and sea – is much larger than in Egypt and Mesopotamia: moreover, the mountains to the south are permeable, and (as in Greece) agriculture depends to a large extent on rain.

145 Anspach (1998) 70–1.

Accordingly political unification of the fertile area occurred much later again, after our period. In our period northern India, like Greece, contained a number of growing cities that could interact relatively easily over a large area (in Greece especially by sea, in India by rivers and plain) and were free to engage in internal and external commerce unhampered by centralising theocracy. That is one factor facilitating, in northern India and in Greece alike, the spread of monetisation – and of a single culture (Brahminical, Hellenic) – across state boundaries.

On the other hand, there are significant geographical differences between the two areas. Greece is well provided with small plains bounded by mountains or by the sea (or by both, e.g. Attica), promoting the development of numerous small but relatively cohesive and stable states. By contrast, the vast Indian plains provided relatively few natural barriers to protect small states, while also being too large to control easily from a single centre.[146] Moreover, during and after the clearance of jungle, the land's fertility attracted arrivals from elsewhere, resulting in the coexistence and layering of a number of ethnic identities that – given the extensiveness of the fertile area – could not be politically united by theocracy (as occurred more easily in the much narrower territories of Egypt and Mesopotamia). Instead, the result was a plurality of populous states with permeable borders, unstable and transcended by various groupings (castes, subcastes, clans, tribes, etc.) that were internally more united by occupation,[147] by ritual practice or by the reality or idea of kinship than by loyalty to territory or state. Political units (mainly kingdoms) came and went within an extensive and (eventually) relatively stable Brahminical culture. Stable ritual power was separate from unstable state power. Brahmins and Kshatriyas formed distinct groups operating a durable joint rule (synarchy).[148]

Crucial to the interaction of the two groups was the sacrificial rite of passage, in which the Brahmins exchanged their expertise for goods, protection and status. In the small Greek polis the cosmic rite of passage (mystic initiation) and animal sacrifice could both be expressions of political community. The Vedic sacrifice, by contrast, was a pivot between the two distinct groups of the synarchy. Whereas in the Greek cosmic rite of passage and sacrifice the individual might be integrated into the group, in the Indian cosmic rite of passage (the sacrifice) there was for the

146 Even jungle might impede centralisation rather than incursion.

147 Caste specialisation (like money) limits the scope of the ancient principle of reciprocity

148 Beautifully expressed at BU 1.4.11. See e.g. Dumont (1980) 71–2, 288–9. I return to the issue of caste in 7§A and 10§D.

individual (characteristically a Kshatriya) no such integration with the officiants as Brahmins. In the sacrifice it was as controller of property, and therefore increasingly – with the development of individual property – as *individual* that the Kshatriya was of interest to the Brahmins. The Brahminical interest was not so much in constituting the Kshatriyas as a group[149] as in promoting the power and eternal well-being of individual Kshatriyas in return for goods and protected status. And so the ideal sacrificer is an autocrat. Even the Brahminical royal consecration was remarkably individualist (5§A), and – conversely – any individual performing the *sarvamedha* (all-sacrifice) was said thereby to 'encompass all beings, pre-eminence, kingship and lordship' (SB 13.7.1.1). Brahminical order, neglecting the state and transcending its borders, regulates the relationship of the powerful individual to the universe.

This broad historical development, in particular the development of individual property and autocracy[150] – and not, as Heesterman proposes, the (unexplained) need to exclude conflict from the sacrifice (5§C) – is the fundamental development behind the pronounced and enduring individualism of the Vedic sacrifice.

In Greece, by contrast, monarchy had in the intellectually advanced cities of our period been largely replaced by a self-governing community, the polis. An individual could sacrifice alone, or as the leader of a sacrificing group. But the Greek sacrifice and mystery-cult were – quite unlike Vedic sacrifice – very often communal in their function and enactment. In its communal distribution of meat (5§A), the Greek sacrifice had no less political and economic importance than the Vedic sacrifice, albeit of a quite different kind. In Homer a communal sacrifice is performed by the military leader Agamemnon.[151] Subsequently sacrifices were funded and organised by and for the polis, on a scale that made them economically significant;[152] and they might serve to affirm, maintain and display the social solidarity essential for the development and survival of the polis, with the result that the polis may be called a sacrificial community.[153] Public inscriptions recorded money allocated by the polis for the purchase of animals for sacrifice, and the dependence of sacrifice (and therefore of the gods) on money even became a joke of comedy (in Aristophanes' *Wealth*). However, whereas in the Vedic sacrifice much wealth might be transferred to the priests or be imagined to be transferred to the gods, in the Greek

[149] The Kshatriyas may have had their own (unrecorded) rituals for that purpose.
[150] On the development of monarchy, see Thapar (1984).
[151] *Iliad* 4.202; cf. e.g. *Odyssey* 3.447–52. [152] Rosivach (1994). [153] Seaford (2004) 41, 49.

sacrifice the gods received no more than the smoke and the priests no more than a portion (sometimes a special portion) of the meat distributed among the group. There is in Vedic sacrifice a cosmic cycle of economic exchange (5§B), whereas in Greece (the smoke and fragrance arising from) animal sacrifices are merely imagined to elicit favour from their divine recipients.

Moreover, the communal distribution of equal portions of sacrificial meat on standardised iron spits was a crucial factor in the emergence in the Greek polis of coinage. What is crucial here is the *combination* of communally sanctioned distribution with individual possession. The word 'obol' (a coin) referred originally to a spit, and 'drachma' to a 'handful' of six spits. Spits were, like precious metal, dedicated to the gods in temples. And so coinage – individually owned communal value – derives, in part, from the element of the Greek sacrifice that is missing from the Vedic sacrifice, the culmination in a communal meal.[154] Did Vedic sacrifice nevertheless facilitate the genesis of Indian money by providing socially sanctioned symbols or units of value (standardised gifts or offerings)? 'Everywhere', notes Graeber, 'money seems to have emerged from the thing most appropriate for giving to the gods'.[155] Perhaps this also happened in India, but there is no evidence for it.

154 Described in detail in Seaford (2004). 155 Graeber (2011) 59.

CHAPTER 6

Inner Self and Universe

6§A From Diversity to Wholeness

In India monism (at least the monism that we know of) is from its beginning closely associated with sacrifice. The only instance of present monism in the *Rigveda* is in 10.90 (from its latest layer), in which what is equated with the universe is man (*puruṣa*) as sacrificial victim, cosmogonically dismembered to form parts of the universe. The combination of fundamental new features in this hymn (4§E) embody a metaphysical transformation.

The metaphysical transformation had further to go. Sacrifice ceased to be merely or mainly an offering designed to obtain from the gods their presence and benefits (as generally in the *Rigveda*), but became also a *rite of passage* for the individual sacrificer, who in the *Brahmanas* aims to become one with the cosmos. Cosmogony is on the whole imagined no longer in terms of conflict between cosmic powers, as between Indra and Vrtra in the main body of the *Rigveda*,[1] but in terms determined, in part at least, by the formation of the individual self. A similar transition occurs, we shall soon see, from the cosmogonic conflict between Zeus and the Titans in Hesiod to the Orphic cosmogony of Zeus absorbing and emitting all things.

In RV 10.90 *puruṣa* was equated with the universe and sacrificed, but was not also the *sacrificer*. Subsequently all three identities are combined. The sacrificer achieves self-integration into the universe by also being – like *puruṣa* becoming the universe in RV 10.90 – the sacrificial *victim*. And so the perfect form of sacrifice would be suicide.[2] Instead, the human

[1] On this conflict as cosmogony, see e.g. Brown (1965). In SB it is mentioned in minor roles (4.3.3.5; 5.2.3.8; 5.3.5.27).

[2] As noted by Lévi (1898) 132–3; Keith (1925) 459: Tull (1989) 54–5, 72–3. On the *puruṣamedha* ('sacrifice of man' – whether real or merely symbolic) see Tull (1989) 55, 143 n.62.

sacrificer was associated or identified with an animal victim,[3] and with the sacrificed Prajapati[4] – thereby becoming everything.[5]

Prajapati, creator of all things, is identified with universe, year, self, sacrifice, sacrificial victim and sacrificer. And (like *puruṣa* of RV 10.90) he *disintegrates*. In illustrating this I will focus on the central part of the *Śatapatha Brāhmaṇa*, which is devoted to the Agnicayana, the building of the fire-altar. We start with the making of a person (by compressing seven persons into one), Prajapati, who is identified with the fire-altar to be built, and generates cosmic elements, gods, mortals, everything that exists. He then 'fell apart' (*vyasraṃsata*)[6] and his prana (vital air, breath) left him. But he was then (in contrast to *puruṣa* of RV 10.90) *restored* (6.1.2.12–13). This mythical sequence, which seems to be a relatively late addition to the various existing accounts of the Agnicayana ritual,[7] is frequently repeated in the following books.[8] Next we learn that (6.1.2.17):

> it was those five bodily parts (*tanvo*) of Prajapati that fell apart (*vyas-raṃsanta*), hair, skin, flesh, bone and marrow – they are these five layers (of the fire-altar); and when he [the sacrificer] builds up the five layers, thereby he builds him up by those bodily parts.

The fragmentation of Prajapati here is bodily;[9] and the building of the layers of the fire-altar restores the fragmented Prajapati: this, too, is a motif that will be frequently repeated.[10]

[3] See E.g. Tull (1989) 46, 74–6; Smith (1989) 172–80.

[4] SB 6.1.2.16; 6.2.1.23; 6.2.2.9; 7.1.1.37; 7.4.1.15; 8.3.4.11; JB 1.41. See e.g. Eggeling (1882–1900) Part 4, xv: 'Prajapati, who here takes the place of the *Puruṣa*, the world-man . . . is offered up anew in every sacrifice; and inasmuch as the very dismemberment of the Lord of Creatures [Prajapati], which took place at that archetypal sacrifice, was in itself the creation of the universe, so every sacrifice is also a repetition of that first creative act. Thus the periodical sacrifice is nothing else than a microcosmic representation of the ever-proceeding destruction and renewal of all cosmic life and matter. The theologians of the *Brahmanas* go, however, an important step further by identifying the performer, or patron, of the sacrifice – the Sacrificer – with Prajapati.'

[5] SB 12.3.4.11; 13.3.1.1; 13.6.1.1; 13.7.1.1; TB 1.4.9.5; Tull (1989) 40 'the sacrificer – like Prajapati, who is the cosmos – realizes his identity with the cosmos'.

[6] Eggeling (1882–1900) comments 'literally, he fell asunder, or to pieces, became disjointed. Hence, when the gods "restored" Prajapati . . . the verb used is *saṃskṛ*, "put together"': Eggeling (1882–1900) on SB 6.1.2.12; Smith (1989) 65.

[7] Proferes (2007) 120. The Agnicayana was itself seemingly a relatively late addition to the early Vedic corpus: Tull (1989) 79; Eggeling (1882–1890) Part 3, xxvi-xxvii.

[8] E.g. 6.1.2.21; 7.4.1.15–17; 7.5.1.16–20; 7.5.1.24; 8.2.1.11–14; 8.2.2.6; 8.3.3.9–10; 8.4.1.6–8; 9.4.2.16.

[9] So also e.g. 8.7.3.1; 8.7.4.19–21; 10.1.2.3–5.

[10] E.g. 6.1.2.29; 7.1.2.9; 7.4.2.3–4; 8.1.1.3; 8.2.1.11–14; 8.2.2.6; 8.3.3.9–10; 8.4.1.6–8; 9.4.1.3; 10.1.1.1–3; 10.4.1.1–2. The restoration may be achieved by other forms of ritual (6.2.2.7; 6.2.2.12; 7.1.2.9–11; 9.4.2.16) or simply by the gods (6.2.2.7; 7.4.1.15–17; 7.5.1.24).

The motif has multiple levels of significance. The fragmented Prajapati is the year,[11] so that the building up of the five layers of the fire-altar is the building up of Prajapati 'with the seasons'; he is the wind, and his five bodily parts the five regions, so that he is built up 'with the regions' (6.1.2.18–19). Building the fire-altar is creative of *cosmos* and of socio-political order.[12] The bricks are identified with the *creatures* that emerge from Prajapati.[13] His disintegration means that 'there was then no firm foundation whatever here' (7.1.2.1). The altar also embodies the immortal inner *self*:

> By assuming that form [of the altar], the pranas (vital airs) became Prajapati;[14] by assuming that form, Prajapati created the gods; by assuming that form, the gods became immortal and what thereby the pranas and Prajapati and the gods became, that indeed he (the Sacrificer) thereby becomes (6.1.2.36).

In laying down the bricks the sacrificer – on the model of Prajapati – establishes his inner self,[15] and makes himself immortal.[16] Laying down the bricks even *unites the subject*:

> Separately he lays down (these ten bricks): what separate desires there are in the breath (prana), those he thereby lays into it. Only once he settles them: he thereby makes this breath one; but were he to settle them each separately, he assuredly would cut the breath asunder (8.1.1.6).

What is said of breath is then said of eye (8.1.2.3), ear (8.1.2.6) and speech (8.1.2.9). The variously placed groups of bricks are holders of the breath, eye, mind, ear and speech (and of various forms of air) (8.1.3.6). The fire-altar is subsequently identified with the mind *(manas)*.[17]

Prajapati sacrifices five creatures, including *puruṣa* (man),[18] separating the heads from the trunks, and then in building up the layers of the altar reunites the heads with the trunks (6.2.1.5–11). Building up the altar follows – and in a sense reverses – the sacrifice:[19] 'one must make the

[11] 10.1.1.2 adds that the joints of the disjointed Prajapati are days and nights.

[12] E.g. 7.1.2.5–8; 8.2.1.1; 8.7.2.1–3; 8.7.4.12–21; 9.4.3.3; 10.1.2.1–2.

[13] 8.2.2.6; cf. 6.1.2.12; 7.1.2.1; 8.1.1.3.

[14] Altar identified with Prajapati: e.g. 7.4.1.1; 7.4.2.3–4.

[15] E.g. 7.2.1.5–6; 7.4.1.15; 8.3.4.11; 8.6.1.1; 8.7.4.16, 19; 10.1.4.1–2; 10.1.4.8–9; 10.4.1.1–2; 10.4.2.29.

[16] 10.1.3.5–7; 10.1.4.1–2; 10.1.4.8–9.

[17] 10.1.2.3, adding that 'as to why the Fire-altar is built first, it is because the mind is prior to the breathings'.

[18] Cf. SB 1.2.3.6; 11.7.1.3.

[19] 'In re-enacting the cosmic man's primordial activity through the construction of the fire-altar, the human sacrificer may be said to approach the ritual in a state of fragmentation – that is, already at what in the creation myth is the second stage of Prajapati's career – and only through completing the altar does he attain a state of wholeness. In the performance of the Agnicayana, these ideas are partly

bricks [for the altar] only after performing an animal sacrifice' (6.2.1.10). Prajapati is also a sacrificial *victim*.[20] The departure and restoration of the pranas, which is inflicted on sacrificial victims,[21] also sometimes happens to Prajapati when he disintegrates and is restored.[22]

According to Proferes:

> A recurring theme within the development of Vedic tradition is that of dispersion and integration. This theme was developed on many levels, and provided a root metaphor ... It could be applied with equal vigor to the economic, social, political and cosmological spheres, and it could be the common principle by which one sphere could be understood in terms of the other.[23]

We have seen that the disintegration and reunification of Prajapati – identified with sacrificer, sacrificial victim and brick fire-altar – expresses the creation or unification of body, subject, universe and society, as well as achieving his immortalisation.[24] A similar configuration attaches to the god Dionysos.

The Greek ritual that assures a passage through death into a happy hereafter is mystic initiation, from which – it has been persuasively argued[25] – there derives the myth of the sacrificial dismemberment and reconstitution of Dionysos embodied in animal sacrifice. The mystic initiate may have imagined his experience in terms of this dismemberment and reconstitution.[26] Similarly, the sacrificial dismemberment and reconstitution of Pentheus in Euripides' *Bacchae* forms one of a whole series of experiences that derive from mystic initiation.[27] The mystic initiand, like the Vedic sacrificer, would experience the dismemberment and reconstitution *mentally* only (i.e. as interiorised[28]), and there are indeed indications[29]

expressed through the peculiar sequence of the ceremony, which places the animal sacrifice (which is a beheading) before the actual construction of the altar': Tull (1989) 98.

20 SB 11.1.8.2–4; PB 7.2.1. 21 7.5.2.8. 22 6.2.2.7; 6.2.2.12; 7.2.1.6; 7.4.2.13; 7.5.1.24.

23 Proferes (2007) 75.

24 Gonda (1975) 389. Cosmos, body and subject are brought together by Tull (1989) 101: 'Prajapati presents the paradigm for man's original state of wholeness. Here, wholeness is defined through a correlation to the existence of the cosmos; that is, the unique events of the cosmogony define an original state of existence wherein man and cosmos are equated on both the planes of "outer" (the physical body, the spheres of the cosmos) and "inner" (the mind and senses, the animate constituents of the cosmos) existence.'

25 West (1983) 140–75. 26 Seaford (1998) 142, 146 n.89. 27 Seaford (1996).

28 5§D; 11§A; e.g. Tull (1989) 46–7.

29 The association of mental and physical fragmentation is implicit at E. *Bacchae* 968–9 (of Pentheus as infant: Seaford [1998] 135), and Pl. *Laws* 672b: 'Dionysos was torn apart (διεφορήθη) by Hera' evokes his bodily dismemberment (especially as Hera prompted the Titans to dismember him), but refers to his *mental* fragmentation, resulting in his creating βακχεῖαι etc. (cf. Plut. *Moralia* 389a); Seaford (2004) 309.

that in Dionysiac initiation the idea of physical fragmentation inspired or expressed a terrifying experience of *mental* fragmentation that was – in the mystic transition from anxious ignorance to knowledge and belonging – replaced by a joyful sense of internal unity. This mystic idea has left its mark on Parmenides (11§D), and (without the bodily fragmentation) on Plato (11§E), and on Neoplatonism, in which there is explicit mention of the dismemberment of Dionysos as expressing the fragmentation of the inner self (resulting from its fall into the world of the senses), and of his reconstitution as expressing its subsequent self-gathering back into unity.[30] (I have elsewhere discussed this theme in its relation to the Lacanian psychology of bodily fragmentation.)[31]

As for the *cosmic* dimension, Dionysos is transformed 'into winds and water, earth and stars, and into the generation of plants and animals', which is said to refer riddlingly to dismemberment, destructions and returns to life.[32] The initiated *group* might have cosmic reach (notably as a chorus of stars).[33] And the *individual* initiand was imagined, like the Indian sacrificer, to go on a journey through the cosmos and back.[34]

And so in the Greek myth-ritual complex, as in the Indian, there are the three levels of body, mind and cosmos: the *bodily* fragmentation and reconstitution of the god are interiorised as a *mental* event and projected as the creation of *cosmic* elements and of creatures. That leaves the socio-political aspect, to which we will come in due course.

In being transformed from one into many, Prajapati disintegrates, like Dionysos. Another form of this transformation is his emission of many things from within himself. For instance:

> This Prajapati, the year, has created all existing things, both what breathes and the breathless, both gods and men. Having created all existing things, he felt like one emptied out, and was afraid of death. He bethought himself, 'How can I get these beings back into my atman (self, body)? How can I put them back into my atman? How can I be again the atman of all these beings?'.[35]

In this second form of his transformation from one to many, described as being 'emptied out', Prajapati resembles not the mystic Dionysos but the

[30] Olympiodorus *In Phaedonem* p. 111, 4–19 Norvin; further refs. and discussion in Seaford (1998) 142. See further 11§E below.
[31] Seaford (1998). [32] Plut. *Moralia* 389a. [33] Seaford (2013) 266–9.
[34] The evidence starts in the fifth century BCE: Seaford (1986). Much later Apuleius includes as part of his mystic initiation (*Metamorphoses* 11.23): 'having been carried through all the elements I returned'.
[35] 10.4.2.2–3; cf. e.g. SB 1.5.3.2 (Gods and Asuras emerge from Prajapati); 9.4.1.2 (beings come from the dismembered Prajapati).

mystic Zeus. In Orphic cosmogony Dionysos' dismemberment and restoration to life is preceded by his father Zeus – on becoming ruler of the world – swallowing all things, and then emitting them in due order.[36]

For both Prajapati and Zeus the polarity between the unity and the diversity of self and of universe is reduced to the capacity of the body to absorb and emit. In both cases what is absorbed is in some versions all things and in others (all) living beings. And in both cases the end result may be described as a compromise between unity and diversity. Before swallowing all things Zeus wonders 'How will all things be one for me and each thing separate?' Prajapati, after feeling emptied out, wonders how he 'can be again the atman of all these beings?', and in another version says to the creatures whom he has emitted 'Return to me, and I will devour you in such a way that, although devoured, you will multiply' (PB 21.2.1).

Whereas Zeus achieves unity-in-diversity by the (ordered) emission of what he had absorbed, Prajapati will it seems achieve it by reabsorbing what has been emitted. This represents the Indian (not Greek) tendency to identify self with universe. However, the difference is eclipsed by a similarity in the *use* made of the myths to affirm the unity of the self, i.e. in the rite of passage.

First, we note the role of ritual in affirming the unity-in-diversity of Prajapati. After he tells the creatures to return (in the passage just quoted), it is by means of ritual chants that they are consumed and caused to multiply.[37] After asking how he can 'be again the atman of all these beings?', he does not in fact reabsorb them but rather constructs for himself an atman by means of the equipment (notably altar-bricks) and utterances of ritual, in which he is imitated by the sacrificer who 'being about to build an altar, undergoes the initiation-rite' (10.4.2.29). In general, we have seen that it is by the building of the altar that the fragmented Prajapati is reconstituted. There is also an economic dimension. In accordance with the identification of the individual (including Prajapati) with his property,[38] we also find the 'emptying out' of the sacrificer's wealth and its replenishment compared to the emptying out and replenishment of his prototype Prajapati.[39]

Prajapati's emission of all things is creation but not cosmogony:[40] there is after the emission still ritual work to do to create ordered unity-in-diversity in the universe as well as in the individual (Prajapati and

[36] West (1983) 72–5; Seaford (2004) 223; frr. 137, 241, 243 Bernabé (= frr. 165, 167–8 Kern; cf. 21a).

[37] The passage is cited by Smith (1989: 64), who also cites PB 17.10.2, in which with ritual the emitted creatures turn towards and encircle Prajapati.

[38] 2§E, 5§B. [39] SB 4.5.8.6–9; 12.8.2.1–2. [40] Smith (1989) 60–2.

sacrificer-initiate), whereas Zeus' ordered emission of all things is a cosmogonic act, performed by a monarch. However, the unity-in-diversity achieved by Zeus' absorption and controlled emission of all things is subsequently achieved for the human inner self – here, too, through the rite of passage. How so?

From an Orphic cosmogonic poem (dated by West to a generation either side of 500 BCE),[41] of which several fragments are quoted in the Derveni papyrus (of the second half of the fourth century BCE), one fragment (in column xvi) quotes the following verses:

> upon him (Zeus) all the immortals grew, blessed gods and goddesses and rivers and lovely springs and everything else that had then been born; and he himself became the sole one.[42]

All living beings growing upon Zeus is a variant of our Orphic myth of Zeus consuming everything. The verses are quoted in order to be explained as having a deeper, allegorical meaning understood only by mystic initiates.[43] The explanation is as follows:

> And as for the phrase 'and he himself became the sole one', by saying this he makes clear that mind (*nous*) being alone is always worth everything (πάντων ἄξιον), just as if the other things were nothing. For it is not [possible] for the present existing things (ἐόντα) to exist [because of] them (sc. the existing ones) without mind. [Also in the verse] after this [he said that mind] is worth everything: '[And now he is] king of all [and will be] afterwards.' [It is clear that] 'mind' and ['king of all' are the] same thing.

Here the cosmic and political content of the Orphic cosmogony (the absorption of everything into the cosmic monarch) is – from the perspective of the mystic initiation – reinterpreted as meaning that mind is alone and always worth everything. I suggest that inner unity-in-diversity – modelled on the reconstitution of cosmic deity (Dionysos) or his absorption of diversity (Zeus) or on building the altar (Prajapati) – is achieved for humans through the cosmic rite of passage (sacrifice, mystic initiation).[44] I will provide further evidence for this suggestion in 11§E.

[41] West (1983) 108–10.

[42] Derveni Papyrus column xvi. I reproduce (here and below) the translation of Kouremenos et al. (2006), based on their edition of the fragmentary Greek.

[43] See e.g. several of the papers in Papadopoulou and Muellner (2014).

[44] In addition to this remarkable and unusual affinity to the SB and early *Upanishads*, the Derveni papyrus is unique among texts of the classical period (a) as a lengthy text put into a tomb, i.e. as of use to the dead, and (b) in the extent of its resemblance to the *Brahmanas* – in identifying deities with other things (Eumenides with souls [col.vi], the phallus with the sun [col.xvi], Zeus with mind [col.xvi], etc.), using (often false) etymologies as explanations, and explaining the particularities of

Finally we come, as promised, to the socio-political aspect. We noted that in the *Śatapatha Brāhmaṇa* the ritual creates socio-political as well as cosmic order. It seems that in our period monarchy grows in importance, but the Brahmins have no interest in imagining a universal divine monarch (like the later *cakravartin*), superior to their own control of ritual, by which they frequently confirm the order of the *castes*.[45] By giving the king a sword that is the (once cosmogonic) thunderbolt of Indra, the Brahmin makes the king stronger than his enemies but weaker than the Brahmin (SB 5.4.4.15). Even in the royal consecration (the *rajasūya*) there is more concern with the king as individual sacrificer than as ruler of the state (5§A). Although Prajapati is a powerful person (he devours others, and those whom he emits resist his 'superiority'),[46] he is not a monarch but the individual sacrificer.

By contrast Zeus absorbs all things after succeeding to the cosmic kingship. The Greek monarchical cosmogony derived in part from the cosmogony recited in the Baylonian new year ceremony.[47] From its role in the ritual of a highly centralised monarchy, it migrated and was transformed into a Greek cosmogony that survived without the support of ritual or of centralised monarchy, but also without the possibility of marginalisation by a priestly caste. It was reunited with ritual, of a different kind: in the mystic initiation indicated in the Derveni papyrus it functions as mythical allegory for the unifying power of the inner self. This unity is imagined as the universal *value* of the mind, as alone and 'always worth everything'. The unifying universality of money is interiorised, here (unusually) *together with* the interiorisation of autocracy (Zeus). Both forms of social power – autocracy and money – are in both cultures interiorised, with the former dominant in India (Chapter 7), the latter in Greece (Chapter 13).

The *nous* (mind) of the Derveni papyrus is solitary and always worth everything, but the other things are not exactly nothing; rather it is '*as if* (my emphasis) the other things were nothing' – an expression of the puzzling power of money to embody the value of everything else. The solitariness of Prajapati is sometimes stressed,[48] and the emptying out and replenishment of Prajapati and of sacrificer are – we have seen – sometimes imagined in terms of property. But the Derveni *nous* – in contrast to Zeus,

ritual as corresponding to an external reality (col.vi: 'they sacrifice innumerable, many-knobbed cakes, because the souls, too, are innumerable').

45 SB 1.1.4.12; 1.3.4.15; 2.1.3.5; 2.4.3.7; 3.1.1.9–10; 5.4.1.3–5; 5.4.2.7; 6.1.2.25; 6.4.4.12–13; 8.7.2.1–3; 9.4.1.3–5; 12.7.3.15; 13.1.5.2–5; cf. e.g. AB 8.24–5; PB 6.1.6–11.

46 PB 6.3.9; 16.4.1–3; 17.10.2; etc.: Smith (1989) 60.

47 Seaford (2004) 221 has references to earlier scholarship.

48 E.g. SB 6.1.3.1

Prajapati and the atman – neither exactly contains nor is exactly identical with all things.

6§B Loka and *Sarva*

Further understanding of why and how sacrifice produces monism is provided by attention to what sacrifice (or *knowledge* of sacrifice) *obtains*, and in particular to the complex term loka.

Loka in the Veda has been studied in great depth by Gonda.[49] The basic meaning of its Indo-European root *louko-* seems to have been a clearing in a wood.[50] Of its thirty-eight occurrences (including compounds) in the *Rigveda* twenty-seven refer to 'room', 'space' or 'place' (generally associated with freedom, safety and comfort) on this earth, often given by the gods. We should imagine the contested open spaces (surrounded by forests or mountains) in which the semi-nomadic people of the *Rigveda*, in the warlike conditions described in 3§A, found the longed-for stability to live freely with their cattle and crops. This territorial aspect of loka reappears much later in a simile: 'As here in this world the possession of a territory won by action comes to an end, so in the hereafter a world (loka)[51] won by merit (*puṇya*) comes to an end' (CU 8.1.4). Lokas continue to be 'won', 'conquered' or 'obtained' long after they have ceased to be real places. For example, at BU 5.4.1 a man who knows brahman 'conquers these lokas'.

There are in the *Rigveda* eleven instances of loka *not* referring to anywhere on this earth. Of these eleven, the late tenth book contains eight.[52] And of these eight, six deserve attention as prefiguring the meaning of loka in later texts.

Of these six, one occurs in our *Puruṣa* hymn (10.90), the other five in rites of passage (funeral, wedding).[53] 10.90.14, uniquely in the *Rigveda*, describes the creation of the four parts of the universe from parts of the sacrificed *puruṣa*, and adds 'thus they arranged the lokas'. In funeral hymns the deceased is to go to the loka the forefathers have made for him (10.14.9) or to 'the loka of good (ritual) performers' (10.16.4), and the widow is told to rise from the corpse of her husband into the loka of the living (10.18.8). In a wedding hymn (10.85) a bride is to be placed along with her husband 'in the loka of the well-performed (sacrifice?)' (24), and at 20 – Doniger explains – 'the chariot that takes the bride to the house of the groom is here

[49] Gonda (1966): for much shorter accounts see Collins (1982) 45–9; Jurewicz (2016a) 373, 432–3.
[50] Gonda (1966) 7–8. [51] Room, space, place, and world.
[52] The other three are: 3.2.9; 3.37.11; 9.113.7. [53] The other two are 10.128.2 and 10.180.3.

assimilated to the world [loka] of immortality that Sūryā [daughter of the Sun] wins in the sky'.

These instances of the non-terrestrial loka in rites of passage, and in the sacrifice of the cosmic man, prefigure the later development of the non-terrestrial loka in the sacrificial (cosmic) rite of passage: the individual obtains through sacrifice or sacrificial knowledge a loka that is generally an imagined rather than a real space, or not even a space but a specific condition, a stable state of well-being or ideal plane of existence that retains its association with freedom and inviolability but is associated with power and with the gods.[54] Loka in such a context may occur in the singular or in the plural. It may be imagined as in this world, as nowhere in particular, as in the spatial beyond, or as in the hereafter – especially as 'celestial (*svarga*) loka'.

As a result of all this, loka is often translated 'world' – which may, however, be misleading: the self-sufficiency of the loka, even of the celestial loka, does not constitute monism. Nevertheless, a tendency towards monism – what may be called present personal reductionism (4§E) – is in this period manifest in numerous passages on the importance of obtaining or conquering a loka or lokas, mainly by means of sacrifice or knowledge of sacrifice.[55] The universe is composed of three lokas (of earth, intermediate space and sky), all of which can be obtained by sacrifice.[56] Prajapati unites many lokas into one, the 'celestial loka'.[57] According to Gonda, the lokas are 'indispensable factors in the process of integration' of oneself into the all.[58] The assimilation of sacrificed man (*puruṣa*), universe and lokas in RV 10.90 describes cosmogony, but is frequent in later texts to express the obtaining of loka (or lokas) by the individual, and his becoming the universe, through the sacrificial rite of passage.

The later sacrifice contrasts with the *Rigveda* not only as a rite of passage but also in that the agent and beneficiary of it is generally an individual; in the *Rigveda* the agents and beneficiaries of sacrifice are referred to much more frequently in the plural than in the singular (although the poet may refer to himself or to a patron in the singular). Three hymns concern a dispute between an individual (Indra) and a group (the Maruts) over the

[54] Gonda (1966) 113: 'ritual techniques enable a sacrificer to become *saloka* – "of one loka with" a power, to gain access to lokas characterised by the "presence" of a particular divine power, to enter into communion with that power, and henceforth to be a "denizen of heaven"'.

[55] E.g. TB 1.4.9.5: the sacrificer is given a firm stand in the terrestrial and yonder lokas and the intermediate space, and 'he who thus knowing performs these rites becomes this all'; SB 2.3.2.3; 12.3.4.11; 13.6.1.3.

[56] SB 12.8.2.32; 13.6.1.3. [57] JB 3.341ff. [58] Gonda (1966) 57; cf. 36, 44, 50–1, 113, 134–5.

right to receive a sacrifice.[59] The late book 10 of the *Rigveda* contains individual rites of passage (funeral, wedding), but even in these we have seen that the cosmic loka obtained is on the whole not merely for an individual: 14.9 the loka the forefathers have made for him, 16.4 the loka of good (ritual) performers, 18.8 the loka of the living, 85.24 the loka of the well performed (sacrifice) for the couple. Even in book 10 the hereafter is more frequently imagined as somewhere in which the dead join a *group*, generally of forefathers,[60] than is the individualised hereafter (and universe) of those later texts – *Brahmanas* and early *Upanishads* – in which furthermore the loka has become more abstract or celestial than was the mainly terrestrial loka of the *Rigveda*.

The relationship between monism and the individual sacrificer can be further illuminated. The sacrificer obtains the terrestrial world, the air, the sky and the regions:

> and, indeed, as much as these lokas and the regions are, so much is all this whole (*sarva*); and the *puruṣamedha* (human sacrifice) is *sarva*: thus it is for the sake of his obtaining and securing this *sarva* (SB 13.6.1.3).

Moreover,

> he who performs (the *aśvamedha*, horse-sacrifice) makes Prajapati complete (*sarva*), and he himself becomes complete (*sarva*) (SB 13.3.1.1).[61]

So the sacrificer, Prajapati, and the universe are each *sarva* (whole, integral). The sacrifice makes Prajapati and the sacrificer whole, and this wholeness or completeness is expressed by the word (*sarva*) that also denotes the universe obtained by the sacrificer. Elsewhere in the *Śatapatha Brāhmaṇa* the sacrificer, Prajapati, and the universe are identified with each other. We may infer that just as Prajapati is a *personal* projection of the *sarva* state of the sacrificer, so 'this *sarva*' (whole, obtained by – or identified with – the sacrifice) is an *impersonal* projection of his *sarva* state. What is this state?

Gonda (1955) describes the development of the meaning of *sarva* from 'whole, complete, integral' (especially of the body) to 'all', especially as in

[59] RV 1.165, 169, 170, 171. Often they share: Jamison and Brereton (2014) 50.

[60] 10.14.7–8, 10 (forefathers); 10.15.12–14 (forefathers); 10.16.1–5 (forefathers); 10.17.3 (forefathers and gods), 4 ('pious'); 10.18.13 (forefathers); 10.135 (gods); 10.154 (forefathers); also e.g. 1.119.4 (forefathers); 9.113.10 (the dead). At 10.14.1 Yama, the god of death, gathers men together. See also AV 4.34.3 (gods); 18.2 (various groups, based on RV); 6.120 (relatives and friends).

[61] Cf. the *sarvamedha* (all-sacrifice) at 13.7.1.1 (quoted 8§B n.23).

'this all' (the universe).[62] When applied to the sacrificer, *sarva* means 'whole', in the way that early on it referred to the wholeness of the body. But it is not corporeal wholeness that the sacrificer obtains through sacrifice. We may infer that what *sarva* describes in the sacrificer is something like *mental* wholeness, (a new) unitary self-consciousness, best expressed by the word that had hitherto expressed the wholeness of the body – a natural extension that we encountered in 6§A.

This inference is confirmed by BU 1.4.9, in which a man by knowing brahman becomes *sarva*, and then asks:

> What did brahman know that enabled it to become *sarva*? In the beginning this world was only brahman, and it knew only itself (atman), thinking: 'I am brahman'. As a result, it became *sarva* ... This is true even now. If a man knows 'I am brahman', in this way, he becomes this whole world (*sarva*).

And again (2.5.10):

> this person ... in the space of the heart, he is just this self (atman), this existence which is not subject to death, he is brahman, he is *sarva*.

The state of being whole (*sarva*) and equivalent to the universe (*sarva*) is in the *Śatapatha Brāhmaṇa* obtained through sacrifice, but in the *Bṛhadāraṇyaka Upaniṣad* through mere knowledge. We will examine this transition from sacrifice to knowledge in more detail in the opening of the *Bṛhadāraṇyaka Upaniṣad* (6§C). What these passages of *Śatapatha Brāhmaṇa* and *Bṛhadāraṇyaka Upaniṣad* together show – for the purpose of our overall argument – is the connection between the advent (within and then beyond the sacrifice) of unitary individual self-consciousness and the advent of (mental) monism.

This new consciousness of oneself as a unitary entity may promote a sense of *universal* control. This resembles the reasoning of Parmenides.[63] The inner self, conscious of being able to think of whatever it chooses, seems to contain within itself *everything*, which – because it belongs to a unitary self – is itself both unitary and under (imaginative) control by the self. The inner self, once it seems to be a separate (unitary) entity, controls – or is identified with – a unitary universe, like Prajapati both creator and creation. The result is mental monism.

[62] Gonda (1955); see also Gonda (1982–3). [63] 11§D, 12§A, 14§A.

6§C Inner Self in *Bṛhadāraṇyaka Upaniṣad* 1.1–4

Despite some indications of the all-importance of knowledge, the *Brahmanas* describe a world in which power is exercised through attention to detail in the performance of sacrifice.

From this world the early *Upanishads* have moved away somewhat. There is still concern with sacrifice, but the power to obtain worlds is now achieved largely by *knowledge* – notably of the equivalence of atman with brahman.[64] The central, cosmic role of the individual self, inherited from sacrifice, remains. The individualism, monism and idea of repeated death[65] found in the late *Brahmanas* are in the *Upanishads* developed to a new plane beyond the performance of sacrifice. And the setting of the discourse is now generally secular.

This transition is illustrated by the opening of what may be the earliest *Upanishad*. The *Bṛhadāraṇyaka Upaniṣad*, which forms the final section of the *Śatapatha Brāhmaṇa*, begins (1.1) with a list of correspondences (repeated from SB 10.6.4.1) between the sacrificial horse (and the sacrificial cup) and parts of the universe.[66] The second section (1.2) is concerned with cosmogonical detail and the creation of atman within the context of the horse sacrifice.

A little later (3.1)[67] we are told that the offspring of Prajapati were the (younger) gods and (older) Asuras (3§B), who competed 'for these worlds'. Speech sang the High Chant for the gods during a sacrifice, thereby procuring for them 'whatever useful there is in speech', and keeping for itself 'whatever is pleasant in what it says'. The Asuras 'rushed at it and riddled it with evil', which is the disagreeable things a person says. And thus it was not only with speech but also with breath, sight, hearing and mind. Only when it is the turn of 'the breath-within-the-mouth' (*āsanya prāṇa*) to sing did the onslaught of the Asuras fail, and they were smashed to bits, with the result that the gods prospered while the Asuras were ruined.

This passage – even though it is not mentioned by Heesterman – embodies the transition he infers, in the sacrifice, from conflict between groups to the centrality of a single individual (5§B), who sings in the sacrifice. And when the individual (breath-within-the-mouth) triumphs, then – for it to become fully empowered as a sacrificial individual – several issues must be resolved.

64 For brahman, see 9§C, 8§A. 65 8§D, 9§C.
66 On the early relationship between sun, power and sacrificial horse, see Proferes (2007) 70–1.
67 Also at CU 1.2.1–9.

Firstly, 'the breath-within-the-mouth' is immortal and immortalising, carrying speech, breath, sight, hearing and mind, called 'deities', beyond the reach of death (1.3.9–16): this is power over *time*. Secondly, in this process speech becomes fire, breath becomes wind, etc. – the components of the individual inner self become components of the universe: this is power over *space*. Thirdly, the breath-within-the-mouth procures – by singing – food for itself (1.3.17), of which the 'other deities' want a share. It tells them to gather around it, and they do so: this is power over *others*. 'Therefore, whatever food one eats through it satisfies also these others' (1.3.18). The components of the inner self form a unity, which is satisfied by food eaten through the breath-within-the-mouth. The text continues:

> When someone comes to know this, his people will gather around him in the same way; he will become their patron, their chief, and their leader.

The internal relation of breath-within-the mouth to the other components of the inner self (gathering around) is the same as the external relation of the individual so constituted to other individuals. Sacrifice bestows on the individual immortality, unity as an individual, implied integration with the universe and power over other individuals.

There follows (1.3.19–27) the identification of the breath-within-the-mouth with the 'essence of the bodily parts', with Brhaspati (lord of speech), with Brahmanaspati (lord of brahman) and with the *Sāman* (a sung liturgical text), providing yet another kind of power, economic power:

> When someone knows the wealth of this *Sāman*, he comes to possess wealth . . . when someone knows the gold of this *Sāman*, he comes to possess gold (26–7).

Next we are told that, as the priest sings, the sacrificer should silently recite:

> From the unreal lead me to the real.
> From darkness lead me to light.
> From death lead me to immortality (1.3.28).

This is reminiscent of Greek mystic initiation, and reminds us that sacrifice was a rite of passage. The silence of the recital indicates interiorisation.[68]

These are the themes of *Bṛhadāraṇyaka Upaniṣad* 1.3. The individual has been constituted and empowered through sacrifice as well as by other actions. But then the extent of his empowerment, so far from making

[68] Silent ritual is associated with the mind at SB 1.4.4.5; cf. 12§D n.6.

him content, creates further needs, which cannot be resolved through sacrifice. These needs are resolved in 1.4, which begins as follows:

> In the beginning the world was just a single atman shaped like man. He looked around and saw nothing but himself. The first thing he said was 'Here I am!' and from that the name 'I' came into being. Therefore, even today when you call someone, he first says, 'It is I', and then states whatever other name he may have.

Here – in contrast to the singing breath-within-the-mouth – is a primaeval individual as mere individual, now unconnected with sacrifice, an atman, which means both body (1.4.1; 1.4.4) and inner self (1.4.8).[69] The first ever event is his establishment, through language, of the primacy of *self-reference* over the name (the latter is used by all, to distinguish a person from others). We are then told that:

> the first being receives a name, *puruṣa*, because ahead (*pūrva*) of all this he burnt up (*us*) all evils. When someone knows this, he burns up anyone who may try to get ahead of him.

Whereas the first ever event establishes the primacy of individualism in *language*, the second establishes intense individualism of *action*.

There then follow two negative consequences of being a solitary individual, fear and lack of pleasure. But both of these can be remedied in a way that preserves the aloneness of the individual. In the first case:

> That first being became afraid; therefore, one becomes afraid when one is alone. Then he thought to himself: 'of what should one be afraid, when there is no one but me?'[70] So his fear left him.

The fear we each have in feeling alone, separate from all others, is prefigured in the fearful solitariness of the primordial being. But he overcame his fear by realising his identity with all ('there is no-one but me'). The integration of the individual into the universe implied in 1.3 is here taken further in what may be called primordial personal monism.

Then:

> He found no pleasure at all; so one finds no pleasure when one is alone. He wanted to have a companion.

[69] For occurrences in the older *Upanishads* of *ātman* meaning 'body', see Cohen (2008) 40, who comments 'this usage eventually falls out of fashion, as the term *ātman* assumes a more spiritual significance'; also Cohen (2008) 134–5 on AU 1–3. The most dramatic rejection of the idea that the atman is the body is at CU 8.7–12.

[70] Already in BU 1.2.7 'death is unable to seize him because death becomes his very atman'.

And so he split his body into two, giving rise to husband and wife. From their copulation sprang human beings and all the animals. It then occurred to him 'I alone am the creation, for I created all this.'[71] Once again, he is identical with all.

There are other cultures in which the primaeval male and female are split or separated from each other. Eve is created from the body of Adam, and in Hesiod's *Theogony* the separation is of male heaven from female earth. What is distinctive about the *Bṛhadāraṇyaka Upaniṣad* cosmogony is its absolute individualism, aetiological of the individual focus on the self as identical with the world.

We then learn that each of the gods to whom people urge sacrifice 'is his own creation, for he himself is all these gods'. This primaeval individual as creator is then identified with brahman (or Brahma): his creation is brahman's (or Brahma's) 'super-creation', because, in another remarkable expression of the autonomous aloneness of the human individual:

> he created the gods, who are superior to him, and being a mortal himself, he created the immortals (1.4.6).

The identity of self with world implies the oneness of the world, which is now expressed by saying that the world was (and is now) 'without real distinctions', being 'distinguished simply in terms of name and form' (1.4.7). This allows a reformulation of the unity of the inner self (atman) that is closer and more explicit than the unity we saw in 1.3. Breathing, speaking, seeing, hearing and thinking are mere names:

> one should consider them as simply his atman, for in it all these become one. This same atman is the trail to this entire world (1.4.7).

We have now reached a conclusion: atman is a unity both internally and with the world. And a man should hold dear only his atman, for only the atman is imperishable (1.4.8).

However, 'the question is raised' (1.4.9) about brahman. How did it become the whole? We might answer this exotic question by saying that brahman is the name given to universal power.[72] But for the *Bṛhadāraṇyaka Upaniṣad* the answer is given by the fact that there is a way of becoming the whole: 'people think they will become whole by knowing brahman'. And so the question is 'what did brahman know that enabled it to become whole?', to which the answer is that:

[71] Cf. BU 4.4.13: 'He is the maker of everything.'

[72] Originally of ritual: 9§C.

> in the beginning this world was only brahman, and it knew only itself (atman), thinking: 'I am brahman.' As a result, it became the whole (*sarva*) (1.4.10).

Hence whoever knows that he is brahman becomes the whole. The aetiological event that consists of the world thinking 'I am brahman' (and so becoming the whole) derives from the practice that it is adduced to explain. Whereas in 1.3 we saw the individual emerging from the sacrifice and acquiring by implication integration with the universe, in 1.4.2 the primaeval atman loses his fear when he realises that he is alone, and this realization becomes, here in 1.4.10, a present possibility.

The autonomy of the individual is taken still further. Not even the gods – created by the primaeval mortal atman (1.4.6) – can prevent a man becoming this whole world, for 'he becomes their very self'. It is an implication of the identification of atman with the Whole that a single atman is shared by all beings, as is made explicit later in this section (1.4.16) and elsewhere.[73] The result is that venerating a deity as separate from oneself is a misunderstanding that makes one a possession of the gods as livestock are of men (1.4.10; 5§C). 'It is his atman alone that a man should venerate as his world (loka)' (1.4.15).

6§D Prana, Atman and *Manas*

In the previous section we encountered – in a sacrificial context – the constitution of the individual by the breath-within-the-mouth; but then, with the sacrificial context left behind, the (primordial) individual was identified with atman. But atman was not the only candidate to embody the emerging concept of the comprehensive inner self or subject. In this section we say more about prana, *manas* and atman as alternative embodiments of the subject, and about the relations between them.

In the *Rigveda* prana occurs ten times (including verbal forms), each time meaning 'breath', which at 3.5.53 leaves the body at death. But subsequently, in pre-Upanishadic texts and in the *Upanishads*, it acquires a range of features similar to that acquired by atman.[74] The life-breath of each individual, it acquires a cosmic dimension when identified with the wind.[75] It is the inner controller[76] and controller of all things; on it everything depends.[77] It is co-extensive with the universe. The sacrificer

[73] BU 1.5.20; 3.4; CU 5.11.6; etc. [74] Connolly (1997) 21–5; Keith (1925) 454.
[75] E.g. SB 10.3.3.7. [76] SB 1.4.3.8; Connolly (1997) 23; CU 4.3.3 breath internal gatherer.
[77] AV 11.4.

Prajapati became breath (prana), and 'breath is everything here'.[78] It is 'this entire creation, everything there is',[79] and the source of all things.[80] It is immortal[81] and incorporeal.[82] It is brahman.[83] It is the physical but invisible intermediary between the universe as corporeal self (RV 10.90) and the universe as inner self.

The plural of prana could mean not only breaths but also 'vital functions' or 'inner faculties': the mind, the various breaths, the five senses (distinct from the *organs* of sense such as eye or ear).[84] The *Brahmanas* repeatedly return to correspondences between elements of the sacrificial ritual and the pranas. In his book-length study of such correspondences in the *Rigvedic Brahmanas* Cavallin[85] concludes that:

> the tendency is that the sacrificer also becomes the goal of the ritual activity. It is, however, not only the sacrificer considered as self, as atman, that is intended, but the focus is upon the constituent principles of the self, the breaths. The efficacy is thereby both dependent on the self – as knowledge of the correspondences is a prerequisite for the attaining of the fruits of the ritual actions – and, at the same time, directed towards it: to the inner principles of the self, among which mind, and also somewhat contradictorily[86] atman, have a place.

The tendency for the individual to become the goal (as well as the agent) of the sacrifice (5§C), which distinguishes the *Brahmanas* from the *Rigveda*, is accompanied by focusing on the breaths or 'inner principles of the self'.

In the early *Upanishads* the superiority of prana as breath over the other components of the subject (pranas) is emphasised not only by the narrative of BU 1.3 (6§C) but also by another narrative (repeated in various versions) in which the only one of the pranas (speech, sight, hearing, mind, semen, breath) that proves indispensable for life is breath (prana), whose superiority they consequently recognise.[87] As a result, in one version they pay tribute to prana, who shares the good quality of each inner faculty, and that is why they are called pranas; in another it is because they decide to become

[78] SB 11.1.6.17. Cf. also JB 1.1–2 on breath and sacrifice, and JB 1.15–16 on breath aligned with mind and good deeds, body with speech and bad deeds.

[79] CU 3.15.4; cf. BU 1.3.22. [80] E.g. TU 3.3; Connolly (1997) 22–3.

[81] SB 6.7.1.11; 10.2.6.18, Connolly (1997) 23–4; BU 1.6.3; 2.3.5; 4.4.7.

[82] *aśarīra*: BU 4.4.7; KB 14.2. *Aśarīra* does not occur in RV (but cf. RV 129.2 breath without wind).

[83] BU 4.4.7; CU 4.10.4–5; BU 2.3.5; KU 2.2; TU 3.3.

[84] SB 8.1.3.1: 'What are the pranas? . . . The pranas are just the pranas.' [85] Cavallin (2003a) 230.

[86] The place of atman among the inner principles is for Cavallin 'contradictory' because atman may also be either the *substrate* or the *container* of the inner principles, which may be ritually instilled in the atman of the sacrificer. Cf. AB 2.21.4; SB 3.1.4.2.

[87] Elsewhere predominance over other inner faculties is given to *speech*: e.g. KB 2.7; at KB 9.3 'in speech and in mind is all this (universe) placed'; see further 8§A n.18.

forms of him that they are named pranas.[88] At KU 2.13 speech, sight, hearing and mind enter the prostrate body, but only the entry of breath makes it get up, with the result that, recognising the pre-eminence of breath, they unite themselves with it, 'which is the self consisting of intelligence (*prajñātman*)'.[89]

The narratives of the pre-eminence of prana over the pranas express the need to reify the new unity of consciousness. The imagined organ of unified consciousness (the subject) is – unlike the eyes and ears etc. – imperceptible. Breath is qualified for the role, because it combines invisibility with fundamentality (life manifestly depends on it). However, though invisible, it is not imperceptible. Although prana is occasionally called incorporeal, the fact remains that breathing is a bodily process, whereas the unified subject seems to be a different kind of thing from the body and its various organs and processes. Another concept is needed to provide absolute abstraction. What 'lies deep within my heart' is the atman (CU 3.14.2–4), the 'immortal and non-bodily atman' that has the mortal body as its abode (CU 8.12.1).

The word atman is generally regarded as deriving from the Sanskrit root *an-* ('to breathe'), and in the *Rigveda* often means breath. The early meaning 'life' of the Greek *psuchē* derived from its etymological association with breath. Perhaps both atman and *psuchē*, as well as prana, were helped by their early association with breath to form a bridge from the physical (objective) self to the abstract (subjective, inner) self.

But atman has also been derived from words meaning 'this I', i.e. the self. In *Rigveda* it sometimes has a broad sense akin to 'self', which becomes more common in the *Atharvaveda* and the *Brahmanas*,[90] and in the *Upanishads* it is generally translated 'self'. The self is the whole person constructed as distinct from other people, i.e. the whole individual person. As such, atman could be object (the whole individual body) or subject (the whole individual consciousness). In the latter sense, it was more suitable than prana to express the new absolute abstraction of an incorporeal entity of comprehensive consciousness, transcendent and yet immanent: beyond its various physical manifestations and yet somehow present in them.

Whatever its etymology, atman unites – like prana – the various pranas: someone who breathes, speaks, sees, hears and thinks 'is incomplete within any one of these. One should consider them as simply his atman, for in it all these become one' (BU 1.4.7). 'It (atman) contains all actions, all desires,

[88] BU 6.1.13–14; CU 5.1.13–15; BU 1.5.21. [89] Cf. AA 2.1.4. [90] 4§C; Deussen (1915) 285.

all smells, all tastes' (CU 3.14.4). Atman, like prana, is an entity of comprehensive consciousness, incorporeal,[91] immortal inner controller,[92] identified with brahman and with all things.[93] Indeed, prana is identified with atman (SB 4.2.3.1); and atman is founded on prana (BU 3.9.26) or consists of prana (TU 2.2.1). Some passages vacillate between atman and prana: e.g. in CU 8.12 the immortal element is first called atman, then (as what leaves the body) prana, but then again (as subjectivity) atman. Both atman and prana became, in different ways, *recipients* of offerings in the self-directed sacrifices known as *ātmayajña* and *prāṇāgnihotra* (5§C n.31). It has been argued that 'in some Upanishadic circles at least, the concepts of atman and brahman were developed on the basis of already existing conceptions of prana'.[94]

Pre-eminence over the pranas is sometimes assigned not to prana but to atman. At BU 4.4.2 the atman of a dying man departs along with his breath, and with his pranas, which throng around the atman like officials 'around a king who is about to depart' (6§B). Another form of the priority of atman over pranas is also expressed metaphorically, at BU 2.1.20:

> As a spider sends forth its thread, and as tiny sparks spring from a fire, so indeed do all the pranas, all the worlds, all the gods, and all beings spring from this atman. Its hidden connection (*upaniṣad*) is 'The real behind the real', for the real consists of the pranas, and the atman is the self behind the pranas.

Thread is very different from a spider, but mysteriously emerges from it, like sparks from fire. This expresses, besides the priority of atman, a close relationship between things different in kind, as does (more abstractly) 'the real behind the real'. The atman is different in kind from ('behind') the pranas that nevertheless emerge from it.

The difference is between subject and object, mind and body: 'This atman of mine that lies deep within my heart – it is made of mind (*manomaya*); the inner faculties (pranas) are its physical form (*śarīra*)' (CU 3.14.2). The statement that atman is 'this person (*puruṣa*) – the one consisting of perception (*prajñānamaya*) among the pranas'[95] looks like an attempt to distinguish what we would call the *subjectivity* of atman from the pranas in general, which include *objects* of perception such as speech and breath. The atman is (imperceptible) pure subject, whereas breath is an

[91] *aśarīra*: CU 8.12.1; *Kauṣītaki Āraṇyaka* 8.3. [92] E.g. BU 3.7.

[93] E.g. BU 2.5; CU 3.14.4; AU 3.3; Deussen (1915) 173, 178–80, 264, 282–8, 324–36.

[94] Connolly (1997): this conclusion is stated at 35.

[95] BU 4.3.7 and similarly 4.4.22. At 2.5.1 the *puruṣa* is an atman within the body.

(invisible) physical entity. A contrast between atman on the one hand and breath and body on the other is implied already in the *Atharvaveda*,[96] but in the *Upanishads* has become much more definite. At BU 3.7.3–23 atman is said to be different from various external things (earth, water, fire, etc.), from the inner faculties (breath, speech, sight, hearing, mind), and from skin, perception and semen. Each of all of these things is said to be the body (*śarīra*) of atman and to be controlled by atman from within, but not to know atman, which is imperceptible (8§C).

Another mode of prioritising subjectivity over breath is at TU 2.3–5. There is an atman consisting of breath, within which there is a different atman consisting of mind, within which there is the atman consisting of *vijñānamaya* (perception, knowledge), within which there is the atman consisting of bliss. Each atman is said to 'suffuse completely' (*pūrṇa*) the atman outside it. Given that something is more fundamental than what it suffuses, the breath atman here is less fundamental than the three subjective atmans within it.

What might be thought to be another potential rival to atman for the role of inner self is mind *(manas)*. In three passages of the late tenth book of the *Rigveda* it is assumed to *travel*, thereby – in Arbman's terminology – adding the function of 'free soul' to its function elsewhere in the *Rigveda* as 'body soul' (4§C). This merger of the two 'souls' promotes the (ethnographically exceptional) idea of a unified inner self that will eventually reach completion as the Upanishadic atman: this is understood by Arbman (1927: 179), who offers, however, no explanation of the merger. I would supplement his account in the following way.

The Upanishadic atman, too, merges the two functions, but with a comprehensiveness that goes beyond that of the travelling *manas*. At CU 6.8.2 *manas* is like a bird tied to a string: it will fly off in every direction, but will return to the breath, 'for the *manas* is tied to breath'.[97] Though it mediates sensations, desire, decisions, etc. (BU 1.5.3), the Upanishadic *manas* is one of the pranas – along with speech, sight, hearing and semen – that acknowledge the pre-eminence of breath (prana).[98] It is lesser than – and springs from – atman,[99] and is what atman is composed of.[100] In contrast to *manas*, the reach of the Upanishadic atman does not require it to move: it is both within the person and everywhere:

[96] AV 5.1.7; 5.9.7; also SB 11.2.1.2: Deussen (1915) 330.

[97] Cf. RV 1.164.37: 'I do not understand what sort of thing I am here: though bound, I roam about in secret by my thinking'; at 6.9.5 the *manas* of Agni is said to fly.

[98] BU 6.1; CU 5.1; etc. [99] CU 7.3–26; cf. BU 4.1.6; Keith (1925) 518, cf. 554–5.

[100] BU 1.5.3; CU 3.14.2; etc.

> This atman of mine that lies deep within my heart – it is smaller than a grain of rice or barley, smaller than a mustard seed, smaller even than a millet grain or a millet kernel; but it is larger than the earth, larger than the intermediate region, larger than the sky, larger even than all these worlds put together. This atman that lies deep within my heart – it contains all actions, all desires, all smells, and all tastes; it has captured this whole world.[101]

The absolute abstraction required for unifying subjectivity is best provided not by *manas* or prana but by atman, which – as imperceptible – must appear to be identical with its *contents* (i.e. with all of which it is conscious). And so – inasmuch as the subject is conscious of everything – the immortal atman *is* everything, the whole world (e.g. BU 2.5). It is as if the ubiquitous subjectivity of the immortal 'free soul' (wandering everywhere independently of the body) has been solidified in its merger with the static subjectivity of the 'body soul', a merger promoted by the interiorisation of sacrifice together with the self-sufficient ubiquity of money.[102] The same merger occurs in a less advanced form, in a society on the point of producing money, in Homer (13§B).

As well as being identified with the whole world, the atman is also separate from it. For inasmuch as the subject also *acts* from *desire*, the atman also *obtains* everything: it 'has captured this whole world', and whoever venerates his atman alone as his world will produce from his atman whatever he desires (BU 1.4.15). The atman is both 'inner controller'[103] and 'the controller of all, the lord of all, the ruler of all'.[104] The identification of atman with brahman is the merging of two universal reified *powers*, the former abstracted from the individual will, the latter from ritual.

Reification of the absolute subject – comprehensive, unified, abstract – as atman makes it seem to contain or control or produce all else, to be ontologically prior to all else. And so what is dear (husband, wife, children, wealth, livestock, priestly power, royal power, worlds, gods, Vedas, beings, the Whole) is dear not out of love for the husband, wife, children etc. but out of love for the self (atman) (BU 4.5.6). In the following sections this is explained: the priestly power, the royal power, etc. reside in the atman, whose relation to them is like that of a musical instrument to the sounds it makes (4.5.7–8). It is – as we might put it – inevitably through the subject that one is aware of all else. But for the *Upanishads* the subject (atman) does

[101] CU 3.14.3. Much of this is already in SB 10.6.3.2; see also SB 12.3.4.11: 'All the worlds have I placed within my own atman' etc.

[102] See e.g. 5§D. [103] Throughout BU 3.7. [104] BU 4.4.22; cf. e.g. 2.5.15; KU 3.8.

not merely *reflect* the world: it *obtains* or *captures* the world, and – if venerated – *produces* all that is desired. The relationship between the atman and all else is modelled – in part – on *possession*. Indeed, the first few items in the list of things said to be dear out of love for the atman are typical possessions: wife,[105] children, wealth, livestock, followed by what can be imagined to reside in the atman (priestly power, etc.). To identify a single abstract entity as the source of value for everything else is analogous to evaluation of all things by money.[106] A comparable structure of thought is found in Plato: things are beautiful only by partaking of beauty in itself (*Phaedo* 100b-e), and derive their usefulness and advantage from the 'form of the good', and so there is no benefit in possessing things without the good.[107]

105 'Husband' is in fact first in the list because Yājñavalkya is at this point talking to Maitreyi, one of his wives.

106 It is also, on the other hand, akin to the ascetic 'search for a contentless self', giving rise to what Collins (1982: 80–1) calls 'the abstraction of value from phenomenal personality which constitutes the aim of religious life and the criterion for its practice'. Cf. the paradox of asceticism in 7§A.

107 *Republic* 505a; for the form of the good see also *Republic* 508a–e, 532b1, *Laws* 965b–966b).

CHAPTER 7

The Powerful Individual

7§A Kshatriyas and Individualism

The historical background to the early *Upanishads*, taken to be from about the eighth to the sixth century BCE, is set out by Thapar (1994). A new economy (based on agriculture and incipient trade rather than herding and raiding) promoted the development of the caste system, of accumulated wealth, of urban centres and of the state. This produced greater wealth and power for the individual Kshatriyas, who accordingly moved away from dependence on sacrificial ritual, possibly preferring to use their new wealth as a basis for other sources of individual power (notably the state) rather than for sacrificial ritual. The result was the decline or interiorisation of sacrificial ritual and a 'new doctrine' (manifest in the *Upanishads*) that 'required discipline, meditation, and concern with the self alone':

> Whereas the sacrificial ritual required the contribution, to a greater or lesser degree, of the clan and thereby underlined clan identity, the new doctrine moved away from this identity and underlined the separation of the individual from the clan.[1]

If Heesterman is right about the advance of individualisation at the expense of reciprocity in the sacrifice, then it was not, as he supposes, orthogenetic (the result of internal rather than external factors), but belonged to the social change described by Thapar. But there is something we need to add to Thapar's account. *Why* did there occur 'the separation of the individual from the clan'? Although she rightly notes that 'the new doctrine first evolved in areas that had experienced an increase in wealth', the growth of wealth does not *in itself* promote individualism. What does do so is the

[1] Thapar (1994) 313, 318.

development of individual *property*, which is facilitated and promoted by *monetisation* (2§E).

This historical approach is required to complement the insights of Heesterman. The gradual advent of a general measure of value (and means of exchange) would facilitate the expenditure of individually owned wealth in an increasing variety of contexts. It would also locate the considerable expense of actually performing sacrifice on a general scale of values, in which it is easily compared to other expenditures, and so might lose its all-importance[2] and tend to be interiorised. Monetisation, together with the advance of commercial relations at the expense of the old codes of reciprocity,[3] promoted *new ways of thinking* – be it about sacrifice, self or universe. I will summarise this case in 9§F; it means neither that monetisation was the *only* factor behind the new ideas nor that ideas can be in any sense *reduced* to money (16§A).

The new form of power inhering in money was uniform, universal, impersonal, automatic, invisible, in principle accessible to everybody and conducive to individual ownership. It was quite different from – and potentially a threat to – the traditional ritual power of the Brahmins. Moreover, its universal power and universal accessibility was antithetical to the absolute differentiation inherent in the idea of caste. Brahminical texts accordingly almost entirely ignored it, just as they ignored commerce and the towns, where money was in all likelihood most prevalent. (This contrasts strongly with the urban milieu and the presence of commerce and money in the earliest Buddhist texts.) On the other hand, a general measure of value, especially if it is also a general means of exchange, *requires for its highly convenient effectiveness* that the everyday life of everybody within its sphere of operation is pervaded with something new, the impersonal power of uniform value. In reality Brahmins could hardly avoid encountering money, or at least the effects of monetisation, and I have given several examples of passages into which money has intruded without being acknowledged or named.

In the late *Brahmanas* and early *Upanishads* interest moves from sacrifice to the view of the world implied and generated by sacrifice, and then to what we may call philosophy; and doctrines are propounded not only by

[2] For Buddhism sacrifices were a waste of resources: 'instead, lay adherents should give donations to the *saṅgha* and kings are encouraged to redistribute their wealth, e.g. to enable trade and commerce (cf. the *Kūṭadanta Sutta*; D 1.127–149)': Schlieter (2013) 14.

[3] From a *psychological* perspective Lea and Webley (2006) argue that money parasitises the human instinct for reciprocity. If so, this process was involved in the *historical* tendency for money to replace reciprocity.

Brahmins but also by Kshatriyas, more specifically rulers (chieftains or kings).[4] And so it has naturally been proposed that these doctrines originated with Kshatriyas, i.e. from a non-Vedic source.[5] The founders of Jainism and Buddhism were also both said to be Kshatriyas.

On the other hand it has been claimed that 'the ideas voiced by the Kshatriya characters, despite what the characters claim, are not particularly new to the Vedic tradition, and that therefore the *motif* of Kshatriya authorship is a literary fiction',[6] with the aim of demonstrating the importance of certain Brahminical doctrines *for* the Kshatriyas. Indeed, this importance is frequently emphasised, no doubt as a means of persuading the Kshatriyas to exercise the generosity to the Brahmins that is also frequently on display in the texts, in a period in which the wealth and power of the Kshatriyas was very likely being monetised.

The precise origin of the doctrines cannot be determined. What we can do is to explore the significance of the *content* of the doctrines associated with Kshatriyas.

There are four places in which the association of a doctrine with Kshatriyas is emphasised, in each case by a Kshatriya. The two passages in which doctrine is most *emphatically* associated with the Kshatriyas (as completely new to Brahmins) are BU 6.2.8 and CU 5.3.7, in both of which King Pravāhaṇa Jaivali says to the Brahmin Uddālaka that 'this knowledge has never before been in the possession of a Brahmin', adding in the latter passage that 'as a result in all the worlds government has belonged exclusively to royalty':[7] the doctrine then expounded is the two-path doctrine (9§D), to which in the second is added what may be the earliest statement of EIR (ethicised indiscriminate reincarnation).[8] These doctrines are versions of the theme 'how to avoid repeated death', which Black notes as a frequent theme of the dialogues between rulers and Brahmins.[9] In 9§D I will analyse the two-path doctrine as privileging (over traditional sacrifice) knowledge, the individual self and permanent escape to brahman from the automatic cosmic food cycle. We will see that it represents a new kind of individual self-sufficiency that is here appropriately propounded by a Kshatriya endowed with the self-sufficiency of (at least partially) monetised wealth.

[4] Black (2007) 101–31.

[5] A strong case for this was made already by Deussen (1906) 8, 18–21, 120–5.

[6] Black (2007) 104.

[7] Thapar (1994) 310 notes that 'this is striking coming from the *rājā* of the Kuru-Pañcāla, an area noted for its learned *Brahmanas* and frequency of the best sacrificial rituals'.

[8] CU 5.10.7, quoted in 9§D (7).

[9] Black (2007) 128. Note also CU 5.11–24, on atman *vaiśvānara* (the self common to all people).

The other two passages in which a ruler emphasises the association of a doctrine with rulers are BU 2.1.15–18 and KU 4.19–20, in both of which King Ajātaśatru accedes to a request from the Brahmin Gārgya to become his pupil, while noting that it is a reversal of the norm for a Brahmin to become the pupil of a Kshatriya. These passages include a comparison of the relation of the inner self to its components with the centrality of a ruler among his people. We will discuss this theme, the interiorisation of autocracy, in 7§B. Here we confine ourselves to a single example of the comparison, from the section of the *Bṛhadāraṇyaka Upaniṣad* (chapters 3–4) known as the *Yājñavalkyakanda.* The Brahmin Yājñavalkya says to King Janaka:

> As soldiers, magistrates, equerries, and village headmen throng around a king who is about to depart, so at the time of death all the vital functions (pranas) throng around this self (atman) as he is breathing his last (BU 4.3.38).

The simile is then followed by two similes for the atman at death passing into something else: as a caterpillar reaching the tip of a blade of grass and drawing itself onto a new foothold, and as a weaver making a new and more attractive design. Further, 'a man turns into something good by good *karman* (action) and into something bad by bad *karman*'. A man who *desires* returns to this world, back to *karman*, but a man who is free from desires 'becomes immortal and attains brahman in this world' (4.4.7). *Karman* basically means 'action', but in its earliest occurrences it refers mainly to actions that follow ritual prescriptions.[10] Even if it here retains an association with ritual rather than referring simply to action in general,[11] the passage is an early precursor of the widespread subsequent metaphysics of karma and individual progress through, and escape from, the cycle of EIR, and as such takes its place alongside the two-path doctrine, and the early statement of EIR, that we have seen attributed to Kshatriyas.

How do we explain the advent of this metaphysics? This question has generated much debate. My own answer will emerge in the course of this book, especially in chapters 9 and 10, in which I set out the relation of the various elements of the new Indian metaphysics to monetisation. But here I must mention – in order to dismiss – the kind of answer that has most recently been proposed by Bronkhorst. This is that the new metaphysics is to be explained by *regional* difference: it originated, he claims, from the distinct culture of Greater Magadha, 'roughly the geographical area in

[10] Gombrich (1996) 31; (2006) 46. [11] Tull (1989) 31; cf. Gombrich (2009) 37–8.

which the Buddha and the Mahavira lived and taught',[12] to the south and east of traditional Brahminical territory.

Rather than presenting the detail of Bronkhorst's argument and the objections that have been made to it,[13] I will go straight to the heart of the matter. Karmic retribution is normally regarded as first appearing in the passages of the early *Upanishads* that I have just discussed. Bronkhorst downdates the final form of these texts to well after the advent of Buddhism and Jainism, and argues that in them the doctrine of karmic retribution 'has been added to material that is devoid of it' (122). The passage I have mentioned from the *Yājñavalkyakanda* is – he claims – designed to reclaim the doctrine as Brahminical. As for the explicitly new doctrines taught to Uddālaka:

> the very earliest references to the doctrine of rebirth and karmic retribution in the Veda – those that are connected with Uddālaka – are also the ones that state quite emphatically that this doctrine is a foreign intrusion into the Vedic tradition (120).

By 'foreign intrusion' he means that the doctrine comes from the king of the old Brahminical heartland of Pañcāla.[14] And so:

> the early *Upanishads* present the doctrine of rebirth and karmic retribution in a Vedic garb. This indicates that the doctrine was 'dressed up' so as to look Vedic. This Vedic presentation is no more than an external veneer, a clothing which does not really belong to it (120).

This is an odd conclusion. If the intention of the *Bṛhadāraṇyaka Upaniṣad* and the *Chāndogya Upaniṣad* was to dress the doctrine up as Vedic, why did they attribute it – unusually and emphatically – to a king?

It is by contrast easy to see why the Brahmins should give their royal patrons prominence in the *Upanishads*, why they should emphasise the importance of Brahminical doctrine for the well-being of their royal patrons, and why – in the same spirit of synarchy (5§E) – they should attribute a doctrine to a royal patron, especially (but not only) if that doctrine was widely known to have arisen in the newly prosperous and powerful urban milieu of the Kshatriyas. In avoiding urban life (2§E) the Brahmins left a new space relatively free of their intellectual domination, especially perhaps in Greater Magadha, where urbanisation flourished most and Brahmins were anyway less established probably than in

[12] Bronkhorst (2007) 4: 'With regard to the Buddha, this area stretched by and large from Srāvasti, the capital of Kosala, in the north-west to Rajagriha, the capital of Magadha, in the south east'.

[13] E.g. by Wynne (2010) and (2011), and Klaus (2011).

[14] BU 6.2.2; CU 5.3.1.

Kuru-Pañcāla. Indeed, the *Yājñavalkyakanda* (though not the *Bṛhadāraṇyaka Upaniṣad* as a whole) was set in the kingdom of Videha in Greater Magadha,[15] and has Yājñavalkya out-talking the Brahmins of Kuru-Pañcāla (e.g. 3.9.19), which seems to express the aspiration of the Brahmins of Videha to rival or outdo the old Vedic heartland of Kuru-Pañcāla. Yājñavalkya is in the *Bṛhadāraṇyaka Upaniṣad* an authoritative figure associated with new and unorthodox thinking, skilled in verbal debate, with a focus on knowledge of the self as opposed to knowledge of the sacrifice.[16] Probably the *Yājñavalkyakanda* was created in the early fifth century BCE, and circulated independently of the Vedic canon for some time.[17]

Neither the Buddha nor the Mahavira were born in Magadha, but they both travelled extensively, and spent time in the city of Rajagriha, the capital of Magadha until the fourth century BCE. Wynne argues that the Buddha gained knowledge of early Upanishadic thought through his teacher Uddaka Rāmaputta, whom other evidence places in or around Rajagriha, and infers that:

> it would seem that a religious group promulgated the teachings of the *Yājñavalkyakanda*, perhaps before it was incorporated into the BU, at the very centre of the ancient kingdom of Magadha during the Buddha's lifetime.[18]

I must emphasise that Rajagriha was 'the largest of all Early Historic Cities' according to Erdosy, who postulates a fifth century date for the 4.5 miles of inner fortifications.[19] As the only major city not on a river, it must have had another reason for its location: this was, suggests Kosambi, because it was close to deposits of iron and on a trade route leading from deposits of iron and copper in the south to the alluvial portion of the Gangetic plain, which had no metal of its own but needed iron to clear its forests and for agriculture and weapons.[20]

The upshot of all this is that there developed – along commercial routes between cities in Greater Magadha and elsewhere, in non-Brahminical milieux – a potent new metaphysics that it was in the interest of the Brahmins to adopt and merge into the Vedic world-view that was itself

[15] Olivelle (1996) xxxix, 308. [16] Black (2007) 67–80.
[17] Wynne (2010) 207–9. Bronkhorst's argument for a much later date for its creation is refuted by Wynne. In particular, Bronkhorst is unable to explain why the dialogue was set in the kingdom of Videha, which was absorbed into the Vriji confederacy by the time of the Buddha's adult life.
[18] Wynne (2010) 207. [19] Erdosy (1988) 109.
[20] Kosambi (1951) 194–5; Erdosy (1988) 109; Chakravarti (1987) 16.

in some ways changing – under the same pressures – in the same direction. Much innovation in the Vedic tradition, notably EIR, can in fact be shown to be a reconfiguration of older elements,[21] rather than requiring the hypothesis of a separate regional origin. The Brahmins innovated with some acknowledgement of the Kshatriyan source of the new metaphysics, but without acknowledging the existence of cities or of money. Other expressions or offshoots of the new metaphysics were Buddhism, Jainism and Ajivikism.

Of course, Greater Magadha was culturally distinct in various respects from Kuru-Pañcāla. Texts that reached their final form centuries later have been used to suggest a distinction in mythological genealogy.[22] And a distinction has been identified in forms of governance: in Greater Magadha instances of the *gaṇa-saṅgha* form ('equal assembly') were in the period of urbanisation absorbed into monarchies associated with wisdom and renunciation, whereas in Kuru-Pañcāla by contrast there were no *gaṇa-saṅgha*s and the king was more likely to be seen as a warrior.[23] But there is nothing in all the evidence presented by Bronkhorst and others that is inconsistent with the view that by far the most important factor behind the new metaphysics was urbanisation, with its consequences. Inasmuch as Greater Magadha contained more not only of the earliest cities but also – crucially – of the earliest coins[24] than did Kuru-Pañcāla, it would be entirely in accord with my perspective that it contributed much to the new metaphysical currents. But we cannot explain the Brahmins' abandonment of their own traditional metaphysics *merely* by their move eastwards to a place that had (inexplicably) a different metaphysics. Pravāhaṇa Jaivali is presented as the source of the new doctrine *and* as king of the old Brahminical heartland of Pañcāla.[25]

To be fair to Bronkhorst, he admits that he does not know *why* the new metaphysics arose (in Magadha).[26] In my view we cannot answer this

[21] 9§C (Blutzenberger), 9§D(1) (Killingley), 10§A (Obeyesekere), 16§A n.1.

[22] Samuel (2008) 63–8.

[23] Samuel (2008) 58, 69–79. The nomadic origins of the warrior king may be still visible in the preliminaries to the *aśvamedha* sacrifice: 3§B n.24.

[24] E.g. Hardaker (2011) 207–8; Gupta and Hardaker (2014) 9, 16 (map of hoard findspots), 19 ('Magadha, one of the largest of these states [the *janapadas*] was one of the first to issue punch-marked coins'), 47: 'the coins of series 0 and I are found in the general region of the Magadhan homeland, but interestingly it is Series 0 that occupies what is considered to be the original heartland of Magadha'. The very earliest coins of the whole Gangetic region may be slightly earlier: Hardaker (2019).

[25] BU 6.2.2; CU 5.3.1.

[26] 'We do not know why and when the belief in rebirth and karmic retribution became part of the culture of Greater Magadha': Bronkhorst (2016) 248.

question if we ignore, as Bronkhorst does, the anthropology of religion, the relationship between religion and societal formation.

EIR is – as a communal belief – found only in beliefs held or originating in ancient India and ancient Greece (10§A). The same is true of abstract monism and mental monism (4§E). How do we explain these striking facts? And why did EIR and abstract monism first appear in India and in Greece at about the same time, after being in both cases absent from earlier texts (the *Rigveda* and Homer)? True, neither the *Rigveda* nor Homer represent the full range of views of their place and time, and so it cannot be excluded with perfect certainty that (a) there were people in northern India or Greece who believed in EIR and abstract (or mental) monism well before they first appeared in extant discourse (and so well before monetisation), and (b) these beliefs were then for some reason adopted – in India by the very people whose sacred duty it was to preserve the earlier Vedic discourse. But no other pre-monetary peoples that we know of have ever devised these beliefs. And it would moreover be a remarkable coincidence if they happened to have been devised by precisely the two peoples who were to be in the future the first monetised peoples in history.[27]

Why has the belief in EIR not only occurred in ancient Greece but has also been – in Jainism, Buddhism, Hinduism and among millions from Christian backgrounds – so remarkably and persistently widespread? Because the ancient traditions of Magadha happened to contain the right formula? Abstract (or mental) monism has also – despite its counter-intuitiveness – been popular, notably in Advaita Vedanta as well as in Greek philosophy. Bronkhorst (2016: 269) writes of the 'enormous divide' that existed between Vedic culture and what he supposes to be the culture of Greater Magadha. Are we content to explain this divide as emerging merely from the (inexplicable) fundamental difference between adjacent Indo-Aryan cultures around 500 BCE? Metaphysical transformations tend to emerge from societal transformations. The societal transformation of this whole region in this very period took the form of urbanisation, commercialisation and monetisation – developments that also occurred at about the same time in Greece, and are still with us.

We have in this section detected – as prominent among the Upanishadic doctrines especially associated with the Kshatriyas and presented as important for their well-being – the (new) self-directed individualism that we have derived in part from monetisation. It represents the Brahmins'

[27] Along with the Chinese (probably): 16§A. For my rejection of the hypothesis that metaphysics explains monetisation, see 13§A.

adaptation (up to a point) of traditional Vedic attitudes and ideas to the changing circumstances (though the Brahmins would not, of course, have described it thus), in which it was as autonomous individuals that their patrons were acquiring and maintaining wealth and power.

The synarchy of Brahmins and Kshatriyas leads not only to metaphysical individualism but also to the repeated insistence in the *Upanishads* on the magnification or empowering of the individual by *mere knowledge* of the new metaphysics (e.g. BU 1.4.10: 'If a man knows "I am *brahman*" in this way, he becomes the whole world'). The Brahminical sphere is not secular power but metaphysics, which must however have the capacity to benefit individuals whose power is secular. And so the mere knowledge that maximises their power and well-being (both based to some extent on money) in this world and the next is – to some extent – knowledge of what is created by the projection (cosmisation) and interiorisation of money.

Moreover, from the *Brahmanas* to the early *Upanishads* we can detect a remarkable development of individualism among the Brahmins themselves. It is in the late *Brahmanas* that 'suddenly it becomes important to link ideas with specific teachers and students'.[28] An essential aspect of the Upanishadic shift from ritualism to knowledge of the self is the new transmission of knowledge between named individuals.[29] Then there are the exchanges known as Brahmodyas. These are at first uncompetitive questions and answers between anonymous priests, in a sacrificial context, not as a debate but as a means of expounding the significance of the ritual.[30] But in the early *Upanishads* they become aggressively competitive debate on a philosophical issue, in a non-sacrificial context, between distinctive named individuals (such as Yājñavalkya), for material reward. All this has been well described by Brian Black.[31] My concern is to emphasise that competition between named individuals for material rewards, familiar though it is to us, was new in Indian texts. I suggest that it is related to the new individualism that I have described as inhering not only in the interiorisation of the sacrifice but also in various *doctrines* expounded in the *Upanishads* by the distinctive named individuals themselves (Kshatriyas as well as Brahmins), and that these developments are symptoms of monetised individualisation. It is at about the same time in Greece that we first find ideas attributed to particular historical individuals (and of competitiveness between them).[32]

[28] Black (2007) 29. [29] Black (2007) 52. [30] E.g. SB 13.2.6.9–17; 13.5.2.11–22.
[31] Black (2007) 59–100. [32] For the competitiveness, see e.g. Hklt. B40 and B42.

I conclude with three specific examples of named isolated sages. Usasti Cakrayana is a pauper who has to beg for food. In order to earn something, he goes to a sacrifice and warns three priests that if they sing without knowing the deity attached to what they are singing, then their heads will shatter. They stop singing, and the *yajamāna* (patron of the sacrifice) employs Usasti to perform the priestly functions, which he does, as well as explaining, by arguments, that the three deities attached to the songs are breath (prana), the sun and food. But first he gets the *yajamāna* to agree to give him the same amount that he gives the priests (CU 1.10–11).

Usasti is a poor man seeking wealth in exchange for his knowledge. His knowledge (of impersonal deity), and his use of the kind of argument that is constantly used in the early *Upanishads*, are set in contrast to the mere performance of ritual. And he offers the *yajāmana* a better result *for the same payment.*[33] This is the kind of calculation characteristic of a monetised society. Black comments:

> Here we see that in the market-place of Upanishadic ideas, Brahmins are pitted against each other as individuals rather than collectively performing rituals together. One Brahmin such as Usasti can perform the jobs of all the priests combined, suggesting that an important incentive for Brahmins to learn Upanishadic teachings is that they reap the same economic rewards as the collective payment for the sacrifice.[34]

Another combination of poverty with wealth acquired through Upanishadic knowledge occurs in my second example, Yājñavalkya, whom we have already seen as authoritative but associated with new and unorthodox ideas, with a focus on the self as opposed to sacrifice. Through his knowledge and skill in debate Yājñavalkya 'amasses more wealth than any other Upanishadic teacher'.[35] But he also associates knowledge of the atman with austerity, fasting, the ascetic life of wandering, giving up the desires for sons and wealth, and mendicancy (BU 4.4.22; cf. 3.5). He then tells us that a man who knows the nature of the atman finds wealth (4.4.24), but at the beginning of the next section (4.5) declares that he is about to become a wandering ascetic.[36] This makes him the first person we know of to be depicted as a renouncer.[37]

[33] Similarly, King Aśvapati offers Brahmin householders the same amount for receiving a teaching from him that he pays the priests for performing a sacrifice (CU 5.11.5).

[34] Black (2007) 91. [35] Black (2007) 95.

[36] It is in this context perhaps that we should understand his ironic 'we are really after the cows, aren't we?' (BU 3.2)

[37] Black (2007) 94–5

Paradoxes are often profoundly revealing. How do we explain this one?[38] A little earlier in the same passage a dreamer:

> appearing to be a god or a king thinks 'I am alone in this world! I am all!' – that is his highest world (BU 4.3.20)

and:

> when a man is successful and rich, ruling over others and enjoying to the utmost all human pleasures – that is the highest bliss of human beings (4.3.33).

However, this bliss is – we are immediately told – vastly less than other forms of bliss, of which the highest is:

> bliss enjoyed in the world of brahman – and, one might add, by those learned in the Vedas who are not crooked or lustful (BU 4.3.33).

The Brahmins value wealth, success and pleasure. However, they are capable of an even higher state (not just for self-respect but in order to be indispensable to their powerful and wealthy patrons). Wealth, Yājñavalkya tells his wife as he prepares to become a wandering ascetic, does not confer immortality (BU 4.5.3), which Brahmins can confer through sacrifice or knowledge of the self. But why choose to be a wandering ascetic?

What the dreamer values about being a god or king is aloneness in the world: 'I am alone in this world! I am all!' The endpoint of monetised individualisation is the individual ownership of everything,[39] reflected in Indian texts as the absorption of everything into the self. But this imagined aloneness is most easily achieved by severing all ties, as a wandering renouncer. The renouncer follows the logic attributed to Alexander the Great, who remarked that – were he not Alexander – he would be Diogenes (the Cynic renouncer).[40] In a fragmentary Greek papyrus of the second or first century BCE[41] Alexander compares the happiness of a forest-dwelling Brahmin with his own fear of those close to him, who are indispensable but constantly scheme against him. He offers gifts (including coins) to the Brahmin, to which the Brahmin replies 'I do not buy anything. I live in solitude. God gives me everything without charge.' Even for (some) Greeks

[38] It is possible that Yājñavalkya's renunciation was a later addition to the text. Even if this were so, it would show merely that the paradox thereby created was acceptable.

[39] Individual ownership of the whole earth was nearly achieved in the story mentioned in 2§E.

[40] Plut. *Alexander* 14; et al.

[41] Berlin Papyrus 13044. The episode reappears (without gaps) about five centuries later in Palladius' *On the Life of the Brahmins*. Both texts are translated by Stoneman (1994).

the isolation of the renouncer is preferable to the isolation of the man of wealth and power.

In Chapter 9 we will pursue further the logic that binds extreme renunciation to monetisation, in India at least. For the time being it is enough to note that the same process of monetised individualism underlies both limbs of our revealing paradox: on the one hand the acquisition of wealth through individual competitiveness in knowledge, and on the other hand ascetic isolation.

My third isolated sage is Raikva.

The wealthy Jānaśruti Pautrāyaṇa had hospices built everywhere, thinking 'people will eat food from me everywhere'. He then overhears the following conversation between two over-flying geese (CU 4.1.2–4):

> '. . . Look, a light like that of Jānaśruti Pautrāyaṇa has spread throughout the sky. Don't touch it, if you don't want to be burnt.'
>
> The other replied 'Come now! Given who he is, why do you speak of him as if he were Raikva the gatherer?'
>
> 'That man – how is he Raikva the gatherer?'
>
> 'As the lower throws all go to the one who wins with the highest throw of the dice, so whatever good things people may do, all that goes to him. I say the same of anyone who knows what Raikva knows.'

Jānaśruti's steward, having failed to find Raikva, is told to 'look for him in a place where one would search for a non-Brahmin'.[42] Raikva is then found scratching his sores under a cart, and is – despite rudely calling Jānaśruti 'sudra' – persuaded by him to reveal his wisdom.[43]

Much here is obscure. What does emerge is that Raikva represents something cosmic and dangerously potent that resembles the ubiquitous generosity of Jānaśruti and is worth knowing. Anyone who knows what Raikva knows is a gatherer. He who throws a higher number wins for himself the lower numbers thrown; in the same way the good things that people do – 'all that goes to him' (Raikva). This explains the word 'gatherer' (*sayugvan*), which Olivelle calls 'probably a technical term of the dice game referring to the gathering up of the winnings'.

The dice game may well have been played for money.[44] In a late hymn of the *Rigveda* it was singled out as the context for the economic ruin of an individual (10.34). And it is itself analogous to monetised commerce:

[42] 'Non-Brahmin' is Rau's conjecture *abrāhmaṇa*, accepted by Olivelle, and makes much better sense (than does 'Brahmin') of what immediately follows.

[43] CU 4.3.1–3, discussed in 8§C.

[44] For dicing producing revenue for the king, see Keith (1925) 343.

numerically based, competitive, self-contained, individualised, rule-governed and yet uncontrollable. Herakleitos, whose cosmology is profoundly influenced by monetised commerce (12§D), described time as a board game (DK22 B52), i.e. a series of competing moves by individuals in absolutely egotistical conflict according to set rules that are independent of the will or identity of the opposed parties (but with more control than in dicing).

Just as the highest throw of the dice (4) gathers to itself the lower throws (3,2,1) to become 10,[45] so Raikva accumulates money from the achievements of others, thereby acquiring a dangerous potency no less cosmic than the gift-giving of Jānaśruti. Raikva is – despite being a vulgar, isolated and disrespectful non-Brahmin – knowledgeable, and eventually provides cosmic wisdom that approaches the four types of reductionism or monism described in 4§E: with respect to the divine sphere, the wind gathers into itself fire, sun, moon and water; and with respect to the atman, the breath (prana) gathers into itself the pranas – speech, sight, hearing and mind.[46] Wind and breath are each called gatherer, *saṃvarga*, which – according to Olivelle – is another technical term from the game of dice with a meaning identical to that of *sayugvan*. What the highest throw becomes (10) is (at CU 4.3.8) equated with the total of five cosmic elements plus five pranas (inner faculties). An invisible component of universe (wind) and of inner self (breath) each 'gathers' (controls, contains, unifies) the other components in a way that is numerically akin to the gathering of the lower numbers of the dice by the highest number. Similarly, in ritual the knower of numerical equivalences achieves power (5§C), and in monetised competition the invisible numerical power of money not only gathers (controls, contains, unifies) what is visible but also gathers the invisible numerical power of money from others into the man who knows.

7§B The Interiorisation of Autocracy

Of the *Brahmanas* and *Upanishads* Bodewitz observes that:

> It is surprising that man as an organism is frequently homologised with the order of the cosmos, whereas the structure and hierarchy of the state hardly received attention in this connection. Only the global division of society into three (or four) classes plays a prominent role and these classes are frequently equated with cosmic and ritualistic entities.[47]

[45] Olivelle (1996: 340) refers to scholarship on this issue.
[46] CU 4.3.1–3, discussed in 8§C.
[47] Bodewitz (1992) 50.

But he goes on to describe an exception, the association of prana with kingship. I confine myself to some instances from the *Upanishads*. Realising the necessity of breath (prana) for life, the other pranas agree to pay tribute (*bali*) to him (BU 6.1.13). And the unity of the pranas in the atman is also expressed in terms of political power. As officials throng around a departing king, pranas throng around the atman of the dying man (BU 4.3.38). A dreamer moves around his body at will, taking the pranas with him, as a king moves around his domain at will, taking his people with him (BU 2.1.18). At KU 4.20 we are told by king Ajātaśatru that:

> to this atman cling these other atmans,[48] as to a chieftain his own people. It is like this – just as a chieftain makes use of his own people, and his own people make themselves useful to a chieftain, so this atman consisting of intelligence (*prajñatman*) makes use of these other atmans, and these other atmans make themselves useful to this atman.

Here it is the chieftain that provides a model for the construction of the inner self. The unity imposed by interpersonal power is interiorised by the mind as a way of knowing itself.

Such knowledge has advantages. BU 1.5.21 narrates the victory of breath in competition with the inner faculties: 'therefore, they are called pranas after him. For this reason, a family is called after a man who has this knowledge', and his rivals wither and die. At KU 2.13 the narrative of the pre-eminence of breath is followed by the conclusion that he who knows this, and recognises the pre-eminence of breath and unites himself with that breath, which is the atman consisting of intelligence, goes to heaven.[49]

The knowledge of the sacrifice led to power through correspondences – of elements of the ritual with elements of the world. Similarly, knowledge of the inner sovereignty of atman may obtain external sovereignty. In BU 1.3.17–18 the deity breath-within-the-mouth obtains a supply of food through singing, with the result that the other deities gather around him; the people will gather around whoever knows this, who will become their leader and a sovereign (6§C). The primaeval conflict between Devas (gods) and Asuras (demons), which in earlier texts occurs by means of – and for control of – the sacrifice, with the Asuras being defeated because of their inferior knowledge of the sacrifice (5§A), is in CU 8.7–12 recast as a contest between a god (Indra) and an Asura for knowledge of the atman. Indra

[48] The atmans here seem to be the pranas (inner faculties) just mentioned as emerging from the atman.
[49] For further examples of knowledge of the narrative of prana's victory leading to sovereignty, see Black (2007) 122.

wins, and is informed that 'when someone discovers this atman and comes to perceive it, he will obtain all the worlds and have all his desires fulfilled'. KU 4.20 states that the relation of atman to the inner faculties is like that of a chieftain to his people, and that:

> as long as Indra did not understand this atman, the Asuras were prevailing over him. But when he came to know it, he smashed the Asuras, conquered them, and secured the supremacy, sovereignty, and lordship over all the gods. A man who knows this likewise wipes off all evils and secures the supremacy, sovereignty and lordship over all beings – yes he does, when a man knows this.[50]

Indra smashing his enemies, as regularly in the *Rigveda*, here depends – this would be inconceivable in the *Rigveda* – on his understanding the atman. By understanding the sovereignty that he has over himself, the autonomous individual is able to extend it over others. Knowledge, whether the old knowledge of the sacrifice or the new knowledge of the atman, leads to power.[51] Accordingly, both kinds of knowledge are – it is clear from the *Brahmanas* and the *Upanishads* – well worth paying the Brahmins for.

But *why* was sovereignty interiorised? The individualisation of sacrifice leads to its interiorisation (5§D). The Agnicayana ritual was once performed only by kings, but subsequently, suggests Proferes, 'attracted the imaginations of all those who longed to overcome the limitations of their social position and who wished to move unfettered in accordance with nothing but their own will, as a great king was imagined to do'.[52] Individual power over (and identification with) the world was bestowed by ritual on the king, and so in being bestowed on others continued to be imagined as kingship. A man dreams of dangers through ignorance but when he dreams of himself 'as a god or a king, and thinks "I alone am this world! I am all!" – that is his highest world' (BU 4.3.20). Proferes[53] discusses 'a substantial number of Upanishadic passages in which metaphors of sovereignty are employed in immediate connection with the identification of the microcosm with the macrocosm'.[54] The interiorisation of kingship

[50] Compare BU 6.3.5: 'He indeed is the king, the ruler, the highest lord. May he make me the king, the ruler, the highest lord'. Similarly, CU 5.2.6.

[51] CU 7.25.2: A man who (by perceiving the atman in a certain way and pleasuring in it) 'becomes completely his own ruler (*svarāḍ bhavati*), obtains complete freedom of movement in all the worlds, whereas those who perceive it otherwise are ruled over by others and obtain perishable worlds'.

[52] Proferes (2007) 137; also 3, 119.

[53] Proferes (2007) 142–50.

[54] Proferes (2007) 143. The passages he discusses include BU 4.3.20; 4.4.17; 4.4.22; 5.3.1; 5.6; CU 2.21.4; 5.2.6; 7.25.2; KU 1.6.

expressed a new sense of individual autonomy, in which a factor was likely to have been monetisation (13§C).

The earliest occurrences of the competition among the pranas (in the *Brahmanas*) do not yet have any connection with kingship,[55] quite possibly because kingship was not yet as important as it became in the time of the early *Upanishads*.[56] But in Greece of our period kingship is in *decline*, leaving correspondingly greater scope for the social power of money. Whereas in India the idea of the autonomous inner self may be influenced by a positive image of the universal individual power of the *king*, in Greece it is influenced by the abstract unifying power of the *money* by which its owner is constituted as an individual.[57] A rare case in our period of Greek interiorisation of sovereignty – in the Derveni Commentary (6§A) – is also one of the rare Greek instances of the unalloyed[58] mental monism that is prominent in the early *Upanishads*. Money bestows power over other beings, and its power is in principle universal; but no individual can possess enough of it to control *everything* in the way that an absolute sovereign – and the Upanishadic individual – may be imagined to do.

Alongside this difference between the two cultures in what is interiorised there is a striking similarity. We have seen that in the *Upanishads* the *interiorisation* of power (sovereignty) creates an inner unity that goes with external power over others. *The same is true of Plato*, except that the interiorised power is of the abstract good (a projection of monetary value): in the *Republic* it is by virtue of their absorption in (in effect, interiorisation of) the abstract good that the philosophers control both themselves and the other citizens,[59] in what may be described as a politically conjoined projection (cosmisation) and introjection (interiorisation) of abstract monetary value.

Finally, in Greece, too, there is an interesting relationship between the power of the autocrat and the new autonomy of the monetised individual. Although kingship was in our period in decline, power in some city-states was seized by a 'tyrant' (*turannos*), whose rule then tended to be arbitrary, unstable and resented as corrupt and oppressive. Towards the end of the sixth century BCE in the newly democratic Athens there emerged with surprising rapidity something entirely unprecedented, a wholly new performance genre: tragedy. Crucial factors in its genesis included the very recent Athenian experience of the tyrant (*turannos*), the recent

[55] Black (2007) 122. [56] E.g. Thapar (2002a) 150–4. [57] Chapter 13.

[58] Unalloyed with material monism or abstract monism (though combination of subject with abstract monism also occurs in the *Upanishads*): chapters 8 and 12.

[59] E.g. Plato. *Republic* 431, 471–521; 15§A.

monetisation of the polis by the introduction of coinage, and the festal amplification by the polis of the communality of mystic ritual.[60]

We may note in passing that two elements of this process, the polis and communal mystic ritual, were in our period lacking in India, as was (accordingly?) any trace of sophisticated drama – despite the wealth, monetisation and sophistication of Indian society. When drama did eventually appear in India, it is impossible to exclude the possibility that the *idea* of drama was an external influence from the West, in other words ultimately from Athens.[61]

But the point to pursue here is that monetisation and mystic ritual were factors not only in the genesis of drama but also – we shall see how in due course – in the Greek emergence of the idea of the individual inner self. It is therefore no coincidence that what we find in tragedy, in the form of *action*, is the unprecedented *isolation* of the individual autocrat (*turannos*[62]) – from the gods and (through conflict) from his own kin – an isolation that is just one of the various features of the new communal genre that can be associated with the new, communal but individually possessed power of money.[63] The power of the recently removed tyrannical family in Athens had been based to a large extent on control of the supply of (now largely coined) money. And the empathetic identification of the individual member of the mass audience with the tragic *turannos* (implicit in Aristotelian theory) may be based in part on the isolating effect of money, that takes an extreme form in the tragic (and historical) *turannos* but may be felt in some measure by everyone who possesses it. The paradigmatically excessive, self-destructive individualism of the *turannos* is staged by the polis, expressed in the *perversion* of household ritual, set against the survival of the anonymous chorus and frequently concluded by the institution of a practice (generally a communal ritual) that brings permanent benefit to the polis, of which in classical Athens the *turannos* was the feared enemy.

In India by contrast there is in this period nothing like the polis, nor any communalisation of Vedic sacrifice. The earliest Indian inner self is constructed, in part, from a positive idea of individual autocracy as well as through the (monetised) individualisation and interiorisation of ritual, resulting in an individually possessed principle (karma) whose universal retributive power precludes the cosmic pessimism sometimes evoked by tragedy. The absolute isolation of the individual, in Greek tragedy an

[60] Seaford (2012a). [61] This has been well demonstrated recently by Bronkhorst (2016: 390–403).
[62] I.e. ruler or tyrant. He is frequently called *turannos* but never 'hero'. [63] Seaford (2012a).

unwittingly self-inflicted horror, is embraced by the Jain monk (9§E). True, in the epic *Mahābhārata* there is – as in Greek tragedy, but not in the (pre-polis) Homeric epic – violent conflict between kin, but in the context of the relation between power and *dharma* (not, as in Greek tragedy, between ruling family and community). Drama appears in India much later than in Greece, and in an entirely different form.

CHAPTER 8

The Formation of Monism

8§A Monism between the *Rigveda* and the *Upanishads*

Having defined the various types of monism and described its exiguous presence in the latest layer of the *Rigveda* (4§E), in this section we look for monism in texts produced after the *Rigveda* but before the earliest *Upanishads*. There is a rough scholarly consensus about what belongs to this period, even though absolute chronology is impossible, relative chronology is obscure and it cannot be excluded that a specific passage is earlier than some material preserved in the late tenth book of the *Rigveda* or later than some material preserved in the earliest *Upanishads*.

In these texts there is a good deal of reductionism, which sometimes goes so far as to produce monism. The examples that follow are classified as in 4§E.

(1) Material Monism

In the hints of *primordial material monism* in the *Rigveda* (129.3; 121.7) the material is water. The statement that 'water was this world' then occurs in the *Taittirīya Saṃhitā*.[1] The *Śatapatha Brāhmaṇa* states that in the beginning there was nothing but water or that the universe comes into being from the waters.[2] In the *Atharvaveda* Skambha ('support') both supports and pervades the universe (10.7.8), the gold of the primordial golden embryo[3] was poured by Skambha (10.7.28) and the residue of sacrifice (*ucchiṣṭa*) is equated with the whole universe (11.7.1–2).[4]

[1] 5.6.4.2 and 7.1.5.1.

[2] 11.1.6.1; 14.8.6.1; cf. 6.1.1.12; 6.1.3.11; 6.8.2.3; 1.1.1.14; etc.: Gonda (1982–3) 10–11; TA 1.23. The identification of all deities to the waters occurs at AB 2.2.16 (vii 6).

[3] Cf. RV 10.121.

[4] Cf. also e.g. AV 13.4.12–13 the gods become one in the sun; SB 10.3.3.5 'the Agni who is everything here'.

(2) Personal Monism

At RV 10.121.10 the lord of creation is identified with Prajapati, who elsewhere in the *Rigveda* has only four mentions (three of them in the late tenth book).[5] Subsequently, however, Prajapati becomes the supreme god. He enters into all beings,[6] and creates the world and all its inhabitants;[7] and all gods and mortals and much else emerge from him.[8] To the extent that this implies that Prajapati was once all there was,[9] this is *primordial personal monism*. This reductionist tendency produces *present personal monism* when it is said that the sacrificing Prajapati is all, the whole (*sarva*).[10] He is sacrificer,[11] identified with the sacrifice,[12] and prototype of the human sacrificer, who repeats the primordial sacrifice in which Prajapati was dismembered and transformed into the universe; and the sacrificer, too, in being identified with Prajapati, may become all (6§A). *Personal monism* (primordial and present) in the *Brahmanas* is *sacrificial*. This is in this period by far the most common form of monism.[13]

(3) Mental Monism

The closest we come in the *Rigveda* to an opposition between the outer (physical) and inner (mental) self is in the *Puruṣa* hymn (10.90),[14] and the closest to (primordial) mental monism is 10.129.4,[15] where – after suggestions of personal (2) and material (3) monism – 'in the beginning from thought (or mind, *manaso*)[16] there evolved desire . . .' In subsequent texts *manas* sometimes has a cosmic role.[17] SB 10.5.3.1–2 identifies the primordial 'neither non-existent nor existent' at RV 10.129.4 with *manas* (producing primordial mental monism), and continues thus:

[5] 9.5.9; and 10.85.43; 169.4; 184.1.
[6] TS 5.5.2.1; *Vājasaneyi Saṃhitā* 8.36; TB 2.2.7.
[7] SB 6.1.2.11; TS 5.5.2.1.
[8] SB 2.2.4; 7.5.2.6; 10.1.3.1; 11.5.8.1; PB 6.1; TB 1.7.1.5; 2.1.6; 2.2.7.
[9] Made explicit at SB 2.2.4.1; 2.5.1.1–2; 6.1.1.8; 6.1.3.1; 7.5.2.6; 11.5.8.1.
[10] SB 1.3.5.10; 4.5.7.2; 5.1.1.6; 5.1.3.1; 7.1.2.6–7; 13.6.1.6: KB 6.15; 25.12; JUB 1.46.2; Gonda (1982–3) 9, 15–17.
[11] His creativity is associated with sacrifice at AB 5.32; PB 6.1; TB 2.1.6, 2.2.7; SB 2.2.4.
[12] SB 1.1.1.13; 1.5.2.17; 1.5.3.2; 1.6.1.20; 1.9.2.34; 2.5.1.7; 4.3.4.3; 4.5.5.1; 5.1.1.2; 5.1.2.11; 5.1.2.12; 5.1.4.1; 5.4.5.20; 5.4.5.21; 11.1.8.3; 11.5.2.1; 14.1.2.8; PB 7.2.1.
[13] Note also the survival at AB 1.1.1 of the special form of personal reductionism that I found in the RV (4§E).
[14] Especially 10.90.13: analysis by Tull (1989) 53.
[15] Cf. RV 10.90.13 'the moon was born from his mind'.
[16] Brereton (1999) describes how the first three verses 'invoke a process of thinking, of developing an idea, and of gradual understanding', leading to the primacy of thought in the fourth verse: this reflects the importance for the priests of their own thought.
[17] Deussen (1915) index s. *manas*.

> This mind (*manas*), when created, wished to become manifest – more defined, more substantial: it sought after an atman. It practised austerity: it acquired consistency. It then beheld thirty-six thousand Arka-fires of its own self, composed of mind, built up of mind: mentally alone they were established (on sacrificial hearths) and mentally built up . . . whatever rite is performed at the sacrifice, whatever sacrificial rite there is, that was performed mentally only, as a mental performance, on those (fires or fire-altars) composed of mind, and built up of mind.

Mind then creates speech,[18] which creates breath, which creates eye, and so on. This primordial mental monism expresses the *interiorisation* of the sacrifice.[19]

To conclude, sacrificial personal monism (the only instance of present monism in the *Rigveda*: 10.90.2) is in this later period more frequent, and there is a striking instance of its interiorisation producing primordial mental monism. On the other hand the indications of material monism are meagre, and there is not yet any abstract monism.

8§B From Correspondences to Monism

We have at several points related the world imagined in the hymns of the *Rigveda* to the specific socio-economic conditions of their production. Here we take the argument further by noting its relation to the context of pre-monetary ritual in which they were performed.

In the society (or section of society) in which the *Rigveda* was created there are two vital kinds of power. One is the physical power of the semi-nomadic community over what is external to it: in particular, the power to create paths and to defeat enemies in battle. The other is internal regulation, the moral power of inherited laws and procedures. Both kinds of power are in the *real* world on the whole both *personal* (embodied in will and action) and *communal* (requiring communal participation). And so in the *imagined* world they are – because of their embodiment of will and action – exercised by personal gods, and – because of their communality – transcendent. When the community summons up or celebrates its power in battle, it imagines the presence and power of Indra, who is also praised

[18] For passages elevating speech (*vac*) to the highest level, see Keith (1925) 444 n.5; 6§D n.14. But at SB 1.4.5.8–11 Prajapati places mind (*manas*) above speech. At SB 11.3.1.1 mind and speech are identical but distinct, 'therefore they tie up the calf and its mother with one and the same rope' – a nice example of a ritual expression of contradiction.

[19] Cf. also TB 2.2.9; KB 26.3; JB 1.20; Keith (1925) 444. Perhaps the earliest indication of the importance of the mind in sacrifice is TS 1.6.8.

for his power to remove obstacles. Internal, moral powers are upheld by the gods, in particular by Varuna (3§B); and as for the fundamental socio-economic principles of distribution and reciprocity, the gods are frequently the agents of distribution among men,[20] and bestow goods and outcomes – reciprocally – on men who give them praise and offerings. The transcendence of *the overall social order* is reified in the untranslatable notion of *ṛta*, which refers to something like order or truth (in universe, society and ritual), but has a wide range of meanings, concrete associations and concrete identifications. Though itself on the whole impersonal, it is nevertheless generally upheld, strengthened, mastered, possessed or promoted by divine persons.[21]

Pre-monetary power is exercised by *personal will*, which – rather than being mediated by the same all-encompassing, impersonal power-substance (money) – is *itself embodied in various actions*. Accordingly, the various powers in the world are – in order to be controlled – not reduced to a single abstract power-substance, but are rather *personified*. There is in the *Rigveda*, in contrast to later texts, no all-encompassing impersonal abstract entity, such as brahman and karma became (and even the broader phenomenon of monism is merely indicated, only four times, and only in late hymns: 4§E). Instead, the world of the *Rigveda* is dominated by a variety of personal powers (gods). Nor is there any all-encompassing mental entity, such as atman became: mind or thought in the *Rigveda* has no ontological distinction, it is merely one among many vectors of power and motion (4§C). What matters most in the universe of the *Rigveda*, as in Homer, is the variety of transcendent personal powers (deities).

The hymns of the *Rigveda* are generally *purposive*, designed to obtain from the gods such benefits as prosperity, victory and offspring. The way of obtaining benefits is twofold: there is *reciprocity* (eliciting benefits from the gods by giving them praise, offerings and hospitality), and there is *ritual*. The obtaining of benefit through ritual may involve making what seem to be inherent correspondences between elements of ritual and elements external to the ritual. The two ladles are heaven and earth (10.82.1), and the firmness of the oblation is associated with the firmness of the universe, of the gods, of the kingship (10.173). If we call such correspondences 'metaphorical', we should be aware that they are metaphorical only in a very broad sense.[22] When, for instance, in the words of Jamison and Brereton, 'the flow of soma over the wooden filter is the destruction of

[20] In 10.84 'battle fury' is praised and invoked to smite the enemy *and* share out the spoils.
[21] Chaturvedi (2016); Jurewicz (2016b). [22] On metaphor cf. 10§C.

Soma's enemies',[23] the felt connection of ritual act with desired outcome is surely more real than illustrative.[24]

Moreover, this kind of imagination extends beyond ritual. Why in the *Rigveda* is the word for 'cow' used for 'the dawn?' For Jurewicz 'the metaphoric mapping enables the poet to reason about the appearance of the dawn light, which is a process difficult to understand, in terms familiar to every cowherd'.[25] No less important is the relative *controllability* of the cow as a source of prosperity. The numerous homologies in the *Rigveda* are, according to Jamison and Brereton, 'not mere poetic embellishments, poetic imagery for its own sake, but an implicit statement of the way things *really are*, the pervasive underlying correspondences unifying apparently disparate elements'.[26] The sacrifice, or the hymn, is a chariot, or like a chariot.[27] The correspondence (or identification) sought and imagined is of the concrete, controllable near-at-hand (ladles, oblation, soma and filter, cow, chariot) with what is otherwise uncontrollable, remote (sometimes invisible), and yet fundamental to well-being: universe, dawn, gods, conflict, journey to the gods.

Such correspondences are subsequently commonplace in the *Brahmanas*, but with important differences. Consider the following passage, chosen at random from the *Śatapatha Brāhmaṇa*:

> As large as the altar is, so large is the earth; and the plants (are represented by) the *barhis* (sacrificial grass); so that he thereby furnishes the earth with plants; and those plants are firmly established in this earth: for this reason he spreads the *barhis* (1.3.3.9).

In the *Rigveda* the correspondences occur in the context of divine power and pervasive reciprocal relations between mortals and deities. The ladles of RV 10.82.7 are the offspring of the god Visvakarman. Soma, whose flow is the destruction of enemies, is a god, who has 'not been drunk without a counter-gift' (8.32.16). In the *Śatapatha Brāhmaṇa* by contrast, numerous correspondences such as the one just quoted occur without any mention of deities: the result can be described as a relative *depersonalisation* of the

[23] Jamison and Brereton (2014) 68. RV 9 has many such passages.

[24] The dissolution of boundaries between what we regard as distinct entities may have been facilitated by the drinking of soma, which creates exhilaration in men and gods. The purified soma juices 'have pervaded our insights with inspiration . . . have pervaded the backs of the two world-halves and this highest airy space': 9.22.3–5; cf. e.g. 8.48.3; 9.107.20; 10.119. Soma confers wholeness in exhilaration, raises the drinker to the sky, bestows power, bestows immortality, is a king, smites the wicked and confers a wide range of benefits: 9.18.1; 10.119; 8.33.4–11; 8.48.3; 9.8.5; 9.79.3; 1.91.

[25] Jurewicz (2010) 42–3. [26] Jamison and Brereton (2014) 24.

[27] E.g. 1.61.4; 1.129.1; 2.18.1; 2.31; 5.2.11; 10.53.7.

sacrificial control of the world. True, the deities remain in a sense the recipient of the sacrifice. But its most prominent beneficiary is now the individual sacrificer, which gives rise to the new kind of correspondence or equivalence – between unitary sacrificer and universe – that we described in Chapter 6. This kind of elaborately interconnective metaphysics makes Vedic ritual very different from Greek ritual.

Our passage from the *Śatapatha Brāhmaṇa* also indicates another difference from the *Rigveda*: the correspondence (of elements of the sacrificial ritual with earth and plants) is made explicit, as the reason for performing the ritual. What matters is not the agency of – or relations with – deity but *knowledge of correspondences.*

In the earliest *Upanishads* the gods have receded even further, and knowledge of correspondences has moved even further to the centre. We still find – as so often in the *Śatapatha Brāhmaṇa* – the correspondence of elements of the sacrificial ritual with elements of the external world.[28] But the correspondences are now differently represented. It is convincingly argued by Falk[29] that the word *upaniṣad* originally meant:

> the generic term [*Oberbegriff*], the effective power that stands behind something else, the principle that on the higher level controls other 'subordinate' terms. In the literary genre known as '*Upanishads*' the point is [*es dreht sich darum*] to seek out the productive powers behind the multiplicity of appearances.

This meaning for *upaniṣad* is approved by Olivelle, who notes that it is 'assumed that such connections are always hidden', and that the term is used with this meaning at CU 1.1.10 and 1.13.4.[30] It was then used as the name for the dialogues of which it formed the central theme, namely to find the hidden but dominant reality behind objects.[31] Already in the *Brahmanas* a correspondence might sometimes involve more than two terms, producing a chain of dependence. But in the *Upanishads* the tendency is for there to be a larger number of items dependent on a single thing, and without any mention of ritual.

There are two basic *modes* of such dependence. One mode is where b depends on c, c on d, and so on, with x at the end of the chain

[28] E.g. the opening words of BU are 'The head of the sacrificial horse is, clearly, the dawn'. See also BU 1.2.1; 1.2.7; 1.3.25–7; 1.4.17; 2.2; 3.1.3–10; 3.2.1–9; 5.3.1–13; 6.3.1–12; 6.4.3; CU 1.1.2; 1.3–7; 1.11.6–9; 1.13; 2.2–22; 3.1–4; 3.12; 3.17.

[29] Falk (1986) 83.

[30] Olivelle (1996) lii-iii. Similarly Black (2007) 6. Cohen (2008: 3–5) proposes the translation 'underlying reality'.

[31] Brereton (1990) 124–5.

(b>c>d> . . . >x), as for example in CU 7.1–25, discussed in detail in 15§C.[32] The other, more recent[33] and more frequent mode represents a tendency towards monism (reductionism): b, c, d, etc. all depend directly on x (bcd . . . >x). CU 7.1–26 combines both modes: after the chain ending in atman, the final section (26) states the direct emergence of each item in the chain (and 'this whole world') from atman.

The dependence takes various forms, of which I confine myself to a few examples taken from BU: b, c, d, etc. are founded on x,[34] identified with x,[35] kept alive by x,[36] reside in x,[37] emerge from x,[38] are forms of x,[39] are fastened to x like spokes to the hub and rim of a wheel.[40] In this new configuration of correspondences x is more fundamental or comprehensive than b, c, d, etc. It has to be sought out not just as hidden but frequently because naturally invisible, or abstract: breath (or wind), atman (often identified with brahman) or brahman itself. All three kinds of text (*Rigveda*, *Brahmanas*, *Upanishads*) aim at well-being, but there is a chronological development that cannot be explained merely by the internal logic of sacrifice. Whereas in the *Rigveda* there are various instances of focus on something visibly at hand as a means of accessing or controlling something beyond (even beyond sight, such as the gods), in the *Upanishads* this relation has not only been transformed by the tendency towards monism but also had its direction reversed: the focus is now not on what is visibly at hand but rather on knowing something that is single, impersonal, abstract (*essentially* invisible), and fundamental to all beings (including what is at hand). In the same way, numerous goods may seem to depend on (as emergent from, sustained by, forms of, identified with, etc.) the abstract value of money: access to various goods is now to be obtained not by a variety of things offered to human or divine persons but through focus on the single abstract universal (of money). Moreover, the transition detectable in the texts from b>c>d>x to bcd>x corresponds perhaps to the transition from the phase in which goods are largely still exchanged for each other (with money fundamental

32 Cf. e.g. BU 3.6; 3.8; 5.14.4; 6.4.1; CU 1.1.2; 1.8–9. In such chains 'the beginning point, the end point, and all points in between can be interpreted as secretly identical' (Jamison [2016] 19).

33 Falk (1986) 87.

34 E.g. 4.1.7: all beings are founded on the heart, which is brahman.

35 E.g. 3.3.2: 'individual things and the totality of things, therefore, are just the wind'; 2.5. 1–14: b, c and d are each 'the honey of all beings'.

36 E.g. 6.1.13: breath keeps alive the other parts of the body.

37 E.g. 2.4.6: the priestly power, the royal power, worlds, gods, beings, the Whole reside in the atman.

38 E.g. 2.1.20. The world, the gods and all beings spring from the atman.

39 E.g. 1.5.21: the vital functions become forms of the central breath.

40 2.5.15: thus are all beings, all the gods etc. fastened to the atman.

only as a measure of value) to the phase in which money has become also a general means of exchange.

Again I suggest that these are not mere analogies, that monetisation was a factor behind the new metaphysics. 'Vedic philosophy turns on the assumption that it is possible to correlate corresponding elements lying on three discrete planes of reality: the macrocosmos . . . the ritual sphere . . . and the microcosmos.'[41] Money tends to occupy and conflate this tripartite structure, being on the one hand cosmised, projected onto the macrocosmos (to converge with brahman) and on the other interiorised into the microcosmos (to converge with atman).

The conflation is complete. The reduction of numerous items to the abstract universals atman or brahman, and the identification of atman with brahman,[42] promotes the coalescence of mental monism with abstract monism (as defined in 4§E). A tendency towards monism in the development of the correspondences is detected by Cavallin already in the *Brahmanas*.

The logical outcome of a process in which interrelated objects more and more come to be considered as identical is some form of monism, and this tendency together with the focus on 'breaths' prefigures the views expressed later in the *Upanishads*.[43]

In the *Upanishads* the breaths tend to be replaced (as embodying the subject) by the more comprehensive and more abstract atman (6§D). It is observed by Smith that:

> in the *Upanishads*, universal resemblance is brought to its logical terminus: universal identity. The complex system of connections between resembling phenomena, the web of *bhandus* [correspondences] integral to Vedic ritualism, and hierarchical distinctions are collapsed in monistic thought into the ultimate connection: the equation of self and cosmos (without the ritual intermediary) formulated as the identity and full equality of atman and the brahman.[44]

The individualisation of the sacrifice, in which the individual becomes destination as well as agent of the ritual, ends in its interiorisation, in which the complex system of correspondences is no longer sustained by the

41 Smith (1989) 46.

42 This has a concrete, sacrificial predecessor at SB 13.7.1.1: Brahman *svayambhu* (the self-existent) 'offering up his own self in the creatures, and the creatures in his own self, compassed the supremacy, the sovereignty, and the lordship over all creatures; and in like manner does the Sacrificer, by thus offering all sacrificial essences in the *sarvamedha* (all-sacrifice), compass all beings, and supremacy, sovereignty, and lordship'.

43 Cavallin (2003a) 227.

44 Smith (1989) 194.

demands of actual practice, and this advances the collapse of the correspondences into universal identity (monism). Interiorisation of the sacrifice is accompanied by the development of monism (especially mental and abstract monism). Rather than depending, as in the *Rigveda*, on reciprocal relations with a variety of gods, or – as in the *Brahmanas* – on a variety of ritual correspondences, well-being now depends on deriving all things from knowledge of the subjective and objective aspects of a single abstract entity. This knowledge, focused on the identification of unitary self (atman) with abstract being (brahman), is not desirable for its own sake, but in order to obtain benefits. The inner self *desires* and *appropriates*, and by uniting the abstract value/power of money to itself (15§B) may obtain all it desires, just as what is identified with (and yet remains in a sense distinct from) atman – abstract brahman – may be imagined as powerful. Black notes as characteristic of the early *Upanishads* (as opposed to the later ones) that they 'make a number of claims as to what kinds of reward this knowledge [understanding atman] can bring,'[45] and mentions cows, gold, power over enemies, as well as immortality. As for its obtaining immortality, this will be the theme of 8§D.

8§C Monism in the Five Earliest *Upanishads*

I here classify and discuss numerous (though not all) instances of reductionism and monism in the five earliest *Upanishads*.[46]

These *Upanishads* contain more monism than do earlier texts. They exhibit a constant tendency, in varying contexts, to reduce the many to the one (*reductionism*), often to the point of *monism*; but it may be difficult to know whether this point has been reached, difficult either (a) because the precise meaning of the Sanskrit is debatable, or (b) because a statement is monist in spirit without being monist in the strict sense,[47] or (c) because the *Upanishads* frequently (and unsurprisingly) imply or assume – sometimes even within a monistic passage – the manifest plurality that is only occasionally[48] explicitly denied. And so our distinction between monism and reductionism (4§E) may sometimes seem artificial. There is, moreover, no reason to expect consistency of doctrine or outlook between the *Upanishads*, within a single *Upanishad*, within a single passage or even

45 Black (2007) 23. 46 *Bṛhadāraṇyaka*, *Chāndogya*, *Taittirīya*, *Aitareya* and *Kauṣītaki*.
47 E.g. BU 1.4.15 'It is his self (atman) alone that a man should venerate as his world'.
48 E.g. at BU 4.4.19–20.

within a single sentence.[49] The usefulness of our classificatory scheme consists of its illumination of the similarities and differences between the monisms developing simultaneously in Greece (Chapter 12) and India. But the *Upanishads* are not conscious of the scheme, and move from one of our four forms of monism to another with fluidity and ambivalence.

Monism does not emerge directly from the data of experience (sensations, mental movements, emotions, etc.), which are inescapably *plural*, but rather from the imagination. True, personal (anthropomorphic) monism – imagining the universe as a person – may depend partly on sense data; and so may material monism.[50] But it is with mental monism and abstract monism, which *exclude* sense data, that the early *Upanishads* are especially concerned. An entity that is universal and abstract (homogeneous, imperceptible) presented an unprecedented challenge to the imagination. There may also be confusion between the outer and inner selves, both of which could be denoted by atman. These difficulties tend to blur the distinction between personal and mental monism.

(1) Material Monism

Among the few hints of monism in the late hymns of the *Rigveda* is the primordial material monism of water. This reappears at BU 5.5.1:

> in the beginning only the waters were here. Those waters created the real (*satya*), the real created brahman, that is Prajapati, and Prajapati created the gods.

We move from a traditional idea (the primordial material monism of water) to an abstract entity (*satya*), thence to something ambivalent between impersonal and personal (brahman = Prajapati), and thence to the unequivocally personal (Prajapati creating the gods).

In the early *Upanishads*, however, I have not found *present* material monism. Material *reductionism* is used as *illustration*.[51] It also occurs at BU 6.2.9–16 (the world up there, a rain cloud, the world down here, a man and a woman are each identified with *fire*),[52] and CU 7.10.1 (various items – including the earth, the intermediate region and the sky – are 'simply specific forms of water': this borders on monism), and something that resembles material reductionism is at BU 3.9.1–9 applied

[49] For instance, at AU 3.3 personal and subjective reductionism are combined: 'Knowledge is the eye of the world, and knowledge the foundation'.

[50] Or rather material reductionism, for I have found no present material monism.

[51] BU 2.1.20; CU 6.1.

[52] Reproduced, with some differences, at CU 5.4–10. See 7§B.

to the gods.[53] It occurs also in the statement that all creatures are born from food and in the end pass into food (TU 2.2).[54]

Material monism, and even material reductionism, have, in contrast to presocratic philosophy, very little importance in the early *Upanishads*, in which the advance of monism is rather almost entirely bound up with the advancing centrality of abstraction in subject and object.

(2) Personal Monism

The early *Upanishads* contain various conceptions of the origin of the universe. We do not find the idea that originally there was more than one entity. Either there was originally nothing, or the universe arose from a single entity (primordial monism). The first chapter of the *Bṛhadāraṇyaka Upaniṣad* implies both conceptions. 'In the beginning there was nothing here at all' (1.2.1): however, we are then immediately told that 'death alone covered this completely'. Death is envisaged as a person,[55] who decides to equip himself with a body (atman). This is something like *primordial personal monism*. Then, as he was performing a liturgical recitation, water sprang from him (here the monism ends), the foam on the water became earth, and as he toiled on her his heat became fire. Death begot (*asṛjata*) the whole world, but 'began to eat whatever he begot' (BU 1.2.5), which looks like a restoration of the monism.

Another version of primordial personal monism occurs a little later. 'In the beginning this world was just a single self (atman) shaped like a man' (BU 1.4.1). He then creates many entities, initially by splitting his own body into husband and wife (6§C). Yet again, at BU 1.4.17 we find that 'in the beginning this world was only atman, only one', who wishes that he had a wife.

At BU 1.4.10[56] primordial monism is restated, but with brahman as the primordial entity: 'In the beginning this world was only brahman, and it knew only itself (atman)'. Brahman is neuter in form, and in the *Rigveda* refers to ritual utterance, but in the *Upanishads* may be personal and is often identified with atman, the self. In the next paragraph, however, the primordial monism of brahman is restated for the sake of explaining that brahman (ritual power) is the womb of the ruling power, so that the king returns in the end to brahman as to his own womb. The monist

[53] A plurality of deities is reduced to one god, who is identified with breath and with brahman. See also KU 2.12–13.

[54] Cf. BU 3.2.10: this whole world is food for death, which is fire and the food of water.

[55] Even though at 1.2.3 his body is that of a horse. [56] Quoted in 5§C and 6§C.

identification in the *Upanishads* of brahman with all that exists seems at least sometimes to combine personal with impersonal monism (undefined as material or as abstract).

How do the many emerge from the primordial one? So far, we have seen the following modes, all of which involve personal agency: during the performance of ritual (liturgical recitation), by the one person splitting his body, by emanation (of heat) from his toiling body, by his giving birth and by thought.

The *primordial* personal monism of BU 1.4 is taken in the direction of *present* personal monism when atman, having created through copulation the male and female of every animal species, says 'I alone am the creation, for I created all this' (BU 1.4.5).[57] Similarly, just as the original brahman by thinking 'I am brahman' became the whole (BU 1.4.10), so – the text continues – 'this is true even now. If a man knows "I am brahman" in this way, he becomes this whole or all (*sarva*)'.[58] At KU 1.6 a man with knowledge tells Brahma that 'you are this *sarva*'. A man may acquire the desirable state of mind in which 'the whole world springs from himself' (atman) (CU 7.5.26).

Similarly to BU 1.4.17, the *Aitareya Upaniṣad* begins 'In the beginning this world was the atman, one alone'. But this looks more like primordial *mental monism*, for the atman immediately created the worlds (lokas) and from the waters 'drew out and gave definite shape to a man', from whose body parts there emerges much else: it seems the first human body is created by the primordial inner self.

(3) Mental Monism

At TU 3.6 brahman forms a single all-encompassing subjective sphere:

> Brahman is bliss (*ānanda*) – for, clearly, it is from bliss that these beings are born; through bliss, once born, do they live; and into bliss do they pass upon death.

At CU 3.14.2–4 atman is a universal, abstract subject:

> This atman of mine that lies deep within my heart – it is made of mind (*manomaya*) . . . space is its essence; it contains all actions, all desires, all smells, and all tastes; it has captured this whole world.

57 Cf. TU 2.6 'He had this desire', to produce offspring, and 'emitted this whole world, everything that is here, and entered that world . . . he became the real, everything that is here'.

58 Cf. e.g. the words uttered in ritual at BU 6.3.6: 'May I indeed become the whole world.'

By knowing the atman one knows the whole world, and the priestly power, the royal power, worlds, the gods, beings and the whole – all reside in the self.[59] This is illustrated by the emergence of sounds from a drum, a conch and a lute, and of smoke from fire. And the organs as the points of convergence of sensations and thought are compared to the ocean as the point of convergence of all the waters. The next illustration of atman is the invisible ubiquity of salt dissolved in water: 'in the same way this immense being[60] has no limit or boundaries and is a single mass of perceptions'. All this is mental monism (or close to it).

(4) *Abstract Monism*

A bridge from ritual to abstract monism is provided by the identification of ritual power in general (brahman) – or of a particular element of ritual such as the sacred sound OM – with the whole world: 'brahman is OM; this whole world is OM' (TU 1.8); 'this whole world *(idaṃ sarvam)* is nothing but OM' (CU 2.23.3). For this purpose sound has the advantage of invisibility. More purely abstract is space:

> 'Where does this world lead to?'
> 'Space (*ākāśa*[61])', he replied. 'Clearly, it is from space that all these beings arise, and into space that they are finally absorbed; for space indeed existed before them and in space they ultimately end' (CU 1.9.1).

Space is abstract enough for this to be called primordial abstract monism. TU 2.1, however, reaffirms what seems to be the more mainstream view by stating the priority of atman over space:

> From this very self (atman) did space (*ākāśa*) come into being; from space, air; from air, fire; from fire, the waters; from the waters, the earth; etc.

Another difference between the *Chāndogya Upaniṣad* and the *Taittirīya Upaniṣad* involves a degree of abstraction greater even than that of space. The former states:

> How can what is existent be born from what is non-existent? On the contrary, son, in the beginning this world was simply what is existent – one only, without a second (6.2.2).

But the latter[62] quotes the verses:

[59] BU 2.4.5–12; also at 4.5.6–15, where the point of the salt image is different: Ganeri (2012) 35.
[60] *bhūtam*, past participle of to become. [61] Free or open space, emptiness, the sky, atmosphere.
[62] TU 2.7; similarly, CU 3.19.1.

In the beginning this world was the non-existent (*asat*),
And from it arose the existent (*sat*).
By itself it made an atman for itself.

The primordial world is imagined in both passages as a single abstraction, be it *sat* or its absence (*asat*). We should note that *sat*, the present participle of the verb to be, may not reach the supreme abstraction of its translation as 'the existent', connoting as it does order and determinateness.[63]

In BU 1.4, which we have seen to contain several expressions of primordial personal monism, we also find that:

> at that time this world was without real distinctions;[64] it was distinguished simply in terms of name and visible appearance – 'he is so and so by name and has this sort of appearance'. So even today this world is distinguished simply in terms of name and visible appearance (1.4.7).

This idea of the universe as a single entity (originally and now), with distinctions within it being merely a matter of name and visible appearance rather than reality, combines primordial monism with present monism. This unitary homogeneous universe implies perhaps abstract monism (no material is specified, and the personal and mental do not have the homogeneity of abstraction).

At BU 3.8 all things are woven back and forth on space (*ākāśa*), which is woven back and forth on the imperishable. This imperishable is characterised negatively ('neither coarse nor fine . . . neither short nor long', etc.); it commands the earth and sky (and other basic things) to stand apart; and it sees (hears, thinks, perceives) but cannot be seen (heard, thought, perceived). This is not quite monism but reductionism, because the image of the loom implies fundamentality not identity, but it is worth noting the carefully formulated abstraction of the fundamental entity.

The stage of pure abstraction is reached at CU 6.9.2, in the statement (approached by a string of metaphors: see below) that 'all these creatures merge into[65] the existent'.[66] And at BU 4.4.18–9 we read that:

The breathing behind breathing, the sight behind sight,
the hearing behind hearing, the thinking behind thinking –
Those who know this perceive *brahman*,
the first,
the ancient.

[63] Halbfass (1992) 26–7. [64] *Avyākṛtam*: unseparated, unexpounded, undeveloped.
[65] *Saṃpad*: meet with, obtain, turn into.
[66] *Sati*, dative of *sat*. Already at CU 6.8.6 we are told that 'the existent, my son, is the root of all these creatures – the existent is their resting place, the existent is their foundation'.

With the mind alone one must behold it –
there is nothing here diverse at all!
From death to death he goes who sees
here any kind of diversity.

As just singular one must behold it –
immeasurable and immoveable.
The self is spotless and beyond space,
unborn, immense, immovable.

The way to perceive brahman is to go behind the various inner processes so as to perceive with the mind alone an entity in which there is no diversity (abstract monism). 'For [or drawn from][67] this intelligence *(prajñā)* all beings become one' (KU 3.4).

(5) Monism and Breath

Breath (prana) gives birth and life to beings, and so is identified with brahman (TU 3.3). And it is material (perceptible), personal, invisible (quasi-abstract) and seems cosmic (as wind). Indeed, with this combination it seems qualified to be the single entity of all our four types of reductionism/monism, or even as a vehicle for their coalescence. There are accordingly passages in which various forms of reductionism or monism are produced by the reduction of various entities to breath. I give some prominent examples:

(a) Those narratives in which the personified subjective functions willingly become forms of prana and are accordingly called pranas (6§D).
(b) In KU 2.12 the deities enter and emerge from breath (*vāyu*, which has as its primary meaning 'wind'),[68] and in 2.13 the deities 'entering the prana and with space as their self went to heaven'.
(c) At CU 4.3.1–3[69] the wind (*vāyu*) gathers perceptible entities (fire, sun, moon and water), and the breath (prana) gathers subjective capacities (speech, sight, hearing and mind). They are both 'gatherers', but are explicitly *differentiated* into two spheres (the divine, and atman).[70] The differentiation distances the passage from monism. On the other hand, the analogy between wind and breath tends to merge the separate spheres, thereby approaching all our four types of reductionism/monism.

67 *Prajñā* is in the dative case; there is an alternate reading in the locative.
68 Olivelle translated this as 'breath' in 1996 but 'wind' in 1998. 69 Discussed also in 7§A.
70 As at CU 3.18.1 (above).

(d) Three forms of reductionism occur sequentially in BU 3.7–8: first the wind is identified as 'the string on which this world and the next, as well as all beings, are strung together' (material reductionism); then the inner controller[71] of this world and the next and of all beings is identified as atman (subject reductionism); and finally all things are 'woven back and forth' on space, which is itself 'woven back and forth' on the imperishable[72] (abstract reductionism).

(e) At KU (3.8) the image of a chariot wheel is introduced by 'there is no diversity in all this': the rim is like ten particles of being (speech, odour, form, sound, etc.) fastened to the spokes (particles of intelligence [*prajñā*]: the speaker, the one who smells it, the one who sees it, the hearer, etc.), which are in turn fastened to the hub, which is *breath*, which is also 'the self consisting of intelligence', bliss, unageing, immortal, and the ruler of the world.[73] This is an elaborate form of reductionism to breath.

(f) More modestly, in KU 4.20 there merges into the breath of a sleeping man a whole series of things: certain veins, his speech with all the names, his sight with all the forms, and so on.

However, breath – unlike perception and thought – is perceptible, and has no object, and was replaced – as the unitary subject or inner self – by the more abstract, purely subjective entity denoted by atman (6§D).

(6) Mental Monism and Abstract Monism Coalesce

Almost immediately after the image of salt dissolved in water as an image for the atman as a limitless 'single mass of perceptions' we learn that 'after death there is no awareness'. This is then explained. When there is no 'duality' (*dvaita*), when:

> the Whole has become one's very atman,[74] then who is there to smell and by what means? Who is there for one to see and by what means? . . . [and similarly for hearing, thinking, greeting, and perceiving][75]

[71] *Antaryāmin*, inner restraint, checking the internal feelings; it means soul in some later texts.

[72] *Akṣara*, imperishable, unalterable (it also means syllable or letter). It is then specified as powerful, beyond measure, perceiving but imperceptible, thinking but unthinkable, et al. Cf. SB 10.4.1.9.

[73] Cf. BU 2.5.15: atman as hub and rim of wheel, with everything else as spokes; RV 1.32.15; the king encompasses different peoples like a rim the spokes of a wheel; cf.1.35.6; 1.129.8; 1.141.9; 2.4.2; 4.1.1; 4.2.1; 4.30.15; 4.36.2; SB 1.4.2.15 (Agni encompassing the gods like the rim the spokes).

[74] Cf. e.g. BU 2.5.1 Atman 'is the immortal; it is brahman; it is the Whole'. Atman is identified with the whole world (*sarva*) already at SB 4.5.9.8: but see Deussen (1915) 173–4. Ganeri (2012: 36) describes the Upanishadic self as 'a sense of being present everywhere; better, a sense of being stripped of a sense of being somewhere'.

[75] BU 2.4.14; also at 4.5.15–16.

The universality of the subject means that there is no object separate from itself, no 'second reality'.[76] The passage continues:

> By what means can one perceive him by means of whom one perceives this whole world? Look – by what means can one perceive the perceiver?

Not only is there no object beyond the subject, but the subject is itself imperceptible:

> You can't see the seer who does the seeing; you can't hear the hearer who does the hearing; you can't think of the thinker who does the thinking; you can't perceive the perceiver who does the perceiving. The atman within all this is this atman of yours.[77]

All we apprehend is the *content* of hearing and thought etc., not hearing and thinking itself. The new unitary, comprehensive inner self (atman) is present in seeing and thinking etc. ('within all this'), and so cannot be identical with any single one of them, either as itself or as its content: neither itself nor its content can be apprehended. It may be imagined only negatively: 'about this atman one can only say "not–, not–." He is ungraspable, for he cannot be grasped'.[78]

And so there is nothing beyond the universal subject, which is imperceptible. Mental monism and abstract monism coalesce to form something else, a single ungraspable abstract entity that transcends the distinction between subject and object[79] and so is neither of them. Atman is brahman.

And yet the entity *is*, inevitably, characterised. The atman is smaller than a mustard seed and larger than 'all these worlds' (CU 3.14.3). 'When a man sees, hears, or discerns no other thing – that is *bhūman*',[80] which is immortal and ubiquitous (CU 7.24): we will discuss this remarkable passage in 15§C.

The ungraspable may be approached by *metaphor* (10§C). We have seen a string of metaphors for atman at BU 2.4.5–12: musical instruments emitting sound, fire emitting smoke, salt dissolved in water. Another string (CU 6.9–13) illustrate the *aṇiman* (minuteness, fineness, smallest particle) that is the atman. Honey[81] is 'a homogeneous whole' (6.9.1) that comes

76 BU 4.3.13–32.

77 BU 3.4.2; similarly 3.7.23 (quoted 6§D); 3.8.11; 4.3.23–30 Deussen (1906) 400, 403–4.

78 3.9.26; BU 4.2.4.

79 CU 2.5.19: Brahman is 'without an inner and an outer', is 'this atman here which perceives everything'.

80 Translated as 'abundance' by Roebuck (2003) and 'plenitude' by Olivelle.

81 Cf. RV 1.90.6–9; 4.57.2–3; BU 2.5; CU 3.1–10. Note the possible role for ritual in generating or transmitting such ideas: it is after uttering verses identifying honey with parts of the cosmos that a man says 'may I indeed become this whole world' (BU 6.3.6).

from nectar from a variety of trees. As honey, the nectar does not know from which tree it has come: this is said to illustrate (the purely abstract reductionism of) 'all these creatures merge into the existent'. Various rivers flow into the ocean, where they do not know which river they are. A huge tree is pervaded by sap, without which it withers away. The tiny seeds of a huge banyan tree are invisible when cut up.[82]

Other passages represent the coalescence of mental monism and abstract monism. The abstract reductionism (almost monism) of the imperishable woven on space is also mental reductionism: it 'sees but can't be seen; hears but can't be heard, etc'. (3.8.11). At CU 3.12.7–9 brahman is identified with space outside a person, which is identified with space within a person, which is identified with space within the heart.[83] Here the distinction between the objective (outside a person) and the subjective (within a person and within the heart) is transcended by the ubiquitous abstraction of space.

At CU 3.18.1 we read that:

> With respect to the atman one should venerate 'brahman is the mind', and with respect to the divine sphere 'brahman is space'. In this way, substitution (*ādiṣṭam*) is carried out in both spheres.

This is not monist, because there are two spheres, and yet it is close to monism in that each sphere is occupied by brahman, with the result that the two spheres may seem like aspects of an all-encompassing brahman, implying a combination of mental monism with abstract monism (space). The Upanishadic doctrine that atman is brahman[84] may approximate to the coalescence of mental monism with abstract monism (with subject and object as the aspects of the same totality), for example at CU 3.14, where it is stated both that brahman is 'this whole world' and that atman is brahman.

At BU.2.1.20 everything springs from atman, and moreover:

> its hidden connection (*upaniṣad*) is 'The real behind the real',[85] for the real consists of the vital functions and the atman is the real behind the vital functions.

Here, too, the identification of atman, as the source of everything, with the abstract 'real behind the real' combines mental monism with abstract monism.

82 Further metaphors for approaching the atman are at BU 2.1.20 and 2.4.7–11.
83 Similarly CU 3.18.1; 8.1.3.
84 Adumbrated at TB 3.12.9. Atman is self-sufficient, immortal, undecaying and autonomous already at AV 10.8.44; see also SB 10.6.3.2.
85 *Satyasya satya.*

This relation between the unitary-comprehensive and the abstract is paralleled in monetisation. Monetary value has to be unitary, comprehensive and abstract. Were it not unitary and comprehensive, it would not be money (in the sensibly narrow sense of money used in this book): it could not perform as a single entity the universal functions of measurement, payment and exchange that define money and make it convenient. But its unitary comprehensiveness also makes its value *abstract*. Like atman, monetary value *must* be negatively imagined as imperceptible (abstract): a universal measure must become detached from everything that is concrete and particular. It is by means of its distinctive abstractness that it seems to exercise control, like the 'inner controller'[86] atman.

This is more than just an analogy. Why did the *Upanishads* embark on the new and difficult task of imagining a comprehensive, unitary subject? Not because nature at this particular moment gave it to them (4§A). The development of such an idea is a historical process, in which some part was played by monetisation. In the *Rigveda* there is a single (late) example of present monism, and it is personal monism. In the *Brahmanas* we found several cases of present personal monism, and a striking instance of primordial mental monism. Most prominent in the early *Upanishads*, by contrast, are present mental monism and present abstract monism. The conceptual development is towards monism, in particular abstract and mental monism. This reflects the development of unitary abstract value; and the coalescence of mental monism with abstract monism reflects the combined introjection and projection (cosmisation) of unitary abstract value that influenced the metaphysics of India and Greece.[87]

8§D Monism and Immortality

Sacrifice conferred immortality on the sacrificer, in part by a journey to heaven or the obtaining of a loka. With the interiorisation of sacrifice, immortalisation remains, but through knowledge. As an example of how this may work, we return to the cosmogony in the opening of BU (6§C). In the beginning there was nothing but death (1.2.1), who – among other things – desires that his corpse become fit to be sacrificed so that he could get a living atman (1.2.7). The

[86] E.g. BU 3.7.23.

[87] Especially Parmenides (14§A) and *bhūman* (15§C); see also 6§A, 7§B, 8§B, 9§F, 13§E, 14§B, 15§A, 15§B, 16§A, 16§C.

corpse becomes a horse, which death sacrifices to himself. The horse sacrifice and the ritual fire:

> constitute in reality a single deity – they are simply death. (Whoever knows this) averts repeated death – death is unable to seize him, death becomes his very atman.

In this passage the merging of opposites – death with the living atman – is there both in the immortalising sacrifice and in immortalising knowledge. Moreover, death is also identified with sacrifice and ritual fire. Sacrifice exercised power (including the power to immortalise) through correspondences or equivalences of elements of ritual with elements of universe and of self (8§B), and when sacrifice is interiorised it is the knowledge of how things *coalesce* into one (reductionism, tending towards monism) that bestows immortality. Immortalisation accompanies monism.

Accordingly, in BU 4.4.18–19 (quoted in 8§C [4]) mortality or repeated death is associated with diversity, in verses introduced as being about the distinction between the corpse (like the sloughed skin of a snake) and the 'non-corporeal (*aśarīra*) and immortal lifebreath (prana)', which is brahman (4.4.7). The verses distinguish between on the one hand an ancient path to the heavenly world followed by knowers of brahman, and on the other hand the blind darkness entered by people who worship in ignorance or delight in learning (8–10). We must discover the atman, which has 'entered this body, this dense jumble' (13). We must know the breathing behind breathing, the sight behind sight etc., so as to perceive the unity of brahman and avoid the repeated death that goes with seeing diversity (18–19). Salvation depends on the monistic vision. Similarly, Parmenides' abstract monism, deriving in part from the unity of the internal content of the mind (12§A), is presented as mystic revelation – i.e. by implication designed to bring salvation – involving choice between a better and a worse path (11§D).

The better and the worse path after death appear again (at BU 6.2 and CU 5.4–10) in the so-called two-path doctrine, with which there is a remarkable set of similarities with Herakleitos (9§D), who – no less that Parmenides – both insisted on the unity of all things (B50) and presented his doctrine as mystic revelation (11§C); and much the same can be said of Plato (11§E).

8§E Chapter 6 of the *Chāndogya Upaniṣad*

I conclude this chapter with an example of the functioning and interaction *in a continuous text* of tendencies and preconceptions that I have hitherto analysed merely by giving isolated examples. It will involve some contextualisation of passages discussed earlier in the chapter. It will also introduce us to an idea complementary to the monism that we have hitherto prioritised, namely the idea that there are a few basic impersonal elements, of which all else (or almost all else) is a mixture. This idea, which I call minimal pluralism, is not as prominent in the early *Upanishads* as is monism. But it had lasting influence in India, as well as in Europe by virtue of its presence in Aristotle.

In a dialogue with his son Svetaketu, Aruni starts by introducing:

> the rule of substitution,[88] by which one hears what has not been heard of before, thinks of what has not been thought of before, and perceives what has not been perceived before (CU 6.1.2).

The rule is illustrated by identifying as real – in different things – their material (clay, copper, iron):

> the transformation is a verbal handle, a name – while the reality is just this: "It's copper" (6.1.4–6).

Svetaketu has learnt all the Vedas and is arrogant, but does not know this 'rule of substitution', rather as Herakleitos (B40), for whom all things are in reality fire, also maintains that 'much learning does not teach understanding'.[89]

The antithesis between names and reality also occurs in the fragments of Parmenides (B8.38–41), and the assimilation of different things to each other by virtue of what is real – their material – resembles the material monism of the Milesian philosophers (12§A) (without there being any attempt by Aruni to reduce *everything* to one material). Aruni then tells his son about the rule of substitution by moving straight on to cosmogony: 'in the beginning this world was simply what is existent – only one, without a second' (6.2.2). For 'how can what is existent be born from what is non-existent?' This argument is also used by Parmenides (B8.7–10) for what exists having no beginning. But for Aruni the abstract monism is (in contrast to Parmenides) merely primordial: the existent 'thought to itself "Let me become many. Let me propagate myself"' (6.2.3). It emitted heat, which emitted water, which emitted food.

88 *ādeśa*, in the grammatical tradition the rule by which one form of a word stands as a substitute for another, with the substitute behaving like the original: Ganeri (2012) 32–3.

89 Cf. also e.g. CU 7.1.3: 'Here I am, a man who knows all the Vedic formulas but is ignorant of the self'; BU 3.5.1; 4.4.21; KaU 2.23.

We have in CU 6.1–2 moved quickly from a suggestion of material monism to primordial abstract monism, primordial personal monism and minimal pluralism. Heat, water and food are then each entered by the deity 'with this living atman' (6.3). Each is fundamental in the sense that the red appearance of fire (and of anything reddish) is in fact the appearance of heat ('so vanishes from fire the character of fire'), and similarly with the white appearance of water and the black appearance of food. The 'rule of substitution' is then restated explicitly: 'the transformation is a verbal handle, a name – while the reality is just, "It's the three appearances"'. Indistinct things are 'a combination of these same three deities' (6.4). We are reminded of the presocratic Empedokles' doctrine of four basic elements (fire, air, water, earth), identified with deities (B6), with all else arising from their mixture (16§B).

CU 6.5. then tells us how each human is constituted by food, water and heat, with mind, breath and speech constituted by the finest food, finest water and finest heat, respectively (compare the Ionian tendency to identify soul or mind with very fine matter, as in Anaximenes, Herakleitos and Anaxagoras). This is then confirmed by considerations adduced in 6.6 and 6.7. In 6.8. just as the bud requires root (food), so food as bud looks to water as root, water to heat and heat to the existent. This is abstract reductionism that approaches monism: 'the existent is the root of all these creatures – the existent their resting place, the existent is their foundation'.

The rest of the chapter consists of eight sections (6.9–16). The first two restate abstract reductionism approaching monism: 'all these creatures merge into the existent', without awareness that they are doing so, just as nectar gathered by bees becomes 'a homogeneous whole' in which it is unaware of its origin in a particular tree, or (6.10) just as rivers that have merged into the ocean are unaware of being particular rivers. Each branch of a tree contains sap, identified with living (*jīva*) atman. When *jīva* leaves the tree, the tree dies, but *jīva* itself does not die (6.11). The seed of a banyan can be cut into invisible parts, which nevertheless account for the huge banyan tree (6.12). This resembles Greek *atomism* (16§B). There follow the invisible pervasion of water by salt (6.13), a wanderer arriving home after being freed from a blindfold, with the arrival interpreted – it seems – as merging into the existent[90] (6.14), an ill man losing consciousness, with his voice merging into his mind, his mind into his breath, his breath into heat and heat into the highest deity (6.15), and finally an

[90] Olivelle (1996) 351.

innocent man in a fire ordeal being prevented by his atman from being burnt (6.16).

It is significant that the chapter consists mostly – despite its diversity – of three kinds of ontological privileging: of (a) the homogeneous, (b) the invisible and (c) the pervasive.

(a) The *homogeneous* – what individual things have in common (copper, heat, existence, water, vital sap, etc.) – is privileged ontologically over the individuals themselves (copper trinkets, red things, creatures, rivers, branches, etc.). Nectar gathered from various trees forms a homogeneous whole in which it feels undifferentiated.

(b) The ontological privileging of the *invisible* takes several forms. Firstly, an *abstraction*, the existent, is the primordial entity, as well as being the root or foundation of all else, and all creatures merge into it. Secondly, there are things in *nature* that are invisible (or not normally visible): the vital sap of a tree, salt dissolved in water. Food, water and heat in their finest forms rise to the top (like the finest part of curd rises to the top to become butter) as mind, breath and speech, i.e. become invisible. This overlaps with the third kind of invisibility, of the inner self (atman), which is identified with very fine matter (*aṇiman*). Finally, the ontological privilege is most explicit in the case of the banyan seeds divided into invisibility:

> This *aṇiman* (minuteness, fineness, smallest particle) here, son, that you can't even see – look how on account of that *aṇiman* this huge banyan tree stands here (CU 6.12.2).

(c) Sap *pervades* the tree, salt the water, existence everything.

There is in all this, as in most presocratic philosophy, no suggestion of any conscious distinction between abstract and concrete or between mind and matter. These distinctions (as we regard them) are ignored or confused in the various forms of ontologically privileged homogeneity, invisibility and pervasiveness. Nectar, rivers, sap, banyan seed and salt are each followed by the refrain:[91]

> the *aṇiman* here that constitutes the atman of this whole world; that is the truth; that is the atman. And that's how you are, Svetaketu.

[91] 6.8.15, though Brereton (1986) argues that the refrain occurred originally only at the end of section 12.

The idea of the finest particle is used here to approach what we would call a transcendent, abstract entity of consciousness that is comprehensive in that it unites all living creatures and is the whole world – as well as somehow underlying or containing the various concrete manifestations of individual consciousness.[92] The *combination* of homogeneity, invisibility and *all*-pervasiveness is confined to the existent and (by implication) the inner self (atman).

To conclude: the ubiquitous power behind the monist/reductionist tendency is illustrated by the *variety* of monism and of reductionism by which even this short chapter of the *Chāndogya Upaniṣad* is pervaded: we find primordial personal monism and abstract reductionism approaching monism, along with striking resemblances to the material monism of Miletos, to the abstract monism of Parmenides, to the minimal pluralism of Empedokles and to Greek atomism. And much or all of this is underpinned, explicitly or implicitly, by the same 'rule of substitution'. To the minimal pluralism and atomism I will return in 16§B.

Especially remarkable is the similarity between CU 6.2.1–2 and Parmenides B8. In both texts we find the distinction between reality and mere naming, together with the replacement of cosmogony by the argument that what exists cannot have arisen from what does not exist.[93] The similarity can be explained neither by influence (2§C) nor merely by the use of reason, but rather by the degree of abstraction with which reason is employed (2§D), abstraction that in turn requires an explanation that applies to both cultures. In 14§B I will provide for this shared novelty the kind of explanation – in terms of monetisation – that accounts for the pervasive monist or reductionist tendency that underlies the other remarkable convergences we have noted between presocratic philosophy and CU 6, as well as more generally the similarities between Indian and Greek thought in our period.

[92] Such transcendent consciousness is – in temporal mode – transmigration: already in the *Brahmanas* (AB 2.1.8); at SB 1.2.3.6 *medha* (translated here 'sap') is said to pass from man into various animals as sacrificial victims and finally into the earth. Cf. AA 2.3.2: atman as sap in plants and consciousness in animals.

[93] True, CU 6 then differs from Parmenides by making the existent become many, so that the abstract monism is merely primordial, but later in the section adopts a reductionism approaching present abstract monism with the repeated observation that 'all these creatures merge into the existent'.

CHAPTER 9

The Hereafter

9§A The Earliest Beliefs

In the semi-nomadic, largely pastoral world of the *Rigveda* there is barely any individual isolation from the community, and the conception of the universe is dominated by the aspiration of positive reciprocity between the offering community and the gods. Of human immortality and the afterlife, in which there is no extensive interest,[1] the dominant conception is of bodily existence (and pleasures) in the sky, with the dead individual generally imagined as irreversibly joining a *community* (of forefathers or gods).[2] Neither in the *Rigveda* nor in Homer is there any indication of the idea found in later texts of both cultures – that life is an inferior state from which escape is desirable.

However, the cosmology and eschatology found in the *Rigveda* are unsystematic. There are indications of the dead under the earth, sometimes for punishment.[3] Especially unusual is a hymn from the late tenth book (16). Verse 3 enjoins the cosmic dispersal of the body (into sun, wind, 'sky or earth', waters, the plants).[4] And verse 5 should be translated, according to a detailed argument by Jurewicz,[5] as follows:

> Release him to his forefathers and again down from them, [him] who, poured into you, travels according to his will. Let him, who wears life, come to his offspring. Let him unite with his body (*tanvā*), Jātavedas.[6]

[1] In the RV *amṛta* ('non-death'), which subsequently meant 'immortality', is not common for humans, and may mean living a complete span of life: Blutzenberger (1996) 68–9; RV 1.125.6.

[2] 6§B; Keith (1925) 406–9. There is the occasional threat of the 'lap of dissolution', from which the dead can be protected or liberated by offerings: 10.19.10; 10.161.2–3.

[3] Horsch (1971) 106; Keith (1925) 409–10: Oberlies (2012) 318–9 notes that the idea of an afterlife in the sky belongs to a later layer of the RV than do the allusions to an afterlife beneath the earth.

[4] This reappears at SB 10.3.3.8 and then in BU 3.2.13.

[5] Jurewicz (2004), (2008), (2010) 305–10: accepted by Gombrich (2013) 30–3. Jurewicz also argues that verse 13 should be translated 'O Agni, sow again the one you burnt [before]!'

[6] Agni as knower of creatures.

This exemplifies, according to Jurewicz, the idea – found in many small-scale societies – that the dead are reborn in their offspring, a form of what I will call 'lineage reincarnation'. At RV 10.14.8 she interprets 'come home again, unite with your body (*tanvā*)' in the same sense. Both passages have been interpreted differently.[7] There are, despite some claims to the contrary, no other passages of the *Rigveda* that substantially prefigure the later Indian doctrine of reincarnation,[8] though there are passages that indicate the idea that offspring represent the continuation of their parents or grandparents.[9] To lineage reincarnation I will return in 10§A.

In the beyond as imagined in the *Rigveda* the *devaloka* (world[10] of the gods) and the *pitṛloka* (world of the forefathers) are indistinct from each other, as are also the paths associated with them, the *devayāna* and *pitṛyāna*.[11] It is only later, in the *Atharvaveda*, that the distinction becomes clear.[12] Later again, in the *Brahmanas*, we see substantial development. The *devaloka* becomes preferable to the *pitṛloka*.[13] Repeated death (*punarmṛtyu*) in the afterlife, for which models are provided by sun and moon, is frequently feared,[14] and at SB 10.4.3.10 it is distinguished from being born after death for immortality. But repeated death (in the beyond) is not yet the same as a repeated (cyclical) passage between this world and the next.

9§B From Ritual Action to Metaphysical Merit

Much of the *Rigveda* is devoted to obtaining the goodwill of gods, whether by requests or through praise or offerings.[15] As for obtaining well-being and immortality in the afterlife, this may be requested directly,[16] or be imagined – at least in relatively late hymns – to depend on what is offered.[17]

An offering has the power to obtain goodwill from the recipient, from which may result (reciprocal) benefit to the donor: the donor acquires

[7] The latter as referring to rejoining the body in the sacrifice.

[8] Other passages of RV that have been claimed to prefigure reincarnation are rightly dismissed by Horsch (1971) 101–5; Keith (1925) 570–2.

[9] 5.4.10; 6.16.35; 6.70.3; 10.1.7; 10.63.13; Blutzenberger (1996) (1998) 69–70; Oberlies (2012) 325–6.

[10] For the complex meaning of loka, see 6§B.

[11] E.g. RV 10.88.15–16; 10.2.3, 7; 10.14.7; 10.16.1–2; Horsch (1971) 110.

[12] AV 12.2.10; 18.4.1–2; etc.; Horsch (1971) 110; Killingley (1997) 16.

[13] Horsch (1971) 110–1; Collins (1982) 44–6.

[14] E.g. SB 2.3.3.9; 10.1.4.14; 10.4.3.10; 11.5.6.9; TB 3.10.11.2; 3.11.8.5–6; JB 1.23; KB 25.1; Keith (1925) 573; Collins (1982) 46–7; Deussen (1906) 326–7; Smith (1989) 118 n.196; Gonda (1975) 366–7.

[15] E.g. 6.28.2: 'Indra aids him who offers sacrifice and gifts: he takes not what is his, and gives him more thereto. Increasing ever more and ever more his wealth, he makes the pious dwell within unbroken bounds.'

[16] E.g. 9.113.7–8; 10.15.4. [17] 1.125.6; 10.107.2; cf.10.14.8; 10.15.4; 10.16.4.

benefit *indirectly*. But to the extent that this power is imagined separately from the recipient, the offering will seem (like money) capable of obtaining well-being *automatically*. There then may develop the idea of an *accumulation* of offerings or gifts that is imagined, separately from any recipient, to promote well-being for the donor.

In the Vedic texts we can detect this development. It is in 10.14.8, a late and innovative passage,[18] that there occurs the only mention in the *Rigveda* of what is accumulated in the next world by action in this one: *iṣṭāpūrta* (described in 5§D). Another term with a similar range of meaning is *sukṛta*, literally '(what is) well done'. It refers to 'the lasting, the effective and positive result of the correct performance of the ritual acts [which] accumulate for the benefit of the performer [in the next world]'. Its opposite, *duskṛta*, refers to 'omissions, negligence or reprehensible behaviour in the ritual or religious sphere', resulting in the diminution or destruction of the individual's afterlife realm.[19] The basic meaning of *sukṛta* and *duskṛta* is good action and bad action respectively, but there is a close relation between action and substance: *sukṛta* is 'lasting merit' that (a) results from actions, (b) accumulates for the benefit of the performer in the future and (c) can also be diminished. In sacrifice wealth was used to obtain well-being in the afterlife. Monetisation promotes the idea of accumulating through action a *store* of wealth (money) with which anything can be obtained, and this leads to the idea of a store of money in the afterlife to obtain or maintain well-being there.

In the *Rigveda* there is reward for good action (*sukṛta*, 10.95.17), and even a loka of *sukṛta* (10.85.24). But it is not until the *Atharvaveda* (roughly speaking) that priests by ritual action reach the loka of *sukṛta* in the afterlife:[20] this implies that what is accumulated by ritual action is stored in the afterlife, independently of the gods. At TS 5.7.7 Agni takes various offerings to heaven for their donors to enjoy after death – an egocentric development of the common practice of making offerings to the dead.

Individual egocentricity or autonomy of this kind is made explicit at SB 6.2.2.27:

> when he becomes initiated, he makes for his atman that loka beforehand, and he is born into the loka made by him: hence they say, Man is born into [or for] the loka that has been made [by him?].

[18] See 4§A, where it is quoted. [19] Gonda (1966) 125–9, quoted by Tull (1989) 31.

[20] Horsch (1971) 128; AV 6.119.1, 120.1, 121.1; 7.83.4; 16.9.2; 11.4.6; 11.14.6. These texts (or parts of them) are in fact found in a number of other texts (see the Commentary on the *Atharvaveda* by Whitney and Lanman [1905]), which may be earlier than their appearance in the AV. See also 18.2.60 treasure in heaven.

The sacrificer eats in the afterlife with a frequency varying with the sacrifices performed (SB 10.1.5.4). For instance 'Verily, he who (regularly) performs the Agnihotra eats food in the evening and in the morning (when he comes to be) in yonder world, for so much sustenance is there in that sacrifice.' Gonda discusses texts in which 'there is a more or less fixed relation between the ritual acts and the merits gained by them on the one hand and the loka resulting from them on the other'.[21] A single offering may obtain a variety of valuable things (AV 9.5.22–36). The quasi-commercial impersonality of the process of assigning good and ill in the afterlife is indicated by the operation there of a pair of scales (SB 11.2.7.33). The good and evil done by the dead are in heaven *quantified* (JB 1.18). What is new about the *Brahmanas* is described by Deussen thus:

> In place of the ancient Vedic conception of an indiscriminate felicity of the pious, the idea of recompense is formulated, involving the necessity of setting before the departed different degrees of compensation in the other world proportionate to their knowledge and actions.[22]

Yet another word that moved from ritual action to general metaphysical merit is *karman* (karma).[23] The principle expressed at BU 3.2.13, 'One becomes good by good action (*karman*) and bad by bad', is generally held to prefigure the classical doctrine of karma.[24]

9§C Metaphysical Merit and Repeated Death

It is not only repeated death that is to be feared in the afterlife but also the diminution or destruction of what has been accumulated there for the well-being (including immortality) of the sacrificer. In SB 2.3.3.8–11 the alternation of day and night destroys sacrificial merit (*sukṛta*), which can however be 'freed' from death by the right ritual. In KB 7.4 the destruction of sacrifice is prevented by *śraddhā* (faith, confidence). The *sukṛta* and loka obtained by some sacrifices are imperishable.[25]

The idea of repeated death (*punarmṛtyu*) occurs only in later Vedic texts. Why did it occur, and why did it occur when it did? Bodewitz (1996) argues convincingly against all the explanations previously offered, before advancing his own. He notes that the problem of *punarmṛtyu* always turns up

[21] Gonda (1966) 137; AV 3.29.3; 9.5.22. [22] Deussen (1906) 324.
[23] Gombrich (1996) 31; (2006) 46.
[24] Even if *karman* here retains an association with *sacrificial* action: 7§A n.11.
[25] SB 1.6.4.16; 2.3.3.11; 2.3.6.1; Gonda (1966) 125–30.

together with its solution, and that 'it is especially connected with the topic of the transitoriness of the (mostly ritual) merits'. And so

> the problem of *punarmṛtyu*, introduced together with its solution and with emphasis on this solution, reflects the reaction of the ritualists to attempts made by non-ritualists to devalue the ritualistic claims. The ritualists probably tried to refute the opinion of other circles that ultimately the merits become exhausted in heaven (36).

But the 'refutations' claimed non-ritual as well as ritual ways of overcoming repeated death, and so it is misleading to ascribe them to 'the ritualists' alone. And why should the criticism be specifically the exhaustibility of sacrificial merit? There are many other, more obvious ways of indicating the inefficacy of ritual. And why did the problem of diminishing merit occur no earlier than it did? To this last question Bodewitz might answer that it was produced by the relative marginalisation of ritual manifest in late Vedic texts. But why then did the marginalisation occur no earlier? Bodewitz (1996: 34) also notes that 'the concept of redeath lost its significance as soon as the concepts of rebirth and release had become accepted. The limited period in which *punarmṛtyu* played a role indicates that it belonged to a period of transition to new ideas.' What caused the transition?

In a detailed discussion Blutzenberger identifies various eschatological conceptions in Vedic texts that, he argues, came together to form the doctrine of transmigration.[26] His description of the development and merging of these conceptions is for the most part as purely intellectual (internal) processes.[27] A crucial step towards the idea of transmigration he describes as follows (107):

> In considering and evaluating the effect of a ritual act, some *Brahmanas* made the disturbing discovery that the individual amount of *karman*, once achieved, was not imperishable, but liable to diminution, and to wearing away (*kṣaya*, e.g. JB 2.53 f.).

It is odd to describe an imagined feature of an imaginary construct as the object of a disturbing discovery. The question should be: why did they take the steps of imagining *karman* as substance and of imagining that it was liable to diminution? And if the 'discovery' of its perishability was so 'disturbing', why did they not imagine – as has so often been imagined of metaphysical entities – that it was imperishable?

[26] Blutzenberger (1996) and (1998).

[27] The only factor he mentions external to the texts themselves is the replacement of inhumation by cremation (already in Rigvedic times).

None of the questions that I have asked in this section can be answered while ignoring the external factor of monetisation. This will become clearer in what follows. Here I confine myself to noting a non-ritual solution to the problem of repeated death. At TB 3.11.8 Naciketas is told to build the fire-altar so as to obtain the indestructability (*akṣiti*) of sacrifice and meritorious work (*iṣṭāpūrte*) and to keep off repeated death.[28] This is a ritual solution, which is followed immediately by a non-ritual solution, the narrative described in 5§D: Prajapati throws gold three times into the sacrificial fire, which was not pleased by the gold, and so he throws the gold into himself, his own heart.[29] Hence gold is the dearest of all valued objects, and the smallest (this refers to the high value of a small amount). The gold is then identified with the *dakṣiṇā* (sacrificial offering or payment), which Prajapati keeps for himself (not having found anybody to give it to), thereby making himself able.[30] Here we have, as in Plato,[31] the individual interiorisation of both ritual and money. What matters for our overall argument is that the individual by interiorising money can avoid repeated death.

9§D Metaphysical Merit and Cyclical Hereafter

This section focuses on a passage that appears with minor variations in both BU 6.2 and CU 5.4–10. It starts with the so-called five-fire doctrine, which consists in the transformation into each other of five fundamental entities through the intermediary of fire, ending with man, who is cremated. There then follows[32] the so-called two-path doctrine, in which the first phase consists of passing into the flame (*devayāna*, path of the gods) or the smoke (*pitṛyāna*, path of the forefathers). The *devayāna* leads ultimately to brahman (CU 5.10.2) or – for some 'exalted people' – 'the worlds of brahman', in which 'they live', and from which 'they do not return' (BU 6.2.15); whereas the *pitṛyāna* leads in both versions eventually to the moon, where they remain 'as long as there is a residue' (CU 5.10.5), then in both versions return to earth and are reborn, and (only at BU 6.2.16) 'rising up again to the heavenly worlds, they circle round in the same way'.

28 Cf. SB 10.4.3.10: a certain kind of knowledge, and the laying down of the fire-altar, make the difference between immortality and repeated death.

29 At AV 10.2.29 the atman is in a golden treasure chest in a citadel. At TU 1.6.1 the immortal person (within the heart) that consists of mind is golden.

30 Elsewhere it is the immortality (SB 4.6.1.6) or life and energy (SB 12.7.2.13) identified with gold that is interiorised.

31 Pl. *Republic* 416e (10§D) and 11§E.

32 The two doctrines are integrated in so far as the cremation fire that concludes the five-fire passage can be seen as the fire that is the first phase of each of the two paths.

The *devayāna* is followed by 'those who know this (the five-fire doctrine) and those there in the wilderness who venerate truth as faith (*śraddhā*)';[33] whereas the *pitṛyāna* is followed by 'those who win heavenly worlds by offering sacrifices, by giving gifts, and by performing austerities' (BU 6.2.16), or 'the people here in the villages who venerate thus: gift-giving is *iṣṭāpūrta*' (CU 5.10.3).

Various points need to be made about this innovative narrative.

(1) Although the fear of repeated death (*punarmṛtyu*) is already present in the *Brahmanas*, the two-path doctrine describes something new: the repeated cosmic cyclicality of the hereafter, from which escape is possible. The newness of this subsequently widespread conception emerges from Killingley's examination of several passages (in the *Brahmanas* and *Upanishads*) that are similar to the five-fire and two-path doctrines.[34] Showing that they were used by a redactor to produce BU 6.2 and CU 5.10, he notes firstly that:

> in all these texts [those similar to the five-fire doctrine] we are presented with a linear series, not a cycle. They were worked into a cycle by our redactor, who clearly did not get all his ideas ready-made from some hypothetical non-Aryan circle, but operated with material derived from the Vedic tradition of ritual and cosmological thought.[35]

He also notes that the Five Fires and the Two Paths occur together only at BU 6.2 and CU 5.10. The redactor's principal innovations, he concludes, were to bring together the two groups of material pertaining to these two doctrines, and to 'transform each of them from a linear series into a cycle'.[36] We may add that a factor in the advent of this cyclical eschatology was surely the debt-driven cosmic cycle to which the sacrificer is subjected in the sacrifice (5§B).

(2) In the *Bṛhadāraṇyaka Upaniṣad* version those who take the *pitṛyāna* are, when they reach the moon, eaten by the gods, and return to earth to be reborn.[37] In the *Chāndogya Upaniṣad* version they (described as giving offerings as *iṣṭāpūrta*) go to the moon, which the gods eat, and

[33] BU 6.2.15; CU 5.10.1 differs by having 'austerity is faith' (cf. BU 4.4.22).

[34] SB 11.2.2.1; 11.6.2; JB 1.45–6; MU 2.1.5; TU 2.1: CU 6.2–5; cf. JB 1.1–2.

[35] Killingley (1997) 13; for the two-path doctrine as combining earlier themes see also Fujii (2011).

[36] Killingley (1997) 17. In later versions the two paths are abridged, so as to focus on the difference of destination: MU 1.2.10–11 states that only on one path is there return to this abject world when they have enjoyed the fruits of their good work atop the firmament, and on the other the permanent final goal through the sun's door; cf. PrU 1.9–10.

[37] The first substantial appearance of rebirth in this world is in the later *Brahmanas*: Horsch (1971) 142–55.

remain there as long as there is a *saṃpāta* (residue of sacrifice) before returning to earth for rebirth. The exhaustibility of what is produced by sacrifice (*iṣṭāpūrta*, *saṃpāta*) is what condemns them to rebirth.[38] Elsewhere we are told that sacrifices, offerings and the performance of austerities all 'come to naught' (BU 3.8.10), and 'in the hereafter a world won by merit (*puṇyajīta*) comes to an end' (CU 8.1.6). Those on the other hand who take the *devayāna* and so escape the cycle do so not by sacrificial offerings or merit but by knowledge.[39]

(3) Those who take the *pitṛyāna* and are eaten by the gods re-enter the cosmic food cycle (becoming food on earth before being reborn, and so on). In several Vedic texts social power, imagined as eating (of the weak by the powerful), is projected as a cosmic food chain:[40] and so permanent escape from the cosmic food cycle (by following the *devayāna*) is a projection of a new kind of self-sufficiency, undisturbed by human relations of power and exploitation.[41] Such self-sufficiency is aspired to in this world and in the hereafter on *both* the paths:

> May we be debtless in this, debtless in the other, debtless in the third, world! What paths there are trodden by the gods and trodden by the forefathers – may we abide debtless on all (those) paths! (TB 3.7.9.8; similarly AV 6.117.3).

In this era the absence of writing with which to record debt may have required debts to be inscribed instead in the minds of creditors and debtors, with enslavement resulting from failure to pay.[42] The metaphysical importance of debt[43] is best understood in the context of the development of settled agriculture and individual ownership, with vast numbers of landless people left permanently in the power of the individual owners.[44]

38 Not (as in the BU version) being eaten by the gods (in CU it is the moon that the gods eat). Olivelle notes that *saṃpāta* generally refers to the residue of sacrifice, but takes it here to mean the residue of the moon being eaten. But this would imply the total disappearance of the moon, which is unlikely (and cf. 'Decrease! Increase!' in BU 6.2.16). There is no reason why *saṃpāta* cannot mean what it normally does: it is giving offerings as *iṣṭāpūrta* that distinguishes these people from those who escape the cycle. The *Bhāgavata Puraṇa* 3.32.1–3 (18.21) states that a man whose merit (accumulated by sacrifice etc.) earns him after death abode in the moon must when the merit is exhausted return to earth. Note also Tull (1989) 35.

39 For a clear statement of the superiority of knowledge to procreation and ritual, see BU 1.5.16.

40 Smith (1990); Black (2007) 126.

41 Cf. e.g. SB 1.6.4.20: 'If one's hateful enemy thrives by trade or through any other means, he continually thrives in order to become food for him who knows this.' The eater of animals might fear being eaten by them in the next world: SB 6.1.2.19; Malamoud (1996) 165.

42 Debt-bondage is already in a hymn of the RV (10.34.4); for its subsequent development see Chakravarti (1985) 39–50. The phenomenon has been widespread: Graeber (2011).

43 5§B, 10§C.

44 Chakravarti (1985) 44–7.

(4) Our two passages are the two early Upanishadic passages most emphatically associated with Kshatriyas (7§A).

(5) The best heavenly destination (for some exalted people) is in the end not the community of forefathers, or even of gods, but permanent access to the abstract universal brahman, which embodies a fusion of the invisible power of ritual with unchanging abstract value.[45]

(6) The elevation of knowledge over ritual and offerings belongs to the individualisation and interiorisation of the sacrifice.[46]

(7) The two-path doctrine contains three basic elements not found in the earliest texts: (a) the repeated cosmic cyclicality of the afterlife, (b) the possibility of escape from the cycle and (c) an imagined substance that can be accumulated and stored in the next world but which runs out, after which there is re-entry into the cycle. This new configuration prefigures – and probably does not predate by much if at all – the classical doctrine of karma and EIR, with (a) corresponding to *saṃsāra*, (b) to *mokṣa* and (c) to karma.

The relationship between store and cycle is not yet developed, and not yet thoroughly ethicised – although EIR *does* appear in the very next passage of the *Chāndogya Upaniṣad*:[47]

> people here whose behaviour is pleasant can expect to enter a pleasant womb, like that of a woman of one of the Brahmin, the Kshatriya, or the Vaisya class, whereas people of foul behaviour can expect to enter a foul womb, like that of a dog, a pig, or an outcaste woman (5.10.7).

Further, BU 4 contains various accounts of reincarnation,[48] culminating in 4.4.6:

> a man who is attached goes with his action (*karman*),
>   to that very place to which
>   his mind and character cling.
> Reaching the end of his *karman*,
>   of whatever he has done in this world –
> From that world he returns
>   back to this world
>   back to *karman*.

[45] 5§C, 16§C.

[46] 5§C. For Tull (1989: 34) the distinction between the *pitṛyāna* and the *devayāna* is 'between a traditional path of worship, one that maintains the relationship between gods, priests, and sacrificers and a path that concentrates on the individual to the point of actually "interiorising" the sacrifice'.

[47] 5.10.7, perhaps a later addition: it comes alongside mention of those who proceed on neither of the two paths and become 'tiny creatures revolving here endlessly' (cf. similar at the end of BU 6.2.16).

[48] 4.3.8; 4.3.35; 4.4.3–5 (cf. 3.2.13); Obeyesekere (2002) 4–7; McDermott (1984) 29.

> That is the course of a man who desires. Now a man who does not desire, who is freed from desires, whose desires are fulfilled, whose only desire is his self, his pranas do not depart. Brahman he is and to brahman he goes.

Like the two-path doctrine, this distinguishes between on the one hand running out of substance accumulated by action and so having to return to this world and on the other hand attaining immortality and brahman. But it is less ritualist, and more general and abstract: *iṣṭāpūrta* and *saṃpāta* (both sacrificial on the *pitṛyāna*) have been replaced by desire and action,[49] and knowledge (on the *devayāna*) has been replaced by freedom from all desires except for desire for the self.

The cyclical combination of five-fire and two-path doctrines is an innovative and comprehensive vision in which immortality, and avoiding repeated death, depend on knowledge of the transformation into each other of five fundamental entities through the intermediary of fire. The better and worse paths appear also in BU 4.4 (8–10) – one to the heavenly world, the other to blind darkness – with the former followed by the knower of brahman, which is 'beheld by the mind alone', whereas the latter is followed by people who delight in learning, and repeated death is undergone by he who sees diversity (8§D). All this resembles the innovative vision of Herakleitos, in which the inner self is transformed from and into fire in a cosmic cycle driven by the transformative effect of fire (13§D), 'better deaths obtain better fates',[50] mere learning is dismissed[51] and the importance of *understanding* is repeatedly emphasised:[52] for instance 'it is wise to agree that all things are one' (B50), a unity perceptible only by the mind. True, the escape from the cycle into permanent well-being (the *devayāna*) has no counterpart in the surviving fragments of Herakleitos, but it is found in many other Greek texts of our period (14§D).

(8) This resemblance prompts me to address the claim by McEvilley (2002), following West (1971), that (yet another) similarity between the five-fire/two-path doctrine and Herakleitos results from *influence* (from India to Greece). This is the 'single specific connection between Herakleitos and Upanisadic doctrine' that according to McEvilley 'demonstrates that philosophical doctrines were in fact travelling between India and Greece in the pre-Socratic period'.

[49] Even if *karman* here retains an association with *ritual* action: 7§A n.11.
[50] B25, B136; cf. B63; KRS 207–8. [51] B40: see 8§E.
[52] Hklt. B1, B2, B17, B32, B50, B41, B101 etc.

Other similarities are, he concedes, not so significant in this respect.[53] To reinforce my rejection of 'influence' in 2§C, I here subject McEvilley's prime exhibit to scrutiny. Anybody already convinced by 2§C will lose little by jumping to 9§E.

The crucial similarity is between, on the one hand, the Herakleitean doctrine that the *psuchē* (soul) is composed (primarily at least) of fire (13§D), together with his B36:

> For *psuchai* (souls) it is death to become water, for water death to become earth, water becomes from earth, and *psuchē* from water;

and, on the other hand, the Upanishadic doctrine represented by the following five passages:

(a) BU 3.2.10, in which 'Death is fire, and it is the food of water.'

(b) CU 6.2.3–4, in which the one (world) emits heat, the heat emits water and the water emits food.

(c) KU 2.11–12:

> Next the 'dying around of the deities'. The brahman shines forth here when the fire is burning; but when the fire stops burning it dies, and its radiance goes to the sun and its lifebreath to the wind.

This is then repeated three times, but with fire/burning replaced successively by sun/shining, moon/shining, and lightning/flashing, and ending:

> When they have entered the wind all these deities do not lose their self-identity but emerge from it again. That was with respect to the deities. Next with respect to the body (atman).

There follows the very same set of observations, but with fire/burning, sun/shining etc. replaced by speech/speaking, sight/seeing, hearing/hearing and mind/thinking, and with 'the wind' replaced throughout by 'one's breath'.

(d) BU 6.2.9–16. In the five-fire doctrine five entities – the world up here, a rain cloud, this world down here, a man and a woman – are each called a fire. Then in the two-path doctrine some people 'pass into' (*abhisaṃbhavanti*) the flame, the day, the fortnight of the waxing moon, the six months when the sun moves north, the world of the gods, the sun and the region of lightning, whence they are led to the worlds of brahman, where

[53] McEvilley (2002) xxxi, 39–44.

they live. Other people (on the other path) 'pass into' smoke, night, the fortnight of the waning moon, the six months when the sun moves south, the world of the forefathers and the moon, where they 'become' food, are eaten by the gods, then 'pass into' into sky, then wind, then rain, then earth, where they 'become' food, are 'again offered in the fire of man, then take birth in the fire of woman' and circle round again.

(e) CU 5.10.3–8. The five-fire doctrine is essentially the same as in BU, and the two-path doctrine is very similar. Some people follow a path similar to that in the BU, to be led finally by a 'person who is not human' to brahman. Other people follow another path (similar to that in BU) to the moon, whence 'they return by the same path they went – first to space, and from space to the wind. After the wind has formed it turns into (*bhavati*) smoke', which turns into thundercloud, which turns into rain cloud, which

> rains down.[54] On earth they spring up as rice and barley, etc., from which it is extremely difficult to get out. When someone eats that food and deposits the semen, from him one comes into being again.

West claims to find in passages (d) and (e) the sequence '*psuchē*, water, earth, water, *psuchē*',[55] which is similar enough to Herakleitos B36 to have influenced it.

One objection to this claim, apart from the considerations advanced in 2§C, is that it selects a small section of the whole cycle, which is itself one of the numerous Upanishadic passages describing sequences of correspondences, emissions and transformations of various kinds. Moreover, there is in the five Indian passages no inner self to correspond with the *psuchē*. What is subject to the cycle is not the inner atman,[56] which is anyway – in contrast to the fiery Herakleitean *psuchē* – not composed of a physical substance (let alone a physical substance that is transformed into other physical substances). Though the idea of a cycle of life and death may promote the idea of an

[54] The idea of a dead person returning to earth as rain is already present in the RV: Jurewicz (2004), (2008).

[55] West (1971) 186.

[56] The word *ātmā* (atman) occurs only once, in passage (c), where it is rightly translated 'body' by Olivelle, referring as it does to the *body within which* the movements of the radiance and lifebreath of brahman occur. It seems – from West (1971) 63–4 – that he has transferred 'soul' from KU 1.2, where the moon is said to wax on the pranas of those who depart from this world: but the word for pranas is translated by Olivelle as 'lifebreaths', and does not appear elsewhere in the passage.

incorporeal inner self, it can exist without it.[57] Indeed, those who go on the two paths are throughout clearly not envisaged as inner selves but as *people*, who are moreover *not* transformed into the various entities but rather are led to or 'pass into' them.[58] The only thing that they ever 'become' is food, which means that they are *eaten*. In the *Chāndogya Upaniṣad* version the wind (which they have entered) undergoes transformations, eventually into rain, and they 'spring up as rice and barley, etc.', to which however is added 'from which it is extremely difficult to get out', implying that they are *contained in* (rather than transformed into) the rice and barley etc. As for the other four passages, in none of them does anything *become* anything else (again in contrast to Herakleitos).

It is easily observed that fire is destructive but absorbed by water (passage [a]), that the world emits heat, that heat emits water (e.g. steam, perspiration) and that water emits food (fertility requires water) (passage [b]). Herakleitos, too, was no doubt influenced by his observation of physical processes; but his entirely unVedic identification of the cosmos and of the *psuchē* with fire has a rationale that reflects the development of Greek cosmology under the influence of mystic doctrine and monetisation.[59] Moreover, this kind of rationale can be extended to provide the context for understanding such similarities as there are (some undetected even in the books of West and McEvilley) between Herakleitos and Indian (Upanishadic and Buddhist) thought.[60]

McEvilley (2002: 40) contrasts Anaximenes' explanation of cosmological change as the rarefaction and condensation of his physical substrate (air) with Herakleitos B36, and claims that

> Herakleitos is in the tradition of Anaximenes, yet his description of the transformation sequence is quite different and, in terms of Greek evidence, unaccountable.

This odd remark expresses the need to find external influence at all costs. The Herakleitean inner self resembles the Anaximenean much more than it does the Upanishadic,[61] and B36 resembles a number of

57 At AB 2.1.8, a passage prefiguring reincarnation, the *medha* (translated here 'sap') that passes from man through a series of sacrificial animals is homogeneous and perhaps invisible but not incorporeal.

58 Olivelle informs me by email – about his translation 'pass into' of *abhisaṃbhavanti* – that "transformed into" is not possible, but "enter" is. A spatial meaning is implicit, because the dead also go to the night, moon, etc.

59 Seaford (2004) and Part D below.

60 See index of this book s. Herakleitos.

61 E.g. the world and inner self are composed of tenuous physical substances – air for Anaximenes (12§A), fire for Herakleitos.

other Greek texts.[62] In general presocratic philosophers, within a shared framework, do markedly differ from each other[63] in ways that cannot be simply called 'unaccountable' (and indeed are often from my perspective explicable).

Most strikingly, McEvilley, following West,[64] supposes Herakleitos to have propounded a dual exhalation of *psuchai* (souls) that corresponds with the two paths in (d) and (e). But if Herakleitos held such a fundamental and memorable belief, it is odd that it is absent from the copious fragments and testimonia. McEvilley depends mainly on a passage about Herakleitos in Diogenes Laertius (9.9–11), derived from Theophrastus, which has a detailed account of two kinds of cosmic exhalation, one bright (producing day and summer), the other dark (producing night and winter). And Aristotle[65] reports that Herakleitos equated *psuchē* with the material principle, namely 'the exhalation from which he compounds the other things'. However, the Diogenes Laertius passage has nothing at all about souls; and the attribution to Herakleitos of *two* exhalations was 'most probably based on a misunderstanding based on Aristotle's own dual-exhalation explanation of meteorological . . . events'.[66] Moreover, imagining the *psuchē* as an exhalation, or associating life and death with a cosmic cycle, could anyway easily occur without external influence.[67]

9§E Renunciation: Ajivikism, Jainism and Buddhism

There is a connection between the individualisation (and interiorisation) of sacrifice (5§C, 5§D) and renunciation (7§A). In controlling the cosmic-sacrificial cycle by interiorising it one may be thought to escape from its effects, and indeed interiorisation of the cycle comes close to renouncing it. According to Heesterman:

62 Seaford (1986).

63 E.g. condensation and rarefaction as explanations of change are – contrary to what McEvilley claims – *not* in fact typical.

64 McEvilley (2002) 41–4; West (1971) 149–51, 187–8.

65 *De Anima* A2, 405a24 = DK22 A15.

66 KRS 202 n.1 with detailed argument. If so, that would explain the absence of souls from the detailed account in Diogenes Laertius.

67 The somewhat different version of the two-paths doctrine at KU 1.2–3 resembles material on the Greek gold leaves (one path leads to reincarnation, another to permanent dwelling with the gods, with the latter reserved for those who answer a question by revealing their divine origin). The resemblances may derive from a common Indo-European heritage or have arisen independently (already at JB 1.18 the deceased is made to answer the question 'who are you?', and his good and bad deeds are *quantified*). McEvilley, following West again, this time derives both texts from the Egyptian Book of the Dead, which, however, has nothing about two paths and nothing about reincarnation.

> The renouncer can turn his back on the world because he is emancipated from the relations which govern it. He is a world unto himself, or rather, he has resumed the oppositions of the world in himself; there is no duality for him any more.[68]

And so

> the difference between classical ritualism and renunciation seems to be a matter rather of degree than of principle. The principle is the individualisation of the ritual, which could not but lead to its interiorisation.[69]

The renunciation of all wealth precludes all future payment of *dakṣiṇās*, and so is, according to Biardeau and Malamoud,

> to withdraw from the cycle of exchanges. The *saṃnyāsa* (state of renunciation) is a rupture with the world: the profane world as well as the sacrificial world; but even this rupture is presented as a sacrifice: the renouncer sacrifices the sacrifice, making it 'mount into him', interiorising his sacrificial fires, and alienating as *dakṣiṇā*, on this occasion, all the goods that would have allowed him to celebrate further sacrifices.[70]

We will now follow these developments into the doctrine of EIR. The doctrine is first indicated in the early *Upanishads* (9§D), and then acquired full form in Buddhism, Jainism and eventually Hinduism. The doctrine did of course take various forms, but our concern is with a core shared by India and Greece.

The fifth century BCE saw the earliest years of the popular and lasting sects of Jainism, Ajivikism and Buddhism, each attributed to a distinct founder. Ajivikism is extinct, but survived for centuries, and has been described as 'the predominant school in eastern India from Buddhist times down to the Mauryan period'.[71] These three 'Sramanic' sects had conceptions of the self that were (or had become) independent of Vedic sacrifice, which they rejected. This rejection is the extreme version of a tendency that is present even in the early *Upanishads*: it transcends the various religious currents, and cannot of course be explained by the birth of a particular individual such as the Buddha.

Money tends to isolate the individual (13§C). The three sects construct metaphysics out of the basic situation of the individual alone, integrated into society neither by ritual nor by kinship, in a monetised world. Here,

[68] Heesterman (1985) 39. Cf. BU 4.5.15. [69] Heesterman (1985) 41–2; (1993) 82.
[70] Biardeau and Malamoud (1976) 177 (my translation of the French). [71] Warder (1956) 44.

for instance, from an early Jain text, is a striking move from reality to metaphysics:

> When the monk realises that he is alone, that he has no connection with anyone and that no one has any connection with him, in the same way he should realise that his self is also alone.

In the same text we are told that

> Man, it is you who are your only friend. Why do you want a friend other than yourself?

These passages are cited by Dundas,[72] who also states that what was distinctive about early Jainism was a special sensitivity to the feelings of all creatures, with 'the resultant desire for, as the Jains put it, friendship with all creatures, which marks out Jainism as a religion with universal concerns at its very beginning'. The apparent paradox is instructive. The individual is isolated – by non-action – from the human group, even from his kin: various Jain texts[73] emphasise that even a person's closest relatives cannot share his karma or suffering. Accordingly, he may feel connected with all creatures. Comparably, 'the Buddha tells the monks that each should live as an island unto himself, guided by the *dharma* which is common to all'.[74] And Herakleitos notes both the fact of individualism and that individualism is contradicted by the communality of the *logos*, which inheres in the inner self.[75] As with money, individual isolation and universality go together.

Karma is important to all three of our sects, but in different forms. For Ajivikan doctrine we are reliant on Buddhist and Jain reports, which polemically misrepresent the doctrine. But where the reported doctrine is neither objectionable nor implausible, then any distortion may well be limited. Our earliest and most valuable account of Ajivikan doctrine is from the Buddhist *Sāmañña-phala Sutta* – karma can be neither brought to fruition nor exhausted by virtuous action, conduct, vows, penance or chastity (1.53):

> That cannot be done. *Saṃsāra* is measured out as with a bushel, with its joy and sorrow and its appointed end. It can neither be lessened nor increased, nor is there any excess or deficiency of it.[76]

[72] *Ācārāṅgasūtra* 1.8.6.1 and 1.3.3.4 (translation by Dundas (2002) 42); cf. Dundas (2002) 101. Cf. liberation from the birth-death cycle as achieving *aloneness* (*kaivalya*): *Kaivalya Upaniṣad* 25.

[73] *Sūtratkṛtāṅga* 2.1.39; *Uttarādhyayana* 4.4, 13.23.

[74] Thapar (1988) 291. On *dharma* as both universal and separating see Halbfass (1988) 317–19.

[75] DK22 B2; 13§D, 14§A, 15§A. [76] Translation by Basham (1951) 14.

Human action has no effect. Living creatures

> are without power, strength, or virtue, but are developed by destiny (*niyati*), chance (*sangati*), and nature (*bhāva*).[77]

On the basis of this passage and subsequent commentary, Basham concludes that

> the only effective cause was *niyati*, which was not merely a first cause, but, in its aspects as *sangati* and *bhāva*, or chance and inner character, was also the efficient cause of all phenomena.[78]

Whereas Vedic literature propounds the numerous correspondences or equivalences that express the specific powers of ritual, here in Ajivikism we see the advent of an idea of *universal regular impersonal causation*. Something corresponding roughly to this description is also found in early Jain[79] and Buddhist[80] texts, albeit in distinct forms: in particular, the Buddhist idea of dependent origination is notably consistent with the idea that all individuals are responsible for themselves. Comparably, in Greece it is in presocratic philosophy that we first see the idea of a single impersonal principle or substance that pervasively controls all else. With the idea of Herakleitos that everything is in constant flux, but happens 'according to the *logos*' (embodied in fire),[81] we may compare the Buddhist idea that everything in our lives changes, but not randomly: everything is process.[82]

For Greece the new idea cosmises the new power – universal, regular and impersonal – of the abstract substance of money.[83] Here I suggest that the Ajivikan *niyati*, which seems to go back to the fifth-century BCE origins of the sect,[84] is a cosmisation of the impersonal omnipotence of money, which renders virtuous action ineffective. The statement in the *Sāmañña-phala Sutta* singles out virtuous action as unable to increase or diminish karma. Nevertheless, the Ajivikan 'six inevitables' that accompany all existence – and that, Roth argues, constitute 'the most ancient and

77 Translation by Basham (1951) 14 and 225. 78 Basham (1951) 227.

79 E.g. Johnson (1995) 15: in the earliest Jain texts activity *inevitably* produces the influx of karmic particles and their bondage to the soul; Schubring (2000) 173: the wandering of the souls, a world law, is caused by their being charged with *karman* once and for ever, and this is also the primary cause of the world structure (equally called a world law).

80 A recent account of the Buddhist doctrine of dependent origination is by Gombrich (2013).

81 KRS 187–8, 199–200; Guthrie (1962) 428–32; cf. West (1971) 124–9.

82 E.g. Gombrich (2013) 10 (cf. 155: the only *dhamma* that does not arise from causes is nirvana). See further 12§D(3).

83 Seaford (2004) 231–42.

84 Basham (1951) 3, 6, 17. On *niyati* generally see Basham (1951) 224–39.

the most primitive doctrine of the Ajivikans'[85] – include gain and loss.[86] The Jain commentator Silanka (ninth century CE) attributes to the *niyatavādins* (surely Ajivikans) the point that the same exertion produces different rewards, and that there can be rich reward 'even when no means of livelihood such as service, etc., is followed', from which they infer that nothing is achieved by human effort:

> Of those who put forth equal effort only one has material success, through the force of *niyati*. Hence only *niyati* is the cause.

The virtuous suffer while the wicked do not, and so only *niyati* is the cause.[87] The fact that virtue and work receive less reward than does rapacity may be attributed to a single cause, the impersonal omnipotence of money, which – as omnipotent – is imagined as a cosmic principle (*niyati*). Injustice of course predates money, but money permits or promotes the idea that injustice results from a single abstract impersonal all-pervasive cause such as *niyati*.

For the Ajivikans there is nowhere the possibility of thwarting the *social power* of money (invisible, impersonal, uniform, universal) cosmised as *niyati*. But there are other aspects of money: it *circulates*, and it is *individually owned or owed*. How are these aspects expressed metaphysically? Circulation influences the idea of a cycle of reincarnation (*saṃsāra*), individual ownership the idea of karma (10§C). Ajivikism has a place for both, albeit – as we would expect – in a form strictly determined by *niyati*: in early Ajivikism *saṃsāra* is *quantified* ('measured out as with a bushel') and *fixed* ('it can be neither lessened nor increased'); and karma is unaffected by virtuous action and the cosmic cycle. 'Ajivika doctrine never wholly excluded karma, but insisted that it operated in an automatic and determinate matter.'[88] I will develop this argument further in 14§A.

Niyati, *saṃsāra*, karma and the impersonal universality of money are all beyond the control of each individual. And so the extreme asceticism of an Ajivikan meant abandoning all action (whether virtuous or otherwise) and therefore escaping altogether not only from the uniform economic cycle in which all action (whether virtuous or otherwise) is mediated by money but also from the tendency for an individual to be constituted by the monetary value of his property. The *Mahābhārata* preserves a story in which one Manki purchases with the last of his property two bulls, which are

85 Roth (1993) 420. 86 Along with life and death, and joy and sorrow: Basham (1951) 255.
87 Silanka on *Sūtratkṛtānga* 1.1.2.2., fol. 30; 2.1.12, fol. 287–8: Basham (1951) 230–4.
88 Basham (1951) 238.

accidentally killed. Manki then utters a chant on the power of destiny, casts off all desires and attains immortality. Basham[89] detects Ajivikan influence on narrative and chant, and suggests that Manki is a corruption of the Prākrit Mankhali (Pāli Makkhali), the founder of Ajivikism. What interests us is that in the narrative the vain desires, the world escaped from, are expressed in *purchase*.

Ajivikism urged non-action, but maintained that neither action nor non-action can control or decrease karma. The Jains too urged non-action, which they mantained decreases karma (as well as not increasing it).[90] For Buddhism, by contrast, action may produce good or bad karma.

On the one hand, if action creates monetary debt or is forced on us by the need or desire for money, to act at all is to submit to the power of money. It is from this perspective, in which money has power *over* individuals, that its universal power is cosmised by Ajivikism as *niyati*. But on the other hand money may also, if accumulated, bestow power *on* some individuals. This ambivalence of money, as both negative and positive, corresponds with the Buddhist idea that accumulated karma can be bad or good. This is consistent with the idea (shared by Ajivikism) that in this world work and virtue are not automatically rewarded, for – in being imagined by Buddhism as karma – money (a) is *ethicised*, (b) drives the cosmic *cycle* of reincarnation (*saṃsāra*) just as on earth it drives the commercial cycle and (c) retains nevertheless the *ambivalence* of its worldly functioning. The ambivalence is now *ethicised*: it is morally good action that produces (good) karma that increases the well-being of the agent, and morally bad action that produces (bad) karma that diminishes the well-being of the agent.

In all three sects – Ajivikism, Jainism and Buddhism – karma was in some sense ethicised, and the ideal was escape from *saṃsāra*, which was also escape from karma. Where the sects differed from each other, at least in the earliest period, was in whether, or how, karma could be influenced by action. In Buddhism good and bad karma could be accumulated or diminished by the (free) action of individuals. This cohered with the Buddhist emphasis on *moderate* asceticism. By contrast the *extreme* asceticism of Ajivikism and of Jainism, which could in principle result in death from starvation, reflected their view that all karma is bad, and so – because all action increases karma – that all action is bad. The idea of actions or karma entering or *sticking to* their agent[91] expresses the status of *self-directed*

[89] Basham (1951) 38–9, 218; Mhb.12,176.5. [90] Bronkhorst (2007) 20–4, 44–5.
[91] Found as early as CU 4.14.3; BU 4.4.22. For the doctrine in Jainism, see e.g. Dundas (2002) 97–9.

(monetised) action as intermediate between self and other (15§B). The Ajivikan view that karma could not be decreased even by non-action makes liberation from *saṃsāra* even more challenging (in principle at least) than it was for Jainism. Another way of avoiding being bound to karma (and to commercial automatism) is to imagine action as *niskāma*, done without desire for the fruits of karma, propounded especially in the *Bhagavad Gītā*.

The extreme asceticism of Ajivikism and Jainism may seem incomprehensible. How to explain it? In general, it is by means of social and symbolic systematisation that people can tolerate the terrible material conditions that have always been faced by most of humanity. It is when those systems fragment or dissolve, without being replaced by anything else, that people suffer the unmediated distress that results in the kind of absolute renunciation that developed in India.[92] Fundamental socio-economic transformation is – I believe – generally a better explanation of such phenomena as renunciation and EIR than is e.g. the likelihood of an increase in disease as a result of mass settlement in the Ganges area.[93] Moreover, there was no special incidence of disease to explain the development of very similar (albeit less widespread and tenacious) ideas in Greece.[94] The isolation and disempowerment of numerous individuals (their place in the universe and the afterlife no longer unequivocally supplied by kinship or ritual) by the impersonal monetisation of the economy promoted uncompromising withdrawal from the all-pervasiveness of money, and so from action, but without the possibility of escape from the isolation.

Against this background, the ideal of extreme asceticism is made more comprehensible by three further considerations. Firstly, to the extent that any self-deprivation was imagined as accumulating the power produced by mortification (*tapas*), this preserved a kind of exchange, albeit now (paradoxically) within the isolated individual. Secondly, such extreme models can be useful as an ideal for their adherents without being fully enacted. Thirdly, the reality of the moderate modes of withdrawal would have certain advantages not only for the individual (freedom from debt and from exploited labour) but also – by endorsing powerlessness even among

92 'Renunciation is born from the need to escape pain': Thapar (1988) 277.

93 This is suggested as a 'contributory cause' to the new negative attitude to life by Gombrich (2006) 59–60.

94 Renunciation (unlike EIR) has occurred autonomously in numerous cultures, and has had various motives: e.g. rejection of the corruption of society and privileging of 'nature' was a more important motive for Greek renunciation (merely incipient in our period) than for Indian. But this investigation is beyond my scope.

the economically active – for the monarchies from which the sects received support.[95] There is symbiosis between monarchy and Sramanic sects, most famously under King Ashoka. The universal orderedness of the state, interpenetrating – as we saw in the *Arthaśāstra* (2§E) – with the universal orderedness of money, is mirrored in the ordered universe imagined by the sects.

The inaction and extreme asceticism professed by Ajivikism and Jainism were from the beginning rejected by Buddhism. But this does not mean that Buddhism was less a reaction to monetisation than were the other two sects. Buddhist monks were banned from handling money, and Buddhism developed two central ideas – the *middle way* and *no self* – that can be regarded as substituting for (or rendering unnecessary) complete inaction.

Firstly, the *middle way* between indulgence and asceticism amounts to a middle way between extreme engagement in the (monetised) economy and extreme rejection of it. The idea was central to Buddhist practice from the beginning (it was, for example, attributed to the Buddha's first sermon), and was subsequently also applied to ontology (between affirmation and denial of existence) and the self (between eternalism and annihilationism).[96] There is a parallel here with Pythagoreanism,[97] which (a) had as a central doctrine the desirability in various spheres (especially ethics and metaphysics) of the middle (*meson*) or measure (*metron*),[98] (b) practised a new way of life, perhaps the first widespread way of life ever to systematically embody conscious departure from tradition, (c) came into being largely as a response to monetisation,[99] (d) at the beginning of its long career was of considerable political significance and (e) propounded EIR.

In all these respects Pythagoreanism resembles Buddhism. As for the *meson* or *metron,* Pythagoreans were not its only Greek advocates. Solon was the first to promote the virtue of moderation or self-control, which will have a long history among the Greeks as a civic virtue.[100] He was appointed to resolve a crisis caused by the unlimited accumulation of individual wealth, and in response produced a metaphysics of limit (15§A). Perhaps for the Pythagoreans, too, the original incentive to privilege and cosmise measure and limit was the unlimitedness of money.[101] Give that Solon

[95] E.g. Basham (1951) 286–7; Warder (1956) 44, 48, 60.
[96] Gombrich (1988) 61–2: see n. 35 below.
[97] For a comparison of the Buddhist middle way with Aristotlelian *mesotes*, see Lyssenko in Lacrosse (2005) 101–19.
[98] Seaford (2004) 281–2; (2012) 283–6, 291–2, 297–8.
[99] Seaford (2004) 266–83.
[100] E.g. the Pythagoreans and Plato: 15§A.
[101] Seaford (2004) 281–2; (2012) 64, 70–1, 291.

urged moderation as part of his radical reforms of the polis, and that Pythagoreans held political power, it is interesting that the third Rock Edict of the reforming King Ashoka, who recognises Brahmins and Sramanas in a society now pervaded by money, recommended 'owning and spending little (*alpa*)'. In both cultures there was a new personal austerity that might take extreme form (in India at least), but could be useful for the merchant.

However, the idea of limiting the unlimited (in universe and in inner self) was much more prominent in Greece than in India, where the reaction against monetisation tended rather to be isolated withdrawal. Solon also freed those enslaved for debt, and his legislation to end the crisis of debt and enslavement was regarded by Athenian citizens as the foundation of their polis. He distinguished the role of the gods, which is to protect the polis, from the greed of the citizens, which is entirely responsible for the crisis (*fr.* 4). The crisis of debt is provided with a dual solution – of individual *self-control* and *political* action – which promotes the idea of a purely secular (human) sphere, such as we do not find in extant texts from ancient India.

Secondly, there is the Buddhist idea of no self (*anatta*), which can be expressed in terms of the middle way.[102] Collins (1982: 263) summarises as follows his account of *anatta*:

> The Buddhist attitude to selfhood, to personality and continuity, is that impersonal mental and material elements are arranged together in a temporarily united configuration. What unifies and prolongs this configuration is desire; it is in desire for the enjoyment of these constituents of personality, and for their continuance, that there arises for the unenlightened man 'the conceit "I am"' (*asmimāna*), a 'conceit; which is not so much asserted propositionally as performed automatically by 'the utterance "I"' (*ahamkāra*). Desire here, indeed, brings about its own object – that is, the continuance of life-in-*saṃsāra*; a form of existence seen from the nirvana-oriented virtuoso perspective as unsatisfactory, as 'suffering'.

Whereas Ajivikism and Jainism recommend non-action and recognise the existence of a self,[103] Buddhism conversely neither recommends non-action nor recognises the existence of a self. To recognise a self and yet not recommend non-action would increase the danger of being drawn into the economic-metaphysical cycle, and none of the three sects do this. In

[102] *Saṃyutta Nikāya* 2.20: 'The same man acts and experiences the result – this is eternalism. One man acts, another experiences the result – this is annihilationism. Avoiding these two extremes, the Enlightened One gives a teaching by the Middle Way' (translated by Collins [1982] 105).

[103] On the inner self in early Jainism, see Dundas (2002) 42–4, 93–4.

other words, there is a sense in which the doctrines of non-action and no self render each other unnecessary.

From a broad historical perspective, the doctrine of *anatta* rejects in particular the atman, the unchanging inner self – an idea that can be seen *developing* in late Vedic texts: we have shown how the late Vedic atman is promoted by the monetisation, individualisation and interiorisation of the sacrificial process through which the individual obtains lokas in this world and the next. This being so, the doctrine of *anatta* coheres with the Buddhist rejection of the Vedas and of sacrifice and with the ban on Buddhist monks using money and owning anything individually beyond minimal property. At the same time the doctrine of *anatta* coheres with a doctrine of all-pervasive unceasing flux that is itself influenced by the newly all-pervasive *circulation* of money, as does Herakleitos' new conception of the ever-changing *psuchē* (13§D). But there was no doctrine of no self in Greece (17§AB).

We have seen in Part C that the atman is central to Vedic doctrine: it came into being in the beginning; it must be known; all that is dear is dear because of it; it is identified with all; it is brahman. Thus atman and *anatta* seem to be diametrical opposites. But the atman is elusive: bigger than 'all these worlds' but smaller than a mustard seed, imperceptible, the abstract undefined something behind (or containing) the various inner faculties. Unlike the variously imagined Greek *psuchē,* it lacks both material existence and internal divisions. To deny its existence is not so big a step as it may seem.

Moreover, like the Greek *psuchē*, it supervenes on earlier texts (RV, Homer) in which there was no unified inner self, no comprehensive organ of consciousness – an absence to which the doctrine of *anatta* may, from a broad historical perspective, be said in a sense to revert. Of course, this comparison of *anatta* with the earlier absence of a unitary subject is in most respects superficial, because the doctrine of *anatta* is philosophical, and was produced in circumstances (including monetisation and the centrality of the atman) quite different from those of the *Rigveda.* But it is not the only feature of Buddhism that seems to perpetuate – albeit in a quite different form – a lost or disappearing past. Another such feature is the minimisation of the individual property of monks and the ban on their use of money: we can detect the historical development of individual property that in a Buddhist text is represented as decline (2§E). Because we claim that the emergence of the unitary inner self is influenced by the development of monetised individual property, it is worth repeating that in Buddhism the rejection of the former coheres with the rejection of the latter. Moreover, the dependence of the monks for food and shelter on the laity, who thereby acquire merit, perpetuates (in a different form) the pre-monetary reciprocity that was (ideally) based on mutual goodwill. Another possibly archaic feature is the *community* of moneyless, propertyless individuals, the *saṅgha*, which may in some respects perpetuate the organisation of the political *saṅgha* of the pre-monarchical state.[104] The individual self of the monk is minimised by the doctrine of *anatta*, by his propertylessness and by his integration into the *saṅgha*.

Further, the importance – in Buddhism and Jainism – both of giving and of taking only what has been given,[105] represents a rejection of the new automatic commercial relation in favour of the (supposedly) voluntary exchange of goods and favours marginalised by the development of commerce. Thapar even suggests that the Buddhist monk, in requesting alms as sharing the householder's wealth,[106] 'was still adhering to the ideals of the earlier system of sharing wealth'.

9§F The Factor of Monetisation

Stephanie Jamison has recently adduced several texts from the *Brahmanas* to illustrate the practice of substituting one kind of sacrifice for another, on which she comments as follows:

> We see in these theological discussions that sacrifice is conceptually fungible. A part can be substituted for the whole, a simpler sacrifice for one more elaborate. All that's necessary is to know the exchange rates of this ritual currency. This type of economic calculation about the value of certain sacrifices and sacrificial acts arises from the same type of reasoning that produced the dispassionate meditations on the hidden connections (*bandhus*) among disparate elements . . . but the economic approach has practical consequences: it allows every Aryan (or every Aryan man) to participate in the sacrificial system and derive the tangible and intangible benefits that sacrifice is supposed to produce for its performer. It is almost the Vedic equivalent of a mutual fund, allowing even the small investor to take part in economic markets.[107]

Jamison informs me that this fungibility 'functions more as a model than a metaphor'.[108] I would go even further and suggest that these new, money-

[104] Warder (1956) 45; Dundas (2002) 16–17; Thapar (1984) 151. It is stated in a canonical Buddhist text (*DN Sutta* 16, 2.73–9) that – as Gombrich [2013] 25) puts it – 'the organisation of the Buddhist *saṅgha* was modelled on that of a tribal republic or oligarchy'.

[105] The second precept of Buddhism is 'I undertake the training rule to abstain from taking what is not given'; Findly (2003); Gombrich (2006) 102; Jainism: Dundas (2002) 30, 174–6.

[106] An idea based on the etymology of Sanskrit *bhikṣu* (Pali *bhikku*, monk): Thapar (1984) 151. Kosambi (1965: 104) calls the new mendicancy 'at base a reversion to food gathering'.

[107] Jamison (2016) 28. [108] By email. On the problematic use of 'metaphor', see 10§C.

like features of sacrifice may arise from the general mode of thinking implicit in – and promoted by – the general monetisation of society (as defined at the beginning of 2§E).

Our account of the late *Brahmanas* and early *Upanishads* has included a variety of new developments that have been described by other scholars, but without any of them being *explained*. In introducing monetisation as an explanatory factor I must emphasise that I neither regard it as the *only* explanatory factor nor propose that the new metaphysics can be *reduced* to monetisation (16§A). But as an explanatory factor monetisation has several advantages. It becomes possible to explain why the new metaphysical developments occurred when and where they did, and why they assumed the form that they did. Moreover, it applies to *all* the major metaphysical developments: they all turn out to be aspects of the same process. And it also works for the remarkably similar (and roughly simultaneous) metaphysical developments in Greece. In this section I bring together an interim summary of the connections I have described – or as yet merely indicated – between the Indian sacrificial-metaphysical developments and monetisation.

In the earliest Vedic texts sacrificers obtain benefits through reciprocity (gift-exchange) with the gods, or through a series of discrete correspondences of the immediate (visible) with the beyond (a with b, c with d etc.). But subsequently the sacrifice is individualised and interiorised, sacrificial reciprocity tends to be replaced by automatism and the sacrificer 'also becomes the goal of the ritual activity' (Cavallin [2003a] 230). The variety of sacrificial correspondences tends to be reduced by monistic thought to a single identification, of the universal abstract subject (atman) with the universal abstract object (brahman). Accordingly, the direction of access to benefit is reversed: knowledge of the abstract (impersonal) entity becomes the key, with the result that the importance of the gods, and of the performance of sacrifice, is diminished. There also develops the idea of a cosmic cycle of redeath and rebirth, along with the idea of metaphysical substance that can through action be accumulated (but also decrease), and that – in its various forms – (a) drives the cycle and (b) attaches its owner to the cycle, but also (c) influences its owner's well-being within the cycle and (d) is a means to escape the cycle.

Everything in the preceding paragraph relates to monetisation. In the pre-monetary world people obtain benefit by being embedded in a *series* of discrete *reciprocal* relations. Monetisation, by equipping each individual with a single universal means of acquisition, promotes *individual autonomy* to an extent that may diminish the need for the *performance of sacrifice* or even for the *gods*. What the individual now needs – in order to obtain a, b, c, d etc – is *knowledge* of the power of a single entity x that is *universal* and *abstract*, that he can through *action accumulate*, and that may also *decrease*. Monetised exchange (in contrast to reciprocity) works *automatically* because the power of money is *impersonal* – and so also seems to merge with the will and intelligence of its user (i.e. is *interiorised*: 15§B), who is also its direct *goal* (without involving the benefit or goodwill of another): it is *self-directed*. From the *cycle* of exchange, which is *driven* by money, *accumulated* money may *free* him (or at least improve his well-being *within* the cycle).

The ideas of metaphysical merit and cosmic cycle (reincarnation) developed together, forming a conjunction that has been widespread and permanent. In order to work, money must be thought to maintain its abstract identity and value everywhere unchanged, but it is only in *circulation* that it works as money. This paradoxical combination of unchangeability and transformation (10§B) is the shape of money.

The other fundamental paradox of money is that it is both an omnipotent universal equivalent and a form (and facilitator) of individual property. As the former it is projected (cosmised), as the latter introjected (interiorised), in both cases as an abstract unifier/controller, which facilitates the identification of the inner self with – or its participation in – the universe.

We shall in due course see that both paradoxes of money are factors in the new metaphysics of both India and Greece. And in both cultures what matters in the newly monetised world, at least for the wise elite, is made explicit: it is not the performance of ritual but action based on knowledge of the (inner and external) abstract universal.

CHAPTER 10

Reincarnation and Karma

10§A Reincarnation: A Cross-Cultural Perspective

I begin by distinguishing between two kinds of reincarnation. One is reincarnation within the kin group: this I call *lineage reincarnation* (LR). The other is *ethicised indiscriminate reincarnation* (EIR, as defined in 2§A). It goes without saying that these are merely useful models (ideal types) of reincarnation: the reality is often less tidy.

The relationship between these two kinds of reincarnation is at the heart of an important study by Obeyesekere (2002), in which he uses terminology that differs from mine but largely overlaps with it. 'Rebirth eschatologies' (which I prefer to group under LR) have been extremely widespread in small-scale societies: he examines them among the Trobriand islanders, the Igbo in Nigeria, various peoples of the north-west coast of America, the Druze of Syria and the Balinese. Common to all these societies is (or was) the idea that 'a dead person will circle back to the same kin group' (xiii). Because 'rebirth eschatologies' have been found all over the world, and in regions unconnected with each other, 'it is likely that they existed in India prior to the complex eschatologies that we now associate with Buddhism and Hinduism'. He also calls these complex eschatologies 'karmic eschatologies'. I prefer to group them under EIR. And from now on I will for the sake of simplicity use my terminology (LR and EIR) rather than his, even when describing his views.

As a communally shared belief, EIR is found in ancient Greece (14§D) and ancient India,[1] in beliefs deriving from India or Greece and – Obeyesekere

[1] Indiscriminate but non-ethicised reincarnation is implicit in Hdt. 2.123 and attributed to Gosala in the *Bhāgavati Sutra* (Basham [1951] 30–1), and perhaps what is indicated at RV 10.16.5 (9§A). Indiscriminate reincarnation is (in both India and Greece) associated with vegetarianism.

claims – nowhere else. Having hypothesised that LR once existed in India, he argues that EIR *grew out of* it there.

The hypothesis was subsequently given support by Jurewicz's detection in the *RigVeda* of what looks like LR (9§A). Moreover, it is stated several times in early Vedic literature that immortality is obtained through offspring; and continuation of the existence of the father in his son is expressed in Vedic ritual.[2] It has been suggested that the relative lack of ideas of the afterlife in the early layers of the *Rigveda* is due to the importance of the family in the cult of the dead, a correlation that occurred also in ancient Rome.[3]

The question of whether the Greeks ever believed in LR is not raised by Obeyesekere. I devote this paragraph to it. In the polis property, self-defence and guilt belonged to the clan (as opposed to the individual) to a greater extent than they do in modernity, and there is evidence that ownership of property by the clan had in the prehistoric past been even greater (2§E). Belief in the transmission of guilt or fault within the family over generations was for centuries widespread among the Greeks,[4] and Proclus combines it with LR.[5] There was perhaps a trace of belief in LR in the ancient Greek practice, still widely followed, of naming children after their grandparents.[6] A more substantial survival of the belief was, I suggest, in the *tritopateres*, who were offered prayer and sacrifice 'for the birth of children',[7] and whose name seems to mean forefathers three generations back.[8] In an Orphic poem of the fifth century BCE, the *tritopateres* are guardians and gatekeepers of the winds, and the soul (*psuchē*) is carried by the winds and breathed in.[9] Subsequently the *tritopateres* are widely identified with winds.[10] True, the souls are not identified in the Orphic poem with the *tritopateres*, but are rather (in Aristotle's report of the poem) breathed in 'from the whole' (ἐκ τοῦ ὅλου). In this there may perhaps be, as Gagné (2007) suggests, some influence from presocratic philosophy. But

[2] References and discussion in Olivelle (1993) 43.

[3] Oberlies (2012) 327. He also (498 n.77) compares the wearing of masks of ancestors at the Roman funeral with the representation of the dead by Brahmins at the ancestor rituals (*Śrāddhas*). For the role of this Roman custom in the development of the Western concept of a person (*persona*, mask), see Mauss (1938).

[4] Glotz (1904); Gagné (2013). [5] Gagné (2013) 27–8.

[6] *Oxford Classical Dictionary*, 4th ed. (2012) s. names, personal, Greek: 'daughters were also often named after family members, but the evidence is less plentiful than for men'.

[7] Phanodemos 325FrGH F6.

[8] Wüst in RE 7A, 325–6; Jacoby ad Phanodemos 325FrGH F6; Bourriot (1976) 1150–3.

[9] F421 (Aristotle *De Anima* 410b27) and F802 Bernabé, shown by Gagné (2007) to belong to the same fifth-century Orphic poem.

[10] E.g. Demon FGrH 327 F2.

this begs the question why – in presocratic philosophy or elsewhere – the individual soul came to be envisaged as belonging to 'the whole' (I indicate an answer in Chapter 12). The combination – in the Orphic poem – of *tritopateres* with 'the whole' may be a symptom of a transition from LR to the indiscriminate reincarnation (involving a *cosmic* cycle) found in Orphic and other texts.

Obeyesekere may well be right to maintain that EIR in India developed out of LR, and I would add that the same may well be true also of Greece. However, he can explain neither *why and how* this development occurred in India and Greece nor why it occurred nowhere else.

It was caused, he maintains, by *ethicisation*:

> When ethicisation is systematically introduced into any rebirth eschatology, that rebirth eschatology must logically transform itself into a karmic eschatology (78) . . .
>
> With ethicisation there is a qualitative change in the structure of continuity such that the rebirth cycle is propelled by ethics that now begin to generate good or bad otherworldly consequences. That too is given a name: karma (126).

But how are we to explain the ethicisation?

> The *Upanishads* produced a great speculative soteriology that was not concerned with ethicisation. What then is the critical feature of religions like Buddhism and Jainism that was conducive to systematically converting a social morality into a religious one?
>
> The answer is that these religions were not simply those of the 'homeless' interested in their personal salvation, as with the Upanishadic virtuosos; they were also concerned with the salvation of the ordinary person tied to a home . . . Buddhists and Jainas established connections with the lay community in a systematic manner and developed stable congregations of lay supporters . . . I suggest that it is in relation to a lay community that the ethicisation of the moral life occurs (111–12).

The establishment of connections with the lay community may have some explanatory power,[11] but is in my view insufficient as well as being itself in need of explanation.

At this point we might expect from Obeyesekere a historical explanation of the revolutionary features of Buddhism and Jainism and of the consequent ethicisation. But Obeyesekere has already ruled this out, in his rejection of the attempt by Kosambi (1965) to relate the expansion of

11 Although the idea of a lay community supporting particular groups of Sramana ascetics in this period may be an anachronism.

Indian thought in our period to 'profound changes in political and economic life'. These changes consisted in the emergence of two empires, Kosala and Magadha, and of new cities, as well as in the development of trade and commerce. New trade routes required policing, which the new empires provided. The emergence of universalising and transcendent religions paralleled the obsolescence of older political communities and the creation of wider ones.

To this Obeyesekere (121) responds that:

> an 'orientation' cannot account for the *content* of a doctrine; therefore a direct tie-in between economic and political change and the thought of the new religion of the Ganges valley is difficult to substantiate.

Similarly, on the one hand he admits that the Western Greeks 'were living in a world rapidly expanding culturally and economically through trade networks'; but on the other hand he states that:

> as with the Indic material, I resist formulating a direct causal tie between social change and eschatological and soteriological beliefs.

Moreover, the two societies are different:

> none of the city-states of Magna Graecia showed the beginnings of grand empires like that of Kosala and Magadha.

However, to characterise the relationship between commerce and cosmic ideas as 'direct tie-in' and 'direct causal tie' is to exaggerate and simplify it so as to make it easier to dismiss. Of course any such relationship is neither 'direct' nor monocausal.

And how then *is* the *content* of the new metaphysics to be explained? If a good or bad rebirth depends on the moral quality of action, then according to Obeyesekere:

> one can no longer guarantee that a person will be reborn into his or her own lineage or family or kin group; there is dislocation consequent to the person's rebirth that, rather than being based on kinship affiliations, is determined by and commensurate with his or her load of sin or merit (80–1).

But this puts the cart before the horse. The basic and initial cause of the dislocation is not the mysterious advent of ethicisation but rather the (explicable) development of differences between the wealth, status and activities of individuals within the lineage, and it is this that results in indiscriminate reincarnation and in ethicisation. The differences demand an explanation, provided by imagining a system of rewards and punishments for good and bad actions in previous lives.[12] But the differences may be too great to be explained by ethical differences between past members of the lineage, and so along with ethicisation recourse is had to the idea that souls may come from outside the lineage (EIR).

But how do the differences arise? Land and animals, in ancient India as in ancient Greece, generally belonged to a group constituted by kinship, the clan or the household. But with the development of commerce, which is more easily conducted by the individual than is agriculture or pastoralism, in both cultures wealth and status come to be possessed less by the lineage and more by the individual (2§E), who may conduct exchanges with numerous other individuals from other lineages, sometimes even at a geographical distance. Individuals begin to interact with individuals from other families both commercially (indiscriminately) *and metaphysically* (through EIR). Commerce promotes *monetisation*, which has four specific consequences tending to further the appeal of EIR at the expense of LR.

(a) Money is unprecedentedly easy to exchange, move around, conceal and store *by the individual*, whom it tends to *isolate*,[13] not least from her or his kin group, by providing the individual autonomy to meet a wide range of needs by transactions that in principle[14] may be with anyone anywhere. The result is that the enclosed solidarity of kinship tends to be replaced by a monetary cycle of unlimited and indiscriminate transactions. Individuals are related to others now less through the corporeal togetherness of kinship and more through the abstract value of money.

A consequence of the individual isolation conferred by the possession of money is that the inner self is reified and united by interiorisation (introjection) of the comprehensively unifying power (over all goods and services) of the abstract (monetary) value on which the identity and autonomy of the inner self depends (13§E). The new, introjected organ of comprehensive consciousness is abstract, unitary and self-contained. Both (b) its abstraction and (c) its self-containment tend to favour EIR at the expense of LR.

(b) Given the perceived physical origin of children in their parents and the physical resemblance among family members, LR is imagined as

[12] Cf. e.g. Iamblichus (*De Mysteriis* 4.5) says that the many doubt providence because of undeserved suffering, but that they cannot know about the crimes of the sufferers in previous lives.

[13] 2§E, 4§D, 13§C.

[14] We refer here to a model or ideal type. In reality most individuals in monetised societies retain unmonetised social links. Nevertheless, our model is much closer to reality in monetised societies than in earlier social forms.

taking place within a continuum that is fundamentally corporeal, however invisible the corporeality of the transmitted spirit. But in *indiscriminate* reincarnation there is no corporeal link or resemblance between the bodies involved, and so the transmigrating inner self may well be imagined as incorporeal (abstract): a soul is unlikely to be imagined as bringing anything corporeal from one kin group to another. Monetisation facilitates indiscriminate reincarnation not only by dissolving the solidarity of lineage but also by supplying, with the interiorisation of abstraction, the idea of the inner self as incorporeal.

(c) In LR the reincarnated person may seem to coexist with the person into whose body (s)he is reincarnated. In Afikpo in eastern Nigeria, for instance, a male body may contain both his ancestor and another spirit, *owa*, which is close to our conception of the self, with the result that 'a male is a composite of incarnated ancestral spirit(s) and his own self'.[15] If a neonate receives the spirit of an ancestor, he is not imagined as subjectively and corporeally identical with his ancestor (often his grandfather), though he may be similar. Rather, he is imagined as being in some sense both his ancestor and himself. This may be an extreme case, but it was surely a general feature of LR that the non-unitariness that is characteristic of the pre-monetary inner self[16] expresses – among other things – the temporal solidarity of the lineage. And so the self-contained unity of the monetised inner self tends to displace the non-unitary subjectivity required for LR.

(d) The egalitarian *procedure* of monetised transactions (one person's money is as good as another's, however different their status) can only intensify any sense of injustice at the massive inequalities of *outcome* that monetised transactions tend to generate.

The more a lineage manifestly consists of a plurality of distinct self-contained individual consciousnesses, along with a plurality of distinct individual states of economic well-being and of interactions with outsiders, the harder it is to reconcile this with the reincarnation of the same spirits or souls within the lineage. *Indiscriminate* reincarnation, on the other hand, explains these pluralities, thereby leaving the lineage with a (limited) self-identity. LR was devoted to perpetuating the *lineage*, whereas in indiscriminate reincarnation what is immortal is the atomised *inner self*, the

[15] Obeyesekere (2002) 26–7. [16] 4§B, 4§C.

abstract atman or *psuchē*, the historically recent organ of comprehensive consciousness.

Two questions may then arise. Firstly, why do we not (on the whole) remember our previous lives? One answer is to introduce an eschatological mechanism, notably the waters of forgetfulness. Secondly, did the atomised soul have a beginning? In Plato's version of reincarnation the soul has always existed.[17] Empedokles imagines himself to be a god who was exiled and subjected to the cycle of reincarnation (14§D).

10§B Cyclicality

Indiscriminate reincarnation differs from LR also by virtue of being, in both India and Greece, imagined as *cyclical*. True, even LR may be imagined as cyclical in so far as the spirit returns to the same kinship group, but this movement is fundamentally linear as well as positive, carrying forward the lineage. And in both Greece and India the cycle of rebirths is *wretched*, with escape from it desirable. To the extent that this escape is linear, it re-establishes an ancient linear movement (to the ancestors in heaven). Imagining this cycle is, I propose, influenced by the circulation of money, and the misery of the cycle owes something to the misery of the new monetised cycle, in which it is easy to feel trapped. According to Gombrich:

> Society with its web of obligations becomes an analogue for the entire cycle of *saṃsāra*, and on the other hand the homeless life with no social ties becomes an analogue for that release from rebirth for which it is conceived to be literally a preparation.[18]

This insightful comment requires two modifications. Firstly, the implication that the social is based on the metaphysical should be reversed: elsewhere Gombrich gets it the right way round ('As money entered the material side of life so the spiritual side came to be treated by many – initially by the laity – in an analogous way'),[19] but his interest in the effect of money is limited to noting this 'analogy': as a 'contributory cause' of the fundamental spiritual change he selects rather *disease*. What Gombrich regards as (merely) 'analogy' I regard as also a causal relationship (or rather as one factor in a complex matrix of causality). In general, the recourse to 'analogy' or 'metaphor' may obscure the reality of causation (10§C).

[17] *Meno* 85d12–86b2. [18] Gombrich (2006) 48. [19] Gombrich (2006) 127.

My second modification is to specify, as a source of *saṃsāra*, the *cycle* of *economic* obligations: cyclical in the sense that goods and services are given up in exchange for money, which is then given up in exchange for goods and services. This cycle seems driven by the power-substance money, just as the cycle of reincarnation is driven by karma (cosmised money: 10§C). The cycle of money is cosmised as the cycle of reincarnation. The desire for debtlessness in the next world accompanies the desire for it in this one (9§D [3]):

> Can a neutral state not be imagined, one in which man would be neither a debtor nor a creditor, but truly freed from the whole system of debt? Such a situation is obviously that of the man who has obtained absolute deliverance (*mokṣa*) and who, blended into the supreme Brahman, aspires neither to rebirth nor even to the endless enjoyment of the delights of the *svarga* [heaven]. The world of the absolute is the world of the absence of debt . . . In this life already man (in fact *dvija* [twice-born], in orthodox Brahminism) can prepare himself for the world that knows neither debtors nor creditors, and he can live it in anticipation. To do so he must embrace the state of a 'renouncer'.[20]

The monetised individual is self-contained and isolated, but depends on interaction. How is this paradoxical interaction to be envisaged? We have seen that the Indian unitary inner self may be imagined under the influence of the *interiorisation* of abstract value, a phenomenon that will be more obvious in Greece (13§E). But the same abstract value persists through the cycle of monetised exchanges, thereby acquiring universal social power, and so is *projected* onto the cosmos. And so the interaction of this (otherwise isolated) abstract unitary individual inner self with the cosmos is imagined as participation in the all-pervasive persistence of abstraction through a universal cycle of transformations. Hence the analogy between indiscriminate reincarnation and the monetised cycle of exchange: in both of them abstraction is projected into a cosmic cycle in which it may be indiscriminately transformed, and in both of them the individual may feel trapped. Even the departure of the soul (death) may be imagined as a monetary transaction (13§C). Whereas LR occurs corporeally within a specific lineage, indiscriminate reincarnation embodies the social universality of the indiscriminate circulation of abstract value.

This is not, however, to say that the cyclicality of reincarnation derived simply from the monetised cycle of exchange.[21] Other factors were the (limited) cyclicality of LR, and the cyclicality of natural processes. But

[20] Malamoud (1983) 35–6. [21] 16§B n.1.

cosmic cyclicality – be it of souls, cosmological processes, time or history – is not found in the earliest texts of India and Greece, and so cannot be explained as *merely* a projection of natural cycles. In sixth-century BCE Greece, too, the power of lineage is being replaced by the power of money. Accordingly the genealogical cosmogony of e.g. Hesiod and Orphic doctrine is replaced by the eternal monisms of presocratic thought, and it is from same period that we have the earliest evidence for Greek reincarnation (14§D). Herakleitos' cosmic cycle is a natural process (of elements transformed into each other) that involves a cycle of souls, and both the cosmic and the psychic cycle are described in terms of monetised exchange (13§D). Comparably, the Vedic sacrificer goes to heaven and back in a cycle that is both an economic cycle (sacrifice is payment of debt, and the sacrificer is identified with his offerings) and the cycle of nature (e.g. the sacrificer may return to earth through rain) (5§B). It is in the context of Vedic sacrifice that we first find ideas of reincarnation (7§A), and the Herakleitean notion of the circulating soul may also have been influenced by the contemporary idea of reincarnation.[22]

The paradox of the monetised individual, isolated and yet indiscriminately transformed, is the paradox of money itself, with its complementary essences: on the one hand money is not money unless it is *possessed* (i.e. as static, self-contained abstract value), but on the other hand it does not realise its value and function as money unless it is being indiscriminately *transformed*.[23] The introjection of money in the construction of the inner self must be the introjection of *both* these essences, mediating the relationship of self-contained self with others but producing a sense of persistent instability.

To conclude, Obeyesekere was right to find Kosambi's historical explanation inadequate to explain the *content* of the new metaphysics, but this is because Kosambi focused on broad political and economic changes and ignored *monetisation*, which was – despite the *political* differences between Greece and India noted by Obeyesekere – a revolutionary *socio-economic* process in the same period as the advent of EIR (in Greece and probably also India: 2§E). Given that the specific and profound doctrine of EIR was adopted at about the same time by only two cultures (remotely from each other), we cannot explain it by

[22] It was taught in mystery-cult, by which Herakleitos was profoundly influenced: 14§D; 11§C.

[23] Marx (1973: 233–4) observed of money that 'as material representative of general wealth, it is realized only by being thrown back into circulation . . . If I want to cling to it, it evaporates in my hand to become a mere phantom of real wealth'. And so, because it is also possessed only by being *withheld* from payment and exchange, money is a 'contradiction'.

imagining metaphysical 'influence' (2§C).[24] We need rather to explain (even if there was some influence) what it was about these two cultures at this time that *both* distinguishes them from other cultures *and* accounts for the appeal of the doctrine. Monetisation does both,[25] while providing for EIR in both societies not only a cause but a model (the all-pervasive cycle of abstract substance), as well as accounting for the ethicisation while not (as does Obeyesekere) leaving the starting point of the explanation unexplained. We have so far said more about the indiscriminate nature of EIR than about its other constituent, ethicisation: this brings us to yet another advantage of my hypothesis – its capacity to explain the historical emergence and the nature of karma.

10§C Karma

Karman basically means 'action', but in its earliest occurrences refers mainly to ritual actions (7§A). It is in the *Bṛhadāraṇyaka Upaniṣad* (9§D [7]) that we first find something approaching what will later emerge as what I call the core concept of karma, that it is an invisible universal power or entity, created by action, that has consequences for the well-being of the agent in this life or hereafter. I here extend to karma my earlier suggestion (in Chapter 9) that the advent of the idea of accumulating metaphysical substance was influenced by monetisation.

The core concept may have been first fully introduced by Jainism and Buddhism.[26] But the earliest surviving Jain and Buddhist discourse cannot be dated with certainty to our period (before 326 BCE), and so I will have to include references that may perhaps be later. My inclusion also of references that are certainly later is to some extent justified by the remarkable and widespread persistence – facilitated perhaps by the irreversible factor of money – of the core concept.

I start with sixteen similarities between karma and money.

(1) They both have *universal*[27] *power*. Karma might even be regarded as the cause of everything.[28]

[24] As is assumed by e.g. Bernabé and Mendoza in Bernabé et al. (2011) 572.
[25] This does not of course mean that money and EIR necessarily go together: 16§B.
[26] Gombrich (2006) 46–9, 68–71; Halbfass (2000) 129–30.
[27] Egge (2002) argues that the Buddhists 'like their Jain and Brahminical contemporaries, invented the idea of karma as a way of unifying the sacrificial and purificatory soteriologies within a single doctrinal system' (11). The comprehensive, unificatory scope of karma emphasised by Egge (e.g. 46–8, 61, 67) corresponds, I suggest, to the same feature of money.
[28] Krishan (1997) 198.

(2) Even autocrats generally need money, and 'even a heavenly being exhausts his stock of good *karman*'.[29]

(3) However, the universal power of money is not absolute. There has been much discussion of the power of karma in relation to other forms of power.[30] Powerful individuals may use their personal power to control money; and accordingly a god may be imagined as dispensing the fruits of karma (*karma-phala-vibhāga kartā*),[31] or as providing escape from karma.[32] In the *Mahābhārata* it is *Kāla* (Time) who dispenses the fruits of karma and is compared to a precise moneylender ensuring the accountability of individuals, with interest accruing over time.[33]

(4) Karma and money are acquired (and accumulated)[34] by *action*.

(5) Both karma and money are – despite their universality – normally acquired, owned, accumulated, exhausted and inherited by *individuals*, in contrast to e.g. the universal principles/powers of *ṛta* or *dharma*. However, money may also be collectively owned, and there eventually occurred the idea of collective karma.[35]

(6) The power of money and karma is *impersonal*. They generally influence the well-being of their owner without the intervention of any other agent, human or divine. Jainism, Buddhism and Ajivikism, as well as most Indian schools of philosophy, give a far more important role to karma than to personal deity.

(7) Money and karma acquired (and accumulated) by an individual influence her or his *future* well-being. The consequences of action are *deferred*.

(8) Both karma and money may be *inherited*. For instance, an early Buddhist text says that 'I am the owner of my karma. I inherit my karma. I am born of my karma. I am related to my karma. I live supported by my karma. Whatever karma I create, whether good or

[29] Gombrich (2006) 48. McDermott (1984) 7: the 'principle of *kamma* is universally applicable, even to the Buddha himself . . . The gods too – and even *Brahmā* – are not immune to rebirth in lower states of existence.'

[30] Documented by Krishan (1997) sections viii and ix.

[31] Shankara on BU 3.7.23, and on BG 7.22 and 8.9; see, further, Krishan (1997) 202–3 239–65. Bronkhorst (2011b: 114) notes that rebirth and karmic retribution are not easy to reconcile with belief in a supreme god, adding that 'even those . . . who introduced the notion of a supreme God in order to render karmic retribution intelligible, accepted a god who was bookkeeper rather than a supreme ruler.'

[32] BG 9.28. [33] 12.34.7; 12.220.96–8; Krishan (1997) 103.

[34] E.g. McDermott (1984) 17, 31; Krishan (1997) 183–93; Halbfass (2000) 264.

[35] Krishan (1997) 489–506. A wife might share the karma of her husband: Krishan (1997) 418–19.

evil, that shall I inherit.'[36] But when a man dies he takes with him his karma not his property.[37]

(9) Money is *ambivalent*: it can empower the individual, whom it can also bind by need and debt. Karma may be good or bad.

(10) Good karma (or metaphysical *puṅya*, 'merit') and money can easily be *transferred* between individuals.[38] The transfer of bad karma and of debt would absolve the undeserving and would not find a willing recipient, and so is much less common.[39]

(11) The *cycle* of exchange seems driven by money, of rebirth by karma.

(12) Coined money is a *material* entity that seems to embody *abstract* value (generally greater than its metallic value) with *invisible* power over goods and services, as does even an unwritten debt. Karma, too, is both material and abstract,[40] with invisible power.[41]

(13) Both money and karma bring everybody into a single system that combines numerous actions into a *cyclical causal chain of automatic reciprocity*.[42]

(14) In fact, the mysteriously invisible power of money is really the power that it bestows on its owner, and so is easily *interiorised*. It depends not on the goodwill of another (as does gift-exchange) but only on the intention of its owner. And so it may seem to merge its invisibility with the invisibility of that intention, with the result that the mind may be imagined in terms of money. Similarly the Buddha allegedly said that 'it is intention that I call karma'.[43] And yet money

[36] *Upajjhathana Sutta* = AN 5.57; also e.g. *Culakammavibhaṅga Sutta* 3 = MN 3.4.5.135.

[37] *Saṃyutta Nikāya* 3.20 (also 3.4). An early Buddhist sentiment is that the wise man cherishes neither life nor death but waits as a servant for his wage: *Questions of Milinda* 2.2.4 = 45 (1.70 Rhys Davids).

[38] McDermott (1984: 44) calls the transfer of merit 'a late addition brought into the Pāli Canon as a result of prior popular acceptance'. But cf. Gombrich (2006: 127) 'the textual evidence strongly suggests that the transfer of merit entered Buddhism round the time of the Buddha's death, close to 400 BCE, or soon thereafter'. See also Gombrich (1971).

[39] Krishan (1997) 417–20; *Laws of Manu* 6.79.

[40] Gombrich (1996) 50–1: Krishan (1997) 33. The physicality of karma for the Jains (Dundas [2002] 38, 98) reflects not only the reduction of (abstract) action to something physical (so Gombrich [2013] 59) but also the strange combination in money of universality and physicality. In this respect they are closer to Thales and Anaximenes than to Parmenides, Anaxagoras and Buddhist (abstract) karma.

[41] On karma as *adṛṣta* (invisible fate), see e.g. Krishan (1997) 149; Halbfass (1991) 309.

[42] Karma is 'the principle of continuity not just from one life to the next, but from one moment to the next throughout our lives': Gombrich (2013) 73. Karma and the law of causation: Krishan (1997) 195–204.

[43] AN 3.415. Cf. Collins (1982) 201: 'perhaps Buddhism's most important contribution to this development of the concept of karma was to have made the crucial act a mental one, a "volition" or "intention" (*cetana*) such that it was the presence of this, rather than the external act alone, which became the karmically significant force'.

and karma are also at the same time *external* processes[44] or entities.[45] Just as the (ubiquitous) power of money 'occupies the boundary between internal and external space' (15§B), so for the Jains (ubiquitous) karma, composed of atoms, is absorbed by action into the soul from the outer world.[46]

(15) Accordingly, both money and karma, despite their universal ordering power and automatic reciprocity, allow *freedom* of action.[47]

(16) Both money and karma simplify what might otherwise be an excessively complex series of transactions.[48]

Ancient (and modern)[49] descriptions of karma use – despite the *opposition* between (amoral) money and (moral) karma – the terminology of money, wealth and debt. I confine myself to a single example,[50] the *Questions of Milinda*, in which karma is represented as a general means of exchange:

> Take with you karma as the price, and go ye up to that bazaar, buy there an object for your thought, emancipate yourselves. Be free![51]
>
> In the Blessed One's bazaar for all manner of merchandise advantages are to be bought for karma according to requirement. Long life, good health, beauty, rebirth in heaven, high birth, nirvāna, all are found for sale here to be bought for karma . . .[52]

In another passage of the same work a prostitute says that she has always given service for cash whatever the status of the payer. On this Gombrich comments that:

> in economic life, cash is the common denominator, the great universaliser.[53] The Buddha's concept of *kamma* is the precise equivalent in the ethical sphere: no matter who you say you are, you're as good as the quality of your *kamma*.[54]

44 'Flow' of karma: e.g. Obeyesekere (2002) 2; McDermott (1984) 111–12.

45 There is no Sanskrit equivalent to the modern idea of a 'law of karma': Halbfass (2000) 31. Similarly, the presocratic cosmos was not subject to 'law'.

46 E.g. Halbfass (2000) 75; Krishan (1997) 54–5.

47 Gombrich (2013) vii, 13.

48 Schlieter 2013: 11: 'Heterogeneous elements (such as actions and their intentions, material giving, time invested into religious practices, etc.) can be converted into a homogeneous and quantifiable "currency"; it helps to visualize how much one might need to pay back certain "karmic debts".'

49 On merit as a 'spiritual analogue of money' see Gombrich (1996) 56. See also McDermott (1984), esp. 31–47; Gombrich (2006) 125–8; Findly (2003) 249–80; Schlieter (2013) 11.

50 See also, inter alia (for payment) Obeyesekere (2002) 134; (for inheritance, possession) McDermott (1984) 2, 9, 21; (for treasure) McDermott (1984) 35–6, 38, 57–8; (for price) McDermott (1984) 119–20. The Buddha allegedly compared certain mendicants' speculations on their fate in the next world to the speculation of traders on their various future acquisitions: MN 2.132; Wagle (1966) 145.

51 5.6 = 333 (2.213 Rhys Davids).

52 5.21 = 341 (2.229–30 Rhys Davids).

53 4.1.47 = 122 (1.184 Rhys Davids); Gombrich (2006) 82–3.

54 Gombrich (2006) 83; Obeyesekere (2002) 184–6; McDermott (1984) 7.

However, in the earliest texts we do not find the idea that good and bad karma may cancel each other out: such cancellation may diminish the fear of acting harmfully, and in the preliterate formative period of karma there were neither bank accounts nor double entry bookkeeping.[55]

Another source of social power, alongside money, was ritual. The expansion of the meaning of *karman* from ritual action to what we call karma (7§A) followed on social changes, notably urbanisation and monetisation, that were likely to produce new spheres of social power and prosperity that did not depend on the ancient Vedic sacrifices. Power and prosperity came manifestly to depend less on ritual and more on money, with the result that the socio-metaphysical power traditionally associated with *karman* was no longer dominated by ritual,[56] but instead was influenced by money. Nevertheless, Brahminism continued after monetisation to assign special power to its Vedic sacrifices, and eventually had to define, as *apūrva*, 'that particular "potency" that gathers and stores the efficacy of Vedic rituals',[57] opposing it to – or integrating it into the general framework of – karma and *saṃsāra*.[58]

It is of course not only money that is used to represent karma. Another factor is another form of wealth, the produce of agriculture.[59] Collins (1982: 221) refers to 'all the metaphorical agriculture of karma'. The life of most Indians in our period was dominated by agriculture. But it also came to be dominated by the circulation of money, which could increasingly buy anything useful, even land.[60] The money-like deferral of benefit imagined in karma is also influenced by the interval between sowing and harvesting. But money is in most respects more suitable than agriculture as a model for the moral cosmic cycle, because it (a) is more simply acquired, stored and spent by an individual, (b) is more universal in its acquisitive power and in the actions that it rewards and enables, (c) seems mysteriously invisible, (d) involves precise quantification, (e) is closer to its owner and (f) is less

[55] The balance of good and bad deeds determining posthumous fate appears already at *Laws of Manu* 12.20–21. The earliest documented instance of the Theravāda practice of 'moral bookkeeping' is in the Mahāvaṃsa (sixth century CE): so Schlieter (2013) 12, 20. Cf. McDermott (1984: 18) on the effects of accumulated good deeds 'superseding' the results of wrongdoing in the *Mahākammavibhaṅgasutta*. The idea of a karmic bank account is common only from the nineteenth century, not least in Western commentators: Schlieter (2013); Krishan (1997) 523–33.

[56] For the Buddha dismissing animal sacrifices and recommending instead (as bearing great fruit) gifts to the deserving, see e.g. McDermott (1984) 48–9.

[57] Halbfass (1991) 301. [58] Halbfass (1991) 291–345.

[59] E.g. Gombrich (1996) 50–1; Collins (1982) 218–23.

[60] Note Anāthapiṇḍika's purchase (2§E) – albeit not of *agricultural* land, the purchase of which is not mentioned in early Pali texts (Chakravarti [1987] 25), but is in the *Arthaśāstra* (e.g. 7.11.41–4); Thapar (2002a) 185.

dependent than agriculture on external factors (weather, disease, security, cooperation, etc.).[61] Accordingly, the universal power of money begins to be projected, in this newly monetised society, as the universal power of karma over this world and the beyond.[62] In other words, the social transcendence of money is imagined as the metaphysical transcendence of karma. Moreover, agriculture long preceded the advent of the idea of karma, whereas monetisation (roughly) coincided with it.

A *metaphor* for karma is what Gombrich calls money and Collins agriculture. They are not wrong, but they fail to make an important distinction.[63] For there to be metaphor there has to be – to use the theoretical jargon – both a target domain, to which the image is applied, and a source domain, from which the image derives. In the metaphor 'this warrior is a lion', the warrior is the target domain and the lion the source domain. But if money (or agriculture) is a metaphor for karma, what is the target domain? Warrior and lion exist – and are known – independently of each other.[64] But *karma* as a target domain does not exist – and is not known – independently of its source domains.[65] *Karma* is known *by virtue of deriving from* money, agriculture, etc. The representation of god as a bearded male sitting on a throne and carrying a sceptre can be called a metaphor (of kingship for god), but a metaphor for exactly *what*? I would prefer to call it cosmisation (cosmic projection) of (the universal social power of) monarchy. Similarly, karma is – in part – a cosmisation of another form of universal social power: money. Another kind of case is Herakleitos' explicit comparison of fire to money (B90). This is a metaphor, for fire and money exist – and are known – independently of each other. But Herakleitean fire is *also* a cosmisation of money: it is identified with the cosmos, exchanged with everything else, contains *logos* and so on.

Our use of 'metaphor', if it obscures such distinctions, allows us the obtuse satisfaction of separating out spheres that are in fact intimately

[61] Schlieter (2013) 10.

[62] Already in earlier Indian texts we find meritorious action rewarded in this world and the next. See e.g. Gonda (1966) 104, 126, 141; CU 1.9.2; 2.7.2.

[63] Cf. 4§A, 8§B, 9§E, 10§A, also 11§A n.5, 14§B.

[64] I have not seen this point insisted on, but it is perhaps approached by Collins himself (1982) 264: 'Whereas Buddhist intellectuals, in the textual tradition, take these patterns of imagery to be merely illustrative of an abstract conceptual account, I take the theoretical constructions of intellectuals to be themselves also illustrations of the underlying, unconscious patterns of imagination to which the imagery found in the textual tradition gives us access.'

[65] An intermediate case is the metaphor 'time is money' (Lakoff and Johnson [2003] 7–9), where the target is *partly* known through the source (to the extent that the abstraction time is shaped and experienced under the unconscious influence of money).

connected, such as king and god, agriculture and karma, or money and karma. Herakleitean fire and karma are reifying projections (cosmisations) of – or constructed from – (inter alia) money, which is not merely a metaphor, a way of illustrating karma and Herakleitean fire but a *component* of them; and this is why money and karma (and money and Herakleitean fire) came into being roughly simultaneously and in the same place. It cannot be emphasised too strongly that I am not proposing the *reduction* of karma to money. Karma is a much more complex phenomenon than money, and takes various forms. I suggest merely that *one of the factors* in the *emergence* of the core concept in northern India from the middle of the first millennium was the simultaneous advent there of monetisation. Once the concept of karma had emerged, it was subject to a myriad different influences.

Both money and karma reify interpersonal relations. But karma takes the reification further, as (in part) the *ethicised cosmisation* of money. But how does the ethicisation occur? We must return to the opposition between the ideal types of gift-exchange and monetised exchange (5§D). The former was based on goodwill, with reciprocity an ethical norm voluntarily chosen. But monetised exchange requires (in principle) no goodwill, just the automatic reciprocity (payment) imposed by supposed external equivalence (of goods, services, money). True, it may involve ethical demands (for a fair price, to fulfil a promise to pay, to describe goods correctly, etc.), but the exchange as a whole seems determined by an *automatic* reciprocity that may seem both to be inherently unjust and to contribute to wider injustice. Monetisation provided for karma not only a model but also a motive, to rectify the injustice associated with money. It follows that ideas of EIR and karma are – with exceptions of course – more likely to be embraced by the numerous victims of injustice than by the wealthy and powerful. Moreover, the metaphysics of the privileged tend to derive more from the (individual) possession of value than from (communal) circulation (14§C). The inscriptions set up by King Ashoka in the mid-third century BCE recognise Sramanas and emphasise the universal order of *dharma*[66] but make no mention of EIR and karmic retribution.[67]

The seemingly automatic reciprocity of monetised exchange, imposed by supposed equivalence, is in fact ultimately a reified interpersonal relation (between the transactors) of *power* that may derive from various factors (inequality of wealth, control of violence, knowledge, need,

[66] On the relation of this to monetisation, see 17§A n.6.

[67] For Brahminism ignoring or rejecting EIR and karmic retribution, see e.g. Bronkhorst (2016) 250.

persuasion, etc.).[68] Nevertheless, a monetised (commercial) transaction requires – unlike e.g. orders given to a slave – the *assent* of both parties (even if the assent arises from there being no other option): otherwise it is theft not commerce. The automatic reciprocity operates only after the assent is given. That is why money, despite its activation and seeming embodiment of automatic reciprocity (13 on our list), depends on intention (14) and permits freedom (15). Karma has these and all the other features of the list; but its automatic reciprocity derives not (as does that of money) directly from a supposed external equivalence but from a *synthesis* of money with the *ethic* of reciprocity that had been lost in monetisation: that is why karma is both objective and subjective (14). Karmic reciprocation resembles monetised reciprocation as *automatic*, but resembles gift-reciprocation as *deferred reciprocation for a voluntary enactment of an ethic* (with the idea of deferral facilitated by the capacity of money to be *stored*). We have already noted that the importance in early Buddhism of giving, and of taking only what has been given, is just one of the respects in which early Buddhism perpetuates pre-monetary practice (9§E). Further, if there was in India an ancient *cohesive continuity* of (lineage) reincarnation, disrupted and atomised by monetisation (10§A), then it was by karma restored as EIR – the vehicle of eventual justice.

As the ethicised cosmisation of money, karma dissolved the distinction between economic and ethical value.[69] But money was not the only source of universal social power. It could be controlled – we noted – by autocracy, with the result that an ethicised cosmisation of the universal power of monarchy, namely a just ruler of the world (*cakravartin*), was also imagined. True, there are important differences. The *cakravartin* is manifestly a ruler whereas karma may seem to have no relation to money.[70] A ruler may be imagined as entirely moral, and good for all his subjects, whereas money *per se* has two negative features and one positive one. Its negative features are that (a) it exercises universal amoral compulsion, is equally powerful whether obtained by (and whether enabling) ethical or unethical action, and (b) as needed or owed (debt) it seems to diminish well-being. Its positive feature is that (c) as an asset it may create well-being. The combination of (a) and (b) underlies the Jain and Ajivikan idea that all karma is to be avoided (by extreme asceticism), whereas the combination of

[68] Hence later Indian philosophers found it difficult to find any mechanical explanation for (this automatic reciprocity projected as) karmic retribution: e.g. Bronkhorst (2011b) 86.

[69] Gombrich (2006) 70: 'if kamma is completely ethicised, the whole universe becomes an ethical arena because everywhere all beings are placed according to their deserts'.

[70] For the reasons for this difference see 4§F.

the opposites (b) and (c) underlies the existence of both bad and good karma in Buddhism and Hinduism. Inasmuch as all karma binds us to *saṃsāra*, there is some inconsistency in describing some of it as beneficial, analogously to the inconsistency of decrying money as a whole while welcoming its benefits. The inconsistency will be diminished in the version of Buddhism in which Nagarjuna relegated karma ontologically: it is 'like a document or a debt that remains unexpired', and accordingly belongs to the realm of truth that is merely provisional, pragmatic and conventional.[71]

The advent of karma was possible only because it also developed pre-existing metaphysical conceptions. One such conception was the idea of the next world as an economic corrective to this one: at AV 3.29.3 the weak in the next world do not pay tribute to the strong, and at SB 11.2.7.33 the scales used in this world and the next to weigh a man's good and bad deeds constitute ethicisation of the commercial process of *weighing*. More importantly, there was metaphysical *debt*.

In the *Rigveda* humans may have debts to other humans and to gods.[72] Subsequently, in the *Śatapatha Brāhmaṇa*, we find a more comprehensive idea of debt, in which in being born the individual incurs a debt (to the gods, to death) to be paid by sacrifice, by which he obtains immortality.[73] According to Olivelle[74] 'the doctrine of debts *became* [emphasis added] an important theological device for legitimating several central religious obligations of the Vedic world'. There are also Greek texts in which human life involves a debt to death.[75]

This advent of transcendent, metaphysical debt must be seen alongside changing conceptions of the afterlife. In the *Rigveda* there was at death a linear (irreversible) path from this world to a permanent abode with the forefathers (or occasionally the gods).[76] Then, in the *Brahmanas*, there was fear of repeated death, which can be prevented by the right sacrifices (even though sacrificial merit may diminish) and by faith (9§C). Then, in a third phase (described in 9§D), in the early *Upanishads* the 'path of the fathers' became subject to cyclicality, which even the sacrifices performed by those who follow it could not prevent, because their metaphysical merit was exhaustible; whereas the 'path of the gods', followed by those who have knowledge and venerate truth as faith, is linear, though leading not in fact

71 Nagarjuna (fl. second/third century CE) *Mūlamadhyamakakārikā* 17; Halbfass (2000) 127, 173.
72 Olivelle (1993) 46–53. The word for debt (*ṛṇa*) could also mean guilt.
73 5§B; sacrifice the source of immortality: Olivelle (1993) 38; Malamoud (1983) 30–1.
74 Olivelle (1993) 53.
75 E. *Alcestis* 419, 782, *Andromache* 1272; Pl. *Timaios* 42e–43a; *Anthologia Palatina* 10.105.
76 6§B n.12.

(as in the *Rigveda*) to the company of the gods,[77] but to the impersonal, 'to brahman' or 'to the worlds of brahman', in which 'they live' permanently.

The posthumous permanent abode with the forefathers (in the *Rigveda*) represents the metaphysical solidarity and continuity of kinship[78] that is subsequently dissolved by monetisation into a universe dominated instead by individual debt, cyclicality and impersonal permanence (brahman) – the three fundamental features of money. Even the continuity of the family, which was perhaps once embodied in lineage reincarnation, came to be ensured by debt incurred at birth by the detached individual (to the forefathers, paid by procreation).[79]

Individual metaphysical debt could initially be paid by the correct performance (*karman*) of sacrifice, which was a transfer of individual wealth. With the increasing spread of money's universal power to create well-being, the relative decline in the importance of the performance of sacrifice, and the concomitant interiorisation of sacrifice, the *karman* that repaid metaphysical debt would surely become itself subject to interiorisation as well as more closely associated with money, which has the remarkable power to repay all debts, worldly or metaphysical. The result of this development was the merger of the metaphysical and *normative* power of *karman* (as correct ritual action) with the universal power of money. For the merger of metaphysical and material economies there is indeed much subsequent evidence:

> The theory of *karman* allows for a sort of general compatibility encompassing material wealth and spiritual merit. If an ascetic or an *agnihotrin* Brahmin dies, leaving profane debts (and should he have no sons to take them over), he loses all the merit earned from his observances, and transfers it to his creditors.[80]

Good karma may create material wealth.[81] The Buddha allegedly maintained that commercial outcome depends on the trader's offerings to mendicants in a previous life.[82] The laity received spiritual merit from Buddhist monks in exchange for material goods. And freedom from

[77] See esp. RV 10.135.

[78] Note also, from the perspective of the forefathers, RV 10.56.6: 'their forefathers have established their own offspring as their paternal power, as their "stretched thread" among the later generations'.

[79] SB 1.7.2.4; TS 6.3.10.5. AT RV 6.61.1 debt is associated with the acquisition of a son, but it is not specified to whom the debt is owed; another possibility is RV 10.135.5.

[80] Malamoud (1983) 39; *Nārada Smṛti* 4.5. Freedom from debt as a Buddhist goal: AN II. 67–68; MN I. 275. On 'karmic debt', especially in China, see e.g. Graeber (2011) 262.

[81] McDermott (1984) 12–13; Rotman (2009) 11: 'the two economies – moral and commercial – do not just mirror each other, they also intersect and interact'.

[82] AN 2.81–2; Wagle (1966) 145–6.

metaphysical debt can be obtained by the freedom from worldly debt achieved by renunciation (10§A).

For Obeyesekere the idea of karma is an inevitable result of the ethicisation of rebirth eschatology (10§A). In what he calls step 1 of ethicisation the other world becomes a place of reward and punishment, and in step 2 *rebirth* is ethically conditioned – so that suffering and happiness in this world are punishment and reward for conduct in a previous life. Plato, he claims, took step 1 of ethicisation but not step 2, and so did not have a theory of *karma*. The only Greek who 'comes close to developing such a theory' is Plotinus, who maintains that there is a cosmic ordinance ensuring punishment in a future life (a ruler who abused his power will be made a slave, etc.). This ordinance is called by Obeyesekere 'a karma-like automatic process . . . hence that awesome word Adrasteia (the inevitable Retribution) – similar to what the Indian Sramanic religion conceptualised as *karma vipaka*, the fruits of karma'.[83]

But Adrasteia is in fact – in contrast to karma – always a person (a goddess). True, there is – in so far as Plotinus imagines an *automatic* cosmic process – a similarity with karma. But karma is *very* much more than an automatic process or a principle of order (it can for instance be owned by individuals). And *why* did Plato not take step 2? Because, according to Obeyesekere, for Plato it is attachment to corporeality that keeps the process of rebirth going, and so takes the place of karma, and that 'his was an exclusive soteriology for the philosopher . . . The philosopher is the only kind of being who can transcend bodily desires and worldly wants, who can glimpse the original pure condition from whence he sprang.'[84] Early Buddhism had a large congregation, whereas Plato did not.

Obeyesekere tries here to explain a difference (the absence of karma in Plato) by concomitant differences (attachment to corporeality as causing rebirth, the exclusiveness of soteriology) that themselves cry out for explanation. But Obeyesekere's explanatory starting point is the ethicisation of rebirth eschatology, which – he claims – produces karma and karmic eschatology. However, the case of Plotinus shows that step 2 of ethicisation does in fact not even necessarily produce karma, let alone what I have called the concomitant differences.

I on the other hand start with the influence of geography on the urbanisations and political formations of Greece and India (5§E), with the relative importance of the polis in the former and of caste in the latter.

[83] Obeyesekere (2002) 288, 295–6. [84] Obeyesekere (2002) 251, 274–5.

I will now continue this line of thought, before eventually addressing directly the question of why the Greeks did not have karma in 17§B.

10§D Lineage and Caste

Romila Thapar notes that in the Vedic sources power was still based on legitimacy through lineage, and that:

> in the Indian situation lineage gave shape and form to caste structure. Lineage elements such as kinship and marriage rules are important to caste . . . The continuation of varna is in a sense the continuance of an aspect of lineage society and of ritual status. The latter becomes the survival of the lineage system . . .[85]
>
> The theoretical construct of caste society was not the simple unfolding of a class society, nor the mechanical measurement of ritual status. It was an attempt at interlocking a series of social units based on diverse rules of functioning but all in the context of a lineage system . . . the emphasis lies in each unit constituting its own method of *comprehending* lineage.[86]

The words most frequently used for caste are *varṇa* and *jāti*. There are four ancient *varṇas* organised in an orderly hierarchy, whereas the hierarchy of the numerous *jātis* is far from orderly:

> The genesis of the *jati* may have been the clan, prior to its becoming a caste . . . There are close parallels between the clan as a form of social organisation and the *jati*. *Jati* derives its meaning from 'birth' which determines membership of a group and the status within it; it also determines the rules relating to the circles within which marriage could or could not take place and rules relating to the inheritance of property.[87]

The Greek Megasthenes (c. 350–290 BCE), in his eye-witness account of the seven occupational groups into which 'the whole population of the Indians' is divided, sometimes employs the word γένος (clan, lineage), which implies kinship.[88]

A difference between the ancient Greek polis and ancient Indian society is the survival in the latter of the pervasive socio-political importance of lineage, especially in the form of what came to be called caste. This is not say that lineage was in our period unimportant for the Greeks, but its

[85] Thapar (1984) 18–19. Knowledge of caste in our period is limited. Moreover, passages descriptive of caste may have been to some extent prescriptive.
[86] Thapar (1984) 51.
[87] Thapar (2002a) 63–4. More on caste and lineage in e.g. Yamazaki (2005) 26–7, 171.
[88] FGrH 715 F19 (ap. Arrian *Ind.* 11), F4 (ap. Diod.Sic. 2.41); cf. Hdt. 2.164.

importance was contained and qualified by being integrated into the polis. The polis was created out of the restriction of the power of the lineage, a transition celebrated in Aeschylus' *Oresteia*. Athens contained a remnant of lineage reincarnation in the *tritopateres* (10§A), but even they received cult not only from lineages but also from the whole polis.[89]

In both societies lineage declined as a principle of ownership, with individual property emerging from clan property, and monetisation tending to detach the individual from the clan.[90] The Greeks of the sixth and fifth centuries BCE comment on the universal power of money, which includes the power to 'mix' γένος.[91] The prostitute who gives service for cash whatever the caste of the payer (10§C) assimilates the indiscriminate impersonality of money to the promiscuity of prostitution, an assimilation that occurs also in Greece and elsewhere.[92] Prostitution, like renunciation, may confound caste divisions.

But the caste divisions remained. The universal principle of *dharma* was *separative*.[93] Ancient India – despite the advent of urbanisation, commercialisation, stratification, the complex division of labour and monetisation – successfully preserved lineage as a fundamental principle of socio-political organisation, in the form of various groups that we call castes or subcastes, and that are held together not by shared property (an important basis for the ancient clan) but by (a) imagined or actual lineage (b) endogamy, (c) shared occupation (or occupations), (d) shared ritual and (e) belonging to a hierarchical system of such groups that is held in place both by ritual and – metaphysically – by myth and by different degrees of imagined pollution/purity.

This survival of the importance of lineage is not the only instance[94] of the conservatism that in India preserved (in part, though more than elsewhere) practices diminished by monetisation. But the survival was not just a matter of conservatism. Lineage was adapted to a new function: caste and EIR were complementary modifications of the basic fact of lineage, forming a system that has survived to the present. Legitimation of caste, provided in the pre-monetary era by cosmogonic myth (RV 10.90), was after monetisation provided by karma, which explains and justifies differences in status and well-being that would otherwise be inexplicable and unjustifiable.

89 Parker (2005) 31–2; Jameson et al. (1993) 111. 90 2§E, 10§A.

91 E.g. Theognis 190 πλοῦτος ἔμειξε γένος.

92 E.g. 'damned earth, Thou common whore of mankind' as the source of gold that unites opposites in Shakespeare's *Timon of Athens* (4.3.43); for Greece see Seaford (2004) 155–7.

93 See e.g. Halbfass (1988) 317–19. 94 Cf. 9§E, 10§A.

A contrast was drawn by Max Weber between India, in which 'it is one of the constitutive principles of castes that there should be at least ritually inviolable barriers against complete commensalism among different castes', and on the other hand the early Christian 'elimination of all ritual barriers of birth for the community of the eucharist'.[95] We may add that even as early as the pre-polis aristocratic society depicted by Homer animal sacrifice is emphatically egalitarian and communal, and that a general commensalism was a feature of the classical polis, where in many festivals sacrificial meat was distributed to all male citizens. It is true that even in the polis ritual was performed by households, clans, demes and so on, and that such ritual frequently expressed and enhanced the solidarity of the group performing it. However, in contrast to India, the rituals did not express the separateness of the group from other groups, nor did the interrelation of the groups involve pollution. The groups were components of the polis, which was united politically by institutions, emotionally by sacred places and by festivals organised and celebrated by the polis and economically by money. Presocratic cosmology reflects the universality of money in the polis. Whereas traditional Greek cosmogony and cosmology were based on lineage, in presocratic cosmology lineage is replaced by the eternal all-pervasive existence of the one (quasi-abstract or abstract) substance. The Herakleitean *logos* is a synthesis of the powers of ritual (mystery-cult) and of money to unite a polis.[96] Mystery-cult might embody simultaneously cosmic and political unity,[97] and Dionysos in Euripides' *Bacchae* requires both mystic initiation of the polis and universal participation in his cult.[98]

Exceptionally, the classes of Plato's ideal republic *are* – like Indian castes – differentiated by both metaphysics and purity. But for Plato the metaphysical differentiation involves neither lineage nor ritual (nor even gender) but merely the ability to absorb a certain metaphysics. Whereas in the *Upanishads* knowledge of the self is 'an esoteric discourse that can be learned only from the proper teacher and in very specific social situations',[99] in the Platonic dialogues it is in principle achievable – by dialogue, reason, introspection and discipline – by anyone.

As for the differentiation of Plato's classes by purity, it consists of the guardians being told that they have divine, unpolluted gold and silver coinage in their souls, and must not 'pollute their possession of that money

[95] Weber (1958) 36–7; NB Paul, *Epistle to the Galatians* 2.11–14. [96] 11§C, 12§C, 14§A.

[97] 6§C; Seaford (2012a) 45–6, 276–7.

[98] *Bacchae* 39–40, 206–9; mystic initiation of the polis also at Plut. *Sol.* 12.5: Seaford (1994) 82 n.30, 227; communality of mystic initiation: 11§C, 12§C, 14§A.

[99] Black (2007) 27.

by mixing it with the possession of mortal gold, for many impious things have been done around the coin of the multitude, whereas theirs is unpolluted'. And so they are to be forbidden contact with gold and silver, from wearing them or drinking from them (*Republic* 416e-7a). Money, which normally unites the polis, is here transcended by the opposition between impurity and purity, i.e. differentiated into impure *circulation* and pure (projected and introjected) abstract *value*. Comparably, early Buddhism, which also did not exclude people from enlightenment on grounds of lineage or ritual (or gender), forbade monks from accepting gold and silver.[100]

From a broad perspective there is a striking transition, at around the same time in both Greece and India, from (a) the initial development of philosophy (presocratics, the *Upanishads*) that is on the whole unethicised and barely mentions money (while cosmising and introjecting it) to (b) philosophy (Socrates, Plato, Buddhism) that is both ethicised and explicitly hostile to the power of everyday money (however difficult it may be to sustain such hostility in practice). However, even in the Platonic utopia the polis is in a sense united by money, albeit only in the limited sense that abstract value is sublimated as the form of the good, to which the guardians have access that benefits the polis as a whole.

[100] Findly (2003) 187.

PART D

Unified Self, Monism and Cosmic Cycle in Greece

CHAPTER 11

Psuchē *and the Interiorisation of Mystery-Cult*

11§A The Interiorisation of Ritual in India and Greece

We have in Part C more than once referred to the way in which the individualisation of the Vedic sacrifice gives rise to its *interiorisation*. The 'logical conclusion' of the process of individualisation is, Heesterman claims, 'the *interiorisation* of the ritual, which makes the officiants' services superfluous'. The knower of equivalences 'resumes in himself the universe and performs in himself and by himself the sacrifice without any outside intervention'.[1] Cavallin, noting that many of the sacrificial correspondences are between ritual and man, more specifically the breaths of man (pranas), infers that:

> there is thus an anthropocentric tendency in Vedic ritualistic thought, something which could explain the final abandonment of the 'outer' aspects of sacrifice in preference for its 'inner' aspects.[2]

Cavallin also distinguishes between three kinds of interiorisation: one is the ritual being performed within the body (for instance a food offering into the fires of the body), another is the ritual being performed mentally (imagined) and the third is intentionality and knowledge being considered as essential for ritual efficacy.[3]

Scholarship has often seen interiorisation of Vedic ritual in our period, but never of Greek. Was Greek sacrifice interiorised? Plato suggested that in sacrifices the gods, rather than obtaining anything advantageous, are gratified by the holiness (τὸ ὅσιον) therein manifested (*Euthyphro* 15b):

[1] Heesterman (1985) 38–9. For the connection between interiorisation and subjective reductionism (cosmogony), see SB 10.5.3.1, quoted in 6§C.

[2] Cavallin (2003b) 20, citing MU 1.2.7–10 and PrU 1.9. Interiorisation was not necessarily the only factor making for the abandonment of the practice of sacrifice.

[3] Cavallin (2003b) 25–6; on interiorisation see also Heesterman (1985) 39, 212n.72.

mental state is more important than what is offered, and the gods cannot be won over by sacrifices from wrongdoers.[4] This is closest to Cavallin's third kind, but still some way from interiorisation: in Greco-Roman antiquity I know of only one pagan[5] instance of the interiorisation of sacrifice (as opposed to sacrifice as a mere metaphor), from well after our period.[6] What does occur in our period is the *rejection* (by some) of animal sacrifice. Reincarnation, which for Empedokles makes animal sacrifice murder,[7] may have motivated the vegetarianism attributed in the classical period to Pythagoras[8] and to Orpheus and the Orphic life.[9] And so the earliest evidence for rejection of sacrifice is from roughly the same era in both Greece and India, and perhaps in Iran.[10] Greek objections to the killing of animals continued, but were always of less historical importance than such objections in India. Nevertheless, in both societies there is – especially in Pythagoreanism and Jainism – a correlation between vegetarianism and mercantilism: the sphere created by traders is beyond traditional (sacrificial) cult, and beyond the need to kill or eat animals.[11]

However, the cosmic rite of passage in which a Greek is ensured well-being in the hereafter is not animal sacrifice but mystic initiation, which *is* – like the Indian cosmic rite of passage (sacrifice) – *interiorised*, by Herakleitos, Parmenides and Plato. Herakleitos was also the first to object to the actual practice of ritual (mystic initiation, and purification by blood).[12]

What will emerge, in this chapter and the next, is that in Greece as in India – in the surviving texts – the dual development of the unitary inner self and of monism, together with the advent of the idea that the living can by acquiring *knowledge* influence their fate after death, all this is inseparable from the *interiorisation of the cosmic rite of passage*.[13]

4 *Laws* 716e, 885b, 905d–6d; cf. *Republic* 364b.
5 For Paul, see Ruin (2016) 211; e.g. *Epistle to the Romans* 12.1–2, which Ruin (211) calls 'not "just a metaphor"': cf. on metaphor 10§C.
6 Iamblichus *De Mysteriis* 5.15.: 'I posit two kinds of sacrifice: those of entirely purified humans, such as would occur in the case of an individual . . . or by some few easily-numbered men, and those that are material, corporeal, and constituted through change.'
7 B128, B136, B137.
8 Other ancient sources deny this: references and discussion in Burkert (1972) 180–3.
9 E. *Hippolytus* 952–3; Pl. *Laws* 782c; Aristophanes *Frogs* 1032.
10 *Yasna* 29; 44.20.
11 And for the settled agriculture that came to dominate the Ganges area the preservation of cattle is indispensable (for plough-pulling, manure, urine and milk).
12 In B14 and B5.
13 We will not be concerned with much later instances of what may be called the interiorisation of mystic ritual, as in Neoplatonism and the Hermetic corpus.

Before examining the texts, it is worth pausing briefly to speculate on the causes of interiorisation. One may imagine causes that were confined to India. The individual sacrificer may have resented Brahminical power over – and the expense of – the actual enactment of the sacrifice. The Brahmins' insistence on the all-importance of knowledge, whether or not intended to confirm their own indispensability in the sacrifice, may have contributed to the marginalisation of its actual enactment. Another possible factor applies to both cultures: the death of the initiand in the rite of passage must be merely imagined, and – whether or not an animal is sacrificed in his stead – this necessary act of imagination is a form of interiorisation. But none of these factors can explain why interiorisation occurred when and where it did. What can contribute to such an explanation is the advance of the idea of the autonomous individual possessed of a substantial inner self closely associated with the universe, an advance that we can observe and explain – independently of interiorisation – in both cultures. This is not to posit a simple causal relationship between individualisation and interiorisation. But the interiorisation of ritual does require the pre-existence of an individual inner space, which it may then help to enrich.

11§B Mystery-Cult and the *Psuchē* Before 400 BCE

Inasmuch as mystic initiation ensures the initiate a happy hereafter, it has to be concerned with that part of him or her that survives bodily death, namely the *psuchē* (soul). In Homer the only role of the *psuchē* in the living person was to leave the body at loss of consciousness – in particular at death, whereupon it departed for Hades. But mystery-cult, because it *pre-enacts* death and the hereafter, provides a focus on the *psuchē* of the *living* as well as of the dead. And this is indeed confirmed by texts of various kinds. I confine myself almost entirely here to the period before 400 BCE.

(1) A series of bone plates found at Olbia (on the Black Sea) seem to have been tokens of participation in sacrifices. Three of them, dating from the fifth century BCE, have inscriptions. One has the words 'life death life' (βίος θάνατος βίος), 'truth', 'Dio(nysos)' and 'Orphic'. Another has 'peace war', 'truth falsehood' and 'Dio(nysos)'; and a third has 'Dio(nysos)', 'truth' and 'soul' (ψυχή, *psuchē*) – possibly along with 'body' (σῶμα).[14] The bone plates were almost certainly

[14] Vinogradov (1991) believed he could detect it.

membership tokens of a group constituted by Orphic-Dionysiac mystic initiation (including animal sacrifice).[15]

(2) The mystic doctrine[16] described in Pindar's second Olympian Ode (467 BCE) maintains that 'those who staying three times on each side had the courage to keep their *psuchē* from all unjust deeds' reached the Isle of the Blessed (68–73). Purity of *psuchē* throughout more than one life[17] ensures arrival at a final happy destination. Mystic eschatology occurs also in fragment 133 of Pindar (14§D).

(3) Aristophanes' *Clouds* contains a parody of Eleusinian initiation, in which Strepsiades as the initiand says that his *psuchē* is fluttering.[18]

(4) The chorus (*thiasos*) of Euripides' *Bacchae* sing (72–5) 'blessed is he who, happy, knowing the initiation rituals of the gods, leads a holy life and θιασεύεται ψυχάν' (joins his *psuchē* to the sacred band called *thiasos*). This certainly refers to mystic initiation.[19]

(5) Gold leaves containing instructions to mystic initiates for the underworld have been found in tombs. One of them (c. 400 BCE) mentions '*psuchai* of the dead going down and refreshing themselves' at a spring in Hades. Another (fourth century BCE) begins 'but when the *psuchē* leaves the light of the sun'.[20]

(6) The inner self or *psuchē* is a central concern in the interiorisation of mystic ritual examined in this chapter.

The *psuchē* of a living person is not (like the heart) a specific part of the body: it may accordingly seem to refer to the whole person, both in life and (in whatever form) after death. It was some such sense of wholeness that may have been induced by the intense experience of mystic initiation. The *psuchē*, even when imagined as separable from the body, or as tenuous, or as invisible, is not necessarily thereby imagined as *incorporeal*: it may for instance be imagined as anthropomorphic, or as composed of (corporeal) air. The *psuchai* in the underworld are incorporeal neither in Homer nor in the mystic instructions in the gold leaves. The idea of incorporeality (or immateriality) is not found in Greece before Plato.[21]

15 West (1983) 17–19.
16 West (1983) 110 n.82; Lloyd-Jones (1985) 245–79; Currie (2005) 347–8, 389, 394 n.277.
17 There has been irresolvable disagreement as to whether 'three times on each side (ἑκατέρωθι)' means life-Hades-life or three sojourns in each place. In my view the latter is more likely.
18 319; for such fluttering as a feature of mystic initiation see Seaford (2009).
19 Seaford (1996) 157–8 et passim.
20 Numbers 1 and 3 Graf-Johnston (2007).
21 This is convincingly demonstrated by Renehan (1980).

11§C The Interiorisation of Mystery-Cult in Herakleitos

The mystery-cult of Demeter at Eleusis was open to all Greek-speakers.[22] It was organised by the Athenian polis, and was envisaged not only as connecting this world with the next but also as expressing the well-being and coherence of the polis: it embodied both cosmic and political unity.[23] According to ancient tradition, it was from Athens that the Ionian city-states were founded. Herakleitos belonged to the Ephesian royal family that – being descended from the Athenian royal family – held the priesthood of Demeter Eleusinia.[24] Hence perhaps his reference (B125) to the *kukeōn*, the sacred drink of the Eleusinian mysteries, as disintegrating if not in motion (i.e. presumably to illustrate his cosmic principle of constant motion).

'The mysteries νομιζόμενα (believed or practised as custom) among humankind are enacted in an unholy way' (B14). The qualification 'νομιζόμενα among humankind' implies the possibility of other mysteries uncorrupted by human performance. Wisdom comes through 'listening to the *logos*' (B50). A 'sacred *logos*' containing secret doctrine might be pronounced in the mysteries.[25] As we will soon see, the *manner* in which Herakleitos presents his *logos*, and the *content* of his doctrine, each independently suggests that he envisages himself as pronouncing a *logos* that – though it does not depend on the *enactment* of mysteries – is in some sense a *logos* of the mysteries. Mystic initiation gives to initiates access to the afterlife by rehearsing their death, and accordingly might involve transformation of their *understanding* (of life, death and the cosmos). Clement of Alexandria, who cites B14, prefaces it by stating the types of people (including mystic initiates) for whom Herakleitos threatens 'the things after death' and prophecises fire: the mysteries are practised 'in an unholy way' because they are practised in ignorance of how cosmology determines eschatology (life, death and the cosmos). Herakleitos, in insisting on the importance of understanding the *logos*, envisages himself as transforming understanding (of life, death and the cosmos) independently of the enactment of ritual. The kind of wisdom revealed in mystic ritual has – with Herakleitos – become detached from its *enactment*, interiorised.

To this transition from mystery-cult to 'philosophy' we might apply, approximately, what Tull (1989: 121) writes of India:

[22] If not polluted by bloodguilt: refs in Parker (2005) [23] Seaford (2012a) 45–6, 276–7.
[24] DK22 A1(6), A2; cf. B125.
[25] E.g. Hdt. 2.51.4; many further refs. in Seaford (2004) 233 n.18; see also Riedweg (1987) 5–14.

> The Brahmanic abstraction of death in the ritual sphere thus seems to have provided the Upanishadic thinkers with the ability to confront death, in whatever context it may have occurred, in the same 'unreal' way in which it was experienced in the context of the ritual performance. This ability, which also allowed the Upanishadic thinkers to move beyond the specific confines of the ritual arena, reflects a process of generalisation, as the structures, paradigms, and principles long established in that arena, were carried outward to a larger world of experience.

In Greece, as in India, the emergence of 'philosophy' accompanies the process of detachment from – or going beyond – the cosmic rite of passage.

Herakleitos' repeated emphasis on knowledge and understanding of the *logos* amounts to interiorisation of the ritual. He resembles the priests (including his ancestors) who transmitted the enigmatic *logos* in mystic ritual, but he transmits it – and his audience or readership receives it – without enacting the ritual.

Enactment of the ritual is replaced by a new version of the knowledge and understanding traditionally revealed in the ritual. This new version is the wisdom that we call philosophy, propounded by Herakleitos. Emphasis on (quasi-mystic) understanding at the expense of enactment, and the interiorisation of ritual that is generally performed by a group, imply the *individualisation* of the ritual. But in fact the communality of the ritual is preserved in Herakleitos' enhancement of the authority of his doctrine by dissociating it from himself: people should listen 'not to me', says Herakleitos, 'but to the *logos*' (B50), which is common to all (B2). To the interaction of individual and communality (at once monetised and mystic) in Herakleitos we will return in 14§A.

It remains to indicate the surviving evidence for my claim, argued in more detail elsewhere,[26] that Herakleitos' discourse resembled mystic doctrine both in the manner of its presentation and in its content.

Herakleitos' discourse is – like the language used in mystic initiation – riddling.[27] Accordingly – and this too resembles mystic discourse – the *logos* that he propounds is, he states, not understood at first hearing.[28] In a later text (*AP* 9.540) the difficulty of Herakleitos' book is imagined as the initial darkness that is in the course of mystic initiation transformed into light. The Olbian mystic inscriptions described above are strikingly similar, in both form and content, to Herakleitean fragments such as B62 'immortals mortals, mortals immortals, . . .' or B67 'god is day night, winter summer, war

[26] Seaford (1986) 14–20; Seaford (2004) 234–8; Schefer (2000).

[27] Seaford (2004) 184, 226 n.36, 233 n.19.

[28] B1, B34; Thomson (1961) 273–5: Schefer (2000) 56–62.

peace, . . .' The similarity is surely due to Herakleitos' use of the riddling style of mystery-cult,[29] a hypothesis proposed well before the discovery of the Olbian incriptions (published in 1978) and confirmed by them.

This brings us to what Herakleitean cosmology shares with the *content* of mystic doctrine, namely four things in particular: the idea that mortals are immortals, the general importance of the unity of opposites,[30] the idea that there are better and worse fates after death and the importance of cosmological elements in the cyclical passage of the *psuchē*. The Olbian 'life death life' resembles Herakleitos in content as well as in style, signifying as it does our transition (as immortal mortals or mortal immortals) through 'death' back to life, thereby also implying the unity of the opposites of life and death.[31] The content of the mystic *logos* was sometimes a myth, which might explain the unity of immortality and mortal suffering in humankind (we are Titans), but also might be interpreted as a riddling account of physical cosmology.[32]

Herakleitos' interiorisation of mystery-cult, the privileging of knowledge over performance, is facilitated by the range of the word *logos*, which could mean not only the discourse delivered in mystic initiation (i.e. part of a *performance*) but also an abstract formula (i.e. an object of *knowledge*). It could in the fifth century BCE, and probably even already in the sixth, also mean monetary account.[33] Because Herakleitos may not have distinguished between these meanings,[34] *logos* formed a bridge between performance, understanding and interiorisation (and even monetisation). The *logos* is presented as if it were the *logos* pronounced in the mysteries, but it is common to all (B2) and inheres in fire, which is an ingredient of the *psuchē*.[35]

This, the earliest extant Greek interiorisation of ritual, is to be found in the thinker who also provided the earliest extant Greek description of the soul (*psuchē*) as an organ of comprehensive consciousness (13§D). As in India, this combination is not coincidental.

11§D The Interiorisation of Mystery-Cult in Parmenides

The fragments of Parmenides contain a narrative in which he journeys to the underworld, where a goddess reveals wisdom to him. The narrative has

[29] If the plates were influenced by Herakleitos (rather than vice versa), which is extremely unlikely, this would require explanation, best provided by the mystic form and content of Herakleitos' *logos*.

[30] The mystic rite of passage involves the unity not only of the opposites of mortal and immortal, and of life and death, but also of male and female and of animal and human: see Seaford (1996) 43–4.

[31] Cf. also B88: 'The same thing in us is the living and the dead . . .'; gold leaf 4.4 Graf-Johnston. More detail in Seaford (1986) 17–20.

[32] As in the Derveni papyrus: Seaford (2004) 233–5. [33] Seaford (2004) 231. [34] Cf. B48

[35] KRS 187–8, 199–200, 203–8; Guthrie (1962) 428–32; Seaford (2004) 232–3, 300.

been shown to correspond in various details to mystic initiation.[36] And there are, I suggest, reasons for believing that – as with Herakleitos – Parmenides' doctrine is influenced by mystery-cult not only in its presentation but also in its content.[37]

Mystic ritual is generally performed by a group, whereas the mystic journey of Parmenides is the mere vision of a mere individual, and as such it individualises as well as interiorises mystic ritual, as does Herakleitos. But with Parmenides the individualisation is unusually marked. He represents the wisdom of the goddess as revealed to himself alone, setting him apart from the ignorance of mortals.[38] Parmenides is carried, as 'the man who knows' (i.e. the mystic initiate),[39] along one path, 'far from the treading of humankind' (B1.2–3, 27), to the goddess, who warns him off other paths, one of which is followed by 'mortals knowing nothing' (B6.3–7).[40]

Similarly, in mystic initiation there is a right path and a wrong path. Funerary gold leaves of the fourth century BCE contain claims that are almost certainly to have been uttered by the mystic initiand on arrival in the underworld: (s)he is of the race of the gods, was subdued by a thunderbolt, has paid the penalty of unjust deeds, has flown from the circle of suffering and desires to be sent by Persephone to the seats of the pure.[41] The circle of suffering refers presumably to the mystic doctrine of reincarnation,[42] and the seats of the pure are presumably a place of irreversible well-being.[43] An initiate is urged to 'journey to the right, to the holy meadows and groves of Persephone'.[44] And a recurrent instruction is to avoid a certain spring, and instead to go further on and drink from the waters of memory: 'thereafter you will rule among the other heroes'.[45] The first spring was presumably the waters of forgetfulness, which probably led – as in Plato (*Republic* 621ab) – to reincarnation. Of the two paths one leads to an unchanging destination, the

[36] References in Seaford (2004) 185 n.58; also 228, 263–5; Burkert (1969); most recently Tor (2017) 267–73.

[37] Seaford (2004) 228–9, 262–3. [38] B1.2–3, 27, 30–2; 6.4–9; 7.2–6; 8.51–2.

[39] Thomson (1961) 289–90; Burkert (1969) 5.

[40] On the two roads as derived from mystery cult, see 14§D.

[41] 2.7; 5.3–5; 6.3–7; 7.3–7 Graf-Johnston. All this is probably based on a claim to be one of the immortal Titans: Seaford (1986).

[42] Graf and Johnston (2007) 127; Zuntz (1971) 321. For Pythagoras the *psuchē* was reincarnated in a circle of necessity (κύκλος ἀνάγκης) according to D.L. 8.14 (probably from Aristoxenos). An Orphic poem referred to escape from the circle (κύκλος) of reincarnation, on which Proclus commented that according to Orpheus it was desired by those being initiated to Dionysos and Korē (*Orphicorum fr.* 348 Bernabé); cf. also Pl. *Phaedo* 72b.

[43] At 5.9 comes the response 'happy and blessed, you will be a god instead of a mortal'. Persephone sends souls to permanent well-being at Pindar *fr.* 133.

[44] 3.5–6 Graf-Johnston. [45] 1.12–14; 2.9–11 Graf-Johnston.

other to undesirable cyclicality, as in the two-path doctrines in the early *Upanishads* (9§D) and in Plato (11§E).

Parmenides, like Plato, gives the two mystic paths a philosophical content, new but not unrelated to mystic ideas: one path leads to the understanding of the permanent unchangingness and abstract uniformity of what exists, whereas the other is followed by ignorant mortals who trust their senses and believe that Being and not-Being are 'the same and not the same, and the path of all is backward-turning (*palintropos*)' (B6.9). *Palintropos* here is generally taken to mean 'contradictory', which it does, but I suggest that it also evokes the path to reincarnation (*turning back* to this world, rather than going to the blessed place): the believer in variety and change is disqualified from permanent well-being. All this is in the part of Parmenides' doctrine called the Way of Truth, but in the Way of Seeming he seems to have propounded reincarnation.[46] The traditionally concrete paths leading (as in India) respectively to eternal being and reincarnation now lead to new abstractions (permanence and contradiction).

Both two-path doctrines (Indian and Parmenidean) concern the hereafter, and they both derive from an opposition that (a) is expressed in a rite of passage to the hereafter, and (b) merges with the opposition between the monetary cycle and escape from the monetary cycle into a place of permanent well-being through the self-sufficiency bestowed by the universal (monetary) value that is projected as the Upanishadic brahman and the Parmenidean One.

Individual isolation, which could occur as a temporary phase in mystic initiation (before integration into the initiated group),[47] is adapted by Parmenides into a permanent state that expresses traditional aristocratic self-sufficiency enhanced by the new seeming self-sufficiency of the monetary abstraction imagined as separate from universal circulation.[48] The chariot in which he makes his mystic journey far from humankind expresses both his isolation and his aristocratic wealth and status.[49]

Similar coalescence of the isolation of the mystic initiand with the isolating effect of money is found in Athenian tragedy. Two important factors in the genesis of tragedy were the mysteries of Dionysos and tyranny, each of which involved the isolation of an individual – the passive isolation of the mystic initiand and the active isolation of the tyrant as man

[46] B12.4; Tor (2017) 237–9. My remarks about Parmenides in this book almost all refer to his Way of Truth: for a good recent account of its relationship with the Way of Seeming, see Tor (2017).

[47] 14§A; Seaford (2004) 299.

[48] Seaford (2004) 244–65, 300; Parmenides a wealthy aristocrat: D.L. 9.21.

[49] Egalitarian banning of riding in chariots on the road to the Eleusinian mysteries: Plut. *Moralia* 842a.

of money.[50] The coalescence of these two opposed forms of isolation is beautifully exemplified by Pentheus in Euripides' *Bacchae*, at once mystic initiand and monetised tyrant.[51] It is their coalescence that produces the unprecedented isolation of the tragic individual.[52]

Inasmuch as the journey imagined by Parmenides is a vision inspired by ritual, it also represents the *interiorisation* of the ritual. Moreover, the goddess urges Parmenides to *introspect*: absent things present to the mind (i.e. objects of thought and imagination) are *continuous* (B4). We will return to this important passage in 12§A and 14§A. For now we emphasise that we have a *dual* interiorisation: within the interiorised mystic revelation there is further interiorisation in the form of introspection. Further, similar terminology is used to describe the continuity of what is introspected and the continuity of what exists (the One):[53] this implies a degree of *assimilation* between the subjective (absent things present to the mind of Parmenides) and the objective (what exists). Given that they are both unitary, this resembles the Upanishadic coalescence of mental with abstract monism described in 8§C (6).

This is not the only instance of such assimilation in Parmenides.[54] He says of the One, 'it is whole-limbed and untrembling and not uncompleted': ἔστι γὰρ οὐλομελές[55] τε καὶ ἀτρεμὲς οὐδ' ἀτέλεστον (B8.24). The uncommon word ἀτρεμής (untrembling), though it describes here the objective One, also implies subjectivity, as it does also more clearly when describing the 'heart' of Truth at B1.29. The same word appears also in the passage of Plato's *Phaedrus* in which he describes pre-natal

> mysteries which it is right to call most blessed, which we celebrated ourselves whole (ὁλόκληροι) . . . with the gaze of our final initiation on whole (ὁλόκληρα) and simple and untrembling *(*ἀτρεμῆ*)* and blessed apparitions in a pure light, ourselves being pure (ἐν αὐγῇ καθαρᾷ, καθαροὶ ὄντες) (250b8-c6).

[50] Cf. 7§B; Seaford (2012a) Part II. [51] Seaford (2004) 307–10.

[52] On Parmenides and the tragic individual see Seaford (2012a) 258–9, 327, 329, 331.

[53] Cf. B4.2 with B8.23–5. [54] Seaford (2004) 227–9, 252.

[55] ἔστι γὰρ οὐλομελές is from the quotation of the line by Plutarch (*Mor.* 1114c; Proclus too quotes it with οὐλομελές). But Simplicius quotes it as οὖλον μουνογενές τε καὶ ἀτρεμὲς ἠδ' ἀτέλεστον, which is generally preferred (with ἠδὲ τελεῖον for the impossible ἠδ' ἀτέλεστον): but we will see (11§E) a hitherto unnoticed respect in which οὐλομελές here makes perfect sense, although it would have seemed to scribes (and still seems) outlandish, and so is by far the *lectio difficilior*, with the bland μουνογενές seeming obviously preferable, despite its inconsistency with ἀγένητον in the previous verse. Owen (1960) urges that Plutarch was often inaccurate in quoting, and misquotes the end of this very line: but so do the other sources for it. Better than τελεῖον is the slighter change οὐδ' (Brandis) for ἠδ': see 11§E.

The combination of wholeness with 'untrembling' in both Parmenides and the explicitly mystic Platonic passage confirms that Parmenides is thinking of the goddess' revelation of the One in terms of mystic revelation.[56] Further, in the Platonic passage 'blessed' (εὐδαίμων) is a word used of the permanent happiness bestowed by mystic initiation on the initiates.[57] Its application here along with 'untrembling' to the apparitions, together with the use of the same words for 'whole' and 'pure' to describe both the initiates *and* what they see, must be taken in conjunction with various passages of Plato and others[58] based on the idea *that the initiates are partially assimilated to what they see or contemplate in mystic initiation.* Plotinus, for instance, implies that in mystery-cult the person who sees is one with what he sees,[59] and Proclus states that some of the initiates assimilate themselves to the sacred symbols.[60] As for 'untrembling', trembling was a typical feature of the suffering of the mystic initiands before their transition to calm,[61] and Proclus describes mystic apparitions as 'full of calm' (γαλήνης μεστὰ).[62] Indeed, the mystic union of subject with object in Plotinus was in an 'untrembling (ἀτρεμής) state' (6.9.11.14). One of the few reliable biographical details for Parmenides is that he was 'converted towards ἡσυχία (calm)' by one Ameinias.[63] Ἡσυχία was achieved in mystic initiation.[64]

Parmenides interiorises mystic ritual. But mystic ritual, even when actually performed, itself might already contain some interiorisation of object by subject. The division between subject and object of the mystic vision would tend to be transcended by partial assimilation between the two, in both directions. In Parmenides, we have seen, the distinction between subject and object is transcended, both in his deductive argument and in his vision of the One as 'whole and of a single kind and untrembling and complete'. The vision results from the 'philosophical' interiorisation of

[56] Parmenides' τέλειον is also associated with mystic ritual (11§E). On the Parmenidean One as like a sphere (*sphaira*: B8.43) and the revelation of a *sphaira* in mystic initiation, rather as Herakleitos takes the mystic *kukeōn* to illustrate the constant motion of the cosmos, see Seaford (2004) 228–9, 238, 263.

[57] E.g. E. *Bacchae* 902 with Seaford ad loc.

[58] *Phaedrus* 249c7, *Phaedo* 79d, 81a, *Symposium* 212a; note also Plut. *fr.* 178; Plotinus *Enneads* 6.9.11.1–7; At Ps.Dionysius *Celestial Hierarchy* 3.1–2 (164d) the beauty worthy of god initiates the initiands by making them an indistinguishable likeness of itself.

[59] *Enneads* 6.9.11. This whole chapter interiorises mystic initiation.

[60] Proclus *In Rempublicam* 2.108.17–24 Kroll.

[61] Seaford (2009) discusses numerous passages; Seaford (2004) 229.

[62] Proclus *In Rempublicam* 2.185.3 Kroll.

[63] Sotion ap. D.L. 9.23. Ameinias is otherwise unknown, and so the detail was unlikely to be invented.

[64] Seaford (1996) 201. Kingsley (1999) associates Parmenides with the practice of incubation.

the ritual interiorisation of what is seen by the mystic initiate. Whereas in India there emerges from the cosmic rite of passage (sacrifice) the 'philosophical' coalescence of mental monism with abstract monism, in Parmenides we see the influence of the cosmic rite of passage (mystic initiation) on a comparable coalescence.

11§E The Interiorisation of Mystery-Cult in Plato

In the extensively preserved dialogues of Plato the ritual and doctrine of mystery-cult are mentioned or evoked more frequently and more explicitly than in the extant fragments of Herakleitos and Parmenides. In these passages the *psuchē* has a central place. It is from '*hosia* and *nomima* here on earth' (almost certainly mystery-cult) that Plato infers the post-mortem journey of the *psuchē* (*Phaedo* 108a). The allegory of the *psuchē* in his *Phaedrus* is full of evocations of mystery-cult.[65] A metaphor in the *Republic* (560e) speaks of purifying the *psuchē* of the person being initiated preparatory to the transformative arrival of a crowned chorus. The followers of Orpheus are said to have taught that the *psuchē* is punished by being imprisoned in the body (*Cratylus* 400c; cf. *Phaedo* 62b). The doctrine of the persistence of the immortal *psuchē* through death and rebirth is attributed by Plato (*Meno* 81ab) to a *logos* told by priests and priestesses (almost certainly in mystery-cult).

Further, Plato uses the structure and vocabulary of mystic initiation to describe the intellectual progress of the philosopher (*Symposium*) and a prenatal experience of the *psuchē* (*Phaedrus*). Because in neither case is ritual enacted, we may say that the ritual has been interiorised. The result – a coherent and influential ethics that (at least for an elite) replaced the performance of ritual with a subtle combination of freedom from (bodily) desire with abstract understanding – in these respects resembled early Buddhism.

We will focus on two closely interconnected aspects of the Platonic interiorisation of ritual: further evidence for the *assimilation of the initiate to what he sees*, and the *wholeness* of the initiate.

In our discussion of Parmenides together with Plato's *Phaedrus* 250b8-c6 (11§D) we detected the implication that in mystic initiation subject and object are assimilated to each other in respect of being pure, blessed, whole and untrembling. According to Plato (*Phaedrus* 249c7):

[65] Riedweg (1987) 30–69.

> He who uses such memories rightly, always being initiated into perfect mysteries (τελέους ἀεὶ τελετὰς τελούμενος), becomes alone truly τελέος (complete, perfect).

'Such memories' refers to a pre-natal mystic vision, which a human remembers by understanding (249b8):

> a general conception going from many sense-perceptions into a unity (εἷς ἕν) collected by reasoning. This is a memory of those things which our *psuchē* once saw when it journeyed with god . . . [i.e. in the mystic vision].[66]

This helps to explain why shortly afterwards, in the passage we discussed above (250b8-c6), Plato insists on the *wholeness* of the mystic initiate. His account in *Phaedo* of the psuchē *gathering itself from all parts of the body*[67] may be one of the ideas that this passage of Plato has taken from mystery-cult.[68] It inspired the Neoplatonist Plotinus' account (*Enneads* 1.6.5) of the longing to 'gather yourselves away from your body' with an excitement that he calls a 'bacchic revel' (ἀναβακχεύεσθε). In Neoplatonism the dismemberment of Dionysos as expressing the fragmentation of the inner self, and his reconstitution as expressing its subsequent self-gathering back into unity, may derive from the reality of mystic ritual, in which the mystic initiand experiences the *bodily* sacrificial fragmentation and reconstitution of Dionysos as a transition from *mental* fragmentation to unity (6§A). Mental fragmentation is naturally expressed by the idea of bodily fragmentation, especially in the pre-Platonic era, in which the mind is imagined as – however tenuously – material. Similarly, the sacrificial fragmentation and recomposition of Prajapati is bodily but also mental, interiorised by the sacrificer (6§A), who makes Prajapati *sarva* (whole) and himself becomes *sarva*, just as the universe obtained by the sacrificer is *sarva* (6§B), rather as in *Phaedrus* the mystic initiates are 'whole' and see 'whole' apparitions.

This is the context in which Parmenides B8.4, in the version I have argued for (11§D n.15), turns out to makes perfect sense: 'it is whole-limbed (οὐλομελές)[69] and untrembling and not uncompleted (ἀτέλεστον)'. This produces a powerfully coherent verse, in which all three descriptions of the One both prefigure later descriptions of it[70] and evoke the *subject at the*

66 For the importance of mystic initiation throughout this passage of *Phaedrus*, see Riedweg (1987) 30–69.

67 67c συναγείρεσθαί τε καὶ ἀθροίζεσθαι, and similarly 80e, 83a. Cf. Augustine *Confessions* 10.11.18.

68 Riedweg (1987) 11, 19, 27, 53.

69 Cf. Empedokles B62.4 οὐλοφυεῖς in the context of the alternation of bodily wholeness and fragmentation.

70 At B8.22–6, 29–30, 38, 42.

conclusion of mystic initiation. Ἀτέλεστος means unperfected (or unfulfilled), or *uninitiated.*[71] Here in Parmenides it applies primarily to the One ('not unperfected') but also evokes the initiatory subject ('not uninitiated'): in both these respects it functions just like οὐλομελές and ἀτρεμές. The triple description (οὐλομελές τε καὶ ἀτρεμὲς οὐδ' ἀτέλεστον)[72] evokes the three fundamental respects in which the initiate who has reached the final phase is similar to a mystic object.

The *Epinomis* (attributed to Plato) associates by juxtaposition the unity of the mystic initiate with the unity of his thought (986d): a εὐδαίμων (happy, blessed) person who admires and learns the movements of the heavenly bodies:

> considering in this way to live the best and most fortunate life, and on death to come to places appropriate for virtue, and having been initiated (μεμυημένος) truly and really, participating, *being one, in one* thinking (μεταλαβὼν φρονήσεως εἷς ὢν μιᾶς) for the remaining time he will continue to be a spectator of most beautiful things . . .

When the *psuchē* is by itself (alone, free from the body), it associates with what it resembles:

> When the *psuchē* enquires by itself, it departs into the pure and everlasting and immortal and unchanging, and being akin (συγγενής) to it remains always with it, whenever it is itself by itself and not hindered, and ceases from its wandering and remains in relation to those things always constant and unchanging, because in touch with such things. (*Phaedo* 79d).

Such a *psuchē*, purified by philosophy, gathers itself into itself from the body and is pure.[73] Again it seems that this is mystic doctrine, for we are in the same passage told that the *psuchē*:

> departs into what is like itself, into the invisible, divine, immortal, wise . . . and, according to the initiated, passes all remaining time truly with the gods.[74]

And those who exchange pleasures and pains etc. for the 'only right currency' (νόμισμα), wisdom, are identified with mystic initiates who in the next world will dwell with the gods (69a-c). In withdrawing from the senses, the *psuchē* is to 'trust nothing except itself in its thought by itself of

[71] E.g. Pl. *Phaedo* 69c; E. *Bacchae* 40.

[72] I do not insist on the initial ἔστι γὰρ, which may be Plutarch's own words.

[73] 80e, 83a. Cf. BU 4.4.23: 'A man who knows this, therefore, becomes calm, composed, cool, patient, and collected. He sees the self (atman) in just himself (atman) and all things as the self'.

[74] 81a. See also 67a, 79d, 80d, 84b, 114c.

what exists by itself', and so 'sees the intelligible and invisible' (83b). It contains its own abstract object of thought, which it sees only when it achieves the purity of withdrawal from the senses,[75] rather as mystic initiation requires exclusive focus on the object to which the inner self of the purified initiate is assimilated.

It is by achieving purity through mystic initiation that the initiate or his *psuchē* attains to what is pure. 'It is not legitimate for the impure to attain to the pure' (67b). In *Phaedrus* the initiates are 'in a pure light, ourselves being pure' (250c6), and in *Phaedo* the immortalising purity bestowed by mystic initiation gives access to a pure place[76] as well the company of pure people.[77] The mention of pure *people*[78] is one of a few slight indications in Plato of the *communal* culmination of mystic initiation.[79]

The influence of mystic initiation is manifest not only in this assimilation to – and vision of – the divine, but also in the choice between ways of life. In *Phaedo* Plato infers from mystery-cult that the path to the underworld has many forks and windings, with different destinations for the good and the bad *psuchē* (soul, 108a-c). Those who are dominated by bodily pleasures and pains etc. are subjected to the cycle of reincarnation (81de, 83d), from which the philosopher escapes by virtue of his absorption in self-sufficient abstract Being. Like Parmenides (11§D), Plato adapts to his philosophy the mystic doctrine of two paths. His cycle is – like the Herakleitean cosmic cycle – a synthesis of mystic doctrine with the cosmisation of the monetised cycle. But from the more communal perspective of Herakleitos there is, so far as we can tell from his surviving fragments, no escape from the cycle.[80]

Finally, in Plato's *Symposium* we find a detailed description of the mystic transition from multiplicity to unity, culminating in an indication of the immortalising assimilation of subject to mystic object. The philosopher's ascent from the multiplicity of particular objects of sense to the 'beauty of the psuchē', and then to beauty itself, is described as a mystic initiation, in which the initiate finally sees a single unitary abstraction of absolute, eternal beauty, through which he finally becomes 'if any other of mankind,

[75] Similar is *Republic* 611e-612a. [76] 80d, 114c; Plut. *fr.* 178.

[77] 67a; Plut. *fr.* 178. Pure knowledge is possible only when the soul is by itself and apart from the body after death (*Phaedo* 66e). And so we should, so far as is possible, keep ourselves pure of the body until god himself frees us (i.e. in death), enabling us to be with the pure: 67, 69c, 79d.

[78] 67a: μετὰ τοιούτων (with no noun) refers – as almost always elsewhere – to *people* (not things), as in its only other occurrence in Plato (*Meno* 90b3): cf. the 'pure men' whom the initiated join in Plut. *fr.* 178.

[79] 14§A n. 14. [80] That he did envisage escape is argued by Guthrie (1962) 481.

immortal, he too'.[81] The perception of abstract unity beyond the appearance of diversity is salvational also in India, for instance at BU 4.4.18–20, quoted in 8§C.

In conclusion, we have seen that for both Parmenides and Plato what is seen as if in mystic initiation (a) is authoritative, even transcendent, (b) resembles the initiate (pure, whole, complete, untrembling) and (c) also resembles and expresses the mental state of the philosopher. (a) and (b) seem to have been features of actual mystic ritual. As for (c), the intensity, wisdom and traditional authority of the death-defying experience of mystic initiation, its power to overcome the separation of subject from object, are deployed to support a new 'philosophical' vision, albeit differently by the two philosophers. For Parmenides the mental state involves individual introspection, yielding an abstract unity that accords with a vision of all that exists (the abstract One). For Plato, a century or so later, a more sophisticated abstract unity is obtained by sustained mental effort of individual abstraction from the corporeal. But in both cases, as in the *Upanishads*, the interiorisation of ritual has led to assimilation between individual abstract subject and universal abstract object.

[81] 212a . . . ἀθανάτῳ καὶ ἐκείνῳ. This reflects the salvational sight of a single object (ear of corn, phallus, etc.) as the culmination of mystic initiation (Seaford [2004] 228).

CHAPTER 12

Monism and Inner Self

This chapter describes the development of Greek monism, and identifies two important similarities with the development of Indian monism. One is the relationship between the development of monism and the development of the idea of the unitary inner self. The other is the overall development – in ideas of the cosmic process – from reciprocity to an invisible monistic automatism.

12§A Greek Monisms

The earliest Greek 'philosophy' was produced in the first half of the sixth century BCE at Miletos. About the three earliest (Milesian) philosophers (Thales, Anaximander and Anaximenes) we are told much by later writers, but of their actual words we possess very little. We do not know whether they were interested in ritual, for example, or in the idea of a unitary entity of individual consciousness. But we do know that each of them propounded a version of monism, with water (Thales), the unlimited (Anaximander) and air (Anaximenes) as the substrate or single principle. The earliest philosophers of whom we possess more than a few *ipsissima verba* are Xenophanes of Colophon, Herakleitos of Ephesos and Parmenides of Elea. These three can all also be called monists, albeit of very different kinds. I propose now to look in these six thinkers, as well as in Plato, for the development of monism (again using the categories described in 4§E) and its connection with the idea of a unitary inner self.

In Homer and Hesiod there is no present monism, and barely any primordial monism (4§E). Presocratic philosophy, by contrast, exhibits all four of the present monisms – material, abstract, personal, mental – that we also find in early Indian texts.

(1) *Material Monism*

The earliest Greek monism was material monism. A clear account of it is by Aristotle (*Metaphysics* 983b):[1]

> Of the first philosophers the majority thought that the causes in the form of matter were alone the principle of all things. For that from which all entities come, from which each thing primarily arises and into which it is at the end resolved, the substance remaining but changing as to affections, this they announced to be the element and principle of all entities.

Aristotle then mentions Thales announcing the principle to be water, Anaximenes (and Diogenes of Apollonia) air and Herakleitos (and Hippasos) fire. Greek material monism sometimes approximates to mental monism, and also has a tendency to abstract monism (to the extent that the unlimited, air and Herakleitean *logos*-embodying fire are quasi-abstract).

(2) *Personal Monism*

Xenophanes of Colophon (circa 565–475 BCE) maintains that all things are one,[2] and that there is one god who is in some sense identical with the universe.[3] To the extent that he envisages this god (in the traditional way) as a person[4] – this is the earliest suggestion of personal monism. But in fact it seems closer to mental monism (see below).

[1] Graham (2006) argues that Aristotle here is so grievously ill-informed or so insensitive to fundamental distinctions (or both) as to be entirely mistaken. Graham makes this remarkable claim by virtue of his dogmatic (and in my view erroneous) assumptions that presocratic thought is (a) purely philosophical, or scientific, and (b) a *single* undertaking, with all the 'philosophers' engaged on basically the same project. The 'philosophical incoherence' of material monism is for Graham evidence that the Milesians were not material monists: instead they merely derived everything from a single generating substance. For Aristotle material monists think that nothing comes to be or is destroyed; and accordingly Parmenides, in arguing (against the Milesians, it is assumed) that nothing comes to be or is destroyed, cannot be arguing against material monism, which was therefore not held by the Milesians. One of the flaws in these arguments is to require strict consistency of expression from the very earliest 'philosophers', whereas it is e.g. obvious both that water becomes ice and that ice is water. The image which Anaximenes chooses to illustrate the transformation of his substrate (air) is felting, in which wool becomes something else (yes, while still being wool) that does not contain anything else. On Herakleitos' statement that the cosmos is an ever-living fire Graham remarks that 'no one has yet defended the traditional reading without convicting Herakleitos of logical incoherence' (142). Well, *of course* Herakleitos is frequently 'logically incoherent'. The key to understanding Herakleitos' vision is not our own precoccupation with 'logical coherence' but his preconceptions. Identifying preconceptions might have saved Graham from the erroneous view that the greater divergence of material monism (than source monism) from everyday experience argues against the Milesian cosmologists being material monists. Everyday observation and logic leads neither to material monism nor to a thousand other seriously propounded beliefs.

[2] DK21 A4, A29, A31, A34-6. [3] DK21 A30; Guthrie (1962) 379–82.

[4] He calls the god 'greatest among gods and men' (B23), which, however, also seems to negate monism.

Roughly contemporary with Xenophanes is an Orphic verse theogony of which fragments are quoted in the Derveni papyrus. In one such fragment (quoted in 6§A) Zeus swallows all things and 'he himself became the sole one'. This personal monism is presumably anthropomorphic. But because later in the narrative Zeus presumably recreated the gods and world out of himself,[5] the monism was only temporary.[6] On the other hand in a fragment of Aeschylus (525–456 BCE) non-anthropomorphic personal monism occurs in the present tense:[7]

> Zeus is aither, Zeus is earth, Zeus is sky.
> Zeus is all things and whatever is above them.

In the fifth-century Pythagorean cosmogony described by Aristotle the cosmos is generated by breathing in, rather as an animal on being born breathes in.[8] This is, or is close to, primordial personal monism. Moving on to the fourth century BCE, we find in the Pythagoreanising cosmogony of late Plato the idea that the universe is a living creature with a *psuchē* and intelligence. In *Philebus* (30a) the body of the universe (τὸ τοῦ παντὸς σῶμα) has a *psuchē*, from which derives the human *psuchē*. In *Timaios* the creator made the universe as a living creature endowed with *psuchē* and mind, and subsequently divided the cosmic *psuchē* into human *psuchai*.[9] At *Statesman* 269 the universe (τὸ πᾶν) is a creature (ζῶον) with intelligence. At *Sophist* 248–9 *psuchē*, mind and life are accorded to absolute being (τὸ παντελῶς ὄν).

(3) Mental Monism

The monism visible in the fragments of Xenophanes has a suggestion of the personal (see above), but is in fact closer to mental monism. The one god identical with the universe is 'quite unlike mortals in body and thought' (B23). 'All of him sees, all of him thinks, all of him hears' (B24). 'He stays always in the same place' (B26) and 'without effort he shakes all things by the thought of his mind' (B25). Whereas in Homer the (physical) *nod* of Zeus shakes *Olympos*, for Xenophanes, using Homeric language and metre,

[5] As was recorded in the later Stoic and rhapsodic versions: West (1983) 90. However, the present identification of Zeus with everything occurs in the later Orphic fragment 243 Bernabé, which identifies parts of the cosmos with parts of his body.

[6] Perhaps therefore we should call it – in our terminology – reductionism; cf. what seems to be temporary personal or mental monism in Empedokles (14§D): in fact, there are four 'roots of everything' (B6; A37).

[7] *fr.* 70; Seaford (2010a). [8] DK58 B30; Huffman (1993) 43–7, 202–14.

[9] *Timaios* 30b, 35a, 36d–37c, 41d, 43d–44b.

it is nevertheless god's *thought* that shakes *all things*. Anthropomorphic deity has been largely replaced by ubiquitously powerful *mind*.

The Orphic verse just discussed in (2) is quoted by the Derveni Commentator, who interprets the phrase 'and he himself became the sole one', as referring to the dependence of existing things on the mind, as if they were nothing, with the mind worth everything (6§A). The temporary personal monism of the Orphic narrative is interpreted by the Commentator as an allegoric reference to something close to present mental monism.

In both Xenophanes and the Derveni Commentator mental monism emerges from personal monism through the mind *of god*. We saw something similar in the dreamer who 'appearing to be a god or a king thinks "I am alone in this world! I am all!" – that is his highest world' (BU 4.3.20; 7§A). There is also what may be called periodic mental monism in Empedokles (14§D).

Mental monism is sometimes associated with material monism. What seems to be the only surviving sentence of Anaximenes is attributed to him by Aetius (B2):

> Just as the *psuchē*,' he says, 'being our air holds us together, so *pneuma* (wind, breath)[10] and air enclose the whole cosmos'.

We also know that for Anaximenes the material substrate of all things is air, which is transformed into other things by being condensed or rarefied. There is some form of assimilation here of the human *psuchē* (composed of air) to the whole cosmos (also composed of air), but how exactly Anaximenes envisaged this – whether for instance he imagined the cosmos as conscious – we cannot know.

Herakleitos has the earliest extant focus on the *psuchē* as a unitary entity of consciousness. The cosmos is an 'everliving fire', and several fragments cohere in implying that the *psuchē*, too, is composed – primarily at least – of fire (13§D). The *logos*, an abstract formula according to which all things happen, is somehow embodied in fire (9§E), and is accordingly both in the *psuchē* and communal.[11] And so, as with Anaximenes, *psuchē* and cosmos are composed of the same universal substrate. But we do not know whether they held that the universal substrate was always in some sense conscious. This does, though, seem to be the view of Diogenes of Apollonia (floruit

[10] For the identification of macrosmic wind with microcosmic breath, cf. CU 4.3.1–3 (8§C), KU 2.11–12 (9§D), Tritopateres (10§A).

[11] B1, B115, B2; also B113, B114.

circa 440–30 BCE), who maintained that 'all existing things are differentiated from the same thing and are the same thing', namely air, which 'has intelligence' and is breathed by men as *psuchē* and intelligence.[12] Here it seems that material monism and mental monism coalesce.

In Anaximenes and Herakleitos the material substrate not only constitutes the entity of individual consciousness (*psuchē*) but also has a controlling or integrating role. Just as the invisible unlimited of Anaximander both encloses (περιέχει) and steers all things as well as being divine,[13] so the invisible air of Anaximenes encloses (περιέχει) the whole cosmos, 'as our *psuchē*, being our air, holds us together'.[14] The *psuchē* resembles the cosmic substrate here not only as consisting of the same invisible substance but also as exercising *unifying* power.[15] As for Herakleitos, he maintains that we should be guided by the *logos*,[16] according to which – embodied as it is in the fire (9§E) that constitutes cosmos and *psuchē* – all things happen.

(4) Abstract Monism

Anaximander stated that the element from and into which everything is transformed is 'the unlimited' (τὸ ἄπειρον).[17] The distinction between material and non-material is unlikely to have been available to Anaximander, but in so far as the ἄπειρον is envisaged as imperceptible, we may be inclined to classify it as abstract monism.[18]

Whereas for Herakleitos all things are in constant flux, for Parmenides in the Way of Truth all differentiation in time and space is illusory: all that exists is one, eternal, unchanging, motionless, homogeneous, continuous and abstract, to be apprehended by *logos* as opposed to the senses. This is present abstract monism.[19]

12 DK64 B2, B4, B5, A19(42). In B2 he regards monism as a *precondition* for interaction (including 'helping' and 'harming') – another analogy with money.

13 Aristotle *Physics* 203b7-9.

14 The statement (if not every word) is Anaximenean: KRS 159–62; Seaford (2004) 243.

15 True, this conception of the unifying soul is not explicit anywhere else before Aristotle, but is simple enough to have occurred to Anaximenes and Diogenes, and may owe something to the old idea of breath as life.

16 B1, B2, B50.

17 A recent attempt to reinterpret (what our ancient sources call) the ἄπειρον as φύσις ἄπειρος is by Kočandrle and Couprie (2017).

18 It is, though, possible that he was (in our terminology) more of a reductionist than a monist, i.e. more concerned with the unlimited as origin and destination of all things than as their persistent substrate.

19 For telling objections to the argument, recently proposed by Sisko and Weiss (2015), that Parmenides was a material monist, see Tor (2017) 290–2.

Parmenides' argument appeals to what he claims to be the continuity of absent things present to the individual mind:[20]

> Look equally with your mind (*nous*) at absent things firmly present; for it will not cut off Being from holding to Being . . .

Here the content of the mind (what is thought or imagined) is described in similar terms to the continuity (and so unity) of all that exists (B8.23–5). It is, like all that exists, unitary and abstract. Parmenides' elevation of thought and introspection over external perception as the key to reality is closely paralleled in the *Upanishads*, where it brings immortality.[21] It is also akin to the Derveni Commentator's idea that nothing can exist outside the mind (mental monism). But Parmenides detaches from the mind its unitary *content*, which presumably he presented as a pointer towards – or confirmation – of abstract monism. In other words for Parmenides, though he has (in contrast to Anaximenes and Herakleitos) no substrate composing the inner self, the mental act of abstraction forms part of his argument for the continuity and unity of the abstract One, an argument to which we have compared the Upanishadic coalescence of mental with abstract monism. Of course, none of this is meant to imply that Parmenides or the Upanishadic authors distinguished between (what we call) mental monism and abstract monism.

Difficult to classify is the Pythagorean doctrine of all things consisting of numbers, which is monist in the limited sense that it propounds a single substrate, but the substrate – number – involves plurality.

12§B From Reciprocity to Monism

In the society depicted by Homer there is no money and the state is weak or absent: relations between people in different households are conducted largely according to codes of reciprocity, whether positive (notably gift-exchange) or negative (notably revenge). Anaximander maintained that the source of things is that into which they perish 'according to necessity (κατὰ τὸ χρεών)', that all things emerge from and pass into 'the unlimited' and that in doing so they 'give penalty and retribution to each other for their injustice according to the disposition/assessment of time'.[22] The things giving penalties to each other are *opposites*:[23] alternations in nature (day-night, summer-winter) are imagined in terms of (negative) reciprocity.[24]

20 B4; 11§D, 14§A. The problematic aspects of the fragment are well handled by Guthrie (1965) 31–2.
21 BU 4.4.18–20, quoted in 8§C; KaU 4.1–2.
22 Anaximander DK12 B1; Seaford (2004) 190.
23 Cf. reports about Anaximander cited in Seaford (2004) 190 n.3.
24 For interpretative detail, see Seaford (2004) 190–1.

Anaximander probably believed that everything (as well as passing from and into the unlimited) also *consists of* the 'unlimited',[25] which also surrounds and steers all things.[26]

Anaximander's imagining of 'the unlimited' involves the cosmisation of money, reflecting the recent monetisation of Miletos (13§A). As for the opposites, they seem to have a certain autonomy, both in perpetrating injustice and even in 'giving penalty and retribution' (even if this is required by the assessment of time). This is the cosmisation of autonomous citizens paying each other (newly monetised) debts of compensation under the incipient control of the polis. This presence of the polis in the earliest Greek philsophical fragment, and the importance of opposites, have no parallel in early Indian metaphysics. But this cannot be said of κατὰ τὸ χρεών: this phrase, which occurs nowhere else, and is the earliest statement of cosmic necessity, is also the earliest occurrence of the word χρεών (neuter), which derives from the same root as χρέος (Attic χρέως), meaning debt or obligation. The Greek notion of cosmic necessity seems, as in India, to have originated in the notion of debt.

A generation later, in the fragments of Herakleitos, we again find a single substrate combined with a cosmic cycle consisting of the reaction of opposites to each other. Herakleitos' explicit monism has survived: fragments state not only that everything passes from and into fire but also that the cosmos *is* ever-living fire.[27] Moreover, the opposites in Herakleitos are not autonomous: instead, they form a unity, or are at the least constantly transformed into each other. All things happen according to the abstract *logos,* as well as 'according to conflict and χρεών' (B80). And the *logos* is somehow (and in contrast to Anaximander's 'assessment of time') embodied in the fire (9§E). The Herakleitean opposites are absorbed into his monism as much as possible while still remaining opposites. All this reflects an advance (since the time of Anaximander) of monism, reflecting an advance in the comprehensiveness of the power of money.

In a third phase, in Parmenides, the element of abstraction has been taken to an extreme to produce extreme monism: there are in the Way of Truth no opposites, and all that exists is one, abstract, invariant in space and time, and held firmly in place by Necessity (B8.30) and by Justice (B8.14) – as if it were a social arrangement. Herakleitos explicitly compares the transformation of all things from and into fire to the transformation of goods from and into gold (B90). But Parmenides' One is a reifying projection (cosmisation) of the ubiquitous constancy of abstract value abstracted even from circulation

[25] See e.g. KRS 105–17. [26] Seaford (2004) 192. [27] B30, B90.

(14§A): it cannot have come into existence from non-being (what is not), for 'what χρέος (debt, obligation) would have driven it to come into being, later or sooner, from nothing?' (B8.9–10). Given that scholars of Greek philosophy generally have no interest in its socio-economic dimension, it is unsurprising that almost all of them commonsensically mistranslate χρέος here as 'need' or 'necessity'. But χρέος means 'debt' or 'obligation'.[28] In the unusual abstract context of the Parmenides passage, unqualified χρέος (without a genitive) cannot be detached from its normal meaning of debt or obligation (14§B [2]).

In the *Rigveda* we find the same combination as in Homer: there is no monism (apart from some indications in its latest layer), and – in a pre-monetary and pre-state society – the relationship of mortals with each other and with the gods is characterised by reciprocity (voluntary requital). In the sacrifice as represented in the *Brahmanas* we have seen (a) a transition from reciprocity and conflict (between autonomous parties) to a cycle driven by invisible necessity, a transition accompanied and followed by (b) the absorption of oppositions into the individual sacrificer and by (c) the advance of monism. Subsequently, in the *Upanishads*, we found the further development of monism (in all four forms) and of (d) the associated idea of an entity of comprehensive consciousness. And we have now found in presocratic philosophy something similar: (a) a transition from reciprocity and conflict (between autonomous parties) to a cycle driven by invisible necessity, a transition that is accompanied and followed by (b) the interiorisation of ritual and (c) the advance not only of monism (in its four forms) but also – we will now see – of (d) the associated idea of an entity of comprehensive consciousness.

12§C Monism and the Unitary Inner Self

We have seen that Greek material monism may also approximate to mental monism, in so far as the material substrate is conscious. For Anaximenes and Diogenes all things (including *psuchē*) are air, and there survives the

[28] Which it frequently turns out to mean even when another translation is used: e.g. A. *Suppliants* 472 (see Fraenkel on *Agamemnon* 1275); S. *Oedipus Tyrannus* 156 (see Dawe ad loc.); E. *Andromache* 337 (see Stevens ad loc.). Even in the (perhaps colloquial) expression 'what (τί) χρέος?' we cannot assume that the notion of obligation is absent (A. *Agamemnon* 85; cf. E. *Herakles* 530, *fr.* 1011). For the meaning 'need' Liddell and Scott (*Greek-English Lexicon*) give only two passages, both of them with an object of the need in the genitive, but neither of them entirely convincing: At Aristophanes *Acharnians* 454 the 'χρέος for a wicker basket' is parody (of the tragic *Telephos*) and so perhaps designed to sound absurd. At Bion *fr.* 5.2 the Doric genitive ἄλλω is a conjecture for ἄλλο, which could equally be restored as ἄλλῳ. On debt in presocratic and Indian cosmology see further Seaford (2019).

statement of Diogenes that air has intelligence. For Herakleitos all things are fire, and fragments of Herakleitos survive implying that the *psuchē* is composed – primarily at least – of fire and that there is a link between consciousness and the material composition of the *psuchē* (13§D). The implication is that – for these three thinkers at least – individual entities of consciousness are conscious by virtue of consisting of part of the material substance (air or fire) of which the cosmos consists. Each *psuchē* is *co-material* with the cosmos. Such a conception of *psuchē*, in contrast to any previous conception, implies a *unitary* entity of consciousness. It consists of a single homogeneous substance, which may be transformed from and into all else. Monism and the unitary inner self go together.

Anaximenes goes further, for he is reported as stating that our *psuchē*, being air, holds us together, just as *pneuma* (wind/breath) and air enclose the whole cosmos. Air (*psuchē*) holds us together: it has a controlling function, uniting what might otherwise be diversity into a single whole, the individual person. On the other hand, there is a sense in which the unitary *psuchē* propounded by Anaximenes, Herakleitos and Diogenes is not self-contained: though homogeneous, it is also a fragment of (and so in a sense belongs to) the substance that pervades the cosmos. Theophrastos attributed to Diogenes the belief that 'air within us has perception because it is a small part of the god'.[29] I will return to these contrary aspects of the *psuchē* in the next chapter.

So much for the emergence of the unitary inner self along with *mental* monism. But it also accompanied *abstract* monism, in so far as Parmenides imagines the inner self in terms of a unitary *content* abstracted from all else – and in this respect just like the One (12§A).

Another feature shared by monism and the inner self in Greece is the increasing importance – as in India – of the *invisible*. Homeric deities may often be invisible to men, as a result of remoteness, disguise or mist. But they are not *inherently* invisible.[30] Present monism is in this respect quite different. Even with present material monism there is invisibility, for what we see is variety, and what is fundamental is (like the inner self) largely invisible. According to Xenophanes 'seeming (δόκος) has been made over all things'.[31]

For Herakleitos all things happen according to the (invisible) *logos* (B1), and 'invisible harmony is stronger than visible' (B54). The tendency towards invisibility culminates in the entirely abstract monism of

[29] DK64 B4, B5, A19(42). [30] An apparent exception is Delusion (Ἄτη) at *Iliad* 19.93.

[31] DK21 B34.4. There is a superficial similarity to the Indian concept of *māya*, which cannot however be dated to our period or investigated here.

Parmenides, whom the goddess enjoins to use *logos* rather than eye and ear (B7).

The inner self is according to the earliest extant Greek accounts of it (by Anaximenes, Herakleitos and Diogenes)[32] a fragment of the (tenuous) material substance of the universe (air, fire), which somehow constitutes or unifies the inner self. The Vedic inner self, too, might be regarded as of a tenuous material substance (prana, breath) that constitutes or unifies the inner self (6§D), and is also manifest as wind. But wind was no more than a *component* of the cosmos, and did not produce the ethical, political and epistemological consequences of the co-materiality of inner self with the Herakleitean universal fire (14§A). There are even in the fragments of Parmenides, despite his being a polar opposite to Herakleitos, a trace of an ethical relation between subject and cosmos: his goddess strongly insists on knowledge of the One (held in place by Justice), whose continuity can be seen by introspection.

How is this difference between Greece and India to be explained? Indian sacrifice was achieved by an individual, with no role for the solidarity of the group, which in Greece by contrast was central to both animal sacrifice and mystic initiation. Accordingly anthropomorphic monism was in our period more common in India[33] than in Greece: the Vedic individual sacrificer was projected as Prajapati, who was identified with the universe. And the monetised interiorisation of sacrifice then gave to its individual performer an irreducibility that was inherited by the philosophical identification of abstract atman with universe. With Herakleitos, by contrast, it is the mystic integration of the individual into cosmic communality that is interiorised and monetised, producing the individual soul (*psuchē*) as defined and governed by the *logos*-embodying cosmic substrate of which it is only a fragment: the Herakleitean projection of the communality of *logos*-embodying money as cosmic substrate combines with the cosmic communality of mystery-cult.

12§D Fire: Herakleitean, Zoroastrian, Vedic and Buddhist

The mastery of fire was a crucial stage in human prehistory, reflected for instance in the myths of Prometheus and Mātāriśvan bringing fire from

[32] I omit Anaxagoras for reasons of space.

[33] And in Egypt and Mesopotamia: McEvilley (2002: 24–7). He claims that in Greece the 'macranthropic concept appears again and again, from Plato's *Timaios* to Stoic thought and after', but he fails to distinguish anthropomorphic from (the more common) non-anthropomorphic personal monism.

heaven. Fire has in most or all societies played a central role in technology and in ritual. This section concerns the divergence in the place and significance of fire in the texts of three Indo-European cultures: Greece, Iran and northern India.

Why did Herakleitos choose fire as his material substrate? It is suggested by West that he was influenced by 'the extraordinary status accorded by Persians to fire'.[34] He cites Persian and Greek texts to show that Persians pray to fire, and Persian texts to show that they honour five different kinds of fire: one resides in rocks and other natural sources, another in the bodies of men and animals, another in earth and plants, another in cloud and the fifth is ordinary workaday fire. And he cites a Persian text stating that Ohrmazd created sky, water, earth, plants, cattle and man, and 'fire permeated all six elements, and the period for which it was inserted into each element lasted, it is said, as much as the twinkling of an eye'.

West acknowledges that:

> this is by no means the same as Herakleitos' theory. Earth for him has not got fire in it, it is fire that has gone out and so changed its substance.

And yet:

> the difference conceals a similarity. The parts of the world that are not fire nevertheless retain the vital forward flow of fire. Fire makes a link between apparently widely separate cosmic districts: this is the essential thought that Herakleitos had to think before he could make use of fire in his cosmology . . .

All West's Persian texts are much later than Herakleitos, but it is not impossible that they preserve pre-Herakleitean beliefs. However, there are two more serious objections. One is that the hypothesis of Persian influence is entirely unnecessary. Herakleitos was not the first Greek material monist, and we will soon see that there are other good reasons why he should have chosen fire as his substrate.

The other serious objection is that West underestimates or ignores three enormous differences between Zoroastrian and Herakleitean fire.

Firstly, the existence of fire in many different things, and its brief primeval insertion into six basic elements, have nothing like the counter-intuitive quality of present monism, in which the cosmos simply *is* fire. Fire can be extracted from rock, there is warmth in living bodies and earth, and so on, but the idea that everything is permanently fire (even though in some places it has gone out) is a preconception of a different order.

[34] West (1971) 170–6.

Secondly, the Persians pray to fire is if it were a person, whereas it is a central feature of Herakleitean cosmology (and an unprecedented feature of presocratic cosmology generally) that his substrate is *impersonal*.

Thirdly, the Zoroastrian temple cult of fire (instituted probably in the fourth century BCE, but with antecedents in the earlier veneration of the hearth fire)[35] points to the most fundamental difference from Herakleitos. West himself notes that the Zoroastrians:

> have always been famous for the holiness they attach to fire. To extinguish it is a sin; to defile it is worse, and to defile it by burning rather than exposing the corpse is a horror.

But such an attitude is based on the *distinctiveness* of fire from all else, a distinctiveness manifest generally in Zoroastrian cult practice. Nothing could be further from the Herakleitean idea that fire *is* all else.

Interestingly, in the very next section West finds in the *Upanishads* something like present material monism:

> As fire in Herakleitos, so wind in this cosmology might be described as the common coin into which other things are changed.

But then he has to concede that:

> There is unfortunately no evidence for the currency of these physical doctrines . . . in ancient Iran.

Quite so. Greek metaphysical ideas are much closer to those found in India than to any found in the vast area (including Persia) between Greece and India (2§C).

Proferes (2007) describes at length the central role of fire in early Vedic ritual and cosmology (especially the *Rigveda*). He observes that the socio-political importance of a threefold *hierarchy* of fires is found both in the Iranian fire cult and in the *Rigveda*.[36] Such a hierarchy, we note, is alien to the Herakleitean (monetised) conception of fire. But Proferes also states that 'despite its distribution in many places, fire was understood to be underlyingly singular' (1), and that 'fire integrates society horizontally as well as vertically' (29). What Agni, the god of fire, represents, 'is nothing less than a universal rule rooted within every hearth' (23).[37] This horizontal universality is closer to the Herakleitean conception.

Subsequently there is a development, described by Heesterman thus:

[35] Boyce (1975); Stausberg (2004) 126–8. [36] Proferes (2007) 24–5.
[37] For more on the potential communality of ritual fire, see Heesterman (1983).

> While Zoroastrianism raised the exterior fire to the transcendent plane as the eternal flame of universal domination, Vedism went the other way and interiorised the fire in the person of the single individual sacrificer. The *agnyādheya* came to mean . . . the founding fire of the inner self as the principle of its immortality.[38]

This Vedic development of the inner fire belongs to the individualisation and interiorisation of the previously agonistic pattern of sacrifice (5§C). A stage in this development is represented by SB 2.2.2.8–20, in which both gods and Asuras were originally without an atman, and so were mortal: the gods were at first defeated in the sacrifice by the Asuras, but then saw the immortal *agnyādheya* (consecrated fire), and 'having set up this immortality in their inner selves (*antar ātman*) they became immortal', acquiring an atman, and defeated the Asuras.[39] Hence he who 'establishes that immortal element in his innermost soul', by 'establishing his fires', becomes immortal and unconquerable (14). 'As long as he lives no one comes between him and that fire which has been established in his innermost soul' (17). Moreover:

> Attendance on (or, the worship of) that consecrated fire (*agnyādheya*) means (speaking) the truth. Whosoever speaks the truth, acts as if he sprinkled that lighted fire with ghee; for even so does he enkindle it: and ever the more increases his own vital energy, and day by day does he become better (19).

On this interiorisation of ritual Heesterman comments:[40]

> Once the fire has been ritually established in the inner self through the *agnyādheya*, it is the sacrificer's inalienable true identity, in short his atman . . . Here the fire disappears behind the atman.

Here the myth that embodies the old idea of sacrifice as conflict legitimates something new, the individualisation and interiorisation of the (material) sacrificial fire, thereby establishing the importance of the (abstract) immortal atman.

With this interiorisation of the sacrifical fire Vedic tradition diverges from (pre-monetary) Zoroastrianism and comes closer still to Herakleitos.

Firstly, it is in the Herakleitean interiorisation of the cosmic rite of passage (11§C) that we find the earliest focus on the living immortal *psuchē*, consisting of the universal *logos*-embodying fire (9§E) that supersedes the

[38] Heesterman (1993) 141.

[39] Alternatively, at AB 4.2 31 the gods defeated the Asuras in the sacrifice by the use of silent praise (a form of interiorisation), which was the only weapon that the Asuras cannot counter.

[40] Heesterman (1993) 216.

notion (as found earlier in Anaximander) of *autonomous* conflicting opposites (12§B). We will suggest below that this inner fire may owe something specifically to the prominence of fire in the cosmic rite of passage (as in India).

Secondly, with the communality of the fiery *psuchē* in Herakleitos[41] we may compare *vaiśvānara* (common to all people) applied at SB 10.6.1.11 and BU 5.9 to fire within the *puruṣa* (man),[42] and at CU 5.11–18 to atman;[43] and in the *Kaṭha Upaniṣad* atman is compared to a single fire that enters living beings and adapts its appearance to match that of each (16§B). As for the external world, for Herakleitos the cosmos is an ever-living fire (B30), and in the Upanishadic five-fire doctrine 'the world up there' and 'the world down here' (et al.) are identified with fire.[44] But these few references in the late Vedic texts are scattered and isolated, unlike the systematic present material monism of Herakleitos and of his Ionian predecessors. The importance of fire in Vedic texts and Zoroastrianism seems to derive ultimately from its importance in ritual. But why did Herakleitos choose fire as substrate?

One factor is that fire has – like the water of Thales, the unlimited of Anaximander and the air of Anaximenes – manifest *cosmic* presence. A second possible factor is that fire has the power to be – like money – constantly and universally transformative: all things, according to Herakleitos, are in flux, and 'all things are an exchange for fire and fire for all things, like goods for gold and gold for goods' (B90). A third possible factor takes us back to the inner self. Fire – with its constant motion, appetitive, insubstantial, but never without content – may seem to bridge the gap between subject and object. The Herakleitean association of fire with consciousness, implied by the fiery composition of the *psuchē*, resembles not only the Vedic inner fire emphasised by Heesterman but also the idea propounded in the Buddhist fire sermon that our senses and mind are on fire. In general, the resemblance between Herakleitean and Buddhist fire deserves detailed examination.

It is maintained by Gombrich that the Buddha made five uses of fire as a metaphor.[45] (1) Consciousness is, like fire, appetitive, and can go out because the fuel is exhausted. (2) Consciousness must, like fire, have an object. (3) Consciousness and its objects are like fire in being not things but processes. (4) These processes are like fire in being non-random. (5) The

41 14§A, 14§D. 42 SB 10.6.1.11; BU 5.9; cf. BU 1.1.1. 43 Cf. BU 1.1.1; 1.4.16; 1.5.20.
44 In BU 6.2.9–16 and CU 5.4–10 (9§D). 45 Gombrich (2013 124–5.

fire should be extinguished by depriving it of its essential fuels: egotism and delusion.

Gombrich also notes a basic similarity between the Buddha and Herakleitos: for both of them 'fire apparently provided the vision of a world of perpetual change'.[46] I propose below four further similarities. But first we should note a significant difference. For Herakleitos fire transcends the distinction between subject and object not only because (as for Buddhism) fire is always in motion and always absorbing objects, but also because souls and cosmos are both composed of fire. Although in late Vedic texts there was some association of consciousness with fire, and we have seen that the interiorisation of the sacrificial fire may have been a factor in the emergence of atman, for Buddhism the ubiquity of fire is a metaphor, whereas for Herakleitos it is a reality. The further similarities (with their differences) are as follows.

(1) Our first similarity, the least consequential of the four, is that in both Buddhism and Herakleitos fire serves as a metaphor for unified multiplicity. To the Buddha is attributed the view that just as fire is classified by what it depends on – a fire that depends on burning wood is classified as a wood-fire, a fire that depends on burning grass as a grass-fire, and so on – so consciousness is classified by what it depends on: if on eye and forms it is classified as eye-consciousness, if on the ear and sounds as ear-consciousness and so on.[47] Similarly, for Herakleitos 'God is day night, winter summer, war peace, satiety hunger. It changes like fire, when it is mixed with spices, is named according to the scent of each of them' (B67), and 'Were all things to become smoke, the nose would distinguish them' (B7).

(2) For both thinkers consciousness, despite being in constant flux (like fire), is nevertheless subjected to a cosmic *cycle*. How is the Buddhist doctrine of *anatta* (no soul or no self) consistent with the doctrine of *saṃsāra*, the cycle of rebirth? If consciousness is a process not a thing, how can it be reborn? An answer given in the Buddhist *Questions of Milinda* is that it is like a flame passing from one lamp to another.[48] Like the flame, the soul is in a sense continuous but in a sense discontinuous with the soul of its previous existence. This resembles the cyclical passage of the fiery soul through the cosmological

[46] Gombrich (2013) 128.

[47] MN 38; Cf in KaU the atman is compared to a single fire that enters living beings and adapts its appearance to match that of each (16§B).

[48] 3.5.5 = 71 (1.111 Rhys Davids); cf. 2.2.1 = 40 (1.63 Rhys Davids).

elements in Herakleitos.[49] Not only do (fiery) *psuchai* undergo the same constant transformation that the whole (fiery) cosmos undergoes, but also each individual *psuchē* consists of a portion of fire, which is not reconstituted by the cycle as the same individual soul. What re-emerges from the cycle is rather the material of souls (fire). In contrast to other versions of the cyclical passage of the soul, neither the Buddhist nor the Herakleitean consciousness maintains any unchanging identity as an individual self or soul, because everything is in flux. Whereas for Buddhism consciousness is like constantly changing fire, the Herakleitean *psuchē* actually *consists* of a mere portion of (is co-material with) the constantly transforming and transformed cosmic fire.

(3) For Buddhism the processes that constitute our experiences are, like fire, non-random. Fire is a causally conditioned process, and karma 'is, as it were, the cause behind causes'.[50] Similarly, for Herakleitos everything happens 'according to the *logos*'. Non-randomness is in Buddhism a given of the process (karma) to which each individual is subjected, whereas in Herakleitos it is an ordering abstraction, the (communal) *logos* that inheres in the fiery *psuchē*.

(4) Both thinkers reject the performance of ritual,[51] and replace it by the importance of right action based on *understanding*.[52] For both of them this means understanding that the individual self-identity of consciousness is illusory, but whereas Buddhism recommends the going out (*nirvana*) of its (metaphorical) fieriness, Herakleitos – for whom its (real) fieriness joins it to the cosmic fire – recommends understanding of the communality of the *logos* that inheres in both cosmos and individual consciousness. Both recommendations have ethical consequences; but once again, at the root of the difference between early Indian and early Greek metaphysics (despite their striking similarities) is the greater importance of communality in the latter – a difference that we have also related[53] to the greater presence in Greece of material monism: here the cosmos is a real fire, in Buddhism fire is a mere metaphor.

Finally, a fourth possible factor in Herakleitos' choice of fire as substrate may have been mystery-cult, by which Herakleitos' doctrines were influenced both in their presentation and in their content (11§C). A central role

[49] B36: see 9§D and 13§D. [50] Gombrich (2013) 125, 128, 10, 21. [51] Hklt. B5, B14, B15.
[52] Cf. 9§D (8). [53] 16§A, 17§A.

in the mysteries, at Eleusis and generally, was played by fire, which was frequently imagined as cosmic (sun, stars, lightning).[54] Characteristic of mystic initiation is a sense of cosmic presence. More specifically, the unity of the initiated group was at least sometimes expressed by their sense of oneness with the cosmos,[55] with the result that we may legitimately speak of the cosmic communality of mystery-cult. Cosmic irruption was staged in the Dionysiac mysteries in the form of the fiery thunderbolt;[56] and for Herakleitos 'thunderbolt steers all things' (B64). In addition, the transformative, cosmic role of fire in sending up to the gods their sacrificial portion was a constant of Greek public life.

Here, too, there may be a connection with the Vedic tradition. In RV 7.88.2 Vasistha asks Varuna to 'lead me to the sun that is in the rock and the darkness, so that I may see the marvel'. This is related by Kuiper (1964) to ancient Aryan cosmology, in which the night sky, containing an inverted mountain, is equated with the netherworld. At the heart of ancient 'Aryan mysticism' is a vision of light in the netherworld in the form of sun in the cosmic mountain. The 'sun in the rock', claims Kuiper, is what is referred to also at RV 9.113.7:

> Where the inextinguishable light shines, the world where the sun was placed, in that immortal, unfading world, O Purifier, place me.

We cannot, admits Kuiper, reconstruct the correlate of this cosmological notion in the religious experience of individuals. But there is, he claims, in RV 6.9 evidence of the ecstasy that accompanied this experience:

> one gets the impression that the seer, by meditating on the sacrificial fire (st.5), attained a vision of the cosmic mystery, the 'sun in the rock' (or Agni in the nether world, into which the sun enters in the evening and arises in the morning, AB 8.28.9 and 13).

Kuiper further suggests that the idea in the *Upanishads* of the atman 'placed in the cavity' is a continuation of the mystic idea of the sun in the rock. He also cites KaU 1.14, in which – in a passage that was subsequently identified as belonging to a ritual death in the initiation of an *adhvaryu* priest[57] – the fire that leads to heaven is located in the 'cave of the heart'.[58] Perhaps, then, ideas of atman and interior fire owe something to the *interiorisation of a mystic vision of the sun in a mountain or netherworld.*

[54] Seaford (2005). [55] Seaford (1986); (2012a) 40–4, 97–101; (2013) 266–9.
[56] Imitated by drums, and perhaps torches: Seaford (2012a) 97–101; Seaford (1996) 195–7.
[57] Helfer (1968) [58] Cf. Ganeri (2012) 20–2.

If so, there would be a striking similarity with Greece. The vision of the sun in the netherworld was a feature of Greek mystic initiation (14§D). And the Herakleitean conception of the fiery *psuchē*, especially in its 'death' as *transformation* and (accordingly) its immortality, is inseparable from the cosmic access bestowed by (interiorised) mystic initiation. I have emphasised the power of money as engendering Greek monism, but we should not thereby ignore the tendency of Greek mystic initiation to transcend the basic divisions of the universe (between sky, earth and underworld),[59] which endows it with a monistic potential comparable to that of Vedic sacrifice.

However, there are also significant *differences* between the Herakleitean and the Indian (Vedic or Buddhist) conceptions of fire. For Herakleitos the cosmos is 'ever-living fire': in being transformed into water, earth, etc., it continues in a sense to be fire. However universal Agni or Prajapati may be, they are not completely devoid of personhood, any more than Hephaistos is completely devoid of personhood when his name means fire in the *Iliad* (2.426). But for Herakleitos fire is neither a symbol nor a personal agent but an impersonal substance, of which all else in a sense consists, and which somehow embodies the *logos*. To this the closest Indian idea is the five-fire doctrine (9§D), which does not however amount to monism and has nothing resembling the *logos*. Further, for Herakleitos *psuchē* (as well as cosmos) is *composed* – primarily at least – of fire (13§D), whereas in the Vedic texts 'the fire disappears behind the atman' (Heesterman). Vedic individualisation led to the explicit *identification* – in the *Upanishads* – of individual atman with brahman, with the statement that atman is brahman implying that they are distinct (as subject and object). But neither the presocratic nor the Platonic inner self is *identified* with the universe. We will return to this difference between the cultures in 15§B and 16§C.

[59] Seaford (1986) 9–23; (2005); (2012a) 26–7, 40–42; cf. (2004) 227–8.

CHAPTER 13

Money and Inner Self in Greece

13§A Money and Universe

In the early sixth century BCE, in the Ionian city of Miletos, we find the first 'philosophy' (as defined in 2§A). In my *Money and the Early Greek Mind* (2004) I argued that an important factor in this intellectual revolution was the advent of the new, all-pervasive, impersonal, abstract power of money. The argument was based on three considerations that are independent of each other.

Firstly, central instruments of social integration tend, at least in premodern societies, to be consciously or unconsciously cosmised. In the absence of experimentation, telescopes, microscopes etc., the unknown can be envisaged only as the known. The trans-individual comprehensiveness of social power is reified as transcendent. This is obvious with the patriarchal monarchy of Zeus, and it would be surprising if it did not occur with the new instrument of social integration, impersonal but seemingly all-pervasive and all-powerful, that began to pervade the polis from the early sixth century BCE.

Secondly, the first substance to function simultaneously as a general measure of value, a general means of payment and of exchange and a general store of value[1] was the coined money that first became generally used early in sixth-century BCE Ionia, of which the commercial centre was Miletos. And so the revolution in thought marked by presocratic cosmology occurred at exactly the same time and in exactly the same place as the first society in history to be pervasively monetised.

Thirdly, the presocratic universe is astonishingly similar in various respects to money, for instance in the idea that the universe is a single

[1] This is not the only possible definition of money, but the most useful one for our purpose. It is (especially on this definition) very unlikely that monetisation occurred earlier in China or India.

entity that is transformed from and into everything else, and in the increasing greater abstraction of the single entity. This does not of course mean that it *is* money or is *reducible* to money. Moreover, in its cosmisation numerous other factors may be involved.[2]

A common reaction to this argument has been to suggest the possibility that abstract thought preceded and made possible the adoption of coined money (rather than vice versa). All I have space for here in response is to note that this is not impossible in principle, but that in my 2004 book I gave a detailed account of the development of coinage that does not require abstract thought as a precondition, whereas I know of no plausible explanation (other than one involving the monetary factor) of why quasi-abstract and abstract monism appeared when and where it did: they are, I maintain, to be understood not as developments purely internal to the intellect but rather as influenced by the practical necessity inherent in the (explicable) universal convenience of monetised exchange.[3] We, too, imagine abstract value as a universal entity detached from its source.

In this chapter I take the argument further by proposing a new understanding of the relationship between monetisation and the development of ideas of the inner self or soul (*psuchē*). The overall aim is to compare this Greek development with the development of the atman, and to relate the similarities and differences to similarities and differences in socio-economic context.

13§B The *Psuchē* of Achilles

In the earliest Greek literary text, Homeric epic, there is no word for an organ of comprehensive consciousness (4§B). The Homeric *psuchē* is merely what departs the body at loss of consciousness. It may therefore be valued as what keeps a person alive, as for instance when Hektor runs – and Achilles pursues – 'for the *psuchē* of Hektor' (*Iliad* 22.161). Now there is one passage of the *Iliad* in which this value of the *psuchē* is described in a way whose significance for the later development of the notion has been ignored. In attempting to persuade Achilles to return to the battle, Agamemnon has offered him numerous gifts. In refusing the gifts Achilles claims that even vast wealth is not equal in value (*antaxios*) to his *psuchē*, not even all the wealth of Troy or of the temple of Apollo at Delphi (9.401–5). The gifts are 'hateful' to him (378).

[2] 16§A; Seaford (2004) 11–12 (esp. n.40).
[3] This is worked out in detail, albeit with some exaggeration, by Sohn-Rethel (1978).

We can easily make sense of this. It would be foolish to exchange life for wealth. But the passage is unique in Homer in explicitly conferring inherent value on the *psuchē*.

What is this value? 'Not *antaxios*' implies that the *psuchē* is more valuable than (and so comparable to) a mass of material goods. On the other hand, because the *psuchē* is invisible as well as fundamental, a different kind of thing from material goods, 'not *antaxios*' implies that its value is incommensurable – beyond equivalence – with material goods as such. This combination of the *psuchē* being both more valuable than all goods and somehow beyond them implies that it *transcends* them.

What has produced this, the earliest focus on the worth of the *psuchē*? It is the isolation of Achilles, arising from the breakdown of economic relations. More specifically, Achilles' rejection of the gifts belongs to a *breakdown of reciprocity* – of the systematic reciprocity (requital that is ostensibly voluntary) that forms a dominant code of social relations in the society described or implied by Homeric epic. Achilles' view is that the distribution of rewards (in return for fighting) has been unfair,[4] that no amount of gifts will be effective and even that he does not *need* the honour of gifts – because he is honoured by the 'distribution of *Zeus*' (9.602–8). For Achilles the breakdown of reciprocity means that gifts are not only ineffective and hateful but even unnecessary.

Achilles does eventually, after his beloved Patroklos is killed, re-enter the war. In both India and Greece the supreme national epic (*Mahābhārata*, *Iliad*) centres on a great war from which a single mighty warrior (Arjuna, Achilles) abstains before – after dialogue with a deity (Krishna, Thetis) – joining the fighting. This basic similarity highlights the instructively profound differences in motivation. In the section of the *Mahābhārata* known as the *Bhagavad Gītā* Arjuna, horrified by the thought of killing relatives and friends, is nevertheless persuaded to fight by the arguments of Krishna concerning the individual salvation that comes from (among other things) knowledge, detached action and devotion to Krishna. In agreeing to fight against his own kin Arjuna in effect follows – albeit for different reasons – the advice given to Orestes in tragedy to persuade him to kill his own mother: 'count all people your enemies rather than the gods'.[5] But in the *Iliad*, which is – in contrast to the *Bhagavad Gītā* – pre-philosophical, the isolation of Achilles, including his isolated relation with god (Zeus), emerges from the breakdown of *social integration* (reciprocity), which is restored by his return to battle: he regrets that he did not save his

[4] 1.162–8, 9.316–9, 330–3; etc. [5] A. *Choephoroi* 902.

companions, is reconciled with the Greek leaders and returns to battle impelled by the desire for revenge for his beloved Patroklos (and for glory), despite being told by Thetis that the revenge will be soon followed by his own death.[6]

In Homeric society, as in many other pre-modern societies, gifts embody interpersonal relations – of honour, loyalty, alliances of various kinds and friendship: the gift continues to be associated with its donor. In withdrawing from the army Achilles isolates himself from such interpersonal relations and from their material embodiment. His identity is now shaped not at all by the relations (of honour etc.) embodied in gifts from mortals, but rather by the unspecified honour provided by 'the distribution of Zeus'. This transcendent abstract honour seals his social isolation, in which his invisible *psuchē* is imagined both in terms of economic value and as nevertheless transcending it.

But why is his *psuchē* so valuable? The reason he gives is that 'cattle and sheep may be seized, and tripods and horses obtained, whereas the *psuchē* of a man cannot be seized or taken to come back once it will pass the barrier of his teeth' (9.406–9). It is clearly imagined as an *entity*, not just as 'life'. And the word translated 'pass' here is in fact ἀμείψεται, 'exchange'. This can taken as a metaphor for the passing of a barrier,[7] in which the *psuchē* exchanges life for death. But given the context, in which the loss of the *psuchē* contrasts with the acquisition of other kinds of object, there is a secondary implication that the *psuchē* is lost by an exchange *transaction*,[8] in which however (in contrast to animals and tripods lost and gained) nothing ever returns. The *psuchē* is not the real person, as for instance in the later ideas of it being imprisoned or entombed in the body. It is rather a *possession of the individual.*[9] As such it belongs entirely to a single owner, from whom – in contrast to gifts and plunder – it undergoes irreversible separation.[10]

In the heroic world, goods circulate by plunder and by gift-giving,[11] which elicit reciprocity (negative and positive): the persistent association of

[6] *Iliad* 18.102–26, 19.65–70. [7] As at *Odyssey* 10.328; A. *Choephoroi* 965.

[8] The only other thing in the *Iliad* that is the object of ἀμείβειν meaning exchange is armour: 6.230, 235; 14.381; 17.192.

[9] It can therefore be 'taken away' from one person by another: e.g. *Iliad* 22.257, 24.754; *Odyssey* 22.444.

[10] Even money can be obtained (though not generally *re*-obtained), as in the monetised version of Achilles' statement at E. *Suppliants* 775–7: 'this is for mortals the only expenditure that once expended cannot be recovered, the mortal *psuchē*, whereas there are means of acquiring money.'

[11] Horses and tripods, contrasted by Achilleus with his soul, are among the gifts offered to him by Agamemnon (9.122–3).

goods (plundered or given) with their original owner demands a reciprocal act (of plunder, of favour or gift). But this is the system of reciprocity that has, in the *Iliad*, broken down: Achilles fights, but is not given his rightful share of the plunder. And to accept the gifts now would be to subordinate himself to their donor.[12] He therefore isolates himself altogether from the power of goods, and accordingly reaches towards a conception of his own *psuchē* as a possession that is isolated from – and contrasts with – the kind of goods that in the heroic world circulate as plunder and as gifts. He rejects reciprocity in favour of a possession of a different kind – of transcendent value, entirely his own and entirely separable from him.

For the anthropology of Arbman and his followers (4§A) the Homeric *psuchē* is a 'free soul':[13] unmentioned when the body is active, it leaves it during swooning and at death and represents the person in the afterlife – all this in contrast to the 'body souls' such as *thumos* and *noos*. Achilles' evaluation of his *psuchē* can be seen as a stage in the merger between 'free soul' and 'body soul' that – in both Greece and India (6§D) – assists the development of an immortal unitary inner self (Platonic *psuchē*, Upanishadic atman). A difference from India is that here in Homer the economic factor in the incipient merger is more visible. In a context of exchange, as response to the breakdown of reciprocity, Achilles has to *evaluate* his *psuchē* highly (as transcendent): but the *value* of the 'free soul' (*psuchē*) for the living can only be as enabling living consciousness, i.e. as 'body soul'. The distinction between 'free soul' and 'body soul' is eroded by the idea of transcendent value.

13§C Death as Economic Transaction

Another strand of anthropology is also relevant here. This, which was initiated by Marcel Mauss and is still thriving,[14] centres on the fact that in (pre-monetary) gift economies the identity of the donor tends to persist in the gift, which thereby continues to connect him subjectively to the recipient with such feelings as honour, friendship, gratitude or subservience. Object and subject seem to interpenetrate. This may take radical forms. Here for instance (to resume a theme of 4§A) is a comment on a 1994 study by four anthropologists of four societies: in the Solomon Islands, the Moluccas, Papua New Guinea and Morocco:

[12] Donlan (1989). [13] Esp. Bremmer (1983).

[14] Mauss (1965); Gregory (1982); Strathern (1988); Weiner (1992); Hénaff (2010); et al. For a good discussion, see Graeber (2001) 33–43; 151–228. For ancient Greece, see Seaford (1994) 13–25. On the identity of the divine donors and their gifts in the Vedas, see Gonda (1965) 213.

> In societies such as these, the authors argue, it is utterly absurd to talk about individuals maximizing goods. There are no individuals. Any person is himself made up of the very stuff he exchanges, which are in turn the basic constituents of the universe.[15]

This is (to develop the opposition described in 5§D) the extreme opposite to *purchase*, which is governed by objective necessity, impersonal equivalence of value, with the result that the separation of the individual transactors from the commodities and money – and therefore from each other – is absolute.[16] There is polarisation: to the absolute (isolated) objectivity of commodities and money corresponds the absolute (isolated) subjectivity of the transactors.

The historical importance of what Achilles says is that – though still in the pre-monetary world – he prefigures this polarisation. The economy implicit in Homeric epic is a gift economy[17] on the point of being monetised. At one pole, in rejecting the interpersonal reciprocity in which reward does not correspond to contribution, Achilles implicitly favours the impersonal equivalence of value. At the other pole, in isolating himself from the social connectivity of gifts, he values instead his own *psuchē*, which consequently seems more like a comprehensive inner self than it does anywhere else in Homer. From the breakdown of the reciprocal economy emerges a self-identical individual. In putting himself beyond the influence of gift-exchange, Achilles implies the idea of an autonomous inner self, which contrasts with – and is isolated from – gift-exchange, with its only form of 'exchange' (ἀμείψεται) irrecoverable loss. Further, the breakdown of reciprocity in the *Iliad* was also a symptom of the decline of Greek monarchy. But in northern India in our period monarchy flourished, a contrast that has metaphysical consequences:[18] in India monarchy was more visibly interiorised (7§B) than was money.

Achilles' *psuchē* is a possession subject to absolute loss, and is greater in value than a mass of goods, which it moreover transcends. The earliest known approximation to the all-important inner self is obtained by the *psuchē* being imagined in terms of transcendent exchange-value that is absolutely alienable. As such, it is analogous to the abstract value of *money*. The implication that Agamemnon's offer is insufficient offends against the old ethics of reciprocity and prefigures the reality of commerce.

[15] Graeber 2001 (19) on Barraud et. al. (1994); see also Graeber (2001) 39.

[16] The distinction between gifts and commodities, most influentially stated by Gregory (1982), is useful in thinking about this issue, even though reality is of course often less tidy. Gregory subsequently defended and restated his 'basic distinction': Gregory (1997), esp. 41–63.

[17] Seaford (1994) 14–17. [18] 3§B, 5§E, 6§A, 10§C.

Although Achilles does not of course express any preference for commerce over reciprocity, and indeed rejects the influence of *all* goods, his isolation does nevertheless prefigure the isolation of the subject of monetised exchange.[19]

What do I mean here by isolation? In order to function, money must have the same power whoever owns it, and so must be entirely impersonal. Having as its sole function the universal impersonal embodiment (absolute reification) of interpersonal relations (of power), it is as historically unprecedented as is the impersonal cosmology that it generates. Moreover, the ease with which coined money is stored, preserved, concealed, transported and exchanged makes it highly suitable for possession and use by the autonomous individual. The isolating effect of money has been confirmed by empirical psychology.[20] In this way the absolute reification of interpersonal relations produces the absolute individual – absolute in the sense that in principle all he seems to need is the impersonal power of money, whereas even the pharaoh had depended on personal relations (loyalty, command of violence, divine charisma, gifts and so on). True, in practice the monetised individual may need, even if wealthy, the loyalty of friends and relatives. But the overall effect of monetisation is undoubtedly to increase the potential or actual autonomy of the individual, and thereby also his practical and emotional isolation. Whereas gifts tend to leave the donor connected to the recipient, a monetised transaction concerns only the equivalence of money with goods, and *qua* monetised transaction leaves the transactors unrelated to each other. Each transactor is completely separated from what the other transactor has received and from the other transactor himself. The monetised transactor is *individualised*. The gift, like kinship or the communal possession of land, unites individuals, whereas money tends to make them autonomous.

The main isolators of human beings are money and death. The idea of death as an economic transaction (and of the *psuchē* as analogous to goods or money) is not confined to Homer. Here I have space only for a few

[19] Even though there is no money in Homer. It is perhaps significant that he mentions the wealth concentrated at Delphi, for dedications of precious metal were important in the development of money (Seaford [2004] 60–7, 75–87, 102–15).

[20] E.g. Vohs et al. (2006): 'The results of nine experiments suggest that money brings about a self-sufficient orientation in which people prefer to be free of dependency and dependents. Reminders of money, relative to non-money reminders, led to reduced requests for help and reduced helpfulness toward others. Relative to participants primed with neutral concepts, participants primed with money preferred to play alone, work alone, and put more physical distance between themselves and a new acquaintance.'

examples.[21] In Hesiod's *Works and Days* the only mention of *psuchē* is in the brief passage on *trade*: men are foolish enough risk their lives by sailing in spring, 'for *chrēmata* (commodities) are *psuchē* for mortals'.[22] In certain mystic texts death is imagined as the payment of a penalty (14§D). According to Pindar, if a man keeps his wealth hidden inside, then he is unwittingly paying *psuchē* to Hades without glory:[23] rather than obtaining glory by risking or paying *psuchē*, as for instance Achilles eventually did, the man is paying *psuchē* but obtaining no glory in return. But in what sense is he paying *psuchē*? Death is inevitable (and so better to gain glory with it), and its inevitability is envisaged as payment of *psuchē*. His unawareness of the payment is suggested both by the invisibility of 'Hades'[24] and by the hiddenness of his wealth: the implication is that hidden wealth cannot be kept intact, for payment (of *psuchē*) is invisibly occurring. Invisible wealth kept 'inside' is analogous to invisible soul. In fact the invisibility of the soul resembles money not only in that money may be hoarded 'inside', kept from public view, but also in that monetary value seems to inhere invisibly in commodities – and especially in coins, for the only function of coins is to embody the power of what seems to be abstract substance. The essence of each coin seems to be the invisible power within it. This provided, I suggest, a historically unprecedented model for the *psuchē* as the invisible but powerful interior essence within each individual. Hence the Greek identification of people, and even of the soul, with coinage (13§E).

My final example is an account of *birth* by a fifth-century Pythagorean, Philolaos: the human being in the womb consists entirely of the hot, but on being born draws in part of the (unlimited) cold air outside and emits it 'like a debt (χρέος)'.[25] Most of what Philolaos wrote is lost: he may have made explicit the consequence that at death the debt is repaid for the last time. This economic transaction is not suggested by the *physical* process, but provides *a priori* the terms for imagining how the individual is constituted. To be born, for Philolaos as for Vedic thought (5§B), is to take on a debt, but for Philolaos – in line with a general contrast between presocratic and Vedic thought – the debt consists of a physical substance (air). Moreover, for Philolaos the macrocosm is created in the same way as the

[21] See also e.g. A. *Psychostasia*, *Agamemnon* 437, *Choephoroi* 518–21 (cf. *Agamemnon* 163–6; Seaford (2010a)); S. *Antigone* 322; E. *Medea* 968, *Phoinissai* 1228; Isocrates 6.109; *Anthologia Graeca*. 7.622.6. Human life involves a *debt* to death: 10§C n.50.

[22] 686; for Solon (13.43–6) the sea-trader is not *sparing* of his *psuchē*. Cf. Tyrtaios 10.14; S. *Electra* 982; E. *Herakles* 1148; Anon. Iamblichi 4.3, 5.3; Isocrates 6.105.

[23] *Isthmian* 1.68–70. Cf. the emendation ψυχάν in Pindar *fr.* 123.7–9.

[24] Ἀΐδᾳ, which could mean 'unseen': Kurke (1991) 239.

[25] A27: Huffman (1993) 289–92, 300; cf. DK58 B30.

microcosm: a central hearth draws in breath (as well as time and the void) from the surrounding unlimited. Here the model is the economy as a whole, in which the household (hearth) is limited but – because it cannot be self-contained – must participate in the unlimited circulation of money.[26]

In Vedic thought one of the debts incurred by birth (to death or to the gods) is discharged by sacrifice. Moreover, the gift (*dakṣiṇā*) to the priest embodies, accompanies or carries the sacrificer on his way to heaven, and even drives the cosmic cycle (5§B). Here, too, as in the Greek imagination, there is no clear distinction between economic transaction and passage to another world. The persistent relationship between donor and gift is exemplified in the persistent relationship between sacrificer and *dakṣiṇā*. But monetisation would tend to transform *dakṣiṇā* from gift into the automatism of payment, and to promote the interiorisation of the sacrifice (5§C, 5§D). Prajapati keeps the *dakṣiṇā*, consisting of gold, for himself (within his own heart, after it is rejected by the sacrificial fire) because he finds nobody to give it to, and thereby increases his own ability.[27] In India and in Greece monetisation promoted a new conception of the inner self and of its relation to the universe.

13§D Herakleitos

The cosmological transformations of fire are described by Herakleitos thus:

> Fire's turnings: first sea, and of sea half (is) earth and half 'burner' (B31).

A similar sequence of transformations is in the following fragment undergone by souls (*psuchai*):

> For *psuchai* it is death (θάνατος) to become (γενέσθαι) water, for water death to becomes earth, water becomes from earth, and *psuchē* from water (B36).

The 'death' of the *psuchē* in becoming water is not annihilation but transformation[28] or 'becoming', and may result in it joining the universal fire.[29] This represents an adaptation of the mystic doctrine of the passage of the *psuchē* through the cosmological elements.[30] Herakleitos reproduces

[26] Seaford (2004) 275–83. [27] TB 3.11.8; 5§D.

[28] Philo *De aet. mundi* 21: Herakleitos called death 'not annihilation but transformation into the other element'. Against the odd idea that B36 refers to physiological processes within the living organism see Schofield (1991) 15–21.

[29] KRS 203–8. [30] 6§A n.34.

the mystic identification of mortals with immortals (11§C). The opposition θάνατος/γενέσθαι in B36 evokes the mystic identification of death with birth exemplified by the (fourth century BCE) mystic formula νῦν ἔθανες καὶ νῦν ἔγενου, 'now you died and now you came into being)'.[31]

As for the normal sense of 'death', namely the death of the body, we can observe that it involves the loss of both breath and heat. For Herakleitos the *psuchē* in observable bodies may well have been composed of both air and fire (in varying proportions),[32] and susceptible to becoming wet, which produces pleasure[33] (B77), loss of consciousness[34] and 'death'.[35] But despite this transformability and variability of the *psuchē*, it remains the case that (a) the cosmos is fire (B30), including therefore *psuchē*, which is subject – like all else – to a cycle of transformation that incorporates all the elements; (b) in B31 and B36 the transformation ('death') is surely between opposites, with fire as the opposite of water; (c) in what survives of Herakleitos it is only fire and *psuchai* that are stated to be subject to (the same) elemental transformations; (d) the 'wisest and best' *psuchē* is associated by Herakleitos with light (and so fire) and/or driness;[36] (e) there is a special relationship between fire and the *logos* and between the *logos* and *psuchē*.[37] And so fire has some essential connection with – is the primary constituent of – the *psuchē* contained in the living human body.[38]

In order to explore this connection further we must first look at the Herakleitean conception of the transformation of the *psuchē* as an *economic transaction*:

> It is difficult to fight *thumos*; for what it wants it buys at the price of *psuchē* (ψυχῆς ὠνεῖται) (B85).

Commentators differ on the meaning of *thumos* here (bodily desire, or anger), but have to agree in identifying the expenditure (loss) of *psuchē* with expenditure of the physical element of which *psuchē* is composed, whether the element be the driness lost through drink or the vapour or fieriness lost through anger. What they do not mention is that the idea of purchase coheres with Herakleitos' comparison of the exchange of fire for all things with the exchange of gold (i.e. money) for goods (B90). Fire is not just the

31 Gold leaf 26 Graf-Johnston. For the gold leaves, see 14§D.

32 Betegh (2007). This is preferable to the view of Kahn (1979: 238–40) that the *psuchē* is simply composed of air.

33 B77; cf. B117 (drunkenness). 34 B117, B118; etc. (KRS 203–8). 35 B36, B77.

36 B118: my 'and/or' reflects a textual problem (beyond my scope here).

37 KRS 186–8, 199–206, 212.

38 Note also B26 as excellently interpreted by Schofield (1991) 27–9.

underlying component of all things, it also drives this cycle of exchange.[39] It is difficult to fight *thumos* because it contains and is driven by the fieriness (dry and airy) of the *psuchē*, whose loss (extinguishing, transformation) is – as in B90 – envisaged as *expenditure*.[40]

B85 and B90 cohere with two further fragments:

> The limits of the *psuchē* you would not find, even by travelling along every path: so deep a *logos* does it have (B45).

And:

> Of the *psuchē* (there is a) *logos* increasing itself (B115).

B45 describes the *psuchē* as occupying unlimited space. Hence, perhaps, B101: 'I sought for myself'.[41] The atman *vaiśvānara* (common to all people), like the Herakleitean *logos*, combines communality with unlimitedness.[42] The *logos* is an abstract formula, and so seems at home in the *psuchē*. But commentators have failed to answer (and generally even to ask) the crucial question of *why* the depth of *logos* is unlimited.[43] A related unsolved puzzle is the nature of the self-increase of the *logos* in B115.

Everything happens according to the *logos* (B1). The *kosmos* is an ever-living fire that kindles in measures and goes out in measures (B30). B31 (quoted above) also contains the words:

> <earth> is dispersed as sea, and is measured to the same *logos* (εἰς τὸν αὐτὸν λόγον) as existed before it became earth.

Balance – the same quantities – is maintained throughout the cycle of transformations. Cycles of transformation in nature – day and night, summer and winter, etc. – are balanced. But something else is introduced by the *logos*, which when used of quantity means quantity expressed as an *abstraction* (formula, measure, reckoning), and could accordingly mean *monetary* account (11§C). The exchange of fire for all things resembles the exchange of money for goods (B90) not just as *unceasing* and *universal* but also as *balanced*.

[39] B64, B66.

[40] In battle internal fieriness, being aroused most completely, may accordingly be completely lost: Herakleitos praises death in battle (B24, B25, B136; KRS 207–8).

[41] Cf. *Kaṭha Upaniṣad* 4.1: 'A certain wise man in search of immortality, turned his sight inward and saw the man within.'

[42] CU 5.18 'measuring a span and beyond all measure'. For the unlimitedness of mind, see also SB 1.4.4.5; 7.2.4.30 14.1.2.8; 6.5.3.7; BU 3.1.9; Tull (1989) 50. Cf. SB 1.4.4.7.4.2.3.1.

[43] The *psuchē* has great depth also, in a practical context, at A. *Suppliants* 407–8.

This helps to explain how the *logos* may increase itself, and is unlimited. The *logos* is the quantitative formula that embodies (e.g. by determining that one vase is four drachmas) the new phenomenon of universal impersonal equivalence that enables the cyclical transformation of fire and money from and into everything else. This process is unlimited in that everything is drawn into it, as well as in that money received for the sale of goods may be used for the purchase – or production – of more goods for the purpose of further sale, and so on. The cycle of commercial exchange may seem to have neither temporal nor spatial limit, especially when vigorously promoted – as in the lifetime of Herakleitos – by the recent invention of coined money. Indeed, the Greeks emphasise the fact that money (and the desire for it) is unlimited.[44] Its dynamic expansion happens according to – and so seems caused by – the *logos*, which therefore seems to be self-increasing and unlimited.

This self-increasing unlimited *logos* seems to regulate the *cosmic* transformation but is located by Herakleitos in the *psuchē*. There is no contradiction here. For *psuchai*, as we have seen, participate in the cycle of cosmic transformation. And to insist that the *logos* (in each *psuchē*) is not limited (to each *psuchē*) resembles his complaint that although the *logos* is communal (ξυνός), 'the many' live as if having individual understanding (B2).

It is presumably this embodiment of the *logos* that gives the *psuchē* the cognitive capacity indicated in B107: 'eyes and ears are bad witnesses for men having barbarian souls (ψυχάς)'. 'Barbarian' here surely suggests failure to understand the *logos* in the broad sense of the abstraction according to which everything happens (B1). In the lifetime of Herakleitos the *everyday* use of coinage (with its mark defining its abstract value) was an exclusively (or almost exclusively) *Greek* phenomenon, not practised or understood by barbarians. Eyes and ears provide sense data, but not the abstract *logos*, which is often misunderstood (B1) or ignored (B2; cf. B72). It is by embodying and using the all-controlling *logos* that the *psuchē* possesses a *comprehensive* consciousness capable of interpreting and integrating the data of the various senses. It is Herakleitos, in this and the other fragments, who provides the earliest extant description of the *psuchē* as an organ of comprehensive consciousness,[45] comparable to the atman. In so far as there is introjection of monetary circulation, as in Herakleitos, the inner self is unbounded. In so far as there is introjection of abstract value, it is bounded.

[44] Seaford (2004) 165–9.

[45] Claus (1981: 125) claims that there are only six occurrences of *psuchē* as a 'psychological agent' before the fifth century; compare Herakleitos B12, 36, 45, 67a, 77, 85, 98, 107, 115, 117, 118; also B26, 88, 136, A16.

To conclude, the Herakleitean cosmological cycle may be regarded as a synthesis of nature, ritual and money: more specifically of the cycle of nature with the cosmic cycle of the (mystic) initiand and with the monetary cycle. The same three cycles merge to form the ancient understanding of the Vedic sacrifice (5§B).

13§E Abstract Value and Inner Self

So far, we have seen that the unitary *psuchē* that emerges in Greek texts from Homer onwards resembles the power of money in various respects that include being an entirely alienable possession, unlimited and endowed with *logos*. Here we begin with further resemblances: they both (a) are invisible[46] (homogeneously abstract), and (b) unify diversity.

(a) Homogeneous abstraction. An immense advantage of coinage, from its very beginning, was that the value of the coin was conventional, determined by its mark rather than by its precise intrinsic value. And from the beginning of coinage the conventional value of coins was – in Greece at least – in general slightly higher than its intrinsic (metallic) value. This tends to favour the idea of coin as the concrete embodiment of quantified abstract value that is also embodied in all commodities. Abstract (invisible) value is homogeneous, the same everywhere, and may seem distinct from the individual coins and commodities in which it is embodied. Souls, too, are invisible, and they too may seem to resemble each other while being distinct from the individual bodies in which they are embodied. Anaximenes, for instance, states that our *psuchē* is air (B2), and so – we may infer – souls are invisible and resemble each other. In an early medical text[47] it is observed that 'the *psuchē* is the same thing in all living creatures, whereas the body of each is different'. For Herakleitos each *psuchē* is co-material with the cosmic fire and contains the abstract (and communal) *logos* according to which all things happen.

(b) The unification of diversity. Anaximenes states in B2 that our *psuchē*, being air, holds us together just as *pneuma* (wind/breath) and air enclose the whole cosmos (B2). The diversity of inner self, and of cosmos, is held together by what it consists of, which is in both cases (invisible) air. Here, too, there is an analogy with the (quasi-abstract)

[46] For more on money as 'identified with the person's generic and invisible inner powers', see Graeber (2001) 99.

[47] Hippocrates *On Regimen* 1.28 (= 144, 18–20 Joly-Byl).

monetary substance, which seems not only to control and pervade the cycle of commodities and coins but also to *unite* them into a single system. The (quasi-abstract) element that unites cosmos and unites *psuchē*, in Anaximenes air, is in Herakleitos *logos*-embodying fire.[48] The *psuchē* in classical Greek thought unites and controls the person.[49] For Plato in the *Phaedo* the *psuchē*, invisible and separable from the body, may nevertheless be 'dragged by the body into things that are always changing, and itself wanders about and is agitated'. But when it rests from this wandering and enquires by itself and is stable and consorts with the pure and unchanging, this is to achieve wisdom (*phronēsis*) (79 cd). The *psuchē* succeeds in being 'by itself' by gathering itself from all parts of the body.[50] We mentioned this passage earlier as embodying the mystic transition from mental fragmentation to unity (11§E), which – we may now add – converges with the mental unity achieved by the interiorisation of money: the internal gathering produces thinking (*phronesis*), described as 'the only right currency (νόμισμα), for which all those things [pleasures, pains, fears] must be exchanged' (69a).

What has emerged is a striking similarity not only between money and the inner self but also between them both and *the cosmos*: in all three, diversity is united by a single homogeneous quasi-abstract entity (monetary substance, the unlimited, air, *logos*-embodying fire) that is also ultimately identified with what it unifies.

Scholars have identified similarities (of various kinds) between *psuchē* and cosmos in Herakleitos, and some have attempted to explain them by the view that the cosmos is constructed out of introspection. For instance, Diels maintained that Herakleitos 'seeks to discover the world-soul from the human soul',[51] and Hussey identifies as a 'Herakleitean principle' that 'to interpret the cosmos it is necessary to study one's own self, and to apply what one finds there to explain the world'.[52] This is not entirely mistaken. But it leaves unexplained *why* the cosmos is based on the inner self, why this self takes the new form that it does, why this new form appeared when and where it did and why it differs so completely from e.g. the Homeric

[48] 13§D; B50, B51, B64 (cf. B66); B41 (cf. B118, B107). Aristotle (*De Anima* 405a25) says that Herakleitos takes *psuchē* as his *archē* (first principle or substrate).

[49] The *psuchē* rules the body: Democritus DK68 B159, B187; Pl. *Alcibiades* I 130ab; Xenophon *Memorabilia* 1.4.9, 4.3.14 (invisible power); in dreams the *psuchē* 'administers its own household' (Hippocrates *On Regimen* 4.86 (= 218, 8 Joly-Byl).

[50] 67c, 80e, 83a. [51] Diels (1909) x. [52] Hussey (1982) 41.

inner self. And can we exclude the possibility that the influence runs the other way, from cosmos to soul?

These questions can be answered only by recognising the historically recent third term in the analogy: cosmos and *psuchē* strikingly resemble not only each other but also the (recent) phenomenon of *money*, which influences the (recent) conceptions of self and of cosmos in a way that explains their (recent) similarities. It is as a *unifying abstract substance* that money dominates exchange, and is *projected* as cosmos and *introjected* (interiorised) as *psuchē*. In the resulting analogy between self, money and universe there is – despite the separation between autonomous subject and impersonal object – a paradoxical element of continuity with the kind of gift economy in which 'any person is himself made up of the very stuff he exchanges, which are in turn the basic constituents of the universe' (13§C).

The Pythagoreans, too, both projected monetary value as universal substrate (number)[53] and interiorised it as *psuchē*.[54] For the Pythagorean Philolaos, microcosm and macrocosm are each generated by the drawing in of air (breath) imagined as an economic transaction.[55] On the absorption of all things into king Zeus the Derveni Commentator writes that 'Mind (*nous*)[56] being alone is always *worth everything* (πάντων ἄξιον), just as if the other things were nothing' (6§A): here the identity of cosmos, mind and value is explicit. The problem of the relation of unity to diversity obtains in various spheres: the political, the cosmic, the mental and the economic. The economic unification of diversity is embodied in *money*. Just as king Zeus absorbs all things, so the mind seems to unite (by embodying the existence of) all else, and money seems to unite (by embodying the value of) all else.

The gift tends to embody interpersonal relations, leaving donor connected to recipient and subject to object, whereas the advent of money tends to isolate the individual. Separation of a single entity out

[53] Seaford (2004) 268–83. Aristoxenos, who was acquainted with Pythagoreans, wrote that Pythagoras 'diverted the study of numbers from the use of traders, likening all things to numbers' (DK58 B2). For the importance in the *Brahmanas* of ritual correspondences based on the identification of entities with numbers, see Gonda (1975) 373–4.

[54] Aristotle *Metaphysics* 985b26; Guthrie (1962) 316.

[55] 10§C. 'Hail the world's soul, and mine!', says the miser Volpone to his gold in Ben Jonson, *Volpone* 1.i.3.

[56] The organ of comprehensive consciousness here is *nous* rather than *psuchē*. Something like comprehensive consciousness may be implied also by *phrēn* (or its plural *phrenes*). But *nous* and *phrēn* are – in contrast to *psuchē* – never equivalent to the self or person, and do not survive independently after death.

from a whole is the creation of a new unity. Accordingly, the separation out of the individual transactor from goods and from all other transactors constitutes him as a unified subject. And because the impersonal and seemingly autonomous power of money is in fact entirely owned by the individual, there may – from the perspective of interpersonal relations – seem to be little difference between money and its owner. The autonomous power to obtain all available goods and services belongs both to the individual subject and to his money. This comprehensive power may seem to pervade thought, with the result that the mind may seem to be subjected – or even assimilated – to money. And so for instance in Sophokles Kreon resists having his *mind* made into an object of trade by Teiresias, who in turn denies being καθαργυρωμένος ('silvered' or 'covered with silver').[57] Plato maintains that the guardians of his ideal state should be told that they have divine coinage in their souls (*Republic* 416e). Parmenides' pupil Zeno was said to have provided, under torture, 'the *logos* of Parmenides in the fire (i.e. for testing) like pure and genuine gold' (Plut. *Mor.* 1126D): internal, reason-based[58] self-sufficiency prevails (like gold) over the constant movement of fire. For Parmenides the abstract unity of things is imagined by introspection. The invisibility of the powerful inner essence of each coin is a model for the invisibility of the powerful inner essence (*psuchē*) of each individual. From the fifth century onwards people are imagined as *coins*, and for Philo the *psuchē* is currency (νόμισμα).[59] The new unified autonomy of the individual (the early Greek soul is a 'self-moving'[60] *substance)* is imagined in a form influenced by – in part modelled on – what makes it possible, namely the seemingly autonomous, unifying abstract substance of money.

The result is a contradiction. Despite this closest of associations between money and subject, money *must* (to be absolutely transferable) be entirely impersonal. This is another[61] factor promoting what I have called – in connection with both Upanishadic and presocratic thought – the coalescence of abstract monism with mental monism. The unprecedentedly

[57] S. *Antigone* 1063, 1077. [58] Parmenides B5 recommends the use of *logos* instead of the senses.

[59] References in Seaford (2004) 298.

[60] The initiation of movement (of itself and of other things) is according to Aristotle (*De Anima* 403b29ff, 404b30, 405b11–12, 31ff.) the primary feature of some early accounts of the *psuchē*. See also Pl. *Phaedrus* 245e.

[61] Other factors are mystery-cult (11§D), and the difficulty of imagining a purely impersonal substance exercising universal power.

impersonal power of money, in being projected onto the cosmos, may not shed entirely its subjective aspect. The 'one thing, the only wise, does not and does wish to be called by the name of Zeus' (Herakleitos B32).

Finally, we are now in a position to return to Homer. How do we explain consciousness that is imagined as multiple – multiple in terms of various relations to other individuals, various distinct organs of consciousness and openness to direct intervention by various gods (4§B)?

The question of whether the mind is a unity or not cannot be resolved by introspection (4§A). Neither unity nor multiplicity is simply given to us by nature. Why, then, does Homeric epic construct a detailed and consistent picture of multiplicity? Varying conceptions of the inner self emerge from varying forms of social interaction, notably in ritual, but also in the long term through historical changes in the organisation of society. An instance of the factor of ritual is provided by the joining of the *psuchē* to the sacred band (θιασεύεται ψυχάν at Euripides *Bacchae* 75) in Dionysiac mystic initiation: the initiand is de-individuated, the boundary between individual and group is dissolved.[62] An instance of the factor of social organisation is provided by the interiorisation of money, another by Plato's conception of the tripartite *psuchē*, into which the best possible (tripartite) order of the polis – including rule by reason (philosophers) – is interiorised.

In Homeric epic there is neither a developed polis nor money available to be interiorised. Interiorised instead – we saw – are *philia*, conversation, subordination, cooperation and gift-giving. These are direct interpersonal relations, mediated neither by reason nor by money. Unmediated, too, is the openness of the consciousness to direct insertions of mental states by the gods (4§B). With monetisation these various direct (unmediated) relations of an individual with others can be replaced by a single (necessarily impersonal and homogeneous) entity that mediates the power to obtain all goods and services at all times and places from anybody.

The interiorisation of money is the interiorisation of the power conferred by the possession of money on the individual agent. But the individual agent is constrained by the money held by others as well as by the modes of thought and behaviour imposed by money as a social institution. The monetised subject is both subjected to the power of money and constituted by it. This converges, we may add in passing, with

[62] For an Indian instance of the relinquishing of *bodies* (not souls) to a single group identity, see Proferes (2007) 55–61 (in the RV and the later Tānūnaptra myth).

a Foucauldian conception of the subject as 'deriving its agency from precisely the power it opposes'.[63] For the subject is produced by subjection. 'Power exerted on a subject, subjection is nevertheless a power assumed by the subject, an assumption that constitutes the instrument of that subject's becoming.'[64]

[63] Butler (1997) 17. [64] Butler (1997) 11.

CHAPTER 14

Community and Individual

14§A Circulation and Abstraction, Community and Individual

The Herakleitean circulation of fire as substrate through the constant exchange or transformation of elements regulated by the abstract *logos* cosmises the constant circulation of money as substrate through the exchange or transformation of goods regulated by the abstract *logos*.

For Herakleitos' younger contemporary Parmenides, by contrast, all that exists is 'One', invariant in time and space (eternal, unchanging, unmoving, homogeneous), abstract, self-sufficient and limited. His poem has been hailed as containing the first extant chain of deductive reasoning. But his conclusion (abstract monism) can be attributed neither to deductive reasoning alone nor to observation, and according to Aristotle[1] it borders on madness. It is surprising therefore that there has been so little interest in identifying and explaining the preconceptions that have entered into his argument and determine his bizarre conclusion.

Both Herakleitos and Parmenides grew up in city-states that had recently been monetised by the introduction of coinage. Money is *valuable* only in payment and exchange (circulation), and yet is *possessed* only by being *withheld* from payment and exchange (10§B). It is money by virtue of being changeable into all goods (as *immanent*), and yet it is money by virtue of permanently maintaining its unitary, abstract, controlling identity (as *transcendent*). These two opposed features of money, which are illusory in the sense that each depends both on the other and on social acceptance, are reified as its dual essence. The (unprecedented) Herakleitean cosmos is a cosmisation of the former, of monetised exchange or circulation[2] regulated by an abstract formula (*logos*). But the (unprecedented) Parmenidean 'One'

[1] *De Generatione et Corruptione* 325a19. [2] Inevitably expressed as *transformation*: 4§F.

is a cosmisation of the latter, of abstract monetary substance that is abstracted completely from exchange, and is therefore unitary, temporally and spatially invariant and abstract. To make this claim is not to deny the contribution made to this vision by the interiorisation of mystic initiation. The power and influence of the vision arise from its overdetermination, as an unconscious synthesis of transcendental unities of distinct origin.

This is the conclusion of a detailed argument that I set out in Seaford (2004). Here I develop it with respect to the relation between cosmos and inner self, for the purpose of comparison with the Indian material.

In Herakleitos the relationship between cosmos and *psuchē* is mediated by regulatory abstraction (*logos*), which is present in both (i.e. both projected and introjected). The abstraction referred to by *logos* is an accounting, formula, proportion or measure that regulates exchange by uniting the items exchanged; it is not itself abstract value imagined in isolation from the concrete items exchanged. The Herakleitean *logos* – in both cosmos (universe) and *psuchē* – is distinct from the concrete, in which it is nevertheless somehow embedded (especially, it seems, in circulating fire).

For Parmenides, by contrast, what is both projected as universe (Being, what exists) and introjected as mind is monetary abstract substance isolated from circulation. Value abstracted from commodity corresponds to mind abstracted from body. We proposed a similar origin for the coalescence of mental monism with abstract monism in the early *Upanishads* (8§C).

Parmenides is especially concerned to reject the view that what *is* also *is not*.[3] This view is exemplified by – for instance – Herakleitos, for whom the cosmos is an ever-living fire that is nevertheless (transformed into) other things. Parmenides responds that it is impossible to think or speak what is not (B2.7–8), that 'it must be completely or not at all' (B8.11), and that what exists can have come neither from what exists nor from what does not exist (B8.6–13). Accordingly, all is full of being (B8.24). He also appeals to *introspection*:

> Look equally at absent things that are firmly present to the mind. For you will not cut off for yourself what *is* from holding to what *is*, neither scattering everywhere in every way in order nor drawing together (B4).

Accordingly, what exists (Being) is *unitary* and *continuous*,[4] as well as *full*, *homogeneous* and *invariant in space and time*.[5]

[3] B6.4–9; B7.1–5; B8.15–16.

[4] B8.6, 25; also B8.33; B8.47–8. It is continuous temporally as well as spatially (despite B8.25): in the thought experiment in B4 (look!) what is imagined (absent) is not restricted to simultaneity.

[5] See esp. B8; Seaford (2004) 240.

I do not intend to describe the well-known detail, sequence, precise meanings and fallacies of Parmenides' argument. Rather, I select for emphasis various of his preconceptions.

(a) Firstly, there is the preconceived identification of the subjective with the objective:[6] 'Understanding and Being are the same thing' (B3).[7]

Then there are various aspects of what Parmenides introspects in B4 and projects onto Being in B8.

(b) *Continuity*. Despite what Parmenides says in B4, the mind may in fact imagine its contents not only as an indivisible whole but also, if it chooses, as diverse, changeable, indeed even scattering and drawing together.[8] But the goddess reveals to Parmenides, as to a mystic initiate, that the contents of his mind is continuous (and so unitary). Introspection discovers what it is predisposed to discover. This expresses – I suggest – the historical newness of the self-conscious abstract unity of the self-contained individual mind. Abstract continuity is both introjected and (in similar vocabulary: B8.23–5) projected onto the One.

Of this preconceived continuity (unity) there are three further aspects worthy of note: abstraction, self-containment and plenitude.

(c) *Abstraction*. In B4 what the mind (*nous*) sees are absent things, which are thus distinct from what is perceived. Coming into being and perishing, being and not being, changing place and altering bright colour – these are merely names given by mortals (B8.38–41). Sight and hearing are misleading; rather 'judge by *logos*[9] the much-contested refutation spoken by me' (B7). This approaches the idea (and ideal) of incorporeality, which will subsequently be made explicit by Plato.

(d) In Plato the incorporeal *psuchē* withdraws into itself and trusts nothing except itself and its self-contained (αὐτὴ καθ' αὑτήν, itself by itself) understanding (νοεῖν) of the αὐτὸ καθ' αὑτό (self-containment) of what exists, and 'sees what is invisible and intelligible' (*Phaedo* 83ab).

[6] For much detail on this identification in Parmenides, see Robbiano (2006).

[7] B3 τὸ γὰρ αὐτὸ νοεῖν ἐστίν τε καὶ εἶναι. Robbiano (2006: 115) shows how this translation is to be preferred, and how the alternative meaning ('the same thing is there for understanding and being') may nevertheless be implied. See also B8.34–6.

[8] The reference to scattering is probably directed against Herakleitos: Seaford (2004) 251.

[9] The precise meaning of *logos* at this stage in its history is unknown, though it must here be a faculty employing abstraction. For the controversy surrounding this passage, see Kingsley (2003: 136–40 and 566–90), and Gemelli Marciano (2013 – especially Mourelatos at 159–77 and Gemelli Marciano at 217–29 and 259–65).

So, too, for Parmenides absent things are 'firmly' present to the mind as one and continuous (B4), and Being is self-contained: it 'remains the same in the same (ταὐτόν τ'ἐν ταὐτῶι) and lies καθ' ἑαυτό, and thus fixed it will remain' (B8.29–30). Here is our fourth preconception: introjected and projected abstract *self-containment*.

(e) The continuity of the contents of introspection in B4 implies *fullness*, which is explicitly identified with thought (B16.4)[10] as well as predicated of Being (B8.24). In CU 7.23–4 the projection and introjection of abstract plenitude (*bhūman*) expresses, as it does in Parmenides, the abstraction of monetary substance from exchange (15§C).

To explain the opposition between Herakleitos and Parmenides we can adduce their cosmisation of the opposed essences of money, Herakleitos its circulation and Parmenides its unchanging abstract value. But this in itself cannot provide a full explanation. In Chapter 11 we considered Parmenides' appeal to introspection, together with passages of Herakleitos and Plato, as examples of the interiorisation of mystic initiation. All three thinkers embody the convergence of mystic initiation with monetary abstraction, but each from a different ideological perspective.

The temporary individual isolation of the mystic initiand becomes in Parmenides a permanent state (11§D): the many remain entirely and permanently excluded from his interiorised mystic initiation. His underworld journey 'bears the man of knowledge' and is 'far from the footsteps of men'. He undertakes it alone, and it is to him alone that the goddess reveals the truth, whereas in the beliefs of mortals, who 'know nothing', there is no true conviction.[11]

For Herakleitos the abstract intersubjectivity of the (mystic) *logos* is interiorised in each individual *psuchē*. 'Thinking is communal to all' (B113), and the *logos*, according to which all things happen and all things are one, is communal, but humans do not at first understand it, and live as if having individual understanding – in both respects like initiands isolated in the first phase of initiation.[12] 'The waking share one common world, whereas the sleeping turn away each into the private' (B89).[13] Both cosmos and *psuchē* are composed of fire that embodies *logos* (9§E, 13§D). The political implications of all this are made explicit. The people must fight for

[10] Translated as '. . . the full (πλέον) is thought': Tor (2017) 176–7. [11] B1.3, 27, 30; B6.4.

[12] B1, B50, B2; Seaford (2004) 233 n.19.

[13] And so – although a sleeper creates light for himself (B26) or becomes his own light (BU 4.3.9) – in BU this gives access to the other world, whereas in Hklt. 'the sleeper contacts the dead person' (merely), although in other Greek texts sleep gives access to the future (e.g. Pindar *fr.* 131).

the law as for a wall (B44) and those who speak with intelligence (ξὺν νόῳ) must rely on what is communal (ξυνῷ) to all, as a polis relies on law, and much more strongly (B114).

Logos in the fifth century could mean both monetary account and mystic instruction. Money belongs entirely to the individual, but in using it he accepts its communally agreed value and has constantly to enter agreements about price. Despite the individualising impersonal power of money, its functioning depends on its being socially created and socially accepted. This is the paradox that underlies Herakleitos' idea that the *logos* in each individual *psuchē* is communal. Money isolates the individual but its *logos* is communal. Analogously, mystic initiation isolates the initiand before incorporating him into the initiated community,[14] who learn from the mystic *logos*. In both monetised exchange and mystic initiation the isolated individual accepts the communal *logos*, and both processes have influenced the communality of the Herakleiteian *logos*.[15]

The unlimitedness of the Herakleitean *psuchē* derives both from the unlimitedness of money (13§D) and from what is exemplified in Euripides' *Bacchae* (13§E): the *psuchē* of the mystic initiate is de-individuated, merged with the initiated community. Mystic doctrine, concerned as it is with the power that transcends post-mortem existence, is *cosmological*. Mystic initiation thereby provided a traditional cosmological paradigm within which Herakleitos was able to encompass – by conscious or unconscious synthesis – the cosmisation of the new transcendent power of money. And just as the communal basis of money is not obvious to the individualised possessor of money, so the communal destination of mystic transition is concealed – in the preliminary phase of mystic initiation – from the fearful and isolated initiand. We have already seen, in Plato's *Phaedo*, synthesis of the unifying effect of money with the unifying effect of mystic initiation (13§E).

It is in the fragments of Herakleitos that we first find a detailed account of the *psuchē* as a substance that has depth and intelligence. Each individual

[14] The mystic transition might be from painful individual isolation to a sense of belonging to a group: Plut. *Moralia* 81de, *fr.* 178 (from individual isolation in the darkness to *sunestin etc.* in the light); *Phaedo* 67a (11§E), 108b (it is inferred from mystery-cult that the pure soul finds gods as companions and guides to the underworld, whereas the impure soul resists, suffers and is dragged to the underworld where it is shunned by all and wanders around bewildered and alone); cf. E. *Bacchae* 72–5, 576–641 (esp. 616–37) with Seaford ad loc., and (on the coherence of the *thiasos*) 693, 748; Aristophanes *Frogs*, (e.g.) 156–7, 450–6; Pl. *Republic* 560de (the new mental state of the initiand is established by the arrival of the resplendent chorus), *Phaedrus* 247a, 250b (with Riedweg [1987] 30–69; Seaford [2013]). To join the mystic group/chorus might be to join the cosmos: 6§A n.34.

[15] Seaford (2004) 231–9.

person has a *psuchē*. And yet Herakleitos emphatically privileges the communal aspect of cognition over its private aspect. The individual is seen from the perspective of the whole. The body of an individual is constituted by narrow physical limits, and yet for Herakleitos the depth of his *psuchē* seems unlimited (13§D), because its *logos* is communal. It may seem paradoxical that the first extant description of the *psuchē* – as the unitary inner self of the individual – insists on its communality in the context of the impersonal unity of all things. This reflects the historical fact that it was the unprecedented unification of all goods and services by an impersonal abstract substrate (money) that in the sixth century BCE promoted unprecedented autonomy for the individual. Individual subjectivity is shaped by the creation of a communal measure of the objective.

By contrast, the individual isolation of the Parmenidean 'knowing man' encounters not the unlimited social universality of the *logos* but rather – through introspection and deduction – the ontological universality of the (limited) One.

Why this opposition between Herakleitos and Parmenides? Why does Parmenides project onto the universe monetary *substance* abstracted entirely from circulation, whereas Herakleitos projects monetary *circulation*? We cannot resort to introspection, which can reveal either self-containment or unlimitedness. We must resort instead to the power of *ideology*.

The Greek ideal of *self-sufficiency* is – in the economic sphere – at least as old as Hesiod,[16] and remains prominent across the range of economics, politics, ethics, metaphysics and theology. For instance, Aristotle states both that 'it is the mark of an *eleutheros* (free man, gentleman) not to live for the benefit of another' and as a general assumption that 'self-sufficiency is an end and what is best', and implies that the individual household should be as self-sufficient as possible.[17]

What was the effect of monetisation on this ideal? In the form of coined money silver circulated much more widely than did the prestige objects of Homeric epic, and – as noted by Aristotle[18] – money equalises the parties to exchange (*qua* exchangers). And so monetisation may seem to threaten the superiority of the aristocratic individual, a threat attested by Theognis. But monetisation also promotes individual autonomy. And the necessary impersonality of money, its tendency to appear as a self-identical thing

[16] *Erga* 31, 364–5, 400–4, 477–8.

[17] Aristotle *Rhetoric* 1367a32; *Politics* 1252b35, 1256a4–58b56; See further Seaford (1994) 200–2; (2004) 247.

[18] *Nicomachean Ethics* 1133a17–21.

independent of all interpersonal relations, may facilitate the sense of self-sufficiency. This sense is of course illusory, because in fact money is valuable only in exchange. But the illusion may be reinforced by the ideology of self-sufficient distance not only from poverty but also from the vulgarity and insecurity of commerce. And the ideology may in turn be sustained and satisfied by the unconscious separation of the value of money from its circulation. Parmenides expresses contempt for the undiscriminating masses (B6), and was said to have been 'of illustrious family and wealth'[19] and to have legislated for Elea.[20] There was a Parmenidean as well as a Pythagorean way of life.[21] It was introspection, into a mind individualised and unified under the influence of monetary abstraction, that revealed to him that Being is unitary and homogeneous and excludes all transformation.[22] The word of Parmenides tested in the fire 'like pure and genuine gold' expresses – as does the intrapsychic divine gold and silver coinage that Plato contrasts with the polluting coinage of the majority – not only self-sufficiency (13§E) but also the aristocratic quality that contrasts[23] with the untested superficiality of circulating coin.

Features of the One that are emphasised by Parmenides, and require explanation, are that it is *self-sufficient* and *limited*:

> It is motionless within the limits of great bonds, without beginning or ceasing, since coming to be and perishing have wandered very far away, and true belief has thrust them off. Remaining the same in the same, it lies on its own, and fixed thus remains (or 'will remain'), for strong necessity holds it in the bonds of limit, which keeps it on every side, because it is right that what is should not be endless; for it is not lacking – if it were, it would lack everything. (B8.26–33).

It is firmly limited, because it is unchanging, and because it is not lacking (i.e. it is self-sufficient); and its self-sufficiency seems to belong to the fullness of its being that was established earlier. The limit is represented as spatial,[24] but seems to be the mark of invariancy in both time and space. The (spatial and temporal) abstract invariancy necessarily attributed to money in circulation forms the basis for imagining its abstraction from circulation. In circulation money (and the desire for it) requires

[19] A1 (Sotion ap. D.L. 9.21). Herakleitos by contrast was said to have resigned the kingship (A1; D. L. 9.6).

[20] Speusippos ap. D.L. 9.23; Plut. *Moralia* 1126a; Strabo 6.1 (252).

[21] [Cebes] *Tabula* 2.2 (Hellenistic). [22] For other possible factors, see Seaford (2004) 245.

[23] On tested or pure gold as an image of aristocratic quality see Kurke (1999) 42–5, 49–54, 57–60, 141–2, 304.

[24] Besides 'the bonds of limit, which keeps it in here on every side', see also 42–3.

transformation and lacks limit, for its value is realised only in exchange and there are always more things for it to seek. But the impersonal convenience of money may foster in its owner the welcome illusion of self-sufficiency, which – by seeming to inhere in the money – produces the imagined separation of abstract substance from unlimited exchange, making it seem limited as well as self-sufficient. It is, again, the ideology of self-sufficiency – reinforced by aversion to circulating money as dissolving class distinctions – that produces the emphatic statements of limit, of 'great bonds', of coming to be and perishing as 'wandered very far away', of the idea that if the abstract One were lacking it would (like money in circulation) 'lack everything', of (a little earlier: 14–16) the One being held in place by Justice – as if it were a matter of economic allocation. I do not know why it would be called 'all inviolate' (48) – implying a surrounding threat – unless this derives from a sense of the sanctity of property. And its eternity is proved by the argument that there is no χρέος (debt, obligation) that could have brought it into being (12§B).

It is only by reference to abstract monetary substance that we can make sense of the particular combination of characteristics found in the Parmenidean One: it is unitary, homogeneous, continuous, abstract, invariant in time and space, self-sufficient and limited. In both Herakleitos and Parmenides the unifying abstraction of money is simultaneously *introjected* (interiorised), represented as if it were mystic doctrine and *projected* into the universe (as impersonal ontology). But each thinker privileges one of the complementary essences of money – Herakleitos (communal) circulation with its *logos*, Parmenides (individual) possession of abstract substance. For both thinkers everything is one, but whereas circulation requires a multiplicity of individual souls (albeit each co-material with the one fire) and a degree of materiality in the objects exchanged, the sense of individual self-sufficiency provided by possession of monetary value depends neither on the materiality of specific objects nor on any other individual: the unitary abstraction observed by introspection may seem to be all there is.

It is as individuals that Herakleitos, Parmenides and the Vedic sacrificer interiorise the cosmic rite of passage. In all three cases philosophy emerges from the (interiorising) effect of monetisation on the cosmic rite of passage. But what distinguishes Herakleitos from the other two is that his communal *logos* is influenced by the eventual integration of the isolated initiand into the group, whereas the Parmenidean mystic vision goes no further than the phase of isolation, and the Vedic sacrificer does not join a group. Accordingly, there is nothing in India, nor even in

Parmenides, comparable to the Herakleitean co-material participation of *psuchē* in universe. Interpenetrating these ritual differences are the corresponding economic ones. Herakleitos privileges the constant circulation of money (albeit governed by an unchanging *logos*), whereas Parmenides privileges its static possessed value, an opposition that correlates – at least in part – with differences in economic milieu.[25]

In India the same opposition, between (transcendent) abstraction and (immanent) circulation, takes various forms, of which here I select three.

(1) Predominant in the early *Upanishads* is the identification of atman with brahman, in which both seem to be unchanging abstract entities. On the other hand the five-fire and two-path doctrine describe subjection to a constant cosmic cycle, with permanent escape to brahman possible only for some exalted people (9§D). The possibility of correlation with differences in economic milieu is suggested by the fact that the doctrine is expounded by a Kshatriya as one that has 'never before been in the possession of a Brahmin' (7§A). It is also possible that the idea of *saṃsāra* (the cycle of reincarnation) was fully developed earlier outside the Vedic tradition (by Jains, Ajivikans or Buddhists).[26]

(2) In fact, the all-encompassing abstract power-entity brahman has two forms (*rūpa*),[27] which are complementary abstract entities. *Tyam*, a demonstrative pronoun denoting an object at a distance, is without fixed shape, consists of air and *antarikṣa* (the space between earth and sky) and is immortal and in motion. *Sat*, meaning what exists, has a fixed shape, consists of everything other than air and *antarikṣa* and is mortal and stationary.[28] The *tyam-sat* opposition (within brahman) is analogous to the opposition between Herakleitos and Parmenides, which it resembles also by virtue of obtaining within the inner self (atman) as well as in the world. From the perspective of individual possession, *tyam* corresponds to amorphous money out there in constant circulation, *sat* to the specific sum of money possessed.

(3) I related the unchangeability of Ajivikan *niyati*, karma and *saṃsāra* to the unchangeable power of money (9§E). But, in fact, Ajivikan cosmology also contains within itself our opposition. On the one

[25] 14§B, 15§A, 17§A. [26] The word *saṃsāra* does not occur in Vedic texts before KaU 3.7.

[27] BU 2.3; Cf. TU 2.6.1; KU 1.6. 'Form' is the usual translation of *rūpa*. Cf. BU 1.4.7: Olivelle (1996) (on BU 1.4.7) prefers the translation 'visible appearances'. But *tyam* (air, breath, space) is *invisible*.

[28] TU 2.6 is more succinct: *sat* is the distinct, the resting, the perceived and the real, and *tyat* the opposite of all these.

hand, as early as the *Sāmañña-phala Sutta* we find ascribed to the Ajivikan sage Pakudha the doctrine of seven unchanging elements (earth, water, fire, air, joy, sorrow, life), such that cleaving a head with a sharp sword is not killing because it passes between the elements. This notion of an unchanging reality behind appearances seems to have influenced the later Ajivikan doctrine of unmoving permanence, *avicalita-nityatvam* (compared by Basham to Parmenides), according to which – given that everything is rigidly determined – every phase of a process is always present, nothing is destroyed, nothing is produced and all change is illusory.[29] On the other hand in early Ajivikism, 'according to the inherent character of that impersonal principle [*niyati*] . . . new entities replaced those which passed away in rigidly determined order. The total content of the universe was always absolutely the same'.[30] This is strikingly similar to the strictly balanced cosmic process imagined by Herakleitos, which he himself compares to the universal monetary cycle, and in which everything happens according to the unchanging impersonal *logos*.[31]

14§B Reason, Mystery and Money

From the previous section three major Parmenidean preconceptions have emerged: that (a) the contents of mind (what can be spoken or thought of) must fully exist; (b) what exists is one and continuous: this is supported by appeal to introspection (B4), and fully stated in B8; (c) *Being*, indicated by repeated *esti* ('is', 'it is', 'there is'), can be abstracted from all other things (leaving them without it). It will therefore easily appear as unitary, full, homogeneous, imperceptible, continuous and unmoving – appearances reinforced by (a).

These preconceptions, together with deduction,[32] produce Parmenides' conclusion, in which the spatially and temporally invariant One is held in chains not only by Justice but also by strong Necessity and Fate.[33] Given Parmenides' conception of the One as not produced by debt and as inviolate,[34] I suggest that Justice here may be the cosmised right to individual property. But what requires the agency of Necessity and Fate?

[29] Basham (1951) 19, 91–2, 236–8, 262–4, 269. [30] Basham (1951) 240.
[31] B30, B31, B90, B1; 13§D.
[32] The deductive aspect of Parmenides has predictably attracted much more attention than his preconceptions: see e.g. recently Wedin (2014).
[33] B8.14 (Δίκη), (Ἀνάγκη), 37 (Μοῖρα). [34] 12§B, 14§A, 14§B.

To this question there are several kinds of answer. First is the logical necessity inherent in the deduction. The second is that the conclusion is so unbelievable as to require strong supernatural support. The third – drawing on the kind of interpretation proposed by Gemelli Marciano (2013) – refers to the necessity that is inherent in the specific context of mystic revelation by a goddess, and that is conveyed by various features of the poem (assonance, alliteration, repetition, etc.) that would have been especially powerful in its *performance*.

There is perhaps some truth in all three of these answers. But they all beg the question: what was the attraction of the preconceptions and of the (preconceived) unbelievable conclusion in the first place?

The only existing answer known to me refers to a certain altered state of consciousness, in which the normal divisions between entities seem dissolved, and there is a sense of perpetual present and of a reality more real than everyday life.[35] This is consistent with the view that Parmenides represents his enlightenment as occurring in mystic initiation, in which altered states of consciousness may well have occurred.[36]

This approach is relevant and important – but also insufficient, because it cannot explain (1) why the Parmenidean vision should have occurred when and where it did; (2) why it was expressed in what seems to be logical reasoning; (3) the place of Parmenidean ontology in the history of Greek thought, both its undoubted relation to previous thought and the considerable persistence of this way of thinking in (and influence on) later thought; (4) why the ontological privileging of unitary abstract Being also occurred at about the same time in India, without any suggestion of mystic ritual or abnormal states of consciousness; (5) various precise details that Parmenides attributes to Being; (6) the *absence* – from Parmenides' description – of the positive features of the reality sensed in altered states of consciousness: e.g. Ustinova supposes the influence on Parmenides of an experience, typical in certain abnormal states of consciousness, of 'eternal, loving unchangeable oneness', and of 'blissful awareness of the shining "unchanging living reality" through which the author lived'.[37] But the dry, deductive objectivity of Parmenides' account of Being could hardly be more different from the love, bliss and personal intimacy regularly reported by those who have experienced the kind of altered state of consciousness attributed by Ustinova and others to Parmenides. Indeed, one of the elements of mystical experience listed by Ustinova is 'a cessation of normal

[35] E.g. West (1971) 222–3; Ustinova (2009) 199–209; Gemelli Marciano (2013) 93–4.
[36] Seaford (2010b); Ustinova (2013). [37] Ustinova (2009) 204, 207.

intellectual operations (e.g. deduction . . .)'.[38] But Parmenides' idea of Being is *depersonalised*, *deductive* mystic vision.

Parmenides' preconceptions and conclusion can be adequately explained neither by observation nor by intuition, nor by data from the study of abnormal psychology, nor by our three ways of answering the question of Necessity and Fate. What is also required is a fourth answer: that Necessity and Fate also express the importance – to the aristocratic ideology of monetised self-sufficiency – of imagining abstract substance abstracted even from circulation. The monetary substance introjected and projected by the earlier presocratics has for Parmenides – the wealthy, aristocratic successor to the Ionian thinkers – become entirely self-sufficient and entirely abstract. The result is the ideologically determined doctrine of abstract Being, unitary, unchanging and self-sufficient.

I must emphasise that this answer is perfectly compatible both with the other three answers and with the elements of Parmenides' vision that can be related to mystic initiation, and that the power and influence of Parmenides' vision derives in part from its overdetermination, producing unconscious synthesis of the abnormal state induced by the cosmic milieu of mystic initiation with preconceptions arising from the interiorisation and cosmic projection (cosmisation) of all-pervasive abstract substance.

From our list of the preconceptions, (a) – the contents of mind must fully exist – is in effect the unity of subject with object, which derives from the experience of mystic initiation (11§D) in synthesis with the interiorisation of money and the ideology of self-sufficiency (14§A). Preconception (b) – the unity and continuity of what exists, established by introspection – is the *projection* (cosmisation) of *introjected* monetary substance. Note that (b) expresses (a): what is observed by introspection is taken to be what exists, the distinction between subject and object disappears.

As for preconception (c) – namely that *Being*, indicated by repeated *esti*, can be abstracted from all else – interpreters cannot agree on whether *esti* is existential or predicative, or on what its subject or predicate might be. Gemelli Marciano sidesteps this problem by maintaining that with *esti* (without a subject) Parmenides does not denote a *thing* but means rather to induce in the hearer a *state* – a sense of totality and completion that occurs in the 'mystic experiences of every culture'; and that is also why *esti* is repeated emphatically and often. I accept the relevance of the mystic sense of totality and completion while also insisting, however, on the fact that *esti*, besides inducing a state, does also imply the existence of a (mysterious)

[38] Ustinova (2009) 18.

abstract *entity*, to which Parmenides then attributes several characteristics, which do not include any – such as beauty or divinity – that would excite admiration or awe, let alone bliss and love. This abstract entity – as strictly impersonal as money has to be – is *inter alia* a projection of monetary substance: indeed repeated *esti* is then a vehicle of the synthesis of the two sources, mystic and monetary, of Parmenides' vision, expressing both a mystic sense of totality and the abstraction of mere Being from all things. Another such vehicle is the assimilation between subject and object, which occurs – albeit in different forms – not only in mystic initiation but also with the interiorisation of money. The historical moment of Parmenides is when the (no doubt ancient) dissolution of boundaries in mystic experience merges with something new that invests it with definable objective reality: the dissolution of boundaries in abstract (monetary) Being.

Gemelli Marciano also claims that the Greek words signifying cause (γάρ, οὕνεκεν, ἐπεί) are used by Parmenides not to express a logical argument but rather to constrain the hearer to focus on *esti*. Again, this is only a partial truth, for Parmenides does also adopt a deductive approach whose purpose is intellectual persuasion. Why does he do so? Or rather, why is it precisely in the context of mystic revelation that there occurs the first extant instance of deductive philosophical argument?

One answer might be that his conclusion is so improbable that he feels obliged to support it with two very different – even opposite – forms of representation, one endowed with emotional power as well as with divine authority as the traditional mode of accessing hidden cosmic reality (mystic initiation), the other endowed with intellectual cogency (deduction). But it is also worth asking what connection there might be – besides strict impersonality – between deduction and abstract value.

For this purpose let us look more closely at the argument, in both Parmenides B8.7–10 and the *Chāndogya Upaniṣad* 6.2.1–2, that what exists cannot have arisen from what does not exist, about which I have maintained that the similarity is to be explained neither by influence nor merely by the simultaneous miraculous advent of reason:[39] what is fundamental is rather the ontological privileging of abstraction.

(1) In both passages we have primordial abstract monism, the use of what looks like pure reason and the (revolutionary) abolition of any cosmogonic act. The point is to understand how closely these three features combine and how the combination arises.

[39] 2§D, 8§E.

Traditionally and cross-culturally, cosmogony is imagined as a concrete act, such as the creation of the world as if it were an artefact, the slaying of a dragon by a monarch or the separation of sky from earth. Such acts are easily imagined as autonomous. However, in a pervasively monetised world, transformative action, be it creating or acquiring artefacts or fighting a battle, is generally at least partly motivated by – and generally also depends on – abstract (monetary) substance, which therefore is imagined to precede and transcend transformative action. The absolute confidence on which the impersonal power of money depends requires that it be imagined as *transcending and so preceding all change*. Moreover, once universal abstract substance (Being) has been abstracted from all else, it is simply the embodiment of existence, and so – at a purely intellectual level – what precedes it must be non-existent (for anything that does exist does *not* precede existence), and so nothing precedes it. It is eternal. This also expresses a natural sense of continuity, which on the other hand does allow *concrete* things to come into being – from other concrete things.

Thus the purely intellectual inference that mere Being cannot have come into existence (from non-Being) coheres with, and may emerge from, the experience of (monetary) abstract substance as preceding all action. In so far as the inference is concerned with what is purely abstract, it is itself purely abstract, the exercise of reason. I emphasise again that the primary step is not the inexplicable simultaneous arrival of abstract reason in two different cultures (why then and there?), but the simultaneous abstraction of Being from all things, which *can* be explained. Fundamental to our combination – of abstraction, eternity and pure reason – is the historical emergence of money.

(2) In B8.9-10 'what χρέος (debt, obligation) would have driven it to come into being, later or sooner, from nothing?' the general mistranslation of χρέος as need or necessity (12§B) derives from assuming that the thought is mere logical deduction. Nor can characterising the One as debtless – and as inviolate, and held in place by Justice and Necessity – be neutralised as mere decoration or metaphor. Metaphor for *what*?[40] Rather, the One is *constructed* and *known* by being imagined in terms of the debtlessness and inviolability that are slightly more concrete aspects of that abstract *self-sufficiency* of the One that is emphasised in the same passage.

(3) This is not to say Parmenides lacks the idea of necessity. The cosmologies of Anaximander and Herakleitos also contain suggestions of debt that,

[40] On the potential for confusion in 'metaphor', see 10§C.

being projected onto the universe, seems to have become a more general necessity (12§B). The cosmological transition from debt or obligation to the less specific and more impersonal concept of necessity is paralleled by the transition in the meaning of *logos* from monetary account to reason. The limitedness of the Parmenidean One, based on its self-sufficiency, is enforced by necessity (B8.30–33), which is in part ideological in origin.[41] But ubiquitously embodied in money is a new kind of (impersonal) necessity, and the two necessities converge to produce what modern commentators on Parmenides (though not Parmenides himself) conceptualise as his sense of logical necessity.[42]

(4) The denial of cosmogony as proposed at Parmenides 8.5–10 and CU 6.2.1–2 is far from typical of Greek and Indian thought of the period. The very next paragraph of the *Chāndogya Upaniṣad* expresses – as do other passages of the *Chāndogya Upaniṣad* and the *Bṛhadāraṇyaka Upaniṣad* – primordial personal monism, and cosmogony as personal agency: the existent decides to propagate itself and emits heat, which emits water, etc. Such ideas may be influenced not so much by the ideal of unchanging value as by the inner power, bestowed by monetisation on the individual, to control and acquire multiplicity. The cosmisation of circulation on the other hand, for instance as *saṃsāra* or the Herakleitean cycle, tends to be without beginning. In both cultures eternity and cosmogony combine in periodic universal destruction.

14§C Ritual and Money

Ritual action tends towards *abstract* action. It tends to be disconnected from the concrete specificities of context and from individual intention. The rules of ritual are, Cavallin maintains, 'general, that is, abstracted from the irrelevant features of specific contexts'. Ritual action 'strives to eliminate the individual idiosyncrasies of the ritual participants'. Further, 'the individual in submitting to ritual norms acts out abstract actions which are part of an inter-subjective repertoire of ideal notions and narratives'. Ritualised actions are 'meant to be instantiations of an archetype'.[43] The point of shaking hands is no more than to instantiate concord.

[41] See further Seaford (2019).
[42] Words indicating necessity occur in Parmenides at B2.5; 6.1; 8.7; 8.11–12; 8.45.
[43] Cavallin (2013) 25–7.

Money and ritual both work by commanding assent to the efficacy of an abstraction – abstract value (money) or abstract action (ritual). And in the origins of Greek coinage they converge. The spits on which meat was distributed to participants in Greek animal sacrifice were of identical shape and size, and so – besides carrying meat – embodied and reinforced the intersubjective abstraction of equal distribution. This embodiment facilitated the use of spits as proto-money, from which evolved coins named after spits.[44] The communally sanctioned equality and distribution of the spits was a factor in their communal circulation as equal proto-monetary objects. An abstract principle of the ritual – absolute equality of distribution – helps the spits to function as proto-money. Money is – like the sacrifice and the sacrificial spits from which it in part emerged – a universally recognised (distinct and stable) paradigm that operates by means of abstraction to coordinate the allocation of goods.

Commercial exchange and mystic initiation are similar in form.[45] In general the act of purchase is ritualised, with communally agreed symbols, actions or words embodying the abstraction of transferred ownership. This combines with what is sometimes called 'real abstraction': commodities are separated from use, from all sensory qualities, from all particularities of place and time, for the purpose of the numerical (monetary) evaluation required for exchange. In the spit becoming proto-money, the abstraction of absolutely equal substance merges with the abstraction of monetary value.

In mystic initiation the revelation of sacred objects, or of secret doctrine or *logos*, was a focus for the group, and might contribute to the new cosmological orientation acquired by the initiates.[46] Mystic

[44] Seaford (2004) 102–15.

[45] Commercial exchange between A and B can be analysed as consisting of three phases XYZ, where in X and Z there is no obligation between A and B, and Y is a (frequently brief) intermediate state in which obligation (debt) has been incurred but not yet fulfilled (paid). Ritual may have the same structure, where two phases of static normality (X and Z) frame the creation of a dynamic phase of tension (Y). This is most obvious in the rite of passage (including mystic initiation), where in the 'liminal' phase (Y) the initiand may be detached from the previous identity but still resistant to acquiring the new identity. Further, the restoration of normality requires the *limitation* of Y. In the case of ritual this is achieved by general acceptance of the power of the (generally traditional) forms of ritual action. But in a monetised transaction it can be achieved only by general acceptance of the power of money. Because it is the money itself that (seems to) contain the power, it makes no difference what actions effect or accompany its transferral. But ritual and money are parallel, inasmuch as they both have the power to limit Y. Such limitation is, seen positively, *completion*: normality is restored, social integration obtained. Indeed, money and ritual each provide a universally agreed paradigm to coordinate numerous social interactions. In addition, rites of passage and money both *mediate contradiction* – the former between the old and new identity, the latter between the parties to the transaction. See further Seaford (2012) 125–7.

[46] 6§A ns.33 and 34.

ritual is de-individuation, and even Plato preserves traces of its communal culmination.[47]

On the other hand in Plato and Parmenides the mystic vision is – like monetary value – interiorised and so individualised. A general contradiction of this kind is noted by Cavallin:[48]

> If ritualization is foremost a process of abstraction which entails a de-individuation of the person, then a focus within a ritual tradition on the human interior seems to go in the opposite direction. As the interior is equivalent to the hidden features of the person, the intersubjective dimension of ritual activity is subjected to a gravitational pull toward the subjective.

On the other hand, interiorisation is facilitated by the abstraction inherent in ritualization:

> It is not only the interior of the human person which is hidden, but also the ideal world shares this elusive nature, despite its being maintained within the social group through such public means as discourse, rituals, and institutions. The ideal entities having shed matter through the process of abstraction are not in a direct sense part of the empirical world . . . the ideal entities of the cultural and religious world are made part of the self, or, with other words, they transform the self in accordance with their nature.

One such ideal entity is the transcendent object of the mystic vision. Another transcendent ideal entity, emerging from the intersubjective process of exchange, is monetary value. Commercial exchange and mystic ritual are both characterised by the negation of isolated individual intentionalities in a single intersubjective abstraction: the consequent ideal entities – monetary value and the object of mystic vision – converge, and are in Plato and Parmenides interiorised and merged.

Consider, for instance, what is 'suddenly' seen at the end of the ascent of the philosopher described in terms of mystic initiation in Plato's *Symposium*. It is 'something amazingly beautiful', eternal, unchanging, unitary, free of all variation, without any sensory qualities. In it, other beautiful things participate, coming into being and passing away while it does not change. The object of the joyful and intense mystic vision is imagined as an unchanging unitary abstract entity, in which mutable things somehow participate. The transcendent object of mystic initiation has here – as also elsewhere in Plato and in Parmenides – merged with the unchanging, unitary, abstract entity of money.

[47] 13§E; 14§A n.14. [48] Cavallin (2013) 96.

The stimulus to interiorisiation comes not from within ritual but rather, I suggest, from the self-sufficiency bestowed on the individual by the historical advent of money. It is only the individual sense of absolute possession of the power of money that is powerful enough to conceal from itself – while interiorising – the essential inter-subjectivity both of monetary value and of the mystic vision. In other words, the contradiction noted by Cavallin, in which the de-individuation inherent in ritual is reversed by the interiorisation of ritual, arises from another contradiction – the individual, self-sufficient appropriation of the intersubjective abstraction inherent in monetised exchange.

The synthesis of the cosmic rite of passage with monetisation also reshapes *temporality*. The permanent passive isolation of the renouncer (*saṃnyāsin*) derives, at least in part, from the temporary passive isolation of the sacrificial initiand (*dīkṣita*):[49] a liminal phase of the cosmic rite of passage becomes permanent.[50] The *saṃnyāsin*, in remaining permanently outside the individualised activity of the sacrificial and profane cycles of exchange, prefigures his eventual release (*mokṣa*) from the *cosmic* cycle. The temporary phase of isolation in the cosmic rite of passage becomes permanent also in the vision of Parmenides (11§D).

But, of course, this significant similarity between the *saṃnyāsin* and Parmenides coexists with fundamental differences. In fact, we may classify the metaphysical relations to the monetised cycle as follows:

(a) The permanent isolation of the *saṃnyāsin* is a complete escape from the commercial cycle – *from below*, into poverty – as an expression and means of escape from the cosmic cycle.

(b) The isolation of Parmenides from the commercial cycle is *from above*: it is influenced by the ideology of monetised self-sufficiency, in which he imagines himself in isolation from the commercial cycle (even though in fact he may indirectly benefit from it). Parmenides is driven ideologically to emphasise that only abstract Being exists (the cycle does not exist).

(c) Plato interiorises the cosmic rite of passage – as do the *saṃnyāsin* and Parmenides. But metaphysically he belongs between the two. So far from (like Parmenides) rejecting the existence of the cycle, he (like the *saṃnyāsin*) endorses escape from it in this world and in the next

[49] Malamoud (1996) 47; similarly Heesterman (1988) 269; Bronkhorst (2007) 81–4, 92–3.

[50] The isolating extension or eternalisation of the liminal phase in the rite of passage occurs also in Greek mythology. And in Athenian tragedy completion of the rite of passage is sometimes deferred in a manner that suggests the unlimitedness of money: Seaford (2012a) 125–36, 144–9, 190–205, etc.

(14§D). Moreover, the latter is for Plato achieved – as often in India – by fundamental knowledge (especially of the self) and freedom from desire, which are already in the *Bṛhadāraṇyaka Upaniṣad* associated with the mendicant, wandering life.[51] But on the other hand Plato privileges (and recommends assimilation to) abstract Being, like Parmenides. His escape from the cycle is not from below, into mendicancy, but *from above*: he *explicitly interiorises* the *possession* of coined money in self-sufficient separation from what he calls the polluting coin of the multitude.[52] This resembles another strand in the *Bṛhadāraṇyaka Upaniṣad*, the two-path doctrine, according to which certain 'exalted people', who have special knowledge, escape the cycle of reincarnation for permanent life in the worlds of brahman (6.2.15). Our familiarity with wealthy capitalists continuing to engage in monetary circulation should not conceal from us the premodern desire to acquire money in order to escape from its circulation.

14§D Reincarnation

We have identified two opposed conceptions of the inner self, the Herakleitean and the Parmenidean, corresponding to the two opposed essences of money, but each emerging from the interiorisation of mystery-cult.

For Parmenides all that exists is the invariant One (or Being). This leaves no room for an independent mind, which therefore seems as if absorbed into the One, an extreme instance of the observer in mystery-cult being assimilated to what is observed.

As for the Herakleitean *psuchē*, we have seen that it is de-individuated in so far as other *psuchai* are also composed of the same material (primarily fire) and contain the (communal) *logos*, and that this corresponds with the merging of the individual *psuchē* into the group in mystery-cult. But it is de-individuated also in another way, over *time*, being transformed through the cosmological elements back into *psuchē*. And this, too, we will now see, corresponds with an idea found in mystery-cult.

The idea is *reincarnation*. In Chapter 10 the main focus was on Indian reincarnation, but here we focus on Greek. Reincarnation as normally understood implies a vehicle of personal identity to make the transition

51 3.5.1; 4.4.22

52 *Republic* 416e. How religion and morality may borrow commercial concepts to protest against commerce is a theme of Graeber (2011): e.g. 89, 186.

between bodies. The vehicle is not necessarily a carefully described soul. But it is not coincidental that the first extant Greek *identification* of a person with his soul is in the context of reincarnation: Xenophanes refers (B7) to Pythagoras recognising the *psuchē* of a friend in the cry of a dog being beaten.[53] In the archaic and classical periods reincarnation was propounded also by Pherekydes,[54] the Pythagoreans,[55] Empedokles,[56] Pindar[57] and Plato,[58] and probably also by Parmenides[59] and in Orphic theogony.[60] It is clear from several passages that it was taught in mystery-cult.[61] We have seen that mystic instructions on gold leaves of the fourth century BCE describe two paths in the hereafter, one leading to unchangingness, the other almost certainly to reincarnation, similarly to the two-path doctrines in the early *Upanishads* (9§D), in Parmenides (11§D) and in Plato (11§E). The fragmentary nature of the evidence means that it is hard to know who maintained EIR, but (in the archaic and classical periods) reincarnation was certainly indiscriminate in Pythagoras and the Pythagoreans, in Empedokles (B117) and in Plato; certainly ethicised where we have complete texts (Pindar and Plato); perhaps ethicised in Pherekydes;[62] and at least partly ethicised in early Orphic theogony[63] and in Empedokles (B115).

Reincarnation and the merging of the *psuchē* in the group both occur in mystery-cult, and they both involve de-individuation (the former over time, the latter at a single moment). True, in reincarnation the *psuchē* may preserve its identity, which may, however, merge with the identity of the person (or animal) in whom it is reincarnated.[64]

The Herakleitean cycle combines these two forms of de-individuation. On the one hand the post-mortem transformation of *psuchē* through the cosmological elements back into *psuchē* resembles the temporal cycle of reincarnation, in which the *psuchē* passes post-mortem from one body to another. But on the other hand for Herakleitos it is not the same individual *psuchē* that passes from one body to another (as generally in reincarnation). Fire, of which *psuchē* and cosmos consist, is subject to

[53] Also Dikaiarchos ap. Porphyry *Vita Pythagorae* 19 (Burkert 1972: 122–3). [54] West (1971) 25–6.
[55] Aristotle *De Anima* 407b20. [56] See below in this section. [57] *Oympian* 2.68–73; *fr.*133.
[58] *Phaedo* 70c, 72a, 81d–82b, 83d, 113a–114c, *Republic* 614–21, *Phaedrus*. 248c–249d, *Meno* 81b, *Laws* 870de, 872e, 903d-904e, *Timaios* 42bc, 91–2.
[59] B12.4: Tor (2017) 237–9.
[60] West (1983) index s. metempsychosis. To Orphism is ascribed the idea that souls enter bodies (Aristotle *De Anima* 410b27; Pl. *Cratylus* 400c), which only requires the idea that they also derive from bodies to be metempsychosis.
[61] Pl. *Laws* 870e, *Meno* 81ab, *Cratylus* 400c (with *Phaedo* 62d); Pindar *Olympian* 2.68–73.
[62] West (1971) 25–6. [63] West (1983) 100–1. [64] See e.g. Pl. *Republic* 619.

a cycle of transformations, through which it somehow retains its identity. And the communality of each individual *psuchē* inheres – at a single moment in time – in its fiery substrate that embodies the unlimited communal *logos*. In this adaptation of mystic wisdom to encompass the power of money, the monetised individual *psuchē*, separated from all others in both time and space, is reintegrated into the communality of the (mystic-monetary) *logos* in both time and space.

In Empedokles we also find the reintegration of the soul in both time and space, albeit in a different form: he calls himself an exiled god who is for thirty thousand years (or seasons) reincarnated in various mortal forms, in a cyclical passage from one cosmological element to another (*aither*, sea, earth, rays of sun, *aither*), undergoing miseries (seemingly including those of the underworld) before eventually rejoining the gods in happiness.[65]

So far, the doctrine is relatively straightforward. But Empedokles also describes a cyclical process of the separation of the four elements (by Strife) and their mixture (by Love), with the latter producing a homogeneous Sphere that Empedokles 'hymns as a god',[66] and which 'rejoices in its joyful μονίη (aloneness)'.[67] The divine is not anthropomorphic but 'sacred indescribable mind alone, darting through the whole cosmos with swift thoughts'.[68] This may be called periodic mental monism, occurring at the point of the cycle in which the diversity of the cosmos has been completely united by Love.

Of these two Empedoklean narratives of divine consciousness, in the first it passes through the cosmic cycle, and in the second it is periodically coextensive with the whole cosmos. Especially since publication of the Strasbourg Empedokles papyrus, we have to suppose that these two conceptions belonged to the same cosmology, and indeed such a cosmology can be imagined.[69] What deserves emphasis here is that – as for Herakleitos, albeit differently – consciousness is de-individuated (unlimited) both temporally and spatially.

This Empedoklean conception is – like the Herakleitean – influenced by the doctrine of mystery-cult, as are other instances of the passage

[65] B112, B115, B118, B119, B120, B122, B124, B126–7, B146–7. Similar is Hdt. 2.123; also 2.47, 61, 170–1; Seaford (1986).

[66] Simplicius *In De Anima* 70, 17.

[67] B27: it has also been interpreted as 'oneness', 'motionlessness' and 'steadfastness': Guthrie (1965) 169 n.3.

[68] B134. Analogously, we think with blood (B105), which is a nearly equal mixture of the four elements (B98).

[69] Martin and Primavesi (1999) 83–6, 346–7; Betegh (2006) 45–6.

through the cosmological elements, notably in the tragic *Prometheia*.[70] An explicit instance of this passage within the actual practice of mystic initiation is provided by Apuleius' *Metamorphoses* (11.23), in which the mystic initiand reaches the threshold of Proserpina (Persephone), and then:

> having been carried through[71] all the elements I returned, in the middle of night I saw the sun shining with bright light.

This is a second century CE account of the mysteries of Isis. But as early as the fifth century BCE there was mystic doctrine that in the underworld the sun shone on the initiated, and torchlight in mystic ritual was associated with heavenly bodies.[72]

Finally, we note the *economic* dimension of the cycle of reincarnation in Greek mystic belief. Pindar states that Persephone will return to the sun above, in the ninth year, the souls of those from whom she will receive ποινὰν παλαιοῦ πένθεος.[73] A ποινά is a penalty or payment, and παλαιοῦ πένθεος means 'for (or consisting in) ancient grief'. Whatever exactly the 'ancient grief',[74] the ποινά may well be the same as the ' ποινά for unrighteous deeds' that – in a mystic formula inscribed on the gold leaves[75] – the dead initiate claims to have paid as he supplicates Persephone to send him to the seats of the pure. Another leaf has 'enter the holy meadow, for the initiate is without ποινά (ἄποινος)'.[76] Is this penalty the death of the initiate (or an ancient cycle of suffering now concluded by the death of the initiate)? In the mystic doctrine found in Pindar's second Olympian the 'helpless spirits of those who die pay penalties (ποινάς) here immediately' (i.e. by dying), before then being sentenced beneath the earth.[77] Finally, In a fragmentary and obscure fourth century BCE gold leaf (4 Graf-Johnston), in which it seems that the mystic experience of death involved the association of deity with the cosmological elements, there occurs ἀνταμοιβή (4: 'exchange'), the very word used by Herakleitos for the transformation of fire from and into all

70 Seaford (1986). 71 Cf. Livy 39.13.13; Merkelbach (1962) 13–14.

72 Pindar *Olympian* 2.61–3 and *fr.* 129; Aristophanes *Frogs* 454–6 (cf. 446–7, 312–14, 340, 350, 154–5); A. *Bassarai* (*Tragicorum Graecorum* Fragmenta, Vol. 3 [ed. Radt], 138); Cleanthes *Stoicorum Veterum Fragmenta*, Vol. 1.538 (ed. von Arnim); etc.: see further Seaford (2005).

73 *Fr.* 133: it adds that from them arise kings and strong and wise men, who are called heroes for the rest of time.

74 One suggestion has been the Titans' dismemberment of Dionysos, the symbolic significance of which we saw in 6§A.

75 6 and 7 Graf-Johnston. 76 28 Graf-Johnston, from Pherai.

77 56–8. For this interpretation of the passage (and against others), see recently Edmunds (2009) 667–9.

things as comparable to the exchange of gold from and into goods.[78] What these passages show is that the idea of the loss of *psuchē* (death) as *payment* (13§C) may in mystic doctrine express the more specific idea that it is payment for an original offence: this implies *metaphysical debt*, and so is comparable to the metaphysical debt paid by sacrificial death in India.[79] Here yet again we encounter the synthesis of cosmic with monetary cycle.

[78] (B90). The gold leaf also contains Ἥλιε πῦρ δὴ πάντα νικᾶι: 'O Sun, fire indeed conquers all things': cf. Hklt. B66. The leaf was folded around another leaf giving instructions to the dead, and this suggests that the cosmological elements, too, belonged to mystic doctrine. It mentioned the abduction of 'chthonic Korē', presumably to the underworld (5–7).

[79] 5§BC, 10§C.

CHAPTER 15

Plato

15§A The Platonic Inner Self

After Herakleitos the next extant philosophical focus on the *psuchē* is in Plato. I will describe and briefly exemplify the several ways in which his conception of the *psuchē* represents something new.

For Plato the *psuchē* is, at least sometimes, (1) incorporeal, thereby contrasting with the body, (2) the organ of *comprehensive* consciousness, (3) composite, (4) the self, (5) a possessor, (6) master of the body as of a slave, (7) self-moving, (8) also a world soul.

(1) Somewhat earlier than Plato, in what survives of Athenian tragedy, *psuchē* occupies both ends of the abstract-concrete (psychological-physical) spectrum.[1] And in the pre-Platonic development of an antithesis between body and *psuchē* a role was probably played by medicine.[2] But the word for 'incorporeal' (ἀσώματος, Sanskrit *aśarīra*) is first used by Plato, who included *psuchē* in what he calls the ἀσώματα.[3] Similarly, the first extant occurrences of *aśarīra* are not until the time of the early *Upanishads*.[4] The idea of the *psuchē* as incorporeal implies the ontological dualism of mind and body, which is by contrast *not* necessarily implicit in the idea of 'spirit' (vel sim.) found in many pre-modern societies.

(2) In the *Republic* the *psuchē* is an organ of *comprehensive* consciousness: it has reasoning, spirited, and desirous *parts*; and in *Theaitetos* (184b–d) the unitary *psuchē* synthesises information received through the

[1] Sullivan (1997) 172, (1999) 213, (2000) 120.

[2] Holmes (2010) 183, 195–6, 201, 204, 208–9, 225–7. For Democritus (B31) wisdom does for the soul what medicine does for the body. There is an interesting focus on the *psuchē* (as susceptible to persuasion) in Gorgias' *Praise of Helen* 1, 8–14, 19.

[3] Demonstrated in convincing detail by Renehan (1980); Plato *Sophist* 247b–d.

[4] BU 4.4.7; KB 14.2 (relatively late?: Gonda [1975] 357–8).

various senses. Even shortly before, notably in Athenian tragedy,[5] consciousness had been for the most part distributed among various organs (*thumos*, *nous* etc.) that were unrelated to each other. Even in Plato the *psuchē* does not always contain all kinds of consciousness: it is sometimes envisaged as mind or intelligence,[6] and in *Phaedo* in particular it is distinguished from bodily sensations and desires, and separable from the body, in which it is as if imprisoned.[7]

(3) Taking the comprehensive nature of the *psuchē* (and its identification with the self) together with our experience of inner conflict, a natural result is the idea that the *psuchē* is *composite*. In the *Republic* the *psuchē* is tripartite, with potential for conflict between the parts, and each part corresponding to a section of the polis. But in the earlier *Phaedo* the psuchē is regarded as non-composite, and 'most like' the uniform.[8]

(4) From the comprehensiveness of the *psuchē* it is a short step to the idea of its identification (whether or not imprisoned in the body) with the *self*, which is often implied,[9] and sometimes explicitly stated: e.g. in *Alcibiades* I[10] it is stated that man (ἄνθρωπος) is *psuchē* (130c). And *Laws* 959ab states that:

> in actual life it is nothing other than the *psuchē* that provides each of us to be what he is, whereas the body is a semblance that follows each of us, it being well said that the bodies of the dead are images whereas the really existing each of us, being called the immortal *psuchē*, . . .

(5) The *psuchē* is envisaged in some early Greek texts as a *possession* (13§B, 13§C). This idea is still found in Plato;[11] however, as a result of the introjection of the increased power of abstract value, the autonomous inner self (*psuchē*) is envisaged as *possessor*, of the body. In *Alcibiades I* it is argued that just as the craftsman uses his tools, so the *psuchē* uses (and rules) the body. The *psuchē* is κύριος of us (controls or possesses us), and he who gets to know something to do with the body knows not himself but 'his things' (τὰ αὑτοῦ). And so, to avoid confusion, τὰ χρήματα (wealth, money) are distinguished from the body as

[5] Sullivan (1997) 173–4, (1999) 212, 215, (2000) 119.
[6] E.g. *Apology* 29d, 30a; *Phaedo* 94b; *Phaedrus* 249c5.
[7] 64a–67e (esp. 65bc, 66bcd), 78b, 79b, 79d, 80b, 82e.
[8] 78c–80b (τῷ . . μονοειδεῖ . . ὁμοιότατον).
[9] Robinson (1970) 4–5, 11–12, 16, 18, 20, 22, 25, 32–3, 46–7, 128, 141 n.6.
[10] This work is Platonic if not by Plato himself.
[11] E.g. *Laws* 726, *Phaedo* 64e8–65e2, 67e6–8 (Robinson [1970] 32).

being 'yet more remote than his things' (129d–131c1). This leads us to a special kind of possession, the slave (6).

(6) The *psuchē*, equated with the person or self, may employ *logos* in the possession and control of his body *and* the body of his slave, for the slave has no *logos*[12] with which to control his body. And so, possessing a slave provides a closer model for the relationship of *psuchē* to body than does possessing mere things. The interiorisation of the master-slave relationship is therefore natural enough, but it extends the range of interiorised relationships from possession of *things* to possession of *people*.[13]

Plato, as did Parmenides a century earlier, interiorises the unity and apparent self-sufficiency of abstract value. But Athens had meanwhile been transformed by the growth of *chattel slavery*, in which numerous individuals *own* other people, over whom their control is *direct*, a kind of *necessity*, albeit still ultimately dependent on abstract value: the monetary purchase of an 'animate instrument'[14] may – along with an overall increase in the pervasiveness of money[15] – strengthen the appearance of individual self-sufficiency. The new, Platonic conception of the *psuchē* – incorporeal, comprehensive, equivalent to the self and self-moving – implies an unprecedentedly self-contained, isolated individual (contrast the communality of the presocratic *psuchē* exemplified in 14§A). And the direct control of slave by master becomes a factor in Platonic ontology.

In what survives of presocratic cosmology power is assigned to the element of which the world is composed (the unlimited, air, fire). This reflects the *impersonal* universal power of money. There is no suggestion of the *direct interpersonal* power subsequently inscribed in the world by Plato, for instance when he says that nature (φύσις)[16] or god[17] made the body δουλεύειν (to serve or be a slave) and to be ruled, and the *psuchē* to rule and be master (δεσπόζειν).[18] And so there is in

12 *Laws* 720, 773e, 966b; Vlastos (1973) 147–8.

13 Graeber (2011) 209 remarks on 'our peculiar habit of defining ourselves simultaneously as master and slave, reduplicating the most brutal aspects of the ancient household in our very concept of ourselves, as masters of our freedoms, or as owners of our very selves. It is the only way we can imagine ourselves as completely isolated beings.' He is led to this conclusion by comparative anthropology, and by the importance of slavery in forming Roman property law (199–201). To this account we should add Plato.

14 ἔμψυχον ὄργανον: Aristotle *Nicomachean Ethics* 1161b4; *Politics* 1253b33.

15 Already Perikles, born two generations before Plato, was said to have decided to sell off all his annual crops as a whole, and then buy from the marketplace each thing as needed: Plutarch *Perikles* 16.

16 *Phaedo* 80a; similarly *Republic* 444b; *Laws* 726, 892a, 896c.

17 *Timaios* 34c, 44d.

18 Plato is conscious of the consequent absurdity of being simultaneously master of and subject to oneself (*Republic* 430e11).

the (few) presocratic fragments on the *psuchē* or mind – in contrast to Plato – no internal conflict.[19] In Plato rule by the *psuchē*, or by the rational part of the *psuchē*, meets resistance,[20] but is necessary for the sake of *order*. Isocrates, a contemporary of Plato, relates the leadership of the *psuchē* over the body – in public and personal matters – to the greater *value* of the *psuchē*. For Plato, too, the *psuchē* is *worth* more than the body.[21]

The cosmisation of the master-slave relationship is not only introjected (interiorised) but also projected (cosmised). This is admirably treated by Vlastos.[22] Cosmogony in *Timaios* occurs through two kinds of cause, one associated with intelligence (νοῦς) and the good, the other with necessity (ἀνάγκη) and with chance and disorder. Whereas the association of necessity with chance and disorder seems to us self-contradictory (we think of necessity in mechanical terms), for the Greeks it arises from the constant association of ἀνάγκη with slavery. The slave is subject to ἀνάγκη, but left to himself is disordered.[23] Causes of the second kind – of physical processes such as cooling and heating, solidifying and dissolving – are used by god as servants (ὑπηρετοῦσι), and have neither reason (λόγος) nor intelligence (νοῦς).[24] The nature of necessity 'submits' to the wise creator god voluntarily and through persuasion.[25] In *Philebus* the relation of the material principle (unlimited) to the (limiting) cause for the purpose of generation is described as slavery.[26]

Platonic ontology has the new aspiration of preserving the Parmenidean self-sufficiency of abstract unity while also – like the Ionians – allowing and explaining diversity. For the Ionians the relationship between (quasi-abstract) unity and concrete diversity is a cosmisation of the transformation of money from and into all goods, as it is to a large extent also for Plato. But Plato introduces into the metaphysics an *interpersonal* relationship of ownership that does not – as would a commercial or reciprocal interpersonal relationship – compromise the self-sufficiency of abstract unity (slaves are possessions acquired by money), and yet expresses the ascendancy of

19 The closest (albeit not very close) are Hklt. B117 and B118.

20 E.g. *Republic* 444b, 442ab.

21 Isocrates *Antidosis* 180 (πλέονος ἀξίαν); Plato *Protagoras* 313a6 (περὶ πλείονος); cf. Pindar *Nemean* 9.32 *psuchai* 'stronger than possessions'.

22 Vlastos (1973) 147–63.

23 On the unruliness of slaves, see *Laws* 777d; Gouldner (1967) 352–60.

24 46cd. They are servants also at 68e4.

25 56c5; 48a2.

26 27a8 τὸ δουλεῦον εἰς γένεσιν αἰτίᾳ.

abstract Being over the corporeal sphere of variety, change and disorder – a sphere of mere (servile) necessity (ἀνάγκη). The cosmos, which for the Ionians was subject to an immanent necessity, in Plato still contains necessity, but the necessity is now servile and subject to a higher, transcendent intelligence. In Greece, as in India, the fundamental social institutions of monarchy and money influenced conceptions of cosmos and of inner self. For Greece we can now add a third influence, the fundamental institution of slavery. In India, by contrast, slavery seems to have had no such influence, perhaps because of the lesser importance there of *chattel* slavery and of the freedom-slavery polarity,[27] but also because of the synarchy of Brahmins and powerful individual Kshatriyas: in the Vedic tradition it was on the whole autocracy that was interiorised to imagine the internal power relation (and freedom and unity) of the inner self (7§B).

(7) For Plato in *Phaedrus* and *Laws* what moves *itself* is *psuchē*, which is accordingly 'cause of all change and motion in all things'.[28] This goes well beyond controlling slaves, implying as it does *autonomous power*, freedom from all internal and external constraints.[29] But it also acknowledges the participation of the *psuchē* in the world of change, and so contrasts with the static version of the *psuchē* found in *Phaedo*. That the *psuchē* is in motion and initiates motion can be observed by introspection. Aristotle attributed to Thales already the view that *psuchē* is κινητικός (a cause of motion).[30] Similarly, for Herakleitos the *psuchē* as fire is in constant transformative motion.

However, *psuchē* may also be subject to external power. In contrast to Plato, for Herakleitos the individual *psuchē* is subject to external power, a universal process that occurs 'according to the *logos*', with the result that thinking is communal. Individuals may imagine that they are absolutely autonomous, but that is because 'although the

[27] Whereas Greeks of the classical period used the simple polarity free-slave (reflected in an observation attributed to the Buddha: n. 38 below), reflecting the widespread phenomenon of chattel slavery, in early India there were various categories of unfree person: Chakravarti (1985). Thapar (1984) 83–4 notes various factors working against the importance of slavery in ancient India (relative to Athens). Megasthenes, who visited Pataliputra circa 300 BCE, wrote (for what it is worth) that there were no slaves in India.

[28] *Laws* 896a–c (and so *psuchē* is 'prior to body, which is secondary and posterior, ruled by ruling *psuchē* according to nature'. Accordingly, god consists of 'soul or souls': 899b5); *Phaedrus* 245c–6a. Cf. Aristotle *De Anima* 404a21.

[29] It does not therefore 'dominate' all else but 'cares for' it: *Phaedrus* 246b.

[30] 'Since he said that the lodestone has a *psuchē* because it moves iron': *De Anima* I 405a19= DK11 A22).

logos is communal, the many live as if having individual understanding' (B2). As universal power-substance that is constantly transformed from and into all else according to a numerical formula (*logos*), money is projected as cosmic fire, which is also – in so far as money is individually owned as well as being universal aim and universal mediator of interpersonal relations – the medium through which each *psuchē* participates in the external world. It is the all-pervasiveness of money that lies at the hidden root of the remarkable Herakleitean unity of the subjective and the objective motion of fire embodying *logos*.

In Plato, by contrast, it is abstract substance detached from circulation that is ontologically privileged both within and beyond the *psuchē*. Whereas power in the Herakleitean cosmos is a projection of the universal *impersonal circulation* of money, Plato imagines the power of abstract substance *over* circulation as (in part) *interpersonal* (master-slave). Within this relation the master is absolutely autonomous, and accordingly the Platonic *psuchē* is initiator (not recipient) of motion and of transformation, and as such is immortal (*Phaedrus* 246a). It is because the *psuchē* has the source of motion within it, and the body does not, that the *psuchē* is prior to the body and by nature rules it (*Laws* 896b–c).

(8) The universe has a *psuchē*, from which human *psuchai* are derived: see the passages cited in 12§A (2).

How do we explain these remarkable Platonic developments in the concept of the *psuchē*? Various historical factors are worth mentioning.

Attica in the lifetime of Plato had numerous slaves,[31] to which monetisation and Athenian power had no doubt contributed. An Athenian work of the late fourth or early third century BCE states that slaves are the first and most necessary kind of property.[32] In his will the aristocratic Plato included two estates (one of which he had bought), four male household slaves, a considerable amount of silver and some gold, and money owed to him; he also freed a female slave, and declared that he owed nobody anything.[33] He was aware that slavery was not consensual, describes the attitude of the properly educated person towards slaves as contempt,[34] and in *Laws* proposes legislation on slavery, the tenor of which has been described as more severe than the actual law of Athens at the time.[35] The projection and

[31] E.g. the latest edition of the Oxford Classical Dictionary s. slavery is not out of line with more recent estimates in suggesting 80,00–100,000, out of a total population of perhaps circa 250,000.

[32] Ps. Aristotle *Oeconomica* I 4.5 (1344a). [33] D.L. 3.41–3. [34] *Republic* 578e, 549a.

[35] Finley (1981) 105.

introjection of the master-slave relationship – into cosmos and *psuchē* respectively – serves to justify not only the master-slave relationship but also Plato's hostility to democracy, for free citizens might lack *logos* no less than do slaves.[36] The 'Old Oligarch', an Athenian contemporary of Plato, complains that the slaves have as much freedom of speech as the free men, who look like slaves,[37]

Athens of the classical period was, among the Greek cities, the leading instance of a form of society that was historically unprecedented in its combination of three basic institutions: a vote for every male citizen, advanced monetisation and pervasive chattel slavery, which largely replaced the other forms of unfree labour found in earlier (sometimes theocratic) societies, thereby producing an unprecedentedly polar opposition between free man and slave.[38] It was in part the individualising effect of this enduring combination that gave rise to the irreversible transition from the universal transformability of quasi-abstract Being (the communal perspective of the Ionians) to the Platonic self-sufficiency of abstract Being accessed by the isolated *psuchē.*

Another distinction is in perspectives on the ideas of limit and the unlimited. In sixth-century BCE Ionia the unlimitedness of money is projected onto the cosmos as the natural order: the substrates of the Milesians Anaximander, Anaximenes and (perhaps) Thales, and (probably) the Ephesian Herakleitos are unlimited.[39] At about the same time, however, for the Athenian Solon the unlimitedness of money, and of the desire to accumulate it, is disruptive and to be restrained, and accordingly the 'limits of all things' are held by wisdom's invisible measure (*metron*), which it is 'very difficult to understand'.[40] Part of the explanation of this contrast may be in the difference between Miletos and Ephesos on the one hand and Attica on the other. Miletos did not possess much fertile land, but was one of the very first cities to have coinage (perhaps as early as the late seventh century BCE) and its excellent position for communication by land and sea helped to make it the leading commercial centre

[36] Vlastos (1973) 152: Plato's 'conception of all government is of a piece with his conception of the government of slaves'. Cf. Aristotle *Politics* 1252a7–9 (perhaps responding to Plato *Politicus* 258e–259d).

[37] Ps. Xenophon *Constitution of the Athenians* 1.10–12.

[38] See e.g. the classic Finley (1963–4). At MN 2.149 (*Assalāyana Sutta*) there is attributed to the Buddha a contrast between Indian ideas and those of Kamboja and Yona (i.e. Greece), where there were only free men and slaves.

[39] Anaximander B1; Anaximenes A1, A5, A6, A7, A9, A10; Thales A13, KRS 94; Seaford (2004) 225; Hklt. B30, B45.

[40] *Frs.* 13.71–3; 4c 3–4; 16.

of the eastern Mediterranean.[41] Ephesos, too, may in the time of Herakleitos have lacked a large agricultural hinterland.[42] Attica had much arable land but in Solon's time was relatively undeveloped commercially, and had silver money but almost certainly not yet coinage. Solon had experience of commerce,[43] but was facing a crisis of monetised greed causing the loss by indebted individuals of their *land*. The unlimited accumulation of monetised wealth was probably more disruptive of traditional ownership in Attica than in Miletos and Ephesos, where it would occur mainly in the commercial sphere.

Moving across to the land-rich city-states of southern Italy, we find, among the Pythagoreans, five resemblances with Solon: (a) they held political power; (b) traditions about fifth-century political conflict put them in the middle ground, opposed both by landowning aristocracy and landless poor; (c) Pythagoras, like Solon, engaged in commerce (expressed in the Pythagorean idea that numbers are universal substrate);[44] (d) they emphasise metaphysical measure or limit, the imposition of limit on the unlimited; (e) I interpret this metaphysical limit – in both Solon and Pythagoreanism – as an expression of the need to control the unlimited accumulation of money.[45]

But there is in southern Italy another form of metaphysical limit, propounded by Parmenides of Elea, namely the limitedness of abstract Being, enforced by necessity (ἀνάγκη) and expressing the monetised self-sufficiency of the aristocratic individual: there was a Parmenidean as well as a Pythagorean way of life (14§A). The Pythagoreans engaged in commerce, but Parmenides was a wealthy aristocrat, and so probably owned enough land to obtain the (monetised) self-sufficiency that was expressed in his metaphysics. He was born about twenty years after the founding (c. 540–35 BCE) of his city Elea, which was being pervasively monetised, so that his land had monetary value.

41 'Next to no arable land': Möller (2000) 87–8; Seaford (2004) 199. The Milesian territory proper ('Milesia') is small and unproductive. It is possible that in the archaic period Miletos also controlled some of the fertile Maiander valley, which was, however, also occupied by other city-states (Myous, Priene, Magnesia) and separated from Miletos by a large gulf. The people of Miletos survived the annual destruction of their crops by the Lydians for eleven years in the late seventh century BC (Hdt. 1.17–18), presumably because they could import food by sea from their numerous colonies.

42 The city was conquered by Kroisos (Hdt. 1.26), and subsequently subjected to Persia. Strabo (14.1.21; 640) reports that the founder of Ephesos settled most of those who had come with him round the Athenaeum and the Hypelaeus, until the time of Kroisos, when 'they came down from the mountainside and lived around the present temple until the time of Alexander'.

43 Plutarch *Solon* 2. 44 13§E n.8. 45 Seaford (2004) 266–83; (2012a) 288–92.

Roughly speaking, then, the unlimitedness of monetary circulation is *affirmed* in Ionian metaphysics, *limited* in Solonian and Pythagorean metaphysics and *excluded* in Parmenidean metaphysics.

Where, in this respect, is Plato? Metaphysically, he expounds – in *Philebus* and *Timaios* – the Pythagorean imposition of limit on the unlimited. But he goes beyond Pythagoreanism, and resembles Parmenides, in systematically separating the abstract (apprehended by the mind) from the concrete (perceived by the senses). His limitation of the latter by the former combines Pythagorean control of unlimited commercial circulation with Parmenidean privileging of abstract substance.

As for psychology and politics, a crucial part in Plato's account is played by the desire for money, which is – beyond even the unruly desires of the body – *unlimited.* This is, as recognised earlier by Solon, potentially disruptive of the polis. Plato recognises that it is also potentially disruptive of *psuchē.* The two superior parts of the *psuchē* – the rational (λογιστικόν) and the spirited (θυμοειδές) – will, he says, preside over the third, appetitive part (ἐπιθυμητικόν), 'which is most of the *psuchē* in each person and by nature most insatiable for money'.[46] It must be controlled by the rational philosophic part of the *psuchē*, just as in the polis the money-making class must be controlled by the class of philosophers.[47] But the appetitive and money-loving element may dominate the inner self (*Republic* 552c). Socrates in the *Apology* (29e) contrasts *maximising* wealth with *perfecting* the psuchē.

The Ionian and Parmenidean cosmologies are projections respectively of the two essential features of money: its constant circulation and its unchanging abstract value.[48] The former is unlimited, whereas the latter is in Parmenides abstracted even from circulation so as to express the necessarily limited self-sufficiency seemingly bestowed by money on the individual. In Plato, an Athenian aristocrat between southern Italy and Ionia, this relationship internal to money, between unitary unchanging abstraction and the movement of concrete particulars, is both projected as metaphysics and introjected (interiorised) within the *psuchē* – either in the form of the master-slave opposition or as monetary exchange (13§E).

Whereas the Herakleitean introjection of the *logos* embedded in monetised *circulation* produces a *psuchē* co-material with the cosmic fire, the

[46] *Republic* 442a; similarly 581a–d; also 434c, 548a, *Laws* 870a, *Phaedo* 6bc1, 82c; Schofield (2006) 253–64.

[47] Cf. the projection (in the *Freudian* sense) of the love of money onto barbarians, to whom people in general are assimilated (*Republic* 436a; cf. S. *Antigone* 1037–9).

[48] This is explained in more detail at Seaford (2004) 248.

Platonic introjection of the *logos* associated with *abstract value* produces a *psuchē* that is (at least sometimes) incorporeal. Incorporeality excludes co-materiality, which does occur however in Plato's *Timaios*, in which the creator *mixed* the *psuchē* of the universe with other material in a bowl before dividing it into numerous *psuchai* (41d). But this unique mention of co-materiality is immediately followed[49] by an account of each individual *psuchē* preserving its identity through the phases of a cosmic journey. And, indeed, the co-materiality does not have for Plato the ethical, political, epistemological and eschatological consequences that it has for Herakleitos. Each individual *psuchē* is for Plato self-contained and isolated, not unlimited (like the Herakleitean), but imprisoned in its body.

The isolation even of the Parmenidean inner self (11§D) is not absolute: because thought is Being and is of Being, which is One, we may infer that all thought is of the same thing (Being). Similarly, the isolation of the Platonic philosophical *psuchē* is qualified by its assimilation to the immortal abstraction to which it will pass after death, an abstraction that is accessible to other philosophical *psuchai* (but excludes all bodies). Each *psuchē* (or its most authentic part) is abstract and realises itself in relation to a single central abstraction (the form of the good), which is more real and more valuable than anything else.

The assimilation to immortal abstraction is – in *Phaedo*, *Phaedrus* and *Symposium* – presented as if belonging to mystic initiation, a ritual that in reality may, besides enacting comparable assimilation, involve both initial isolation and eventual incorporation into a community (of this world and the next). But in Plato (as in Parmenides) the mystic progress and discovery is an affair of the individual. Plato's use of chariot imagery for the psuchē (17§A) is no less telling than that of the aristocratic Parmenides for his mystic journey. Whereas in mystic ritual the isolation of the individual, expressed as people trampling on each other, was a prelude to joining a peaceful community,[50] in the mystic process in *Phaedrus* by contrast many *psuchai*, after trampling on each other, simply go away 'uninitiated in the vision of Being'.[51] True, Plato does occasionally hint at the post-mortem community of pure initiates (11§E). But the monetised individual reaches (as imprisoned *psuchē*) a new level of isolated self-containment.

Nevertheless, the aristocratic ideal of (monetised) individual self-sufficiency in Plato does combine with aristocratic concern with the polis. In his ideal polis Plato has to regulate the relationship between the

[49] As noted by Betegh (2006) 47.
[50] Plutarch *fr.* 178; *Moralia* 81de.
[51] 248b1–5; Riedweg (1987) 65–7.

majority, who use polluting human currency, and the guardians, who are told that they have in their souls divine gold and silver coinage from the gods. Correspondingly, in the hereafter we find both cycle (reincarnation) and an unchanging state, along with the possibility of rising – through philosophy – from the former to the latter. Plato does not, like Parmenides, merely cosmise abstract value, but rather cosmises the relationship between abstract value and circulation (however difficult or even impossible it is to specify the relation from his perspective). He is accordingly aware not only of the power of money to pollute but also of its *ordering* power.[52] Whereas Ionian monism projects the circulating substance of money from a communal perspective, and Parmenidean monism projects the substance of money from the perspective of self-sufficient individual possession, completely abstracted from circulation, Platonic idealism occupies an intermediate position, projecting the substance of money abstracted from circulation while also trying to give an account of its relationship to the various changing particular things in the world, thereby combining the perspective of self-sufficient aristocratic ownership with a more communal perspective that acknowledges circulation.

15§B Reflexivity and Subjectivity

In Homer reflexive constructions are infrequent, and never occur in a psychological sense.[53] Subsequently they become much more frequent, occur in a psychological sense (e.g. the Herakleitean 'I sought for myself') and are especially important in Plato. Part of this development of reflexivity in language is the emergence of the idea of a unitary self. The absence of this reflexively derived self in Homer complements and confirms the argument first advanced by Snell to the effect that there is no unitary inner self in Homer (4§B).

All this has been demonstrated in much convincing detail by Jeremiah (2012). At several points in his book he relates it to socio-economic (especially urban) development. But about the nature of this development he says very little, and nothing at all about money. He does however ask a good question:

> Is the construction of a reflexive self dependent on the institution of private property? Does power over what is one's own lead, through ineluctable metonymy, to power over oneself? This would amount to an internalisation of the relation between subject and private property . . . (170).

[52] *Laws* 918bc. Cf. Noutsopoulos (2015) 10. [53] Jeremiah (2012) 8, 18–20, 61, 69–70.

Rather than appealing to 'ineluctable metonymy', we should imagine the process of constructing a unitary inner self: it is hard to see how this could be done without interiorising (introjecting) something external. The interactions within Homeric inner space are interpersonal relations (conversation,[54] dominance, gift-giving, etc.) interiorised (4§B). What is interiorised in the imagining of the *unitary* self?

Individual property promotes social recognition of the individual as an individually acting agent, and occupies a unique place intermediate between his inner will and the external world. Jeremiah provides much evidence for the connection between the self and its property (often described reflexively as 'the things of himself', τὰ ἑαυτοῦ, or 'the things of myself', τὰ ἐμαυτοῦ). In Alkaios, whose poetry may contain the first extant mention of coinage,[55] there are two examples of the reflexive turning something communal towards the individual: one is 'you will be *tamias* for yourself',[56] where *tamias* originally meant 'distributor' (of food) before meaning 'treasurer'; the other is 'sharing with yourself the youthfulness ...'[57] In the *Theognidea* (895–6) possession is interiorised in the idea that a man has nothing better than intelligence in himself (αὐτὸς ἐν αὐτῶι). Herodotus writes of democratic Athens as a place in which 'each man was eager to work for himself'.[58] In Euripides' *Medea* we find the idea that each person loves himself more than his neighbour, 'some justly, some also for the sake of gain (*kerdos*)' (86–7). In the *Constitution of the Athenians* (39.1), attributed to Aristotle, we find the significant conjunction 'being in charge of themselves and reaping the proceeds of the things of themselves (τὰ αὑτῶν, i.e. their property)'. In Plato τὰ ἑαυτοῦ is juxtaposed with 'oneself' (ἑαυτός),[59] in a movement from plural to singular. Jeremiah concludes from these and many other passages that:

> essence and property are mutually dependent, so that the differentiation of an individual requires the differentiation of what belongs to it, and in an important way the differentiation and determination of the former takes place through the latter (263).

And he compares Hegel's logic, in which – Jeremiah paraphrases – 'my property collapses into me'. We may add that οὐσία meant both property and essence or Being.

[54] The *psuchē* converses with itself also in Plato: *Theaitetos* 189e6–190a6; *Sophist* 263e3–5.
[55] Seaford (2004) 89. [56] *Fr.* 317aL-P: Σὺ δὲ σαύτωι τόμιαις ἔσῃ (τόμιαις is the Aeolic form).
[57] *Fr.* 317bL-P: . . σαύτω μετέχων ἄβας . . . [58] 5.78.1; similarly S. *Ajax* 1366–7.
[59] *Republic* 443cd; *Timaios* 72a5, 77bc.

Jeremiah also indicates in early Sanskrit the same link between the developments of the concept of a person and of the reflexive system (notably in the reflexive pronoun atman):

> The old reflexive of Vedic Sanskrit, *tanū-*, which, just as in the early stages of pronominal reflexivity in Greek, does a limited amount of reflexive work, leaving much of it to the verbal system, is pushed out of this role by atman as Vedic morphs into Classical Sanskrit.[60]

The world and self originate as a reflexive act:

> In the beginning this world was just a single atman shaped like a man. He looked around and saw nothing but himself. The first thing he said was, 'Here I am' and from that the name 'I' came into being.[61]

But what is this 'I', this atman? The subject (atman) can be apprehended neither by the senses nor by thought: it is unknowable (8§C[6]). For this there may be various reasons: (a) if the subject is the whole world, it can have nothing as object; (b) the unitary subject (like e.g. the eye) cannot directly perceive itself; (c) the atman (unlike the eye) is an abstraction (characterised in the *Upanishads* as the inner controller, 'behind' the senses and faculties) and so imperceptible – either incorporeal (6§D) or a special kind of object, invisible and ubiquitous like salt dissolved in water (8§C); (d) I can see a tree but I cannot see the seeing of it: subjectivity, though it may seem to contain the whole world, is imperceptible.

This unknowability of the abstract (incorporeal) atman does not apply to the abstract (incorporeal) Platonic *psuchē*. Why not? One answer might be that only the subject that is identified with the whole world (i.e. the atman) attracts our problem (a). But a fuller explanation requires us to recapitulate and compare the development of the inner self in both cultures.

In early Vedic and in presocratic thought the inner self is composed of a tenuous material (breath, air, fire), by which it is also unified. But a difference between the Vedic and the presocratic accounts is that only in the latter is the material also the substance of the whole universe, and in the most detailed extant account, Herakleitos', this co-materiality requires a certain ethics and understanding of the inner self. The difference derives – in part at least – from the distinction between the individualism of the Vedic cosmic rite of passage and the communality of the Greek one: in the latter

[60] Jeremiah (2012) 63–4, citing Lehmann (1992), Hock (2006) and Kulikov (2007). For more on the relation of reflexives to vocabulary related to the soul in various languages including Sanskrit, see Orqueda (2015). For the (different) issue of the *origin* of atman, see 4§C.

[61] BU 1.4.1; Jeremiah (2012) 100 n.123.

the individual inner self may (to some extent) merge with other participants, with sacred objects, or with the universe.[62] Subsequently, in both cultures there supervened a new conception of the inner self as abstract or even 'incorporeal': the Upanishadic atman and the Platonic *psuchē* (in some of their versions). The latter, however new in conception, inherits from the distinct Greek tradition not only the location of the (controlling) inner self within the body but also the ethical and epistemological consequences of its kinship with the external, ontologically privileged everlasting reality (12§C), which is for Herakleitos the *logos*-embodying cosmic fire, for Parmenides the One held in place by Justice, for Diogenes intelligent air; for Plato it is the form of the good – but also what the philosophical *psuchē* is 'akin' to: the pure, everlasting, unchanging, invisible, divine and wise (11§E). Moreover, the master-slave relationship (imposed by nature or god as the control of *psuchē* over body) is – in contrast to the autocratic power interiorised by the Upanishadic inner self – not only inscribed in the Platonic cosmos but also central to the everyday life of Greek citizens. The Platonic *psuchē* is accordingly knowable. Above all, as we saw in Chapter 11, Greek mystic initiation provides a model – and *experience* – of the assimilation of subject to divine object, of the external representation of subjectivity. For Parmenides knowing is Being.[63] As for the fiery Herakleitean *psuchē*, the impossibility of reaching its limits results from the depth of its *logos*, which requires *communal* understanding (13§D).

The mystic assimilation evoked by Parmenides and Plato represents the interiorisation and individualisation of what was in practice a communal experience. This individualisation is taken to its extreme by Plotinus: the interiorisation of mystic initiation produces the merging (unity) not only of subject with object but also of the individual with the One.[64] In this respect Plotinus, in whom the legacy of the polis has finally disappeared completely from philosophy,[65] is closer to Upanishadic thought than is any other Greek thinker.[66]

62 6§D, 11§D, 11§E, 12§C, 13§D, 14§A (esp. n.14).

63 14§A. The imperceptibility of subjectivity is imagined by Parmenides not as the imperceptibility we find in nature (such as of dissolved salt in the BU) but as the imperceptibility of *its own abstract object*. Similarly, for Aristotle 'the *nous* (mind, intellect) thinks itself by participation in the *noēton* (object of thought, intelligible): for by touching and thinking it (the *noēton*) it becomes *noētos*, so that *nous* and *noēton* are the same' (*Metaphysics* 1072b19–21).

64 E.g. *Enneads* 1.6.7; 5.5.8; 6.7.34–5; 6.9.10–11. For the individual subject there are no other subjects, and finally not even itself.

65 Plotinus' justice (*dikē*) is set in a natural principle that – rather than regulating interpersonal relations – ensures that each individual moves spontaneously to its appropriate place.

66 Hatab (1992).

To return to Jeremiah: he compares the unknowability of the Upanishadic subject with the Kantian idea that I cannot know as an object that which I must presuppose in order to know any object. Kant observes that:

> in attaching 'I' to our thoughts, we designate the subject only transcendentally ... without noting in it any quality whatsoever – in fact without knowing anything of it either directly or by inference.[67]

In this respect Kantian individualism[68] is (despite its obvious differences) closer to the *Upanishads* than to Plato. However, Jeremiah maintains that Kant's transcendental category of the self is not in fact given as a universal category of experience (as it is for Kant himself). In this we agree with Jeremiah, on the principles described in 4§A. It is rather, he continues, 'created or constructed by certain types of events, namely reflexive psychological acts', for instance as described in the Herakleitean 'I sought for myself' (B101). In such a statement there is:

> some relation of identity between the referent of the reflexive pronoun and the referent of its antecedent. This relation of identity takes place on one level, while another, transcendental level of the subject is brought into being over and above it.[69]

Similarly the *psuchē*, though an organ of comprehensive consciousness, may seem nevertheless to be independent of the subject, as if a possession of the subject. But the 'types of events' giving rise to the transcendental category of the self are – *pace* Jeremiah – surely not *merely* 'reflexive psychological acts'. But what other type of event is relevant here? Whence the 'reflexive psychological acts'? At this point, bearing in mind Jeremiah's association between the reflexively constructed self and individual property, we may be tempted to see the identity-cum-split of transcendental subject with reflexively constructed self as a synthesis of indeterminate consciousness with the determinateness of interiorised individual property. The person is described by Sorabji and others as 'owner' of his thoughts etc. (4§A). But how can such interiorisation occur? Jeremiah cannot provide an answer.

67 Kant (1787) A355; Jeremiah (2012) 32–5.D.
68 For Kant's transcendental unity of the self-consciousness as 'itself an intellectual reflection of one of the elements of the exchange abstraction, the most fundamental one of all, the form of the exchangeability of the commodities underlying the unity of money and of the social synthesis', see Sohn-Rethel (1978: 77), who does not, however, sufficiently distinguish between the socio-economic conditions of early Greek and of Kantian thought: Seaford (2012b).
69 Jeremiah (2012) 33–4. Cf. 73, 117.

The expression τὰ ἑαυτοῦ moves from plural to singular. The unitary self can be constructed out of the plurality of individual property (furniture, animals, land, etc.) only by interiorising that plurality as *pervaded and controlled by a single, abstract entity.* Χρήματα, property, can also mean money. The single, invisible, homogeneous power that inheres in money is uniquely responsive to my will, and so occupies the boundary between internal and external space, closer to my inner self than are the objects I possess. Indeed, the inner self is easily assimilated to money (13§E). Money seems to unite abstract subject with universal object, and in this respect[70] resembles karma, and – in the *Upanishads* – atman identified with brahman.

The inner self may be a unity while consisting of parts. The Platonic *psuchē* is imagined sometimes (notably in *Republic*) as the abstract entity together with physical sensations and attachments, but sometimes (notably in *Phaedo*) purely as the abstract entity itself, imprisoned in the body. What is interiorised is a *relation*, between the abstract power of money and the concrete variety of what it may command,[71] with the variety either within the *psuchē* or relegated to the body.

Jeremiah describes the reflexive interiorisation of other-directed relations and activities, their replacement by self-directed relations and activities.[72] This is – I suggest – to be explained by the tendency of other-directed relations and activities to become dependent on the *self-directed* accumulation of money. Rather than performing what are imagined for the most part as other-directed activities – such as communal herding or agriculture, or doing favours (in return for other favours), or fighting in the army (to defend or advance the community) and so on – I act to appropriate *for myself* an entity (money) that has no direct connection with any particular good but – in mediating the acquisition of all goods and services – seems to embody a universal relation (of invisible power) with goods and people, and so to resemble my inner self, to mediate numerous transitive relations, to be uniquely and entirely responsive to my will, and to be all I need, rendering direct personal relations *in principle* unnecessary. In this way, I suggest, other-directed relations and activities are absorbed into 'the self as an inherently reflexive structure', the being 'which engages

70 This goes well beyond (a) imagining thought in physical terms, which is found in numerous cultures and in the RV, and (b) more specifically, imagining Agni (fire personified) as both subject and as object in the RV (Gombrich [2013] 117–18).

71 For the power exercised by the in-itself and by the transcendental subject, see Jeremiah (2012) 92, 97.

72 Jeremiah (2012), e.g. 9, 39, 109–10, 142, 219, 259; 40 'the increasing reduction of other directed relations to self-relations'.

in reflexive acts, whether it be thinking about itself, helping itself, promoting itself, determining itself . . .', the 'human agent as a source of action onto itself'.[73]

And so, in the 'types of events' from which Jeremiah derived the transcendental category of the self it is crucial to include money-directed thoughts and actions. Self-consciousness is of a construction (the self) that partakes of consciousness and yet must be (as its *object*) somehow also distinct from it. It is only when constructed as monetary value that individual property acquired the transcendent unity and autonomous invisibility that allowed its synthesis with these very same qualities of consciousness – while remaining nevertheless (as possession) determinate and distinct from consciousness.[74] Money, we have seen, like brahman and karma, bridges the mysterious gap between subjectivity and the object. It both promotes the autonomous inner self and provides it with a model for its (a) relationship to the person (*ownership*), (b) abstract unity and (c) mysterious synthesis of subjectivity with objectness.[75] This is a powerful combination. And in (c) it resembles another process that promotes the inner self, mystic initiation, in which subject is assimilated to object.

Finally, Jeremiah observes from time to time that it is not only the emergence of the unitary self that accompanies the growth of reflexivity:

> The thing-in-itself of fundamental ontology comes into being alongside the soul as that which moves itself . . . (4)
>
> The important conclusion for us is that these philosophical foundations or ἀρχαί are acquiring reflexivity just as the human subject which thinks them is acquiring it also (239–40).
>
> It is interesting that the reduction of the human being to a unified self accords with the reduction of the cosmos to the influence of a single god (35 n.59).
>
> As an object of thought, the thing-in-itself takes another thing-in-itself, the soul, as its subject (259).
>
> [In Plato's *Phaedo*] A self-relating subject thinks self-relating entities (204).
>
> [On Plato's *Timaios*] Why is it that the soul should take on the same characteristics as Being, or indeed the cosmos as a whole? (89)
>
> [On presocratic philosophy] Mind (νοῦς) attracts the qualities of Being (τὸ ὄν) and vice-versa (93).

[73] Jeremiah (2012) 3, 30.

[74] In Hklt. B115 and B45 (both quoted in 13§D) the *unlimitedness* of monetised exchange/accumulation is interiorised in synthesis with the unlimitedness of consciousness.

[75] While concealing, however, the concrete *production* of its abstract value.

The idea of the self-sufficiency and unity of Being[76] emerges along with the idea of the self-sufficiency and unity of the inner self, as part of the growth of reflexivity. But it is easier to see how the latter (unity of inner self) emerges along with reflexivity than does the former. Abstract Being, Being in general, the cosmos: none of these is a frequent or natural subject of reflexive propositions. If on the other hand we regard not just urban commerce or private property but monetisation as the key development, then we are provided with the best explanation of the simultaneous development of the unitary self-sufficiency not only of the self but also of Being and universe: the all-pervasive power-substance of money, including its seeming self-sufficiency (so welcome to its owner), is both cosmised (as Being) and interiorised. The theme of self-sufficiency takes us back, in the next section, to India.

15§C Chapter 7 of the *Chāndogya Upaniṣad*

Individual self-sufficiency is in Greece often enabled by money, in India also by renunciation, which – we have argued – is intimately connected to monetisation.[77] For another illustration of this connection we will look at a continuous passage, from the seventh chapter of the *Chāndogya Upaniṣad.*

It starts with a long chain of dependences, in which each item is said to depend on the next: speech depends on mind, which depends on intention, which depends on deep reflection, which depends on perception, which depends on strength, and so on. Towards the end, action depends on (7.22) *sukha* (happiness, well-being), which is (7.23) identified with *bhūman* (abundance, plenitude).[78] We then read (7.24) that 'where a man sees, hears, or discerns no other thing, that is *bhūman*', which is immortal. But is this the end of the chain?

> On what is *bhūman* based? On one's own greatness. Or maybe it is not based on greatness. Cattle and horses, elephants and gold, slaves and wives, farms and houses – these are what people here call greatness. But I don't consider them that way; no I don't, for they are all based on each other.[79]

There follows an alternative conception:

[76] See also Jeremiah (2012) 196–206. [77] 7§A, 9§E.

[78] It is 'abundance' in Roebuck (2003)'s translation (Penguin), 'plenitude' by Olivelle (1996)'s (Oxford World's Classics).

[79] This is Olivelle's translation of *anyo hy anyasmin pratiṣṭhita iti*, i.e. literally 'for another is based/founded on another', a single syntactic unit referring to the things listed in the previous sentence. Roebuck translates: 'That is not what I am saying. I say' he said 'that it is other, and rests on something other.'

> that (i.e. *bhūman*) extends over the whole world. Now, the substitution of the word "I" . . . I extend over this whole world. Next, the substitution of *ātman* . . . the *ātman* extends over the whole world?

Through 'substitution' the atman has replaced greatness and property as what *bhūman* is based on, as the final item in the chain of dependence. This is then immediately justified by the claim that someone who sees, thinks and perceives it thus, and (*inter alia*) attains bliss in the atman, becomes completely his own master and obtains complete freedom to move in all the worlds; the items in the chain of dependence, and the whole world, spring from his atman; whereas those who perceive it otherwise are ruled over by others and obtain perishable worlds (25–6).

Action, on which ultimately all other things depend (in the chain of dependence), itself depends on well-being, which depends on something (*bhūman*) that people regard as based on possessions. This makes practical sense: posessions are fundamental, it is on possessions that intention, performing rituals and everything else in the chain depends. However, we are also told that *bhūman* is where someone perceives no other thing, in other words that it involves somehow the unity or assimilation of subject and object, and that this is immortal. Further, *bhūman* extends over the whole world, and is substituted by atman, which extends over the whole world; and devotion to atman brings self-sufficient freedom (not being ruled by others). The self-sufficient freedom brought by *bhūman* is normally based on possessions, but is here redefined.

And so, at the end of the chain of dependences, plenitude (*bhūman*) is both *projected* (as co-extensive with the world) and *introjected* (interiorised) as atman, which is also co-extensive with the world. This is how immortal *bhūman* assimilates object to subject. It is with remarkable similarity that – as we have seen – in early Greek metaphysics money is both projected and introjected, involving the immortalising assimilation of object to subject. As for the meaning of *bhūman* ('plenitude'), Parmenides both projects and introjects the continuous *plenitude* of abstract substance (14§A).

Note the reason for rejecting possessions as the greatness on which *bhūman* is based: the possessions listed are 'all based on each other', whereas true *bhūman* extends over this whole world. This expresses the truth that, after the advent of a universal measure of value and means of exchange, the value of each possession remains based on the value of other possessions, and only abstract (monetary) value itself is inherently universal. Monetary value seems to acquire its true Being – fundamental and transcendent – only if universal, projected (onto the cosmos) and introjected, whereas possessions, however various or valuable, can never equal this transcendent universality of monetary value.

Moreover, this reinforces the unsatisfactoriness of the cycle of commercial exchange and of its cosmisation as the cycle of reincarnation (*saṃsāra*).[80] With the introverted focus on atman we should compare the Platonic *psuchē gathering itself from all parts of the body* as producing thinking (*phronesis*) described as 'the only right currency (νόμισμα), for which all those things [pleasures, pains, fears] must be exchanged' (69a); whereas attachment to the body means entering the miserable cycle of reincarnation (81c–e).

80 9§E, 10§A.

PART E

Conclusion

CHAPTER 16

The Complex Imagining of Universe and Inner Self

16§A Monetisation and Other Factors

My project has been to explain the intellectual transformations in India and Greece in a way that does not ignore socio-economic processes. Inasmuch as my privileging of the effect of monetisation may – I know from experience – generate misunderstanding, I will now provide six clarifications of how I envisage this effect.

(1) My emphasis on the factor of monetisation implies not that it was the *only* factor, rather that monetisation has been *ignored*. Examples of other detectable factors are:

- (a) the importance in both cultures of *ritual*, specifically the cosmic rite of passage, and of its synthesis with monetisation
- (b) the influence of *autocracy* on the idea of the self in the early *Upanishads* (7§B)
- (c) various factors – all found within the earlier Vedic tradition[1] – promoting the cosmic cycle and (more specifically) reincarnation[2]
- (d) the Platonic interiorisation of the master-slave relationship (15§A)
- (e) the *fear* that is overcome by the realisation of one's identity with all else (6§C)
- (f) the influence of *mystic experience* on the Parmenidean One (11§D).

[1] Horsch (1971) 155; Killingley (1997) 13. For reincarnation as a purely Vedic development, see Blutzenberger (1996) and (1998); nor is there any reason to suppose external influence on any other of the features of Indian EIR (10§A).

[2] (1) The belief in survival as animals or plants (RV 10.16.3; SB 13.8.1.20; e.g. Durkheim [1915] 168–9); (2) the cyclical pattern of nature (SB 1.5.3.14; Horsch [1971] 120); (3) rebirth in offspring (RV 10.16.5; AB 7.14; SB 2.2.4.7–8; AU 2.1–3); (4) the sacrificial cosmic rite of passage (Horsch [1971] 120–6).

This list is not meant to be exhaustive.[3] In order to be as complete as possible, my explanation would thoroughly explore all potentially relevant factors such as geography and linguistic and cultural inheritance. But a complete investigation of all the potential factors is beyond the scope of a single monograph. Moreover, there may be factors that have disappeared without trace.

(2) There is no sense in which ideas can be *reduced* to money. Rather, ideas are the product of complex processes in which money may be a factor, as may other ideas.

(3) To identify socio-economic processes as a factor in the creation of metaphysical ideas is not to deny that metaphysical ideas may influence socio-economic processes.

(4) To identify the preconditions (economic or otherwise) for an intellectual development is not in itself to cast doubt on its content. For instance to claim that monetisation was a precondition for Pythagorean mathematics is not to deny its validity. Monetisation may help to crystallise or promote new beliefs that are useful, valuable, true or even (to us) obvious. But these advantages of the beliefs were not always sufficient cause for them to be held.

(5) It has become obvious from our argument that there is not a single mode of projecting (cosmising) or introjecting money. In particular, we have seen how the dual essence of money (value and circulation) contributes to differing (even opposed) conceptions of the universe and of the inner self. We have associated value with the perspective of individual possession (e.g. in Parmenides) and circulation with the perspective of community (e.g. in Herakleitos). But value and circulation are in fact so inextricably linked, each entirely dependent on the other, that they may also generate an individual perspective on circulation and a communal perspective on value. This produces various modes of cosmisation (and introjection), which are complex enough to require a section of their own (16§B).

(6) Cosmisation and introjection are complex processes. Distinct phenomena may be projected (cosmised) or introjected together, for instance money and autocracy are together projected into the god

[3] For instance Allen (2016) argues that Indo-European social trifunctionality (cf. 2§B) should be supplemented by 'a separate category relating to transcendence, totality and creation'. If so, then – inasmuch as the traditional social trifunctionality (from which the merchant is absent: Hénaff [2010] 68–9) is transcended most effectively by money – I suggest that the separate category was colonised by monetisation, initially in the two earliest Indo-European societies to be pervasively monetised (Greece and northern India).

of Xenophanes and (differently) introjected into the Upanishadic inner self.

(7) The spread of monetisation since the sixth century BCE, resulting eventually in today's monetised world, has clearly not resulted in each monetised society producing a new metaphysics. Does this not call into question my connection between monetisation and metaphysics? This raises a large issue, on which I can here only sketch the following basic points.

Monetisation (as defined in 2§E) may be *endogenous* (i.e. developed within a society with little or no external influence), but in most cases has been *exogenous* (i.e. introduced from outside).

The earliest societies to produce coinage for general use were the Greek polis, northern India and China, all around the middle of the first millennium BCE. Indian coins differ considerably from Greek coins in their appearance and production technique (though not in their material: silver), and in this period Indian society shows no other sign of Greek contact or influence of any kind: Greek and Indian culture in my period developed separately from each other. Nevertheless, a very likely idea to be transmitted along trade routes is the idea of coinage, which may indeed have arrived in the Gangetic region indirectly all the way from the Greek polis. But such an isolated component of Greek culture would have taken root only if there was already a place for it in Gangetic society, either as already monetised or at least commercialised to the point of being ripe for monetisation. Indeed, the endogenous monetisation of northern India almost certainly occurred before – perhaps long before – its adoption of coinage (2§E), and the same can probably be said of both Greece and China. Greece and northern India were each characterised by many cities engaging in internal and external commerce unhampered by centralising theocracy. By contrast, endogenous monetisation did not occur in the irrigation-based centralised states of Mesopotamia,[4] Egypt, the Indus valley and Mesoamerica.

When monetisaton was – as so often – introduced from outside, it generally came with other elements of the introducing culture: traders, settlers, literature and art, sometimes even a whole way of life complete with religion and metaphysics.[5] For instance, from the Greek city-states

[4] For Mesopotamia and Egypt, see Seaford (2004) 318–37.

[5] In some cases exogenous monetisation may – rather than *importing* ready-made metaphysics – be better described as promoting metaphysical *transformation* of traditional culture. These extremes delimit a spectrum of possibilities, with the origins of Islam – at the intersection of a monetised (and largely monotheistic) and a pre-monetary (and largely polytheistic) world – towards the latter end.

coinage eventually spread directly or indirectly, with other elements of Greek culture, to numerous other societies (including Rome), and from Rome – again with other elements of culture – to those parts of the Roman empire that had not already acquired it.

In Greece and northern India (and China), by contrast, societies pervasively monetised *from within*, we see *the unalloyed reaction of a pre-monetary culture to monetisation*, without influence from an external monetised culture.[6] It is surely not coincidental that it is these three cultures alone that produced a new *kind* of elite metaphysics.

The metaphysics thereby produced varies not only according to the specific mode of monetisation but also according to the pre-existing social formation with its ritual and cosmology. For instance, the existence in China – as among the Roman elite – of a strong state together with a tenacious cult of ancestors (both resistant to the development of the kind of individualism that we find in India) would tend to prevent the development of EIR, for which monetisation may be a necessary but is not a sufficient condition. Greece in this respect falls somewhere between China and India, and accordingly produced a form of EIR less widespread and tenacious than the Indian.

The case of abstract monism is rather different. Once money has been established (whether exogenously or endogenously), its unthinking usage is enabled by previous usage. But during the initial phase of endogenous monetisation, and during the first use of endogenous coinage, a certain mental operation may be required: to imagine the abstract value-substance – ubiquitous, permanent, omnipotent – embodied in the money (as its only or main purpose). This mental operation may, in engagement with pre-monetary cosmology, be conducive to monism. We do find in China in the wake of monetisation[7] the advent of a formless entity (*qi*) comparable to brahman and to the presocratic single substrate, perhaps as – in part – a cosmisation of money. As in Greece and India, there is in China

[6] In our (Achaemenid) period there were relations between Persia and the Indus area, but the Achaemenid empire was not pervasively monetised (i.e. with ubiquitous low-value coinage).

[7] Our understanding of monetisation and the early development of coinage in China have recently been much advanced by archaeology and by the systematic studies of Emura (2011) and Kakinuma (2011), both in Japanese but sympathetically reviewed (in English) in detail by von Falkenhausen (2013 and 2014). Emura shows that coinage began to be used in about 550 BCE, a time for which archaeology has revealed significant change in numerous aspects of material culture, including substantial growth in the size of urban settlements. Kakinuma argues (von Falkenhausen disagrees) that the (earlier) shells did not function as money. Most recently von Glahn (2016: 62) states that 'bronze currency in the shape of knives and spades first appeared c. 600 BCE', and that before 500 BCE currency had spread over a very large area. Fan Li, who resigned as prime minister of Yue in 473 BCE, was said to have travelled to Qi and there earned 'several hundred thousand coins' (64).

a rejection of the practice of ritual along with an 'inward turn', which, in the words of Ying-Shih Yü:

> took a giant step forward in the fourth century BCE with the emergence of the new cosmology of *qi*. According to this new theory, the *qi* permeates the entire cosmos. It is in constant movement and, when differentiated and individuated, all things in the world are formed.

And like brahman and the presocratic single substance, its all-pervasiveness includes the inner self. For:

> only by turning inward to nourish the most refined *qi* in the heart can one hope to attain oneness with the cosmos.[8]

It is by virtue of being an *entity* that is both *all-pervasive* and *interiorised* that the presocratic substrate, brahman and *qi* differ from such pre-monetary universal principles of order as Indian *ṛta* and Egyptian *ma' at* and from the kind of pre-monetary power known as *mana*. Comparably, the *dao* – after the time of Confucius – was used to mean the source and totality of all things, 'a symbol of the transcendental world in contrast to the actual world of everyday life . . . the *dao* functions everywhere but is hidden'.[9] But the *dao* is *ethicised*, and so in this respect is closer to *dharma* and karma than to brahman or the presocratic single substance.

In all societies people pursue wealth and conduct exchange. But money is specifically an all-pervasive substance that seems to contain within itself universal impersonal invisible power. The first three societies to be monetised in this sense (Greece, India, China) were also the first three societies to produce – at about the same time, and despite their profound *political* differences – the idea of a fundamental cosmic principle (entity or power) that is impersonal, abstract, all-pervasive, imperceptible and interiorised.

16§B Differing Perspectives on Money

Money has value only when immanent in *circulation* (payment or exchange), but on the other hand seems to be a stable, value-embodying substance only as a transcendent entity, by being *withheld* from circulation, *possessed* (10§B). Circulation is necessarily communal, whereas possession is generally by the individual. Our thinkers (whether Greek or Indian) vary in the extent to which their cosmisation of money is of circulation (i.e. from a communal perspective) or of value (i.e. from

[8] Yü (2003) 72, citing Mencius 2A: 2. [9] Yü (2003) 71–2, 67.

an individual perspective). In this section we will describe these cosmisations in descending order of their prioritisation of circulation over value, starting with the extreme prioritisation of circulation by Herakleitos and ending with the extreme prioritisation of value by Parmenides. But each of the two essences of money (exchange and possessed value) produces when projected into the world an unacceptably one-sided account (Herakleitos excludes stable identity, Parmenides excludes motion and multiplicity). This presents an intellectual problem.[10] But in practice money must both have value and the power to circulate: the two aspects *interpenetrate*. And so we shall see that in fact cosmisations of circulation cannot exclude value, and cosmisations of value cannot exclude circulation.

(1) Early Ionian Cosmology

In early Ionian monism the substrate is the cosmisation of the abstract or semi-abstract substance of money. In other words, the cosmisation does not and cannot exclude value. But at the heart of the universe is the transformation of the substrate from and into everything else. The early Ionian cosmologist of whom the most fragments survive, Herakleitos, emphasises the communality of the abstract formula (*logos*) that governs the constant, cyclical transformation of elements and opposites[11] into each other, amounting to prioritisation of circulation over value. This cosmisation of monetary circulation represents the communal perspective of the polis, by which coinage was produced and legitimated. The earliest mass coinage was an institution of the polis, and the Ionian cosmologists were citizens of the prosperous poleis that were the first to be pervasively monetised by coinage. Their perspective is limited largely to the Greek archaic period.

Subsequent thought addresses the problem of how to combine the fact of changing concrete multiplicity (corresponding to the fact that value does circulate) with the Parmenidean logic of unchanging abstract monism (corresponding to the fact of individually possessed value). Once again, I must emphasise that what is generally regarded as a purely intellectual

[10] Precluded in the semi-mythical thinking at SB 11.2.2.3: 'Then the Brahman itself went up to the sphere beyond. Having gone up to the sphere beyond, it considered, "How can I descend again into these worlds?" It then descended again by means of these two – Form and Name.'

[11] On the connection between opposites and monetary circulation, see Seaford (2004) 238–40. The opposites were also crucial for the monetised metaphysics of the politically and commercially engaged followers of Pythagoras (15§A), who was born and bred on the prosperous Ionian island of Samos but emigrated to southern Italy.

problem of inexplicable provenance cannot be fully understood by ignoring monetisation. The tendency towards abstract monism was a *preconception* that had already begun in Ionia before its extreme form was reinforced by Parmenidean logic. The quasi-abstract Ionian substrate-in-circulation and unchanging abstract Parmenidean Being were – albeit from opposite perspectives – both cosmisations of the all-pervasiveness of monetary value. Other, intermediate perspectives, involving the synthesis of change and multiplicity with the unchangeable, were provided in different forms – we shall see – by Empedokles, atomism and Plato.

(2) *Empedokles*

Empedokles propounded constant cyclical change, but not a single substrate. Everything is composed of four unchangeable 'roots of all things' (B6) – earth, air, fire and water, which are brought together and apart by Love and Strife. Empedokles himself, as an exile from the gods, passes in a cycle of reincarnation from one cosmological element to another (14§D). This is much like what in the early *Upanishads* I called minimal pluralism.[12] It allows him to cosmise unchangingess (as does Parmenides) *and* circulation (as do the Ionians). And, indeed, in describing the unchangeability of each of the four elements he uses language reminiscent of Parmenides.[13]

(3) *Atomism, Greek and Indian*

Investigating the indivisible immutable particles of which the world is composed (atomism) is in premodern cultures neither natural nor inevitable nor widespread. Moreover, Greek atomism takes a specific form: it explains the multiplicity of appearances by the varying shapes, sizes and arrangements of (ontologically prioritised) atoms, which are qualitiless, invisibly small, indivisible, immutable and impenetrable.[14] Once again we

[12] 8§E; AU 3.3 (five elements). Passage through the cosmological element also at CU 5.10.5–6; BU 6.2.16; 9§D. Successive elements in cosmogonies, with the first item a person or atman: BU 1.2.2; CU 6.2.3–4 (8§E, 9§D); TU 2.1.1; cf. CU 6.2.3: accordingly, the earliest order of the elements seems to be determined by the progressive embeddedness of the inner self in matter (McEvilley [2002] 305); in the much later *Śvetāśvatara Upaniṣad* (6.2) the order is reversed. Once detached from polytheism, the elements may be closely related to the inner self. Both Empedokles (B6) and CU 6 (3.2) do also call the basic elements deities, but this is marginal to their conception as physical elements.

[13] DK31 B17.34–5; B12; B17.12–13.

[14] Democritus DK68 A6, A14, A37, A41, A49, A57, A59, A124, A125.

have a metaphysical construction created neither by observation nor by experimentation nor by (mere) logic.

Monetary value is, *qua* possessed, (transcendent) undivided abstract substance, but in the process of *exchange* this (now immanent) abstract substance *must* be divided into determinate quantities. True, the five drachmas that I pay for olive oil have some of the qualities of Parmenidean Being (limited, abstract, homogeneous, unchanging), but they do not have the *indivisibility* that Parmenides explicitly (B8.22) attributes to Being: in the practice of exchange they are divided from my remaining money, and five drachmas can be divided into five single drachmas or thirty obols.

But the divisibility of monetary value is not unlimited. Every currency has its smallest unit. Aristotle mentions the *tetartemorion* (quarter of an obol) as if it were the cheapest coin.[15] In the United States it is one cent, in the *Arthaśāstra* a half-kakani. Units of account (e.g. the 'mill') can always be imagined with lower value than the cheapest coins, but *infinitesimal* units would have no practical purpose. In exchange, every sum of money is an aggregate of indivisible abstract units (unless it be itself the indivisible unit). Abstract Being can maintain *even in exchange* the unchanging indivisibility (as well as the homogeneity, limitedness and self-sufficiency) that Parmenides attributes to it, but *only in the smallest monetary units*. As invisible, unitary and qualitiless, the atom is as close as possible to the Parmenidean abstract One while also functioning as the basic component of material multiplicity. And, indeed, atomism has been represented, from Aristotle onwards, as reconciling Parmenidean ontology with multiplicity.[16]

Aristotle also remarks[17] that the atoms' 'substance (φύσις) is one, as if each were a separate piece of gold': the simile is in a sense inept (the atoms lack sensible qualities), so why does he employ it? Because it is as appropriate as Herakleitos' comparison of the 'exchange' of fire for all things to the exchange of gold for goods (B90). Herakleitos and atomism cosmise money from a communal perspective (entailing change and multiplicity), but whereas Herakleitos' focus is mainly on circulation, the atomist focus is mainly on value. It goes without saying that none of this is to claim that the cosmisation of money is the *only* source of Greek atomism.[18]

15 *Politics* 1323a31. This is not to say that coins of even lower value were nowhere or never produced.

16 *De Generatone et Corruptione* 325a2. Cf. Melissos DK30 B8: 'If there were plurality, things would have to be of the same kind as I say the One is.' Guthrie (1965) 389–92; KRS 407–9.

17 *De Caelo* 275b31.

18 Another possible source is the conception of the individual person: ἄτομον can mean individual as well as indivisible. I have no space for the issue of whether the basic unit of value was also *introjected*, except to note that the atomists valued imperturbability of the individual soul: Democritus DK68 A1 (45), A167, A169; Epicurus: D.L. 10.136; etc.

It was in the fifth century BCE that atomism was first propounded in Greece. In India our evidence for systematic atomism was all written much later than our period, in which it perhaps did not yet exist. It may have developed under Greek influence, although I emphasise again that such fundamental beliefs are not transmitted unless there is already a place for them in the recipient culture. Systematic doctrines of atomism were held by the Jains, Ajivikans, Buddhists and Vaisesikas. Here I can no more give a full account of them than I can of Greek atomism, or of the substantial differences between Indian and Greek atomism. Instead, I will select a few points relevant to my overall argument.[19]

A proto-atomist mode of thinking appears already in the passage of the *Chāndogya Upaniṣad* (6.12) that we discussed in 8§E. The banyan tree depends on the invisible *aṇiman* (minuteness, fineness, smallest particle) produced by Svetaketu cutting up a tiny seed, and the *aṇiman* that 'constitutes the atman of this whole world' is 'how you are, Svetaketu'.

Although this bestows ontological privilege on invisible particles, it is far from being fully fledged atomism. Despite the cutting up, the concern here is not *indivisibility* (still less the nature of the indivisible, as in atomism) but the ontological priority – in self and universe – of *invisibility* over visible multiplicity, which also underlies, in the very same chapter, similarities with the material monism of the Milesians, the abstract monism of Parmenides and the minimal pluralism of Empedokles (8§E). It is from this kind of ontological matrix, in India as in Greece, we may surmise, that there emerged fully fledged atomism, sustained by the continuing introjection-with-projection of money and atomisation of the individual inherent in monetisation and renunciation.

In Jainism karma composed of atoms is literally (physically) interiorised (10§C). In Ajivikan atomism the personal dimension of the eternal atoms is explicit: they are of seven elemental categories (earth, water, fire, air, life, joy and sorrow), which are barren, and do not have any effect on the joy or sorrow of each other, or injure each other.[20] However, even atomised individuals cannot – from a communal perspective at least – escape all interrelation with others, in a world controlled by money. The combination of multiplicity with unchangeable essence (i.e. from a communal perspective on value) leaves unexplained what it is that controls the movement and interrelationship of atoms (each in its isolated self-sufficiency); and so an explanation is provided by a force that resembles money as

[19] For a detailed discussion of Indian atomism, see Keith (1921) 16, 262–3; Gangopadhyaya (1980).
[20] Basham (1951) 262–3; McEvilley (2002) 318.

abstract, impersonal, universal and external to individuals (atoms). In Greek atomism it is *anangkē*.[21] In some versions of Nyāya-Vaiśeṣika atomism it is *adṛṣṭa*,[22] and in some versions of Ajivikan atomism *niyati*,[23] although in other versions *adṛṣṭa* tends to merge with karma[24] (as does *niyati*)[25] or with the atoms themselves.[26] I have associated all three of these Sanskrit concepts with money.

(4) Karma

In India metaphysical power-substances are accumulated and owned by – and influence the well-being of – individuals (Chapter 9), in particular karma (10§C). Such power-substances represent cosmised monetary *value*. But there are three ways in which they are influenced by *circulation*.

Firstly, the karma possessed by an individual may decrease or accumulate, which happens to money as a result of circulation. Secondly, merit (*puṅya*), or good karma, could be transferred between individuals. Thirdly, projected into karma is not only the positive power of possessed monetary value but also the negative power of money-driven circulation (e.g. as debt): accordingly, there is desire for escape from cosmic circulation (*saṃsāra*) and from the cosmic money (karma) that drives it. The same kind of misery may have influenced the idea of escape from cosmic circulation also in Greece. As for Herakleitos, the circulation of *logos*-embodying fire expresses the circulation not only of money (from a communal perspective) but also of souls (*psuchai*); but there is in his fragments no mention of escape from it, and he explicitly privileges the communality of the *logos* over life lived according to individual understanding.

(5) Plato

At the centre of Platonic metaphysics is Being that is unchanging and abstract. There is a (Parmenidean) tendency in Plato to imagine that the source of what truly exists and is truly valuable is a single abstract entity. But he also ontologically prioritises *forms*, which are abstract, unchanging and untransformable into anything else: in these four respects they resemble not only the Parmenidean One but also the invisible, qualitiless atoms.

21 'Necessity': Leukippos DK67 A1, A10, A24, B2; Demokritos DK68 A1, A37, A39, A66.
22 Keith (1921) index s. Adṛṣṭa; Gangopadhyaya (1980) 36–9; Halbfass (1991) 311–13.
23 Basham (1951) 263, 266. 24 Halbfass (1991) 311–17. 25 Basham (1951) 266.
26 Gangopadhyaya (1980) 39.

This threefold resemblance derives from the fact that all three are shaped by the projection of abstract monetary *value*.

However, the Platonic forms are – unlike the Parmenidean One – *multiple*. In this respect they are like the atoms, which differ, however, from the Platonic forms by virtue of being physical (albeit qualitiless) components of what can be grasped by the senses. This distinction initiates the long-lasting philosophical polemic between idealism and materialism.[27] We note here merely that in this initial phase it reflects different ideological perspectives on money. Whereas the perspective of Plato is that of the individual possessor of abstract value who also recognises multiplicity, the atomists are heirs to the communal Ionian tradition that assumes the material multiplicity inherent in circulation based on a material (albeit tenuous) substrate. Democritus was from Abdera, an Ionian colony. His (lost) encyclopaedic writings are evidence for a wide range of interest in the material world. Diogenes Laertius records (9.35–7) that as the third son he divided up the family property, and chose the smallest portion because it was 'in currency' (ἐν ἀργυρίῳ) needed for his extensive travels, and that he had 'all experience in τεχναί (practical skills)'.

Given its provenance in the Ionian tradition, why does early atomism adopt a more Parmenidean substrate? In response, it is often claimed, to Parmenidean logic. A substrate may not simultaneously also be something else. But a substrate of atoms that are immutable and untransformable accounts for variety and change (by their varying shapes, sizes and arrangements), as well as for multiplicity, while retaining the materiality of the Ionian cosmos.

But it is not just a matter of Parmenidean logic, the conclusion of which Aristotle regarded as bordering on madness.[28] Behind that logic is the historical advent of the idea of abstract value that – being distinct from its metallic vehicle and from all other commodities – can bestow self-sufficiency on its possessor, and so is imagined as self-identical, untransformable into anything else. That advent helps to account for the origin and long-term popularity of the priority of immutable abstract Being; and it may also have been a factor in the imagining of atoms as immutable and almost abstract (qualitiless) while being in fact (conveniently[29]) material. Platonism and atomism endured (along with the opposition between idealism and materialism) because they represent the first sophisticatedly

[27] See esp. Plato *Sophist* 256a–c; Furley (1987). [28] *De Generatione et Corruptione* 325a19.

[29] As avoiding the problem (e.g. in Plato) of the relation between ontologically prioritised abstract entities and material realities.

systematic cosmisations of not just one but both the essences of money, with Platonism prioritising one of them (value) and atomism the other (circulation). In India by contrast there is in our period no evidence for a systematic doctrine of philosophical materialism.[30]

(6) The Early Upanishads

The individual possession of abstract value is expressed, in the early *Upanishads*, in the concept of brahman, which has developed – in one of its meanings – into an unchanging, abstract, universal entity that an individual may become or attain.[31] I argued in Part C that this development was promoted by monetisation. But the cosmisation of value in these texts does not exclude the cosmisation of circulation. The attainment of brahman is in one passage (BU 6.2.15) represented as – for some 'exalted people' – a permanent exit from cosmic circulation. And I have related the opposition between two forms of brahman, *sat* and *tyam*, to the opposition between value and circulation (14§A).

(7) Parmenides

The abstract monism of Parmenides expresses not only the individual *possession* of value, abstracted from goods and from circulation, but also the ideology of individual self-sufficiency, now reinforced by the power of money to unite all else in abstract value. But even from this perspective circulation is not entirely excluded. In these respects the Parmenidean One resembles *brahman*, from which, however, it differs in ways that deserve a separate section (16§C). The problem of the relationship between the Way of Truth, which excludes change and multiplicity, and the Way of Seeming, which accepts and describes them, has generated much inconclusive discussion. The irresolvability of contradiction can only be fully understood, I suggest, as an expression of the contradiction inherent in Parmenides' *ideology*. The insistence on the One being held in place by Justice, on it being 'all inviolate', on coming-to-be and perishing as having 'wandered very far away', with true belief having 'thrust them off': all this and more expresses the artificial but necessarily irresolvable separation – driven by the ideology of monetised individual self-sufficiency – of value

[30] On the history of materialist attitudes in India, see Chattopadhyaya (2006).

[31] E.g. BU 1.4.10; 3.4; 4.4.5–7; CU 3.14; 8.14. For Brahminism ignoring or rejecting the metaphysics of *circulation* (karmic retribution in EIR), see e.g. Bronkhorst (2016) 250.

from circulation (14§A). It is only by understanding the source and force of this absolute separation that we will cease to be puzzled by the absolute separation of the Way of Seeming from the Way of Truth.

16§C Brahman and the Parmenidean One

In so far as it is an abstract, unchanging, universal entity that (in contrast to the Ionian substrate) is *not* transformed into other things, the Parmenidean One resembles brahman, from which however it also differs in various respects.

The first difference is that brahman (unlike the One) has a range of meanings, mostly deriving from its origin in ritual. Secondly, brahman is invisible and yet specific, neither material substance (as Ionian substrate) nor purely abstract Being (as Parmenides). Thirdly, whereas the Parmenidean One is kept entirely separate from multiplicity, brahman is often related or identified with various entities, compared to which it is generally more comprehensive or fundamental. For instance, BU 2.5 contains a long list of entities arranged in sections, with each section starting with a basic element (such as the wind, the sun, space, *dharma*) and ending with the words 'It is immortal; it is brahman; it is the Whole.'

Further differences relate to the different relation of money and ritual to *agency*. In order to circulate, money requires agency, but must also be imagined to contain its invisible unitary power as value entirely within itself. This, together with the Greek aristocratic ideology of individual self-sufficiency (isolated from circulation), enables and promotes the imagining of unitary monetary value as all that exists, and therefore as the One, or Being – rather than as power or value, which depend on circulation.

Vedic ritual, from which the concept of brahman derives, has a different relation to agency. However central the individual to the sacrificial ritual, it is a traditional social act, in which the individual depends on the knowledge and actions of Brahmins, whom he rewards. Even when the ritual is interiorised, salvation may depend on acquiring (metaphysical) knowledge from others. In the concept of brahman the traditional comprehensive invisible power of ritual comes to be reinforced by the new comprehensive invisible power of money. Although the latter power tends to merge subject (atman) with object (brahman),[32] the ritual origin and associations of brahman ensure that it does not entirely exclude the independent existence of subjects (as the Parmenidean One does, except in so far as the subject is

[32] 13§E, 15§B.

revealed by introspection): this is our fourth difference between brahman and the Parmenidean One.

The individual subject (the all-pervasive atman) can become or attain (all-pervasive) brahman: this accords with the influence, on both concepts, of (interiorised) ritual in which the individual obtains the world, and has no counterpart in Parmenides. This is our fifth difference. In this respect the *Upanishads* are closer to Ionian cosmology: Anaximenean air and Herakleitean fire[33] is each also the substance of the inner self (*psuchē*). Underlying the similarity is that the impersonal power of money depends for its realisation on the inner self, to which it is easily assimilated. But this Ionian cosmology represents a communal perspective on circulation, and so each soul is merely a fragment of the universe, not identical with it. Different again, though similar in origin, are the mental monism (with *god* as subject) in the Derveni papyrus and Xenophanes, and the *cosmos* as subject in Empedokles and Plato.[34]

The identity of atman with universe (as brahman), which – it is worth repeating – contrasts with the Ionian conception of the soul as a material fragment of the universe, has the implication that there is only one universal atman identical with everybody and everything.[35] This is our *sixth* difference. *Vaiśvānara* ('common to all people') is applied in the *Śatapatha Brāhmaṇa* to Agni (i.e. fire) within the *puruṣa* (man),[36] and then in the *Chāndogya Upaniṣad* to atman *as* 'measuring a span and beyond all measure';[37] and 'as the single fire, entering living beings, adapts its appearance to match that of each; so the single atman within each being adapts its appearance to match that of each, yet remains quite distinct' (KaU 5.9). But this doctrine is peripheral to the early *Upanishads*: it is there without the (ethical and salvational) importance to which it is adapted in later Indian thought, and without the ethical and political implications of the similar doctrine in Herakleitos; but on the other hand it does not approach the purely

33 There are even passages of the early *Upanishads* that associate the atman with fire: BU 1.2.3; 2.4.10; CU 3.13.8: Jurewicz (2007) 123–5. But the Herakleitean *psuchē* is quite different: it shares its substance (fire) and *logos* with the universe.

34 12§A (2), 14§D.

35 'The true self is not the individual self, but rather the identity that one shares with everything else. There is no true distinction among living beings, for they all emerge from being and retreat into it. All things, both animate and inanimate, are united in being, because they are all the transformations of being': Brereton (1990) 124.

36 SB 10.6.1.11: 'whosoever thus knows that Agni Vaiśvānara as *Puruṣa*-like, as established within the *Puruṣa*, repels death . . .'

37 CU 5.18.1; cf. 8.1.3.

monetised hyper-individualism that accompanied the universality of the Parmenidean One.

These differences all relate to the fundamental difference that whereas the Parmenidean One is a cosmisation of the comprehensive invisible self-sufficiency of money, brahman derives in part from the (traditional) comprehensive invisible power of ritual (influenced by the new comprehensive invisible power of money). More will emerge about this difference in the next section (17§A).

CHAPTER 17

Ritual, Money, Society and Metaphysics

17§A Universe and Inner Self

In this section we will recapitulate the relation between ritual and money as factors in the intellectual transformation that we crudely summarise as follows.

In both the *Rigveda* and Homer a society pre-dating cities, states and money is ruled by warriors, and:

(1a) There are several deities, who may embody or control forces of nature. Humans, individually or in groups, make offerings and prayers in the hope of eliciting from them goodwill and benefit. I call this polytheist reciprocity.

(1b) There are organs of consciousness, which have thought and emotion and initiate action. But none of them is ever subject to focus or description, let alone ontological privilege. None of them is explicitly or implicitly comprehensive. And there is no incorporeality.

(1c) Death is a linear transition to the place of the dead from which (on the whole) there is no return.

Subsequently, in India the warrior caste rules, but 'the priestly power (brahman) is the womb of the ruling power' and the king 'returns in the end to brahman as to his own womb' (BU 1.4.11). Plato in his ideal state in the *Republic* subordinates the warriors to the intellectuals. For an elite, in the early *Upanishads* and in early Greek philosophy:

(2a) Polytheist reciprocity is largely replaced by monism of various kinds.

(2b) There is a focus on an unchanging inner self, a unitary organ of comprehensive consciousness (prana, atman, *psuchē*, *nous*), and on its relation to the universe. Human aspiration is expressed not so much in reciprocal polytheism as in individual knowledge of this organ and of the unity of the universe.

Further:

(2c) The early *Upanishads* have indications of the belief in EIR that we also find in Greek texts of the period and which is subsequently widespread in India.

(1a) and (1b) imply changeability and plurality, which in (2a) and (2b) are replaced by the unchanging and the unitary. However, (2c) implies – in contrast to (1c) – repeated cyclical movement. This creates in both cultures a contradiction between the ideal of the unchanging and the unitary on the one hand and belief in the circulation of souls on the other, and in both cultures the contradiction is resolved by the desirability of escape from the circulation to a haven of unchanging well-being.

Ritual and money both mediate relations between the individual and the world, deploying collective confidence so as to reduce haphazardness to predictable and durable order. To do so they must both seem to embody invisible power, to generate the ideas of invisible power that are required for their practice. Such invisible power embodied in sacrificial ritual *may* be impersonal and comprehensive,[1] and in money it *must* be impersonal and comprehensive. It is on the basis of this fundamental similarity that in India there occurred a fusion of sacrificial with monetary power.[2] At the same time it was the impersonal omnipotence of money that tended – for an elite in both cultures – to promote the interiorisation of ritual and to marginalise the power of the gods.

There is a cultural and historical similarity between our two cultures: the cosmic rite of passage is in India and Greece monetised at about the same time. This forms the background to the strikingly similar transformation of metaphysics. But there are also cultural and historical differences, which go some way to explain the metaphysical differences. I will (a) summarise the cultural and historical differences, and (b) relate them to the metaphysical differences.

(a) The cosmic rite of passage was in India sacrifice but in Greece mystic initiation. The Greek sacrifice culminated in a communal meal that – in large-scale sacrifice – could unite a whole community. The communal

[1] On the invisible power embodied and carefully articulated by Vedic sacrifice it is still worth reading Hubert and Mauss (1898): for an example of such power as comprehensive and both personal and impersonal see pp. 42–3.

[2] 5§D, 8§B.

meal, indeed communality generally, is absent from the Vedic sacrifice. The Greeks did not have a priestly caste or class, whereas at the centre of the Vedic sacrifice was the traditional relationship (synarchy) between the two dominant castes, between the Brahmin priests and the Kshatriya individual sacrificer. This difference, whatever its origins (5§E), meant that whereas presocratic thought was produced by *citizens* of the recently monetised polis, Upanishadic thought was produced by *priests*, who were relatively (but not entirely) resistant to the monetisation occurring around them.

In Vedic sacrifice Brahmins controlled access to the gods and heaven, and the Kshatriyas brought wealth. This tradition remained neglectful of – and even hostile to – the urbanisation that was widespread in northern India by the time of the Buddha, along with a degree of commercialisation and monetisation. At the same time the effects of monetisation, notably the idea of uniform universal value and the autonomy conferred on the individual by possession of that value, could hardly fail to influence ideas surrounding the wealth brought to the sacrifice. From being a gift designed to elicit reciprocal benefit, moveable wealth in a world that is being monetised tends to become rather an embodiment of universal value and individual power.

Greeks dedicated valuable and permanent offerings to the gods in the public space of temples, but in animal sacrifices the gods received very little, and access to well-being in the beyond was created not (as in India) by the accumulation of offerings but by the experience of mystic initiation. Even what could be buried with the dead was limited by legislation.[3] What is offered in the Greek sacrifice does not, as in the Indian, acquire or become an imagined world for the individual sacrificer, but is flesh roasted on spits and distributed among the participants for a communal feast. This contributed to the emergence of coined money:[4] the communally sanctioned but individually possessed egalitarian share of the sacrificed animal (on its standard metal spit) develops into the communally sanctioned but individually possessed standard piece of metal (the obol coin, named after the spit), which by virtue of the confidence generated by its continual widespread use becomes entirely detached from sacrifice.

[3] Seaford (1994) 74–86. [4] 5§E, 14§C.

(b) The metaphysical differences are in conceptions of the inner self, kinds of monism and the variety of relationships between permanence and circulation.

In Greece the introjection and projection of money by citizen cosmologists occurred relatively independently of the cosmic rite of passage (mystic initiation), by which it might nevertheless be influenced. In mystic initiation participation is both individual and communal. And so, two practices that combined individual and community – monetised exchange and mystic ritual – both influenced the imagining of inner self and of cosmos. The inner self was assimilated to and isolated by (its individual share of) *money*, which was, however, constituted by communal confidence and communal practices. Analogously, in the cosmic rite of passage (mystic initiation) the inner self might also be influenced by the potentially isolating assimilation of subject and object to each other, and by confrontation with its own immortality and separability from its body, before reaching the culminating communality of the ritual. However, even in the individualist Parmenides this synthesis produces (so far as we know from the fragments) not mental monism but abstract monism: subject is absorbed into universal object (money projected as abstract Being) rather than vice versa.

The Vedic unitary inner self also emerged under the influence of monetisation, but (in contrast to Greece) *from within the cosmic rite of passage* (sacrifice by and for an individual). This difference coheres with several contrasts between Greek and Indian belief. Firstly, it produces a tendency in India for universal object to be absorbed into person or subject (personal or mental monism). The individual sacrificer obtaining the loka, when he interiorises the sacrifice, absorbs the world into himself. Secondly, whereas early Greek monism was a cosmisation of the controlling all-pervasiveness of money, in which all things seem to be constantly transformed from and into money, Vedic monism derived from the (money-influenced) collapse of the old (mysteriously controlling) *sacrificial* correspondences or identities[5] into a single unchanging correspondence or identity (8§B). Thirdly, the individual Vedic sacrificer was generally a man of wealth and power, and sometimes an autocrat. The (to some extent monetised) power of the autocrat was accordingly interiorised in India so

[5] This legacy is still manifest in the metaphysics of the early *Upanishads*: e.g. in CU 1.7 the Rg verse and the Sāman chant are successively identified with various parts of the person, until finally 'the person one sees within the eye' is identified with brahman; in 1.8 Sāman leads to sound, sound leads to breath, and so on, until the list ends at heaven ('one should not take it beyond the heavenly world . . . for heaven is the place from which Sāman is sung').

as to imagine unity within the emerging inner self (7§B), whereas in the Greek polis, which post-dated kingship, the social relation interiorised for this purpose was primarily the power of money. Fourthly, in India the individual may through sacrificial offerings accumulate merit in the beyond: there is a historical transition, influenced by monetisation, from offerings to the gods (to elicit their goodwill) to offerings that accumulate in the beyond as a single metaphysical substance for the general well-being of the individual offerer. Fifthly, the *universal* power of money promotes and interiorises a metaphysical substance that is produced by *all* (not just sacrificial) action,[6] but remains (like sacrificially earned metaphysical substance) individually accumulated and owned: karma.

Just as early Greek monism is largely material or abstract rather than personal or mental, so correspondingly the early Greek inner self is generally imagined either as a *co-material* fragment of the impersonal universal (Anaximenes, Herakleitos, Diogenes of Apollonia) or as *sharing form* with the impersonal universe (Parmenides, Plato) or even with the polis (Plato *Republic*). In other words, the introjected (inner self) and the projected (universe) share substance or form but are distinct. From this emerges the idea of a purely human sphere on the one hand and of impersonal nature or cosmos on the other. But early Indian monism, being largely personal or mental rather than material or abstract, does not generate such an idea. Atman as mere subject is unknowable (8§C [6]), without specific substance or form; rather than participating in the universe, it emerges from a sacrificial process in which the universe is what the individual acquires or absorbs, with the result that projection (cosmisation) of abstract Being is generally inseparable from its introjection. Brahman, too, tends to be without specific substance or form.

Nevertheless, we find in both cultures the same remarkable *metaphor* for the inner self. The metaphor of the soul as a chariot famously appears, with some remarkable similarities, in both the *Kaṭha Upaniṣad* and Plato's *Phaedrus*.[7] The most significant difference is the idle passenger or owner (distinct from the charioteer) identified with the inner self (atman) in the *Kaṭha Upaniṣad*: in Plato there is no passenger, and the inner self (*psuchē*) is compared to the composite of a charioteer with a pair of horses. How do we

6 For the monetised kingdom of Ashoka the importance of *dharma* and respect for all religions (in his inscriptions) reflect the universality of monetisation (against the particularity of rituals, which are unfavourably compared to *dharma* in Rock Edict 9). On the universalisation of karma, see e.g. Gombrich (2013), esp. 44, 58.

7 The *Kaṭha Upaniṣad* may date to well after 326 BCE, and so may have been indirectly influenced by Plato. Magnone (2016) argues for influence in the other direction.

explain this difference? Partly, perhaps, by the Upanishadic interiorisation of the autocrat, who would have had his own charioteer.

But there may be another factor. For early Greek thought a model for the inner self is provided by abstract value-substance, which is imagined as self-sufficient, separate from – but also as both *goal* and *controller* of – the production and exchange of commodities. Accordingly, for Plato the *psuchē*, or its most authentic part, should aspire to separating itself from bodily experiences while also *controlling* them (like slaves): the interiorisation is based on everyday experience. The atman, too, is constituted – in part – by the interiorisation of power (of the autocrat), but also, reflecting Brahminical experience, by its passive interiorisation of the world-controlling sacrifice (sometimes imagined as a chariot), and it appears accordingly not as controller of the chariot but as detached passenger. The opposition between inner self and body, which is fundamental to Plato (with the body associated with the slave), can also be important in the early *Upanishads*,[8] in which, however, a more fundamental opposition is between the self (atman, which can mean body as well as inner self) and what it may attain.

The control exercised within the Platonic *psuchē* was sometimes over the *unlimited*, which in turn might be associated with *money*. This is just one instance (the culmination perhaps) of the Greek interiorisation of money. Any influence of monetisation on the idea of the atman, by contrast, was mediated by the interiorisation of the sacrificial obtaining of the world. The Greeks frequently emphasise, from a communal perspective, the dangerous limitlessness of money and of the desire for it, which for Plato must – along with other desires – be limited within the soul. This basic antipathy to money is not found in Indian texts, and the atman is neither a bounded entity nor a site for limiting the unlimited. The Upanishadic inner self – imagined as the inner faculties' acceptance of and merging with prana (6§D) – consists of the unity of the inner faculties, not the control of desires. In Greece early asceticism emphasised self-control, in India isolated withdrawal.

Money, as an embodiment of universal value and individual power, promotes the individualisation, automatisation and interiorisation of the sacrifice. The absorption of the sacrifice (and of the lokas it obtains) into the individual contributes to the idea of an atman that has the permanence and invisible ubiquity of the abstract value by which the monetised individual is constituted. What the *yajāmana* (sacrificer) once obtained

[8] Notably at CU 8.7–12.

through giving wealth he begins to obtain through the autonomous power of his mind. The sacrificial fire, notes Heesterman, 'disappears behind the atman' (12§D).

This process reflects the individual ownership of universal value, not the experience of communal monetary circulation, from which the sacrificial milieu is somewhat removed. But this does not mean that the early *Upanishads* were entirely immune from the influence of monetary circulation, which may indeed have been an influence (along with natural cycles and the rite of passage) on the sacrificial cosmic cycle. In the two-path doctrine, people whose worship is marked by offerings to the gods return after death (and after the residue of offerings runs out) to Earth, and enter the cycle of rebirth; whereas those who have knowledge follow after death a path that leads ultimately to the world of brahman, from which they do not return (9§D). The latter path prefigures *mokṣa*, escape from *saṃsāra* (the cycle of rebirth). The opposition between these two kinds of post-mortem fate may be influenced by the opposition between those trapped in the cycle of commercial exchange and those who are able to escape from it.

The two-path doctrine adapts a tradition associated with ritual (the cosmic rite of passage) to the prioritisation of *knowledge*. Parmenides does the same. At the heart of his mystic revelation is the distinction between on the one hand the path taken by the mass of the ignorant and on the other the path that provides knowledge of what truly exists (eternal and unitary). We have seen that this adapts the distinction in mystic ritual between the path that leads to reincarnation and the path that leads to permanent well-being (11§D), and the same kind of adaptation is found in Plato (11§E). In both Greece and India the idea of two paths, deriving from the rite of passage to the hereafter, merges with the opposition between the monetary cycle and escape from the monetary cycle through the self-sufficiency of unitary abstract value, cosmised as brahman and the Parmenidean One.

However, in 16§C we described six differences between brahman and the Parmenidean One. How to explain these differences? They all reflect the basic difference that whereas Greek monism – including the Parmenidean One – is a *direct* cosmisation of monetary value, the universal abstract brahman emerged in a context of the monetisation, individualisation and interiorisation of the world-obtaining cosmic rite of passage (sacrifice): the power (brahman) of the sacrifice to obtain or absorb various things (expressed in correspondences or identifications of elements of the ritual with things external to it) was (incompletely) assimilated to the power of a single abstract all-powerful thing (money) that depends not on the performance of ritual but on the inner self of its possessor. The ideological imperative is not to separate value from circulation (as with Parmenides) but rather to maintain the access of privileged (Vedic) knowledge to universal power even without the actual performance of sacrifice. The power of the sacrificer becomes, with the possession of money, the inner ability to absorb the world (loka or brahman) directly into himself.

Parmenides, by contrast, is a citizen of the newly monetised polis. And yet here, too, there is a role for the cosmic rite of passage. The totality of the transcendent abstract One produced by monetisation in the aristocratic mind of Parmenides could not be expressed in any ordinary way. And so, the fundamental cosmic reality hidden from the multitude presented itself to him as the fundamental hidden cosmic reality revealed only to mystic initiates by the goddess (in this case to him alone). This should be seen not as a literary device but as the attempt to convey a genuine experience and to give it traditional authority (14§B). However, there is a significant difference here between this cosmic rite of passage and the Vedic one (sacrifice). Whereas mystic initiation gives individuals a preview of the happiness that they will have – often as a group – in the next world, Vedic sacrifice by contrast is a socially central context of *exchange* producing individual possession or control. Accordingly, although the goddess appeals to Parmenides' introspection as evidence for the (continuous) nature of the One, as well as hinting at the mystic assimilation between subject and object, nevertheless the self-sufficiency of the One ensures that – unlike brahman – it remains separate from the subject. And so the abstract monism of Parmenides contrasts with the personal and mental monism, and the identification of atman with brahman, that we find in the *Śatapatha Brāhmaṇa* and early *Upanishads*.

Despite these differences, we find both in the early *Upanishads* and in Parmenides the ontological prioritisation of the (permanent) *value* or *substance* of money, from the perspective of the individual possessor (16§C). But in early Buddhism and Herakleitos we find the ontological privileging of its *circulation*: in both of them not only is everything in constant flux, associated with fire (12§D), but also there is no self-identical enduring inner self.

In both Greece and India the earliest focus on the individual inner self takes two opposite forms: one insisting on its unchangingness and self-identity, in Parmenides, Plato and in the *Upanishads*; the other, on its changefulness and lack of self-identity, in Herakleitos and Buddhism. The unchanging unitary inner self (atman) described in the earliest *Upanishads* is prefigured in the *Śatapatha Brāhmaṇa*, but not found in earlier texts (notably the *Rigveda*). And so what the Buddhist doctrine of *anatta* ('non-self') denied, the *unchanging*[9] atman of the early *Upanishads*, was a relatively recent idea, which – I argued in Chapter 5 – emerged under the influence of the individualisation and interiorisation of the sacrifice, which were in turn promoted by monetisation. Perhaps the doctrine of *anatta* can be seen broadly as a reaction against the advent of the new, monetised individual, along with other Buddhist reactions to monetisation such as banning the monks from handling money. Herakleitos makes the connection between the circulation of money and the non-self-identity of the fiery *psuchē* explicit: the cosmic cycle driven by fire is imagined as the monetary cycle and the individual *psuchē* is imagined as spent in purchase.[10]

Here again, along with the striking similarities, we will also try to explain the fundamental metaphysical differences between Buddhism and Herakleitos, as we did the differences between Parmenides and the early *Upanishads.* Here the explanation must start by noting that the socio-historical condition for the metaphysical prioritisation of circulation, in both India and Greece, was a degree of engagement in pervasive monetary circulation that was rejected by Parmenides and the early *Upanishads.* Early Buddhist texts are the first Indian texts to describe society as a whole, beyond the narrow Vedic milieu. The society that they describe is monetised. The Buddha is represented as preaching to vast numbers, and his lifetime in all likelihood coincided with the rapid spread of numerous coins of value low enough for everyday usage. The same can be said also of the lifetime of Herakleitos. The sixth-century monetisation of the Ionian city-states coincided with – and was probably a factor in – their remarkable economic and cultural flourishing and their commercial prosperity. We may note en passant that this far outstripped the polis of Parmenides, the recently founded colony of Elea, whose economy was monetised in his lifetime but probably precarious – as dependent on fishing, passing ships and some agriculture.

These are, crudely summarised, the conditions for the metaphysical prioritisation of circulation in India and Greece. Now for the difference. In 16§B we distinguished between the *communal* perspective on circulation represented by the Ionian cosmologists (including Herakleitos) and the *individual* perspective on circulation represented by the doctrine of deliverance through karma from the miserable cosmic circulation called *saṃsāra*, a doctrine shared by early Buddhism. We cannot in fact be sure

[9] E.g. Gombrich (2013) 9. [10] 13§D; B90; B85.

that the Ionians did not in one or more texts now lost propound such a doctrine of deliverance, as some Greeks certainly did. But there is no indication of it in the substantial evidence for Herakleitos: if, indeed, he did not propound it, how would we explain this significant difference (despite the striking similarities) from early Buddhism?

The communal consciousness that Greek coinage derived from its early association with the communal ritual of sacrifice is expressed in the practice of each polis issuing coins with its own distinctive emblems (like the Ephesian bee or Athenian owl). By contrast, the punchmarks on early Gangetic coins provide no evidence for the association of money with communality or with any particular community: this coheres with the absence of community from the Indian texts of our period. Here we touch on a profound difference from the India of the Buddha. The communal identity, strength, prosperity and splendour of Ephesos owed much, surely, to the circulation of coinage, which derived from communal sacrifice and joined it at the heart of the polis, whereas early Gangetic coins may have been introduced from above, under the influence of a remote culture, to pay soldiers. Mid-sixth-century BCE Ephesos was embellished by the construction of the temple of Artemis, and what is almost certainly a record of the monetary expenses of building it has survived.[11] Here, in this central public place, Herakleitos deposited his (quasi-mystic) *logos*. As a member of the royal family that held the priesthood of the Eleusinian (mystic) Demeter (11§C), he resigned the kingship.[12] From his metaphysical privileging of circulation from a *communal* perspective there was perhaps no possibility or need to escape. Instead, a model for *communal* salvation was provided by civic mystery-cult, the actual practice of which he seems to have rejected (11§B) along with a privileged individual role therein for himself.

The cosmic rite of passage interiorised by Herakeitos is communal, whereas the cosmic rite of passage interiorised by late Vedic thought is highly individualised. The Herakleitean *logos* (in universe and inner self) is *communal*, whereas karma (in universe and inner self) is accumulated by individuals. In Greek thought there is – we noted in 10§C – nothing comparable to karma, even among those who believed in the need for escape from the cycle of reincarnation. Indeed, the Greeks never even mention the karma of the Indians, even after the opening up of communications between the two

[11] Detailing silver and gold 'weighed out' from various sources: Seaford (2004) 79, 94.
[12] DK22 A1(6), A2.

cultures after 326 BCE. Why this absence? The answer deserves a new section.

17§B Why Did the Greeks Not Have Karma?

Part of the explanation for the absence of karma from Greece is that in Greece EIR was supplemented and then marginalised by other forms of compensatory metaphysics. Punishment in the hereafter[13] and inherited guilt[14] became more prominent in Greece than in India, reflecting the greater strength and ideological importance of the Greek state with its comprehensive judicial function.[15]

Another part of the answer is the importance of the individual Vedic sacrificer: we have seen that the power of his action contributes to the development of the concept of brahman, and that the power of his action and of the wealth that he thereby transfers to the divine sphere contributes to the development of the concept of karma. There is nothing corresponding to this in Greek ritual. Both terms are, in being reified, abstracted from the practice of ritual, and yet retain the autonomous power, specific but imperceptible, that derives from ritual – in metaphysical synthesis with the imperceptible universality of monetary power-substance. This development produces on the one hand brahman, whose imperceptible *universality* is *unchanging*, and on the other karma, which is a metaphysical synthesis of (ritual) action with the power of *individually accumulated* monetary substance to drive *circulation*. Brahman and karma polarise, corresponding respectively with Parmenidean Being and Herakleitean *logos*-embodying fire.

The latter resembles karma as a cosmisation of the universal impersonal power of money creating ordered cosmic circulation that includes the inner self, with ethical implications (karma as intention, *logos* as calculation or understanding). Moreover, karma ensures ultimate justice, and so perhaps

[13] For India, see Horsch (1971) 106; Keith (1925) 409–10.

[14] The Indian evidence is slight and confined to the earliest texts, esp. RV 7.86.5; Oldenberg (1894) 289; Krishan (1997) 417. Greek inherited guilt (2§E n.100) may combine with EIR (Gagné 2013: 27–32, 147); and it was occasionally associated with inherited wealth: i.e. inherited wealth might affect the individual (if unjustly acquired) negatively (albeit metaphysically); but the wealth is (unlike metaphysically inherited karma) real: Gagné (2013) 31–4; Proclus *In Cratylum* 93 (in 395c); Hermias *In Phaedonem* 96.9–11 (in 244d). Athenian tragedy approaches this idea, notably A. *Septem*: Seaford (2012) 158–77.

[15] This function was cosmised, but also tended to replace the collective responsibility of the clan with individual responsibility, leaving a gap that was then filled by the idea of *divine* punishment for the offspring or descendants of transgressors (2§E) – perpetuating the old idea of clan responsibility (albeit only at the metaphysical level) as well as accommodating the undeserved suffering of the innocent and the impunity of the criminal.

does the *logos*.[16] This makes the *logos*-embodying fire the closest early Greek idea to karma.

But it is not very close. At the centre of the Vedic cosmic rite of passage, and so of metaphysics, is the irreducible self, which even grows in importance by interiorising the world controlled by sacrifice. Karma, emerging from this process, is a power (in contrast to Parmenidean Being) and (in contrast to Herakleitean fire) imperceptible and untransformable into other things. At the centre of the Greek cosmic rite of passage, by contrast, is the absorption of the individual into the group, and at the centre of Greek sacrifice is the communal meal, which in its division into equal portions contributed to the genesis of coinage. Greek sacrifice conspicuously legitimated the absolute ownership by individuals of equal portions (on spits, which gave their name to coins) of sanctified communal wealth. And so, the metaphysical power-substance of Greek monism derives – in part and indirectly (via money) – from the communal substance (spits with meat) distributed in the sacrifice. Karma, on the other hand, originates in the individual's correct performance of the sacrifice, by which he could accumulate *iṣṭāpūrta* and *sukṛta* (9§BC), which karma eventually surpassed as what could be accumulated by non-sacrificial action. And so individual accumulation distinguishes karma from Herakleitean fire (as well as from brahman).

Especially illuminating of the absence of karma in Greece is the account of EIR in Plato. Whereas in India the relation between the individual and EIR is mediated by karma, in Plato there is no such mediation. How do we explain this difference?

Plato cosmises both unchanging abstract Being (like Parmenides) and monetised circulation (like Herakleitos): it is the absorption of the philosopher in self-sufficient abstract Being (abstracted from circulation) that allows him to escape from the attachment to corporeality and so from the cycle of rebirth, just as in everyday life it is possession of abstract, seemingly self-sufficient *ousia* (money, Being) that promotes and permits his lofty detachment from the cycle of money. In imagining the permanent abstract self-sufficiency of monetary value, Plato unconsciously provides himself with a model for the escape of the philosopher from the cycle of rebirth.[17] Of the two opposed and complementary essences of money, the unchanging abstraction attained by philosophy is ontologically privileged over

[16] If the point of B102 ('for god all things are fine and good and just, but men have supposed some things unjust and some just') is the human failure to understand the communal *logos* (B1, B2, etc.).

[17] *Phaedo* 80d–84b; *Phaedrus* 248c–249d.

circulation, and this structure is also projected on to the afterlife, in which escape from the cycle of reincarnation to permanent well-being is attained by philosophy.

Whereas the first step of Upanishadic thought is 'who am I really?', the first step of early Greek philosophy is 'what really exists?' But the latter cannot be simply explained as somehow the natural first step of philosophy. It is rather the basis for the cosmisation of the abstract power-substance by which the prized self-sufficiency of philosophers and other privileged citizens is constituted. Reality turns out to have at its heart the single abstract power-substance from which they live. True, money is in Plato both projected *and* ethicised (as is karma), for the projected abstract power-substance is identified as the 'form of the good'.[18] But whereas karma arises from the interaction of ritual *karman* with money in circulation, the abstract form of the good arises from the cosmisation of unchanging monetary value.

The Indian renouncer, in contrast to Plato, rejects the world as a whole. What we know of the Indian sages in the period before and during the emergence of Buddhism suggests a withdrawal from the monetary cycle in the opposite direction, not into the self-sufficiency conferred on the Greek aristocrat by his possession of abstract value but rather into homeless renunciation, into release from the cycle of monetised relations as analogous to release from the cycle of rebirth, as preparation for the world that knows neither debtors nor creditors (10§A).

Buddhism arose in a commercial milieu: there is evidence for early Buddhist monks associating with merchants, and the reinvestment of income and commercial intelligence are praised in early Buddhist texts.[19] And yet it seems that from the earliest times the monks refused to accept money and to buy or sell.[20] Accordingly, the rise of Buddhism has been interpreted by some as legitimating, and by others as rejecting, the commercial values of the new society. Gombrich appositely observes that 'having it both ways is precisely what religions excel at'. Satisfying very different needs may promote success.[21] We may add, more specifically, that Buddhism rejects the new monetary cycle in this world while ethicising it in the next. Buddhist metaphysics provides an ethicised cosmisation of the commercial milieu in which Buddhism originated and flourished: monetisation creates

[18] See 6§D n.34. [19] DN 3.188; AN 1.116. [20] Gombrich (2006) 104–5.

[21] Gombrich (2006) xii, 14. Cf. Marx (1973) 232 (written as early as 1857–8): 'The cult of money has its asceticism, its self-denial, its self-sacrifice – economy and frugality, contempt for mundane, temporal and fleeting pleasures; the chase after the *eternal* treasure. Hence the connection between English Puritanism, or also Dutch Protestantism, and money-making'.

not only the problems (isolation, injustice) but also a metaphysical model for their solution. The early Buddhist conception of the inner self is formed neither within the Vedic sacrificial tradition (whatever it may have taken from it) nor – like the Greek inner self – through introjection of money. Rather it rejects not only the practice both of sacrifice and of monetised relations but also – with the doctrine of *anatta* (no self) – the irreducible unitary inner self promoted by both kinds of practice. And yet Buddhism is also influenced by the new all-pervasive circulation of money, which it metaphysically ethicises and interiorises. A monk removing an inner hindrance is compared to a businessman paying off a debt.[22]

Platonic metaphysics is constructed from ontologically prioritising one of the opposed essences of money over the other (an *intramundane* opposition). The unchanging abstract Being of money provides a model for detachment from all that attends monetary circulation in this world and from the miserable cycle of reincarnation in the hereafter. But the Indian renouncer, in rejecting this world *as a whole*, adopts an *extramundane* perspective.[23] And so what he ontologically privileges is an imagined world that corrects this one, an ethicised version of this (monetised) world *as a whole*, including the power of money to drive and determine circulation. The cycle of reincarnation is – as it is for Plato – as miserable as the monetary cycle, and escape from both is desirable. But because the circulatory power of money is not (as it is for Plato) rejected in favour of abstract Being, it is in the invisible world ethicised, synthesised with the autonomous power-substance that derives from the power of sacrificial ritual (*karman*), and endowed with features of money that include being accumulated so as to improve well-being within the cycle and to facilitate escape from it.

In India the two fundamental powers that seem to determine the fate of the individual – lineage (expressed in family and caste) and money – are cosmised as reincarnation and karma. This invisible symbiosis holds in place the same symbiosis in this world, by providing (a) ethical and metaphysical justification for the vast differences that developed in our period between the status and wealth of individuals and of lineages

22 MN 1.277 (*Maha-Assapura Sutta*).

23 Dumont (1985) distinguishes the individualism of the Indian renouncer, as an *outworldly* individual, from modern (inworldly) individualism, which originated in a fusion of Christianity with the outworldly individualism that began with Hellenistic philosophy (especially Stoicism). For an explanation of this Hellenistic outworldliness 'we should look first of all to philosophy itself', which 'fosters individualism, because reason, universal principle, is in practice at work through the particular person who exercises it' (97). The obvious difference of this approach from mine deserves exploration, which I cannot provide here.

(including castes), and (b) the hope of return (through good action) to this world in a better individual position or a better lineage (including caste). The traditional structure of caste lineage is protected – by the ethicised cosmisation of money – against the dissolving and atomising power of money in this world. A result of all this is that the Indian solution differs sharply from the Greek not only by virtue of karma but also by virtue of the lasting centrality of the idea of reincarnation.

Bibliography

Aglietta, M. and Orléan, A. (1998) *La Monnaie Souveraine*. Paris: Jacob.

Akin, D. and Robbins, J. (1999) *Money and Modernity: State and Local Currencies in Melanesia*. Pittsburgh, PA: University of Pittsburgh Press Association of Social Anthropology in Melanesia Monograph Series.

Allen, N. J. (2016) 'The Common Origin Approach to Comparing Indian and Greek Philosophy', in Seaford (2016), 12–27.

Anspach, M. (1998) 'Les fondaments rituels de la transaction monétaire, ou comment remercier un boureau', in Aglietta and Orléan, 53–83.

Arbman, E. (1926) and (1927) 'Untersuchungen zur primitiven Seelenvorstellung mit besonderer Rücksicht auf Indien'. Parts I and II, *Monde Oriental*, 26 (85–226) and 27 (1–185).

Arora, U. P. (1996) *Greeks on India: Skylax to Aristoteles*. Bareilly: Indian Society for Greek and Roman Studies.

Bailey, G. and Mabbett, I. (2003) *The Sociology of Early Buddhism*. Cambridge: Cambridge University Press.

Barraud, C., de Coppet, D., Iteanu, A. and Jamous, R. (eds.) (1994) *Of Relations and the Dead: Four Societies Viewed from the Angle of Their Exchanges*. Explorations in Anthropology. Oxford and Providence: Berg.

Basham, A. L. (1951) *History and Doctrines of the Ājivīkas*. London: Luzac.

Bayne, T. (2010) *The Unity of Consciousness*. Oxford: Oxford University Press.

Bechert, H. (ed.) (1995) *When did the Buddha Live?* Delhi: Sri Satguru.

Bechert, H. (2001) 'Die Entdeckung der Heiligen Schriften des Buddhismus entlang der Seidenstraße und ihre Bedeutung für die Buddhismusforschung', *Akademie-Journal*, 2/2001. (Union der deutschen Akademie der Wissenschaften, Mainz), 36–41.

Beckwith, C. (2015) *Greek Buddha: Pyrrho's Encounter with Early Buddhism in Central Asia*. Princeton, NJ: Princeton University Press.

Bellah, R. N., and Joas, H. (eds.) (2012) *The Axial Age and Its Consequences*. Cambridge, MA: Harvard University Press.

Berger, P. (1967) *The Sacred Canopy: Elements of a Sociological Theory of Religion*. New York, NY: Doubleday.

Bernabé, A., Kahle, M. and Santamaría, M. A. (eds.) (2011) *Reencarnación: La Transmigración del las Almas Entre Oriente Y Occidente*. Madrid: Abada.

Betegh, G. (2006) 'Eschatology and Cosmology: Models and Problems', in M. M. Sassi (ed.) *La costruzione del discorso filosofico nell'età dei Presocratici*. Pisa: Edizioni dell Normale. 29–50.

(2007) 'On the Physical Aspect of Herakleitos' Psychology', *Phronesis*, 52.1.3–32.

Bhandare, S. (2012) 'From Kautilya to Kosambi and Beyond: The Quest for a 'Mauryan/Aśokan' Coinage', in P. Olivelle, J. Leoshko and H. P. Ray (eds.) *Reimagining Aśoka: Memory and History*. Oxford: Oxford University Press. 93–128.

Biardeau, M. and Malamoud, C. (1976) *Le sacrifice dans l'Inde ancienne*. Paris: Presses Universitaires de France.

Black, B. (2007) *The Character of the Self in Ancient India*. Albany, NY: State University of New York Press.

Blezer, H. (1992) 'Prana', in van den Hoek et al., 20–49.

Blutzenberger, K. (1996) and (1998) 'Ancient Indian Conceptions on Man's Destiny After Death: The Beginnings and the Early Development of the Doctrine of Transmigration', I and II, *Berliner Indologische Studien*, 9/10.55–118 and 11/12.1–84. Berlin.

Bodewitz, H. (1973) *Jaiminīya Brāhmana I. 1–65*. Leiden: Brill.

(1985) 'Yama's Second Boon in the Kaṭha Upaniṣad', *Wiener Zeitschrift für die Kunde Südasiens*, 29.5–26.

(1991) *Light, Soul, and Visions in the Veda*. Poona: Bhandakar Oriental Research Institute.

(1992) 'King Prāna', in van den Hoek et al., 50–64.

(1996) 'Redeath and its Relation to Rebirth and Release', *Studien zur Indologie und Iranistik*, 20.27–46.

Bourriot, F. (1976) *Recherces sur la nature du Genos*. Paris: Champion.

Boyce, M. (1975) 'On the Zoroastrian Temple Cult of Fire', *Journal of the American Oriental Society*, 95.3.454–65.

Braude, S. (1995) *First-Person Plural*. Lanham, MD: Rowman and Littlefield.

Bremmer, J. (1983) *The Early Greek Conception of the Soul*. Princeton, NJ: Princeton University Press.

Brereton, J. (1986) '*Tat Tvam Asi*' in Context', *Zeitschrift der Deutschen Morgenländischen Gesellschaft*, 136.98–109.

(1990) 'The Upanishads', in W. T. de Bary and I. Bloom (eds.) *Approaches to the Asian Classics*. New York, NY: Columbia University Press. 115–35.

(1999) 'Edifying Puzzlement: Ṛgveda 10. 129 and the Uses of Enigma', *Journal of the American Oriental Society*, 119.2.248–60.

Briant, P. (2002) *From Cyrus to Alexander: A History of the Persian Empire*. Winona Lake, IN: Eisenbrauns.

Bronkhorst, J. (1999) '*Why is There Philosophy in India?*' Amsterdam: Royal Netherlands Academy of Arts and Sciences.

(2007) *Greater Magadha*. Leiden: Brill.

(2011a) *Buddhism in the Shadow of Brahmanism*. Leiden: Brill.

(2011b) *Karma*. Honolulu, HI: University of Hawai'i Press.

(2016) *How the Brahmins Won: From Alexander to the Guptas*. Leiden: Brill.

Brown, W. N. (1965) 'Theories of Creation in the Rig Veda', *Journal of the American Oriental Society*, 85.1.23–34.

Burkert, W. (1969) 'Das Proōmium des Parmenides und die Katabasis des Pythagoras', *Phronesis*, 14.1–30.

(1972) *Lore and Science in Ancient Pythagoreanism* (translation). Cambridge, MA: Harvard University Press.

(1983) *Homo Necans* (translation). Berkeley: University of California Press.

(1985) *Greek Religion, Archaic and Classical* (translation). Oxford: Blackwell.

Burley, M. (2013) 'Reincarnation and Ethics', *Journal of the American Academy of Religion*, 81.1.162–87.

Butler, J. (1997) *The Psychic Life of Power: Theories in Subjection*. Palo Alto, CA: Stanford University Press.

Caland, W. (1931) *Pancavimsa-Brāhmaṇa: The Brāhmaṇa of Twenty-Five Chapters*. (Bibliotheca Indica 255). Calcutta: Asiatic Society of Bengal.

Carrithers, M., Collins, S. and Lukes, S. (eds.) (1985) *The Category of the Person: Anthropology, Philosophy, History*. Cambridge: Cambridge University Press.

Cavallin, C. (2003a) *The Efficacy of Sacrifice*. Göteborg: Institutionen för religionsvetenskap.

(2003b) 'Sacrifice as Action and Actions as Sacrifice', in T. Ahlbäck and B. Dahla (eds.) *Ritualistics*. Abo, Finland: Donner Institute for Research in Religious and Cultural History. 19–35.

(2013) *Ritualization and Human Interiority*. Copenhagen: Museum Tusculum Press.

Chakravarti, U. (1985) 'Of Dasas and Karmakaras. Servile Labour in Ancient India', in U. Patnaik and M. Dingwaney (eds.) *Chains of Servitude: Bondage and Slavery in India*. Hyderabad: Sangam Books. 35–75.

(1987) *The Social Dimensions of Early Buddhism*. New Delhi: Munshiram Manoharlal.

Chattopadhyaya, D. (2006) *Lokāyata: A Study of Ancient Indian Materialism*. 8th edition. New Delhi: People's Publishing House.

Chaturvedi, A. (2016) 'Harmonia and ṛta in the Ṛgveda', in Seaford (2016), 40–54.

Clarke, M. (1999) *Flesh and Spirit in the Songs of Homer: A Study of Words and Myths*. Oxford: Clarendon Press.

Claus, D. (1981) *Toward the Soul*. New Haven, CT: Yale University Press.

Cohen, S. (2008) *Text and Authority in the Older Upanishads*. Leiden: Brill.

Collins, S. (1982) *Selfless Persons: Imagery and Thought in Theravāda Buddhism*. Cambridge: Cambridge University Press.

Connolly, P. (1997) 'The Vitalistic Antecedents of the Atman-Brahman Concept', in Connolly and Hamilton, 21–38.

Connolly, P. and Hamilton, S. (eds.) (1997) *Indian Insights: Buddhism, Brahmanism and Bhakti: Papers from the Annual Spalding Symposium on Indian Religions*. London: Luzac.

Cribb, J. (2005) *The Indian Coinage Tradition: Origins, Continuity and Change*. Nashik: IIRNS Publications.

Currie, B. (2005) *Pindar and the Cult of Heroes*. Oxford: Oxford University Press.

Davies, J. K. (1988) 'Religion and the State', in J. Boardman, N. G. L. Hammond, D. M. Lewis and M. Ostwald (eds.) *The Cambridge Ancient History*, Vol. IV, 2nd edition. Cambridge: Cambridge University Press. 368–88.

Deussen, P. (1906) *The Philosophy of the Upanishads* (translation). Edinburgh: Clark.

(1915) *Allgemeine Geschichte der Philosophie: mit besonderer Berücksichtigung der Religionen,* Vol. 1.1. *Allgemeine Einleitung und Philosophie des Veda bis auf die Upanishads*. Leipzig: Brockhaus.

Diels, H. (1909) *Herakleitos von Ephesos*. 2nd edition. Berlin: Weidmannsche Buchhandlung.

Doniger, W. (1981) *The Rig Veda*. London: Penguin Classics.

Donlan, W. (1989) 'The Unequal Exchange between Glaucus and Diomedes in Light of the Homeric Gift Economy', *Phoenix*, 43.1–15.

Dumont, L. (1980) *Homo Hierarchicus* (translation). Chicago, IL: University of Chicago Press.

(1985) 'A Modified View of our Origins: The Christian Beginnings of Modern Individualism', in Carrithers et al., 93–122.

Dundas, P. (2002) *The Jains*. 2nd edition. London and New York: Routledge.

Durkheim, E. (1915) *The Elementary Forms of the Religious Life* (translation). London: Allen and Unwin.

Edgerton, F. (1965) *The Beginnings of Indian Philosophy*. London: George Allen and Unwin.

Edmunds, L. (1992) 'A Hermeneutic Commentary on the Eschatological Passage in Pindar Olympian 2 (57–83)', in U. Dill and C. Walde (eds.) *Antike Mythen: Medien, Transformationen und Konstruktionen*. Berlin and New York, NY: de Gruyter. 662–77.

Egge, J. (2002) *Religious Giving and the Invention of Karma in Theravāda Buddhism*. Richmond: Curzon.

Eggeling, J. (1882–1900) The *Satapatha*, 5 parts (translation). *The Sacred Books of the East*, Vols. 12, 26, 41, 43, 44. Oxford: Clarendon Press.

Emura, H. (2011) *Shunjū Sengoku jidai seidō kahei no seisei to tenkai*. Kyūko sōsho vol. 96. Tokyo: Kyūko Shoin.

Erdosy, G. (1988) *Urbanisation in Early Historic India*. British Archaeological Reports International Series 430. Oxford: British Archaeological Reports.

(1995) 'City States of North India and Pakistan at the Time of the Buddha', in R. Allchin (ed.) *The Archaeology of Early Historic South Asia*. Cambridge: Cambridge University Press. 99–122.

Falk, H. (1986) 'Vedisch upanisad', *Zeitschrift der Deutschen Morgenländischen Gesellschaft*, 136.80–97.

(1991) 'Silver, Lead and Zinc in Early Indian Literature', *South Asian Studies*, 7.111–17.

(1993) *Schrift im alten Indien*. Tübingen: Gunter Narr.

Fauconnet, P. (1928) *La Responsabilité*. 2nd edition. Paris: Alcan.

Findly, E. B. (2003) *Dāna: Getting and Giving in Pali Buddhism*. Delhi: Motilal Barnasidass.
Finley, M. (1963–4) 'Between Slavery and Freedom', *Comparative Studies in Society and History*, 6.233–49.
(1981) *Economy and Society in Ancient Greece*. London: Chatto and Windus.
Fränkel, H. (1975) *Early Greek Philosophy and Poetry*. Translated by M. Hadas and J. Willis. Oxford: Blackwell.
Fujii, M. (2011) 'The Recovery of the Body After Death: A Prehistory of the Devayāna and Pitryāna', in B. Tikkanen and A. M. Butters (eds.) *Purvaparaprajnabhinandanam: East and West, Past and Present. Indological and other Essays in Honour of Klaus Karttunen*. Helsinki: Finnish Oriental Society. 103–20.
Furley, D. (1987) *The Greek Cosmologists*, Vol. 1. *The Formation of the Atomic Theory and Its Earliest Critics*. Cambridge: Cambridge University Press.
Fynes, R. (2015) 'Coined Money and Early Buddhism', *The Journal of the Oxford Centre for Buddhist Studies*, 8.146–54.
Gagarin, M. (1981) *Drakon and Early Athenian Homicide Law*. New Haven, CT: Yale University Press.
Gagné, R. (2007) 'Winds and Ancestors: The Physika of Orpheus', *HSCP*, 103.1–24.
(2013) *Ancestral Fault in Ancient Greece*. Cambridge: Cambridge University Press.
Ganeri, J. (2012) *The Concealed Art of the Soul*. Oxford: Oxford University Press.
Gangopadhyaya, M. (1980) *Indian Atomism, History and Sources*. Atlantic Highlands, NJ: Humanities Press.
Gaskin, R. (1990) 'Do Homeric Heroes Make Real Decisions?', *Classical Quarterly*, 40.1.1–15.
Geertz, C. (1984) '"From the Native's Point of View": On the Nature of Anthropological Understanding', in *Local Knowledge: Further Essays in Interpretive Anthropology*. New York, NY: Basic Books.
Gehlen, A. (1964) *Urmensch und Spätkultur*. Frankfurt: Athenäum Verlag.
Geldner, K. F. (1951) *Der Rig-Veda*. 3 vols. Cambridge, MA: Harvard University Press.
Gemelli Marciano, M. L. (2013) *Parmenide: suoni, immagini, esperienza*. Eleatica 3. Sankt Augustin: Academia Verlag.
Ghosh, A. (1973) *The City in Early Historical India*. Simla: Indian Institute of Advanced Study.
Giovinazzo, G. (2000/1) 'Les indiens à Suse', *AION*, 60.59–76.
Glotz, G. (1904) *La solidarité de la famille dans le droit criminelle en Grèce*. Paris: Fontemoing.
Gombrich, R. (1971) '"Merit Transference" in Sinhalese Buddhism', *History of Religions*, 11.2.203–19.
(1996) *How Buddhism Began*. London: Athlone Press.
(2006) *Theravāda Buddhism*. 2nd edition. London and New York: Routledge.

(2013) *What the Buddha Thought*. Corrected edition. Sheffield: Equinox.
Gonda, J. (1950) *Notes on Brahman*. Utrecht: Beyers.
(1955) 'Reflections on *Phaedra-* in Vedic Texts', *Indian Linguistics*, 16.53–71. H.
(1965) *Change and Continuity in Indian Religion*. The Hague: Mouton.
(1966) *Loka. World and Heaven in the Veda*. Verhandelingen der Koninklijke Nederlandse Akademie van Wetenschappen, Afd. Letterkunde, n.r. 73.1. Amsterdam.
(1975) *Vedic Literature. A History of Indian Literature*, Vol. 1. Wiesbaden: Harrassowitz.
(1982–3) 'All, Universe and Totality in the *Śatapatha Brāhmaṇa*', *Journal of the Oriental Institute*, (Baroda), 32.1–17.
(1991) *The Functions and Significance of Gold in the Veda*. Leiden: Brill.
Gouldner, A. (1967) *Enter Plato*. London: Routledge and Kegan Paul.
Graeber, D. (2001) *Toward an Anthropological Theory of Value*. New York and Basingstoke: Palgrave.
(2011) *Debt: The First 5000 Years*. New York, NY: Melville.
Graf, F. and Iles Johnston, S. (2007) *Ritual Texts for the Afterlife*. London and New York: Routledge.
Graham, D. (2006) *Explaining the Cosmos: The Ionian Tradition of Scientific Philosophy*. Princeton, NJ: Princeton University Press.
Grassmann, H. (1873) *Wörterbuch zum Rigveda*. Leipzig: Brockhaus.
Greenfield, P. M. (2009) 'Linking Social Change and Developmental Change: Shifting Pathways of Human Development', *Developmental Psychology*, 45.2.401–18.
Gregory, C. A. (1982) *Gifts and Commodities*. London: Academic Press.
(1997) *Savage Money*. Amsterdam: Harwood Academic Publishers.
Griffith, R. T. H. (1926) *The Hymns of the Rigveda*. 2 vols.Benares: Lazarus.
Gupta, P. L. (1966) 'The Chronology of Punch-Marked Coins', in Narain and Gopal, 1–18.
Gupta, P. L. and Hardaker, T. (2014) *Punchmarked Coins of the Indian Subcontinent: Magadha-Mauryan Series*. Revised edition.Mumbai: IIRNS Publications.
Guthrie, W. (1962) *A History of Greek Philosophy*, Vol. 1. Cambridge: Cambridge University Press.
(1965) *A History of Greek Philosophy*, Vol. 2. Cambridge: Cambridge University Press.
Hahn, R. (2001) *Anaximander and the Architects*. Albany: SUNY Press.
Halbfass, W. (1988) *India and Europe: An Essay in Understanding*. Albany, NY: State University of New York Press.
(1991) *Tradition and Reflection: Explorations in Indian Thought*. Albany, NY: State University of New York Press.
(1992) *On Being and What There is: Classical Vaiśeṣika and the History of Indian Ontology*. Albany, NY: State University of New York Press.
(2000) *Karma und Wiedergeburt im Indischen Denken*. Munich: Diederichs.
Hale, W. E. (1986) *Asura in Early Vedic Religion*. Delhi: Motilal Barnasidas.

Hardaker, T. (2011) 'Aspects of Human Society from the Earliest Punchmarked Coins of the Indian Subcontinent', in S. Bhandare and S. Garg (eds.) *Felicitas: Essays in Numismatics, Epigraphy & History in honour of Joe Cribb*. Mumbai: Reesha Books International. 203–21.

(2019) *Punchmarked Coinage of the Indian Subcontinent: Non-Imperial Series North of the Deccan*. Mumbai: IIRNS Publications.

Harrison, A. R. W. (1968) *The Law of Athens: The Family and Property*. Oxford: Oxford University Press.

Hatab, L. (1992) 'Plotinus and the Upanishads', in R. Baine Harris (ed.) *Neoplatonism and Indian Thought*. Delhi: Sri Satgura. 27–43.

Havelock, E. (1963) *Preface to Plato*. Cambridge, MA: Harvard University Press.

Heesterman, J. (1957) *The Ancient Indian Royal Consecration: The Rājasūya Described According to the Yajus Texts and Annoted* (sic). The Hague: Mouton.

(1959) 'Reflections on the Significance of the Dakṣiṇā', *Indo-Iranian Journal*, 3.241–58.

(1983) 'Other Folks' Fire', in J. F. Staal (ed.) *Agni. The Vedic Ritual of the Fire Altar*. 2 vols. Berkeley, CA: Asian Humanities Press. 2.76–94.

(1985) *The Inner Conflict of Tradition*. Chicago, IL: University of Chicago Press.

(1988) 'Householder and Wanderer', in Madan, 251–71.

(1993) *The Broken World of Sacrifice: An Essay in Ancient Indian Ritual*. Chicago, IL: University of Chicago Press.

Helfer, J. (1968) 'The Initiatory Structure of the Kathopanisad', *History of Religions*, 7.348–67.

Hénaff, M. (2010) *The Price of Truth* (translation of *La prix de la vérité*, Editions de Seuil, 2002). Palo Alto, CA: Stanford University Press.

Hock, H. (2006) 'Reflexivisation in the *Rig-Veda* (and beyond)', in B. Tikkanen and H. Hettrich (eds.) *Themes and Tasks in Middle Indo-Aryan Linguistics: Papers of the 12th World Sanskrit Conference*, Vol. 5, 19–44. New Delhi.

Holmes, B. (2010) *The Symptom and the Subject*. Princeton, NJ: Princeton University Press.

Horsch, P. (1971) 'Vorstufen der Indischen Seelenwanderungslehre', *Asiatische Studien (= Études Asiatiques)*, 25.99–157.

Hubert, H. and Mauss, M. (1898) *Sacrifice: Its Nature and Functions* (translation). Chicago, IL: Chicago University Press.

Huffman, C. (1993) *Philolaus of Croton*. Cambridge: Cambridge University Press.

Hussey, E. (1982) 'Epistemology and Meaning in Heraclitus', in M. Schofield and M. C. Nussbaum (eds.) *Language and Logos: Studies in Ancient Greek Philosophy Presented to G. E. L.Owen*. Cambridge: Cambridge University Press. 33–59.

Hutchinson, S. (1996) *Nuer Dilemmas: Coping with Money, War, and the State*. Berkeley, CA: University of California Press.

Jackson, P. and Sjödin, A.-P. (2016) (eds.) *Philosophy and the End of Sacrifice*. Sheffield, and Bristol, Connecticut: Equinox.

Jacoby, F. (1944) 'ΓΕΝΕΣΙΑ: A Forgotten Festival of the Dead', *Classical Quarterly*, 38.65–75.

Jahn, T. (1987) *Zum Wortfeld "Seele-Geist" in der Sprache Homers*. Munich: *Zetemata* 83.

Jameson, M., Jordan, D. and Kotansky, R. (1993) *A lex Sacra from Selinous. Greek, Roman, and Byzantine Monographs* 11. Durham, NC: Duke University.

Jamison, S. (1996) Review of Heesterman (1993), *Method and Theory in the Study of Religion*, 8.1.103–8.

(2016) 'The Principle of Equivalence and the Interiorization of Ritual', in Jackson and Sjödin, 15–32.

Jamison, S. and Brereton, J. (2014) *The Rigveda*. 3 vols. Oxford: Oxford University Press.

Jeremiah, E. (2012) *The Emergence of Reflexivity in Greek Language and Thought*. Leiden: Brill.

Johnson, W. J. (1995) *Harmless Souls: Karmic Bondage and Religious Change in Early Jainism with Special Reference to Umāsvāti and Kundakunda*. Delhi: Motilal Banarsidass.

Jurewicz, J. (2004), 'Prajapati, the Fire and the Pancāgni-vidyā', in P. Balcerowicz and M. Mejor (eds.) *Essays in Indian Philosophy, Religion and Literature*. Delhi. 45–60.

(2007) 'The Fiery Self: The Rgvedic Roots of the Upanishadic Concept of Atman', in D. Stasik and A. Trynkowska (eds.) *Teaching on India in Central and Eastern Europe*. Warsaw: Dom Wydawniczy Elipsa. 123–37.

(2008) 'Rebirth Eschatology in the *Rigveda*', *Indologica Tauriniensia*, 34.183–210.

(2010) *Fire and Cognition in the Rigveda*. Warsaw: Dom Wydawniczy Elipsa.

(2016a) *Fire, Death and Philosophy. A History of Ancient Indian Thinking*. Warsaw: Dom Wydawniczy Elipsa.

(2016b) 'The Concept of ṛta in the Rigveda', in Seaford (2016), 28–39.

Kahn, C. (1979) *The Art and Thought of Herakleitos*. Cambridge: Cambridge University Press.

Kakinuma, Y. (2011) *Chūgoku kodai kahei keizaishi kenkyū. Studies on the History of the Monetary Economy of Ancient China*. Kyūko sōsho vol. 92. Tokyo: Kyūko shoten.

Kant, I. (1787) *Critique of Pure Reason* (translation by N. K. Smith, 1964). New York, NY: St. Martin's Press.

Karttunen, K. (1989) *India in Early Greek Literature*. Helsinki: Finnish Oriental Society.

Kaye, J. (1998) *Economy and Nature in the Fourteenth Century*. Cambridge: Cambridge University Press.

Keith, A. B. (1921) *Indian Logic and Atomism*. Oxford: Oxford University Press.

(1925) *The Religion and Philosophy of the Veda and the Upanishads*. 2 vols. Cambridge, MA: Harvard University Press.

Killingley, D. (1997) 'The Paths of the Dead and the Five Fires', in Connolly and Hamilton, 1–20.

Kingsley, P. (1999) *In the Dark Places of Wisdom*. Point Reyes, CA: The Golden Sufi Center.

(2003) *Reality*. Point Reyes, CA: The Golden Sufi Center.

Klaus, K. (2011) Review of Bronkhorst (2007), *Zeitschrift der Deutschen Morgenländischen Gesellschaft*, 161.1.216–22.

Kočandrle, R. and Couprie, D. (2017) *Apeiron: Anaximander on Generation and Destruction*. Berlin: Springer.

Koch, H. (1993) *Achaemeniden-Studien*. Wiesbaden: Harassowitz.

Kosambi, D. (1951) 'Ancient Kosala and Magadha', *Journal of the Bombay Branch of the Royal Asiatic Society for 1951*, 180–213.

(1965) *The Culture and Civilisation of Ancient India in Historical Outline*. London: Routledge and Kegan Paul.

Kouremenos, T., Parassoglou, G. M. and Tsantsanoglou, K. (2006) *The Derveni Papyrus*. Florence: Leo Olschki Editore.

Krishan, Y. (1997) *The Doctrine of Karma*. Delhi: Motilal Banarsidass.

Kuiper, F. B. J. (1960) 'The Ancient Aryan Verbal Contest', *Indo-Iranian Journal*, 4.4.217–81.

(1964) 'The Bliss of Asa', *Indo-Iranian Journal*, 8.2.96–129.

(1971) 'An Indian Prometheus?', *Asiatische Studien, Zeitschrift der Schweizerischen Gesellschaft für Asienkunde*, 25.86–98.

(1975) 'The Basic Concept of Vedic Religion', *History of Religions*, 15.2.107–20.

Kulikov, L. (2007) 'The Reflexive Pronouns in Vedic: A Diachronic and Typological Perspective', *Lingua*, 117.1412–33.

Kurke, L. (1991) *The Traffic in Praise: Pindar and the Poetics of Social Economy*. Ithaca, NY: Cornell University Press.

(1999) *Coins, Bodies, Games, and Gold*. Princeton, NJ: Princeton University Press.

Lacey, W. K. (1968) *The Family in Classical Greece*. London: Thames and Hudson.

Lacrosse, J. (2005) *Philosophie Comparée: Grèce, Inde, Chine*. Annales de l'institut de philosophie de l'université de Bruxelles. Paris: Vrin.

Lakoff, G. and Johnson, M. (2003) *Metaphors We Live By*. Chicago, IL: University of Chicago Press.

Lea, S. and Webley, P. (2006) 'Money as Tool, Money as Drug: The Biological Psychology of a Strong Incentive', *Behavioural and Brain Sciences*, 29.161–209.

Lehmann, W. P. (1992) 'SWAES: From the Middle to Pronominal Reflexive Markers', in C. Blank et al. (eds.) *Language and Civilisation vol.1*. Frankfurt: Peter Lang. 139–46.

Lévi, S. (1898) *La Doctrine du sacrifice dans les Brahmanas*. Paris: Leroux.

Lincoln, B. (1981) *Priests, Warriors, and Cattle. A Study in the Ecology of Religions*. Berkeley, CA: University of California Press.

LiPuma, E. (1998) 'Modernity and Forms of Personhood in Melanesia', in M. Lambek and A. Strathern (eds.) *Bodies and Persons*. Cambridge: Cambridge University Press. 53–79.

Lloyd, G. E. R. (1979) *Magic, Reason and Experience: Studies in the Origin and Development of Greek Science*. Cambridge: Cambridge University Press.

Lloyd-Jones, H. (1985) 'Pindar and the Afterlife', *Pindare. Entretiens de la Fondation Hardt*, 31.245–79.

Loeschner, H. (2012) 'Kanishka in Context with the Historical Buddha and Kushan Chronology', in V. Jayasval (ed.) *Glory of the Kushans – Recent Discoveries and Interpretations*. New Delhi: Aryan Books International. 137–94.

Lubin, T. (2005) 'The Transmission, Patronage, and Prestige of Brahmanical Piety from the Mauryas to the Guptas', in F. Squarcini (ed.) *Boundaries, Dynamics and Constructions of Traditions in South Asia*. Florence: Firenze University Press. 77–103.

Macpherson, C. B. (1962) *The Political Theory of Possessive Individualism*. Oxford: Oxford University Press.

Madan, T. (ed.) (1988) *Way of Life: King, Householder, Renouncer. Essays in Honour of Louis Dumont*. 2nd edition. Delhi: Motilal Barnasidass.

Magnone, P. (2016) 'Soul Chariots in Indian and Greek Thought: Polygeneisis or Diffusion?', in Seaford (2016), 149–67.

Malamoud, C. (1983) 'The Theology of Debt in Brahmanism', in C. Malamoud (ed.) *Debts and Debtors*. New Delhi: Vikas. 21–40.

(1996) *Cooking the World*. Oxford: Oxford University Press.

(1998) 'Le paiement des actes rituels dans l' Inde védique', in Aglietta and Orléan, 35–52.

Martin, A. and Primavesi, O. (1999) *L'Empédocle de Strasbourg (P. Strasb. gr. Inv. 1665–1666). Introduction, édition et commentaire*. Berlin and New York: de Gruyter.

Marx, K. (1973) *Grundrisse: Foundations of the Critique of Political Economy (Rough Draft)* (translation).London: Penguin.

Mauss, M. (1938) 'Une Catégorie de l'Esprit Humain: la Notion de Personne, Celle de "Moi"', *Journal of the Royal Anthropological Institute*, 68.263–281 (translated in Carrithers et al., 1–26).

(1965), *The Gift: Forms and Functions of Exchange in Archaic Societies* (translation of Essai sur le Don, 1925). New York, NY: Norton.

McDermott, J. P. (1984) *Development in the Early Buddhist Concept of kamma/karma*. New Delhi: Munshiram Manoharlal.

Merkelbach, R. (1962) *Roman und Mysterium in der Antike*. Munich and Berlin: C. H. Beck.

McEvilley. T. (2002) *The Shape of Ancient Thought: Comparative Studies in Greek and Indian Philosophies*: New York, NY: Allworth Press.

Meikle, S. (1995) *Aristotle's Economic Thought*. Oxford: Oxford University Press.

Minkowski, C. (1996) Review of Heesterman (1993), *Journal of the American Oriental Society*, 116.2.341–4.

Möller, A. (2000) *Naukratis: Trade in Archaic Greece*. Oxford: Oxford University Press.

Nanamoli, B. and Bodhi, B. (1995) *The Middle Length Discourses of the Buddha*. Boston: Wisdom Publications.

Narain, A. and Gopal, L. (eds.) (1966) *Seminar Papers on the Chronology of the Punch-Marked Coins*. Varanasi: Banaras Hindu University.

Noutsopoulos, T. (2015), 'The Role of Money in Plato's Republic, Book i. A Materialistic Approach', *Historical Materialism*, 23.2.131–56.

Oberlies, T. (2012) *Der Rigveda und seine Religion*. Berlin: Verlag der Weltreligionen.
Obeyesekere, G. (2002) *Imagining Karma*. Berkeley, CA: University of California Press.
Oldenberg, H. (1894) *Die Religion des Veda*. Berlin: Wilhelm Hertz.
Olivelle, P. (1993) *The Āśrama System*. New Delhi: Munshiram Manoharlal.
(1996) *Upanishads*. Oxford: Oxford University Press.
(1999) *Dharmasūtras. The Law Codes of Ancient India*. Oxford: Oxford University Press.
(2013) *King, Governance, and Law in Ancient India: Kautilya's Arthaśāstra*. New York, NY: Oxford University Press.
Orqueda, V. (2015) 'Semantic Change of *ātman-* in the *ṛgveda* and the *atharva-veda*', *Alfa. Revista de Linguística*, (São José Rio Preto), 59.2 São Paulo.
Owen, G. E. L. 1960. 'Eleatic Questions', *Classical Quarterly*, 10.84–102
Pande, G. C. (1995), *Studies in the Origins of Buddhism*. 4th edition. Delhi: Motilal Barnasidass.
Papaodopoulou, I. and Muellner, L. (2014) (eds.) *Poetry as Initiation*. Cambridge, MA: Harvard University Press Center for Hellenic Studies.
Parfit, D. (1984) *Reasons and Persons*. Oxford: Oxford University Press.
(1999) 'Experiences, Subjects, and Conceptual Schemes', *Philosophical Topics*, 26.217–20.
Parker, R. (1983) *Miasma: Pollution and Purification in Early Greek Religion*. Oxford: Oxford University Press.
(2005) *Polytheism and Society at Athens*. Oxford: Oxford University Press.
(2011) *On Greek Religion*. Ithaca, NY: Cornell University Press.
Parry, J. and Bloch, M. (1989) *Money and the Morality of Exchange*. Cambridge: Cambridge University Press.
Pinchard, A. (2009) *Les langues de sagesse dans la Grèce et l'Inde anciennes*, Geneva: Droz.
Prasad, M. (1966) 'Literary Evidence on the Chronology of Punch Marked Coins', in Narain and Gopal, 161–70.
Proferes, T. N. (2007) *Vedic Ideals of Sovereignty and the Poetics of Power*. New Haven, CT: American Oriental Society.
Rau, W. (1957) *Staat und Gesellscaft im Alten Indien nach den Brāhmaṇen-Texten dargestellt*. Wiesbaden: Harrassowitz.
(1997) 'The Earliest Literary Evidence of Permanent Vedic Settlements', in Witzel (1997), 203–6.
Renehan, R. (1980) 'On the Greek Origins of the Concepts Incorporeality and Immateriality', *Greek, Roman and Byzantine Studies*, 21.105–38.
Rhodes, P. J. (2006) 'The Reforms and Laws of Solon: An Optimistic View', in J. H. Blok and A. P. M. H. Lardinois, (eds.) *Solon of Athens*. Leiden: Brill.
Rhys Davids, T. W. (1890) translator, *The Questions of King Milinda*. 2 vols. *Sacred Books of the East*. Vols. 35 and 36.
Riedweg, C. (1987) *Mysterienterminologie bei Platon, Philon und Klemens von Alexandrien*. Berlin and New York: de Gruyter.
Riedweg, C. (2005) *Pythagoras* (translation). Ithaca, NY: Cornell University Press.

Robbiano, C. (2006) *Becoming Being: On Parmenides' Transformative Philosophy*. Sankt Augustin: Akademia Verlag.
Robinson, T. M. (1970) *Plato's Psychology*. Toronto: University of Toronto Press.
Roebuck, V. J. (2003) *The Upaniṣads*. London: Penguin.
Rosivach, V. J. (1994) *The System of Public Sacrifice in Fourth-Century Athens*. Atlanta, GA: Scholars Press.
Roth, G. (1993) 'Gosāla Mankhaliputta's Birth in a Cow-Stall, Including Notes on a Parallel in the Gospel of Luke', in R. Smet. and K. Watanabe (eds.) *Jain Studies in Honour of Josef Deleu.*Tokyo: Hon-no-Tomosha. 413–55.
Rotman, A. (2009) *Thus Have I Seen: Visualising Faith in Early Indian Buddhism*. New York and Oxford: Oxford University Press.
Ruin, H. (2016) 'Sacrificial Subjectivity: Faith and Interiorisation of Cultic Practice in the Pauline Letters', in Jackson and Sjödin, 197–218.
Russo, J. (2012) 'Rethinking Homeric Psychology: Snell, Dodds and their Critics', *Quaderni Urbinati di Cultura Classica*, 101.2.11–28.
Samuel, G. (2008) *The Origins of Yoga and Tantra: Indic Religions to the Thirteenth Century*. Cambridge: Cambridge University Press.
Schefer, C. (2000) 'Nur für Eingeweihte! Heraklit und die Mysterien', *Antike und Abendland*, 46.46–75.
Schlieter, J. (2013) 'Checking the Heavenly "Bank Account of *karma*": Cognitive Metaphors for *karma* in Western Perception and Early Theravāda Buddhism', *Religion*, 43.4.1–24.
Schlumberger, D. (1972) 'De la pensée grecque à la pensée bouddhique', *Académie des Inscriptions et Belles-Lettres. Comptes rendus des séances de l' année 1972*. Janvier-Mars. 188–9.
Schubring, W. (2000) *The Doctrine of the Jainas*. 2nd edition. Delhi: Motilal Banarsidass.
Schofield, M. (1991) 'Heraclitus' Theory of Soul and its Antecedents', in S. Everson (ed.) *Companions to Ancient Thought*, Vol. 2: *Psychology*. Cambridge: Cambridge University Press. 13–35.
(2006) *Plato*. Oxford: Oxford University Press.
Seaford, R. (1986) 'Immortality, Salvation, and the Elements', *Harvard Studies in Classical Philology*. 90.1–26 (reprinted as Seaford (2018) Chapter 9).
(1994) *Reciprocity and Ritual*. Oxford: Oxford University Press.
(1996) *Euripides: Bacchae*. Warminster: Aris and Phillips.
(1998) 'In the Mirror of Dionysos', in *The Sacred and the Feminine in Ancient Greece*. London and New York: Routledge. 128–46.
(2004) *Money and the Early Greek Mind*. Cambridge: Cambridge University Press.
(2005) 'Mystic Light in Aeschylus' Bassarai', *Classical Quarterly*, 55.602–6.
(2009) 'The Fluttering Soul', in U. Dill and C. Walde, *Antike Mythen. Medien, Transformationen und Konstruktionen*. Berlin and New York: de Gruyter. 406–14 (reprinted as Seaford [2018] Chapter 18).
(2010a) 'Zeus in Aeschylus: The Factor of Monetisation', in J. Bremmer and A. Erskine (eds.) *The Gods of Ancient Greece*. Edinburgh: Edinburgh University Press. 178–92.

(2010b) 'Mystic Light and Near-Death Experience', in M. Christopoulos and E. Karakantza (eds.), *Light and Darkness in Ancient Greek Religion*. Lanham, MD: Lexington. 201–6.

(2012a) *Cosmology and the Polis*. Cambridge: Cambridge University Press.

(2012b) 'Monetisation and the Genesis of the Western Subject', *Historical Materialism*, 20.1.1–25 (reprinted as Seaford (2018) Chapter 17).

(2013) 'The Politics of the Mystic Chorus', in J. Billings, F. Budelmann and F. Macintosh (eds.), *Choruses Ancient and Modern*. Oxford: Oxford University Press. 261–79.

(ed.) (2016) *Universe and Inner Self in Early Indian and Early Greek Thought*. Edinburgh: Edinburgh University Press.

(2017) 'The *Psuchē* from Homer to Plato: A Historical Sketch', in R. Seaford, J. Wilkins, and M. Wright (eds.), *Selfhood and the Soul: Essays on Ancient Thought and Literature in Honour of Christopher Gill*. Oxford: Oxford University Press.

(2018) *Tragedy, Ritual and Money in Ancient Greece: Selected Essays*, edited by R. Bostock. Cambridge: Cambridge University Press.

(2019) 'Cosmic Debt in Greece and India', in J. Weisweiler (ed.), *Debt: The First 3000 Years*. Oxford Studies in Early Empires. New York, NY: Oxford University Press.

Sharma, B. R. (1972) *The Concept of Ātman in the Principal Upanishads*. Delhi: Dinesh.

Sharples, R. W. (1983) '"But Why Has My Spirit Spoken With Me Thus?" Homeric Decision-Making', *Greece and Rome*. 30.1–7.

Singh, D. (2018) *Divine Currency: The Theological Power of Money in the West*. Palo Alto, CA: Stanford University Press.

Sirkar, D. C. (1968) *Studies in Indian Coins*. Delhi: Motilal Barnassidas.

Sisko, J. E., and Weiss, Y. (2015) 'A Fourth Alternative in Interpreting Parmenides', *Phronesis*, 60.1.40–59.

Smith, B. (1989) *Reflections on Resemblance, Ritual and Religion*. New York, NY: Oxford University Press.

Smith, B. (1990) 'Eaters, Food and Social Hierarchy in Ancient India: A Dietary Guide to a Revolution of Values', *Journal of the American Academy of Religion*, 57.2.177–205.

Smith, K. (2012) 'From Dividual and Individual to Porous Subjects', *Australian Journal of Anthropology*, 23.1.5–64.

Snell, B. (1960) *The Discovery of the Mind* (translation). New York, NY: Harper and Row.

Sohn-Rethel, A. (1978) *Intellectual and Manual Labour. A Critique of Epistemology*. London and Basingstoke: Macmillan.

Sorabji, R. (2006) *Self: Ancient and Modern Insights about Individuality, Life, and Death*. Oxford: Oxford University Press.

Spiro, M. (1970) *Buddhism and Society*. New York, NY: Harper and Row.

Stausberg, M. (2004) *Die Religion Zarathushtras*, Vol. 3. Stuttgart: Kohlhammer.

Stoneman, R. (1994) *Legends of Alexander the Great*. (Published as Everyman Paperback 2012 by I. B. Tauris).

Strathern, M. (1988) *The Gender of the Gift*. Berkeley, CA: University of California Press.
Sullivan, S. D. (1988) *Psychological Activity in Homer: A Study of Phrēn*. Ottawa: Carleton University Press.
(1995) *Psychological and Ethical Ideas. What Early Greeks Say*. Leiden: Brill.
(1997) *Aeschylus' Use of Psychological Terminology*. Montreal: McGill-Queen's University Press.
(1999) *Sophocles' Use of Psychological Terminology*. Ottawa: Carleton University Press.
(2000) *Euripides' Use of Psychological Terminology*. Montreal: McGill-Queen's University Press.
Taylor, C. (1989) *Sources of the Self*. Cambridge: Cambridge University Press.
Thapar, R. (1984) *From Lineage to State*. Oxford: Oxford University Press.
(1988) 'The Householder and the Renouncer in the Brahmanical and Buddhist Traditions', in Madan, 273–98.
(1994) 'Sacrifice, Surplus, and the Soul', *History of Religions*, 33.4.305–24.
(2002a) *The Penguin History of Early India*. London: Penguin.
(2002b) 'Army and Exercise of Power in Early India', in A. Chaniotis and P. Ducrey (eds.), *Army and Power in the Ancient World*. Stuttgart: Franz Steiner. 25–37.
Thomson, G. (1961) *The First Philosophers*. 2nd edition. London: Lawrence and Wishart.
Todd, S. C. (1993) *The Shape of Athenian Law*. Oxford: Oxford University Press.
Tor, S. (2017) *Mortal and Divine in Early Greek Epistemology*. Cambridge: Cambridge University Press.
Tull, H. W. (1989) *The Vedic Origins of Karma*. Albany, NY: State University of New York.
Ustinova, Y. (2009) *Caves and the Ancient Greek Mind*. Oxford: Oxford University Press.
(2013) 'To Live in Joy and Die with Hope: Experiential Aspects of Ancient Greek Mystery Rites', *Bulletin of the Institute of Classical Studies*, 56.2.110–23.
van den Hoek, A., Kolff, D. H. A., and Oort, M. S. (1992) *Ritual, State and History in South Asia. Essays in Honour of J. C. Heesterman*. Leiden: Brill.
van der Mije, S. (1991) Review of Jahn (1987), *Mnemosyne*, 44.3–4.440–45.
Vinogradov, J. G. (1991) 'Zur sachlichen and geschichtlichen Deutung der Orphiker-Plättchen von Olbia', in P. Borgeaud (ed.), *Orphisme et Orphée en l' honneur de J. Rudhardt*. Geneva: Recherches et Rencontres. 3.77–86.
Vlastos, G. (1973) *Platonic Studies*. Princeton, NJ: Princeton University Press.
Vohs, K. D., Mead, N. L. and Goode, M. R. (2006) 'The Psychological Consequences of Money', *Science*, 314.5802.1154–6.
von Falkenhausen, L. (2013) Review of Emura (2011), in *Tōyōshi kenkyū*, 72.2, 139–148 (English version posted on *Academia.edu*).
von Falkenhausen, L. (2014) Review of Kakinuma (2011), *Zhejiang University Journal of Art and Archaeology*, 1.278–92.
von Glahn, R. (2016) *The Economic History of China*. Cambridge: Cambridge University Press.

von Simson, G. (1995) 'Historical Background to the Rise of Buddhism and the Problem of Dating', in Bechert (1995), 169–77.

Wagle, N. K. (1966) *Society at the Time of the Buddha*. Bombay: Popular Prakashan.

Warder, A. K. (1956) 'On the Relationship Between Early Buddhism and Other Contemporary Systems', *Bulletin of the School of Oriental and African Studies*, 18.1.43–63.

Weber, M. (1958) *The Religion of India* (translation by H. H. Gerth and D. Martindale, original edition 1921). New York, NY: The Free Press.

Weber, S. A. (2003) 'Archaeobotany at Harappa: Indications for Change', in S. A. Weber and W. R. Belcher (eds.), *Indus Ethnobiology*. Lanham: Lexington Books. 174–98.

Wedin, M. V. (2014) *Parmenides' Grand Deduction*. Oxford: Oxford University Press.

Weiner, A. (1992) *Inalienable Possessions: The Paradox of Keeping-While-Giving*. Berkeley, CA: University of California Press.

West, M. L. (1971) *Early Greek Philosophy and the Orient*. Oxford: Oxford University Press.

(1983) *The Orphic Poems*. Oxford: Oxford University Press.

Whitaker, J. L. (2011) *Strong Arms and Drinking Strength: Masculinity, Violence, and the Body in Ancient India*. Oxford: Oxford University Press.

Whitney, D. W. and Lanman, C. R. (1905) *Atharva-veda Saṁhitā. Translated with a Critical and Exegetical Commentary*. Harvard Oriental Series, vols. vii and viii. Cambridge, MA: Harvard University Press.

Williams, B. (1993) *Shame and Necessity*. Berkeley, CA: University of California Press.

Witzel M. (1997) *Inside the Texts, Beyond the Texts. New Approaches to the Study of the Vedas*. Proceedings of the International Vedic Workshop. Harvard University, June 1989. Cambridge, MA.

Witzel, M. (1997a) 'The Development of the Vedic Canon and its Schools: The Social and Political Milieu', in Witzel (1997). 257–345.

Wright, R. (2010) *The Ancient Indus: Urbanism, Economy, and Society*. Cambridge: Cambridge University Press.

Wynne, A. (2010) 'The Buddha's "Skill in Means" and the Genesis of the Five Aggregate Teaching', *Journal of the Royal Asiatic Society*, 3.20.2.191–216.

(2011) Review of Bronkhorst (2007) on H-Buddhism, July 2011.

Yamazaki, G. (2005) *The Structure of Ancient Society: Theory and Reality of the Varṇa System*. Tokyo: Toyo Bunko.

Yü, Ying-Shih (2003) 'Between the Heavenly and the Human', in Tu Weiming and M. E. Tucker (eds.), *Confucian Spirituality*, Vol. 1. New York: Crossroad. 62–80.

Zaehner, R. C. (1961) *The Dawn and Twilight of Zoroastrianism*. London: Weidenfield and Nicholson.

Zuntz, G. (1971) *Persephone: Three Essays on Religion and Thought in Magna Graecia*. Oxford: Clarendon Press.

Index of Principal Ancient Passages

Acārāngasūtra
1.3.3.4: 182
1.8.6.1: 182
Aeschylus
fr. 70: 237
Aitareya Brāhmaṇa
8.21: 20
Aitareya Upaniṣad
1.1: 154
Alkaios
fr. 317: 305
Anaximander
B1: 239, 240
Anaximenes
B2: 238, 239, 265
Aṅguttara Nikāya
3.415: 204
5.57: 203–4
Apuleius
Metamorphoses
11.23: 292
Aristophanes
Clouds
319: 222
Aristotle
Metaphysics
983b: 236
Arthaśāstra
2.12.24: 28
5.3.14: 29
8.1.42–5: 29
Atharvaveda Saṃhitā
3.293: 210

Bṛhadāraṇyaka Upaniṣad
1.1.1–2: 114
1.2: 153, 161–2
1.3.1: 114
1.3.9–28: 115
1.3.17–18: 138
1.4: 153–4, 306
1.4.1–8: 116
1.4.6–10: 117–18
1.4.7: 120, 156
1.4.9: 113
1.4.10–11: 88, 118
1.4.15: 88, 118, 123
1.5.15: 20
1.5.21: 138
2.1.15–18: 128
2.1.18: 138
2.1.20 : 121, 160
2.4.5–12: 155, 159
2.4.14: 158–9
2.5: 329
2.5.10: 113
3.2.13: 170
3.4.2: 159
3.7.3–23: 122
3.7–8: 158
3.8.11: 160
3.9.1–9: 152–3
4.2.33: 135
4.3.7: 121
4.3.20: 135, 139, 238
4.3.33: 135
4.3.38: 128, 138
4.4.2: 121
4.4.6: 175
4.4.7: 128
4.4.7–13: 162
4.4.8–10: 176
4.4.18–9: 156, 162, 234
4.4.22: 20, 134
4.4.24: 134
4.5: 134
4.5.3: 135
4.5.6–8: 123–4
5.4.1: 110
5.5.1: 152
6.1.13: 138
6.2: 172

6.2.8: 127
6.2.9–16: 152, 177–8, 289
6.2.16: 93

Chāndogya Upaniṣad
1.9.1: 155
1.10–11: 23, 134
2.23.3: 155
3.12.7–9: 160
3.14: 160
3.14.2: 121
3.14.2–4: 120, 154
3.14.3: 123, 159
3.14.4: 120–1
3.18.1: 160
4.1.2–4: 136
4.2.4–5: 20
4.3.1–3: 157
4.3.38: 137
5.3.7: 127
5.4–10: 172
5.10.3–8: 178
6.1–2: 163–4, 166
6.2.2: 16, 155, 283
6.3–16: 164–5
6.8.2: 122
6.9–13: 159–60
6.9.2: 156
6.12.2: 165, 325
7.1–25: 149
7.5.26: 154
7.10.1: 152
7.22–6: 311–13
7.24: 159, 274
8.1.4: 110
8.3.2: 90
8.7–12: 138–9
8.12.1: 120
11.2: 22

Constitution of the Athenians
9.2: 35

Curtius Rufus
Life of Alexander
8.12.42: 30

Derveni Papyrus
Col. xvi: 108, 237–8, 267

Diogenes Laertius
9.9–11: 180

Empedokles
B6: 164, 323

Euripides
Bacchae
72–5: 222, 269

Herakleitos
B2: 224, 264, 298–9
B14: 223
B25: 223
B30: 248, 262–3
B31: 261–3
B32: 269
B36: 177, 261–2
B40: 162
B45: 263
B50: 176, 224
B52: 137
B54: 243
B62: 224
B64: 251
B67: 224–5, 249
B80: 243
B85: 262–3
B89: 274
B90: 243, 248, 262–3, 292–3
B101: 263, 308
B107: 264
B114: 275
B115: 263

Herodotus
3.38: 10
3.98–105: 11
4.40: 11

Hesiod
Theogony
116: 63
535–60: 73
Works and Days
686: 260

Homer
Iliad
9.401–5: 254
9.406–9: 256
9.602–8: 255
14.244–6: 63
15.204: 46
21.412–3: 46
22.169–72: 48
23.65–92: 57

Inscriptiones Graecae
1.104: 35

Jāiminīya Brāhmaṇa
2.69–70: 84
2.278: 93

Kaṭha Upaniṣad
1.14: 251
2.3: 25
5.9: 330

Kauṣītaki Brāhmaṇa
7.4: 170
Kauṣītaki Upaniṣad
1.6: 154
2.11–12: 177
2.12: 157
2.13: 120, 138
3.4: 157
3.8: 158
4.19–20: 128
4.20: 138, 139, 158

Mahābhārata
12.34.7: 203
12.176.5: 185
12.220.96–8: 203
Manu, Laws of
9.111: 92
Megasthenes
FGrH 715 F18a: 18

Nagarjuna
Mūlamadhyamakakārikā 17: 251

Pañcaviṃśa Brāhmaṇa
18.3.2: 23
21.2.1: 107
Parmenides
B1: 226
B4: 228, 240, 272, 274
B6.3–7: 226
B6.9: 227
B7: 244, 273
B8.4: 228, 231
B8.7–10: 16, 166, 272, 283
B8.9–10: 242
B8.26–33: 277
B8.29–30: 274
B8.30–33: 285
B8.38–41: 163, 273
Philolaos
A27: 260, 267
Pindar
Isthmians
1.68–70: 260
Olympians
2.56–8: 292
2.68–73: 222
fr. 133: 292
Plato
Alcibiades I
129d–131c1: 295–6
Epinomis
986d: 232
Euthyphro
15b: 219–20
Laws
959ab: 295
Meno
81a-b: 230
Phaedo
69a-c: 232–3, 266
79d: 232, 266
81a: 232
83ab: 273
108a: 228, 233
Phaedrus
248b1–5: 303
249b8: 231
249c7: 229–30
250b 8-c 6: 228, 231
Republic
416e: 24, 215–6, 268
442a: 342
560e: 228
Symposium
212a: 233–4, 287
Timaios
41d: 303
Plotinus
Enneads
1.6.5: 231
6.9.11.14: 229
Plutarch
Life of Solon
18.5: 35
21.2: 34
Prometheus Bound
511–18: 47

Questions of Milinda
5.6 = 333: 205

Rigveda
1.89.10: 64
2.12: 42
3.5.53: 118
4.42: 46
6.9: 251
7.11.5: 43
7.83.9: 45
7.88.2: 251
8.28.4: 41
9.113.7: 251
10.14.8: 66, 166, 169
10.16: 59, 66, 167
10.34: 136
10.90: 64–7, 102–3, 110
10.107: 80, 93
10.117: 91
10.129.4: 144

Sāmañña-phala Sutta
1.53: 182–3
Śatapatha Brāhmaṇa
1.3.3.9: 147
1.7.2.1– 2: 78
1.9.3.1: 81
2.2.2.6: 79, 91–2
2.2.2.8–20: 247
2.3.3.8–11: 170
2.3.4.4: 73
3.3.3.1–7: 24–6
3.6.2.16: 79
3.6.2.26: 73
4.5.8.6–9: 107
4.6.1.15: 20
5.4.3.24–6: 27
5.4.4.15: 109
5.5.5.16: 26
6.1.2.12–13: 103
6.1.2.17: 103
6.1.2.18–19: 104
6.1.2.36: 104
6.2.1.5–11: 104
6.2.1.10: 104–5
6.2.2.27: 169
7.1.2.1: 104
8.1.1.6: 104
8.1.3.6: 104
9.5.2.12–13: 90
9.5.2.16: 92
10.1.5.4: 170
10.4.2.2–3: 106
10.4.2.29: 107
10.4.3.10: 168
10.5.3.1–2: 144–5
10.5.4.16: 87
11.2.2.5– 6: 80
11.2.6.13–14: 87–8
11.2.7.33: 210
11.4.4.1–7: 89
11.7.1.3: 79
13.3.1.1: 112
13.6.1.3: 112
13.6.2.9: 20
13.7.1.1: 100
13.7.1.15: 20
14.1.1.32: 27
14.3.1.32: 27
Solon
fr. 4: 188
fr. 16: 300
Sophokles
Antigone 1063–77: 268

Taittirīya Āraṇyaka
6.1.1: 92
Taittirīya Brāhmaṇa
6.2.16: 96
3.7.9.8: 174
3.11.8: 172, 261
Taittirīya Saṃhitā
2.2.1: 20
Taittirīya Upaniṣad
1.8: 155
2.1: 155
2.2: 153
2.3–5: 122
2.7: 155–6
3.6: 154

Vinaya
1.152: 28
2.158–9: 28

Xenophanes
B7: 290
B23-6: 237
B34: 243

Yasna
32.3: 46

Index

Achaemenid empire, 10
Achilles, 48, 57, 254–257, 258–260
Aditi, 47, 64
Adityas, 45–47, 84
Adrasteia, 212
Advaita Vedanta, 132
Aeschylus, 28, 47, 214, 237
afterlife, 59, 66–67, 80, 97, 105, 110, 111, 167–192, 221, 223, 226–227, 232–233, 257, 290, 304, 344
Agamemnon, 48, 100, 254, 258
Agni, 43, 59, 60, 66, 169, 246, 251, 330
Agnicayana, 103, 139
Ajātaśatru, 128, 138
Ajivikism, 131, 180–190, 203, 209, 279–280, 325–326
Alexander the Great, 7, 10, 30, 135
Alkaios, 305
Anāthapiṇḍika, 28, 31
anatta (no self), 188–189, 249, 340, 345
Anaxagoras, 164
Anaximander, 235, 239–241, 248, 300
Anaximenes, 164, 179, 235, 236, 238–239, 242–244, 248, 265, 300, 336
Anspach, M., 98
Arbman, E., 51, 58–59, 122, 257
Aristophanes, 100, 222
Aristotle, 12, 16, 34, 141, 163, 180, 236, 271, 276, 298, 324, 327
Arjuna, 255
army, 29, 31, 341
Aruni, 163
Ashoka, 21, 187, 188, 208
asu, 57–60
Asuras, 74, 83, 114, 138
atman, 20, 57–60, 61, 63, 66, 79, 80, 90, 102–124, 128, 134, 138–139, 149, 150–151, 153–156, 157–162, 164–166, 177, 178, 189, 191, 199, 244, 247–249, 251, 252, 254, 263, 264, 279, 306–307, 312–313, 325, 329–330
ātmayājin, 87, 93
atomism, 164, 166, 323–326, 327–328
autocracy, 47, 75, 100, 109, 137–142, 194, *See* monarchy

Basham, A, 185, 280
Baylon, 109
Bayne, T., 50
Berger, P., 67–69
Bhaga, 47, 60
Bhagavad Gītā, 186, 255
Black, B., 133, 134
Blutzenberger, K., 171
Bodewitz, H., 137, 170
Brahma, 117, 154
brahman, 88–90, 117–118, 121, 127–128, 149, 150–151, 153–155, 157, 160, 162, 279, 315–331, 332, 336–339, 342–343
Brahmins, 17, 20, 23, 24, 26, 27, 33, 74, 78, 79, 83, 99–100, 109, 126–137, 139, 188, 206, 211, 221, 279, 298, 329, 334, 337
Brereton, J., 146
Bronkhorst, J., 14–16, 28, 60–62, 65, 131–132
Buddha, the, 18, 21, 31, 129, 130, 182, 187, 204, 205, 211, 248–249, 334, 340
Buddhism, 14, 16, 21, 28, 127, 131, 132, 180–190, 235–252, 279, 325
Buddhist texts, 17, 19, 20, 24, 28, 126, 182, 189, 203, 249, 340, 344

caste, 78, 109, 167–192, 212, 332, 334, 345, *See varṇa*
Cavallin, C., 85, 87, 119, 150, 191, 219, 220, 285, 287, 288
Chakravarti, U., 17, 19
chariot, 78, 81, 147, 158, 227, 303, 336, 337
China, 7, 8, 14, 52, 319–321
clan, the, 19, 34–36, 125, 194, 213–215
Clement of Alexandria, 223

coinage, 17, 19, 23, 27–31, 33, 37, 101, 131, 141, 204, 215, 253–254, 259, 260, 264, 265–266, 268, 271, 276, 286, 289, 300, 304, 305, 319–320, 322, 324, 334, 340–341, 343
Collins, S., 188, 206, 207
commerce, 17, 18, 19, 21, 24–26, 31–32, 44, 52, 61, 78, 90, 94, 97–99, 126, 130, 136, 185–186, 190, 196–197, 209, 210, 211, 220, 258, 264, 268, 280, 286, 287, 288, 300–302, 313, 319, 344
cosmisation (cosmic projection), 12, 48, 67–69, 82, 106, 112, 133, 140, 150, 161, 174, 183–185, 187, 192, 200, 207–208, 209, 216, 233, 241, 244, 253–254, 267, 269, 271–272, 274, 275, 280, 282, 285, 297, 304, 311, 313, 315–331, 335, 336, 338, 342, 343–346
cows, 22–27, 147
Cribb, J., 30
Ctesias, 11
cyclicality, 5, 81–82, 172–181, 184–185, 191–192, 199–202, 204, 210, 227, 233, 249–250, 263–265, 271–293, 313, 338, 343, 345

dakṣiṇā, 22, 23, 26–27, 77, 83, 93, 94, 96, 97–98, 172, 181, 261
dao, 321
Darius I, 10
debt, 78–79, 82, 94, 174, 185, 188, 200–201, 204, 209–212, 241–242, 260, 278, 280, 284–285, 293, 345
Democritus, 327
Derveni papyrus, 108, 109, 140, 237, 238, 240, 267, 330
Deussen, P., 170
Devas, 46, 74, 138
devayājin, 87, 93
devayāna, 168, 172, 174, 176
dharma, 142, 182, 203, 208, 214, 321, 329
Diogenes Laertius, 180, 327
Diogenes of Apollonia, 236, 238, 242–244, 307, 336
Diogenes the Cynic, 135
Dionysos, 105–107, 108, 215, 221, 227, 231, 251, 269
dismemberment, 105–107, 231
Drakon, 35

Egypt, 9, 18, 19, 98, 99, 321
Elea, 277, 301, 340
Eleusis, 97, 223, 251, 341
Empedokles, 164, 199, 220, 290–291, 323, 325, 330
Ephesos, 223, 341
Erdosy, G., 18, 20, 31, 130
Erinues (Furies), 46–48
Euripides, 105, 215, 222, 228, 275, 305

fire, 68, 73, 96, 103, 121, 152, 172–179, 207, 236, 238, 243–252, 261–264, 268, 271–272, 298, 330, 342–343
Foucault, M., 270

Gagné, R., 194
Gārgya, 128
Gemelli Marciano, M., 281, 282, 283
Glotz, G., 34
gold, 22–27, 28, 30, 96, 115, 143, 172, 215, 241, 261, 268, 277
gold leaves, funerary, 222, 226, 290, 292
Gombrich, R., 199, 205, 207, 248, 344
Gonda, J., 110, 111, 112, 170
Graeber, D., 101
Greenfield, P., 32

Hahn, R., 14
Halbfass, W., 75
Hardaker, T., 31
Havelock, E., 14
Heesterman, J., 77, 81, 83–87, 90, 93, 94, 98, 100, 114, 125, 180, 219, 246, 247, 248, 252, 338
Hekataios, 11
Hektor, 28, 48, 254
Hephaistos, 252
Herakleitos, 23, 137, 162, 163, 178–180, 182, 183, 189, 201, 207, 220, 223–226, 233, 236, 238–240, 241, 254–259
Herodotus, 10, 11, 305
Hesiod, 43, 45, 62, 63, 73, 74, 117, 260
Homer, 33, 35, 41–48, 54, 60–62, 63, 77–78, 100, 132, 146, 167, 215, 221, 235, 237, 240, 242, 243, 254–259, 269, 304, 332

immortality, 22, 23, 25, 27, 57, 104, 105, 115, 120–121, 123, 128, 135, 151, 161–162, 172–180, 185, 194, 210, 224, 232–234, 247–248, 251–252, 299, 303, 312
incorporeality, 7, 26, 119, 120, 178, 198, 222, 273, 294, 303, 306
individualisation, 20, 33, 82–90, 94, 97–101, 125, 133, 135, 139, 141, 150, 175, 180, 219, 224, 226, 247, 252, 307, 337
Indo-Europeans, 8–9, 44, 245
Indra, 42, 45, 48, 60, 66, 67, 109, 111, 138, 145
Indus valley civilisation, 18
inheritance, 20, 34, 36, 203–204
interiorisation (introjection), 52, 87, 94–96, 106, 109, 125, 133, 137–141, 145, 150, 161, 172, 180, 191–192, 197, 201, 211, 216, 219–234, 244, 247–249, 264, 267, 269, 272, 274, 278, 287–289, 296, 305, 308, 318, 325, 335, 337
iṣṭāpūrta, 66, 169, 173, 176, 343

Jainism, 127, 131, 132, 180–190, 195, 202, 203, 205, 209, 220, 279, 325
Jamison, S., 146, 190
Janaka, king of Videha, 23, 128
Jeremiah, E., 304–306, 308
jīva, 57–60, 164
Jurewicz, J., 147, 167, 194

Kant, Immanuel, 308
karma, 15, 128–129, 141, 170, 171, 175, 182, 183–186, 195, 200, 214, 250, 325–326, 336, 341–346
karman, 89, 128, 170, 171, 175, 202, 211, 344, 345
Kausambi, 18
Killingley, D., 173
Kosala, 18, 196
Kosambi, 130, 195, 201
Krishna, 255
Kshatriya, 20, 78, 99–100, 125–133, 175, 279, 298, 334
Kuiper, F., 251
Kuru-Pañcāla, 129–130, 131

Lacanian psychology, 106
LiPuma, E., 52
Lloyd, G., 14, 15–16
logos, 182, 183, 207, 215, 223–225, 236, 238, 239, 241, 243, 244, 247
loka, 79, 110–112, 168, 169
Lysias, 36

Magadha, 31, 32, 128–132, 196
Mahābhārata, 142, 184, 203, 255
Mahavira, 129, 130
Malamoud, C., 76, 80, 81, 97, 181
manas, 57–60, 123, 144
Maring, of New Guinea, 52
Mātāriśvan, 74, 244
Mauss, M., 257
McEvilley, T., 14, 176, 179
Megasthenes, 18, 213
Melanesia, 51
Mesopotamia, 19, 98, 99, 319
Miletos, 241, 253, 300
Mitra, 45
Moira, 47
mokṣa, 175, 200, 288, 338
monarchy, 29, 42, 44, 45, 67–68, 75, 100, 108–109, 128, 131, 135, 137–142, 153, 187, 238, 267, *See* autocracy
monism, 7, 48, 61, 62–67, 94, 102, 110, 111, 112, 114, 137, 143–166, 201, 220, 230, 235–252, 304, 322, 332, 335, 338, 343
  abstract, 15, 62, 132, 145, 150, 151, 152, 155–157, 158–161, 162–163, 166, 236, 239–240, 243, 254, 268, 271, 272, 283, 320, 322, 325, 328, 335, 339
  material, 62, 143, 145, 152–153, 166, 236, 238, 239, 242, 243, 246, 248, 250, 325
  mental, 62, 113, 132, 140, 144–145, 150, 151, 152, 154–155, 158–161, 230, 235, 236, 237–239, 240, 242–243, 268, 272, 291, 330, 335, 339
  personal, 62, 64, 116, 144, 145, 153–154, 161, 164, 166, 236–237, 238, 285, 336, 339
  present, 63–67, 102, 144, 145, 154, 156, 161, 235, 238, 239, 243, 245, 246, 248
  primordial, 63, 116, 143–145, 152, 153–154, 155–156, 161, 164, 166, 235, 237, 283, 285
monotheism, 64
mystic initiation, 97, 99, 100, 105–110, 141, 162, 215, 221–234, 244, 250–252, 260, 261, 269, 271–293, 303, 307, 310, 333–335, 338, 339, 341

Naciketas, 172
Nagarjuna, 210
necessity, 82, 94, 240, 241, 280, 282, 285, 297
Neoplatonism, 106, 231, *See* Plotinus
niyati, 183–184, 185, 279, 326
nous, 108, 109, 267

Oberlies, T., 45
Obeyesekere, G., 201, 212
Ohrmazd, 245
Olbia, 221, 224
Olivelle, P., 17, 20, 136, 148, 210
Orestes, 255
Orphic belief, 102, 107, 108, 194, 201, 221, 237, 238, 290

Parfit, D., 49–51
Parmenides, 13, 15–16, 106, 113, 162, 163, 166, 225–234, 239–240, 241, 243–244, 268, 271–290, 301–302, 303, 307, 312, 315–331, 335, 338–340, 342
Pataliputra, 18
Patroklos, 57
Pentheus, 105, 228
Persephone, 226, 292
Persepolis, 10
Pharaoh, the, 259
Philo, 268
Philolaos, 260, 267
Pinchard, A., 9
Pindar, 222, 260, 290, 292
pitṛyāna, 168, 172, 173, 176
Plato, 9, 24, 34, 57, 94, 106, 124, 140, 167–192, 199, 212, 219, 226, 228, 230–234, 237, 266, 268, 269, 273, 286, 287, 288, 290, 294–313, 326–328, 332, 336–337, 343–345
Plotinus, 212, 229, 231, 307
Plutarch, 34, 35
Poseidon, 46

Prajapati, 20, 74, 81, 84–85, 89, 96, 103–110, 111–112, 114, 118, 144, 152, 172, 231, 244, 261
prana, 57–60, 102–124, 137, 138, 157–158, 162, 244
Pravāhaṇa Jaivali, 127, 131
Proclus, 194, 229
Proferes, T., 86, 105, 139, 246
Prometheus, 47, 73–75, 244
property, individual, 19–22, 32, 33–36, 52, 53, 100, 107, 126, 184, 189, 192, 214, 278, 280, 299, 304–313
psuchē, 56, 58, 61, 120, 177, 178–180, 189, 194, 221–222, 230–233, 235–252, 253–270, 271–293, 294–304, 336, 340
punarmṛtyu, 84, 168, 170, 173
puruṣa, 64, 65, 66, 102–103, 110–111
Pythagoras, Pythagoreanism, 9, 187, 220, 237, 240, 260, 267, 290, 301–302, 318

qi, 320

Raikva, 136–137
Rajagriha, 18, 130
rajasūya, 75
Rau, W., 19
reason, 14–16, 113, 166, 268–269, 271, 280–285, 297
reciprocity, 41–48, 61, 77–78, 84–86, 90–95, 125–126, 146–147, 189, 191–192, 204, 208–209, 240–242, 255–259, 332
reincarnation, 7, 66–67, 175, 184, 185, 193–202, 220, 226–227, 233, 289–293, 313, 323, 345
  ethicised indiscriminate (EIR), 7, 193, 197, 208, 214, 290, 320, 342, 343
  lineage (LR), 168, 193–200, 209, 211
renunciation, renouncers, 134–136, 180–190, 288, 344
Rigveda, 17, 41–48, 57–62, 63–67, 76–78, 86, 88, 102, 110–112, 118–122, 132, 139, 143–149, 167–169, 194, 210, 246, 332
Rome, 194, 320
Roth, G, 183
ṛta, 45, 46, 203, 321

sacrifice, 20, 22–26, 41–44, 64–67, 73–101, 125–127, 133–134, 138–139, 144, 145, 147–148, 150, 161, 170, 172, 181, 189, 190–192, 201, 206, 211, 215, 221, 231, 242, 244, 247, 261, 286, 288, 333–346
saṃsāra, 175, 182, 184–186, 199, 279
sarva, 112–113, 118, 144, 154, 155, 231, *See* wholeness
self-sufficiency, 27, 61, 127, 174, 227, 276–278, 282, 284, 288, 301–304, 311, 328–331, 343
Silanka, 184
silver, 22–24, 25, 30–31, 215
slavery, 174, 188, 296–298, 337
Smith, B., 89, 150
Snell, B., 54, 304
Socrates, 216
Solon, 34, 35, 36, 187–188, 300–302
soma, 24–25, 42, 146–147
Sorabji, R., 49–51, 308
soul, 50, 53, 54, 57–59, 63, 122, 123, 180, 197, 198, 205, 247, 249–250, 257, 265, 266, 268, 278, 290, 292, 296, 303, 310, 326, 330, 333, 336, *See psuchē*
sukṛta, 89, 169, 170, 343
Sullivan, S.D., 54
Sūryā, 111
Svetaketu, 163, 325

Thales, 235, 236, 248, 298, 300
Thapar, R., 19, 125, 190, 213
Themis, 47
Theophrastus, 180
Thetis, 255
Todd, S., 34
tragedy, Greek, 47, 57, 140–142, 227, 255, 294
Tull, H., 223

Uddaka Rāmaputta, 130
Uddālaka, 127, 129
urbanisation, 17–19, 36, 46, 129–132, 212, 304, 311, 334
Usasti, 23, 134

Vaisesikas, 325, 326
varṇa, 64, 65–66, 213
Varuna, 45–47, 60, 61, 146, 251
Visvakarman, 147
Vlastos, G., 297
Vrtra, 42, 102

Weber, Max, 215
West, M., 108, 178, 179, 245–246
wholeness, 102–110, 112–113, 222, 229, 230–231, *See sarva*
writing, 21, 24, 174
Wynne, A., 130

Xenophanes, 235–237, 243, 290, 319, 330

Yājñavalkya, 23, 130, 133, 134–135
Yājñavalkyakanda, 128–130
Yama (Death), 66, 84
Yü, Ying-Shih, 321

Zeus, 43–48, 67, 73, 102, 106–110, 237, 253, 255–256, 267, 269
Zoroastrianism, 46, 244–248

Printed in the United States
by Baker & Taylor Publisher Services